UNIX® Papers

♯♯♯
HOWARD W. SAMS & COMPANY/HAYDEN BOOKS

Related Titles

Advanced C Primer++
Stephen Prata, The Waite Group

**C Programmer's Guide
to Serial Communications**
Joe Campbell

MS-DOS® Bible
Steven Simrin, The Waite Group

Discovering MS-DOS®
Kate O'Day, The Waite Group

MS-DOS® Developer's Guide
*John Angermeyer and Kevin Jaeger,
The Waite Group*

Tricks of the MS-DOS® Masters
*John Angermeyer, Rich Fahringer,
Kevin Jaeger, and Dan Shafer, The Waite Group*

Inside XENIX®
Christopher L. Morgan, The Waite Group

UNIX® Primer Plus
*Mitchell Waite, Donald Martin,
and Stephen Prata, The Waite Group*

**Advanced UNIX® —
A Programmer's Guide**
Stephen Prata, The Waite Group

UNIX® Shell Programming Language
Rod Manis and Marc Meyer

UNIX® System V Bible
*Commands and Utilities
Stephen Prata and Donald Martin,
The Waite Group*

**UNIX® System V Primer,
Revised Edition**
*Mitchell Waite, Stephen Prata,
and Donald Martin, The Waite Group*

UNIX® Communications
*Bart Anderson, Bryan Costales,
Harry Henderson, The Waite Group*

**C Primer Plus,
Revised Edition**
*Mitchell Waite, Stephen Prata,
and Donald Martin, The Waite Group*

Turbo C Programming for the IBM
*Robert Lafore, The Waite Group
(forthcoming)*

Quick C Programming
*Carl Townsend
(forthcoming)*

**C With Excellence:
Programming Proverbs**
Henry Ledgard

VM/CMS Handbook
Howard Fosdick

Hayden Books
UNIX System Library

UNIX® Shell Programming
Stephen G. Kochan and Patrick H. Wood

UNIX® System Security
Patrick H. Wood and Stephen G. Kochan

UNIX® System Administration
David Fiedler and Bruce H. Hunter

Exploring the UNIX® System
Stephen G. Kochan and Patrick H. Wood

UNIX® Text Processing
Dale Dougherty and Tim O'Reilly

Programming in C
Stephen G. Kochan

Topics in C Programming
Stephen G. Kochan and Patrick H. Wood

*For the retailer nearest you, or to order directly from the publisher,
call 800-428-SAMS. In Indiana, Alaska, and Hawaii call 317-298-5699.*

UNIX® Papers

Edited by
The Waite Group

HOWARD W. SAMS & COMPANY

A Division of Macmillan, Inc.
4300 West 62nd Street
Indianapolis, Indiana 46268 USA

FIRST EDITION
FIRST PRINTING—1987

International Standard Book Number: 0-672-22578-6
Library of Congress Catalog Card Number: 87-81111

The following people contributed to the publication of this book:

From The Waite Group, Inc.:
Developmental Editor: Mitchell Waite
Managing Editor: James Stockford
Series Editor: Harry Henderson

From Howard W. Sams & Company:
Acquisitions Editor: James S. Hill
Copy and Production Editor: Brown Editorial Service
Illustrators: Wm. D. Basham, Don Clemons, Ralph E. Lund
Cover Artist: Kevin Caddell
Compositor: Impressions, Inc.

Printed in the United States of America

To my Dad, James Waite, who gave me the freedom to explore the unknown and the courage to say what I discovered.

Mitchell

Contents

Preface

UNIX Papers is a compendium of exciting ideas, methods, programs, tips, tutorials, and insights into UNIX written for UNIX power users, software developers, and programmers:

- It provides the newest information on subjects not available in the popular UNIX literature.

- Tutorials on USENET, C++, programming the new UNIX shells, release 3 enhancements to System V UNIX, RFS and streams, and real-time UNIX will take you to the cutting edge of this powerful operating system.

- The reasons behind UNIX's style and why it appeals so much to a certain type of user. This will help you understand the purpose of a UNIX program, the approach required for using it properly, and how to avoid the weaknesses of UNIX.

- A look into the future of UNIX as an open system standard, the IEEE POSNIX project, XINU, and AU/X will help you see where UNIX is headed so you can make the right decisions now.

- A look at porting UNIX to three different microprocessors will give you a better idea of how to interface to UNIX running on the 80286, 80386, and MC68030.

- The book appeals to a broad range of readers and has information for intermediate to advanced UNIX users and programmers.

The Waite Group has been developing UNIX books since 1982 when *UNIX Primer Plus* was first published. Since then we have published more UNIX books, but have had to carefully watch the UNIX topics we publish.

The UNIX topics we wrote about had to have sufficient interest to support the large financial investments computer books require. Because UNIX is an operating system of renowned complexity, scope, and detail, we found ourselves in a quandary. How could we write a book about some of the more esoteric but very interesting side issues of UNIX, such as USENET and uucp, mailers, device drivers, shells, streams, remote file systems, tightly coupled multiprocessor implementations, 80386 and 68030 ports of System V, the C++ language or real time UNIX?

In the summer of 1986, I posted a message on the USENET system about the viability of a collected work of UNIX topics. (USENET is a computer network linking thousands of professionals using UNIX computers around the world—see Harry Henderson's paper in this book). The response was an overwhelming number of email messages: "Yes! Do it," "I'd buy it," "These topics need to be described," "How do we find out more?" A more detailed proposal for *UNIX Papers* (with the subtitle "for UNIX Developers and Power Users") was posted on USENET in August 1986. Our charter was to make each chapter in *UNIX Papers* a complete tutorial, as fine in quality and content as all our other books, and to make sure the paper taught something new and something useful about UNIX. We did not want the pedantic and overly dry technical articles that typify some of the UNIX trade journals. We wanted an organization that also offered something for the user (nonprogrammer), the lightweight programmer, and the heavy duty programmer/hacker.

From the more than 100 mail messages from potential contributors, we narrowed it down to 15 authors, each with a subject that fit well into the book's concept. Over the next 5 months these 15 dedicated individuals wrote several drafts of their essay, sending it back and forth between editor and reviewers, debating the contents with us by email, and fine tuning the paper until it was smooth and polished.

To make the book accessible to the widest variety of readers and to allow these readers to easily find the articles they are interested in, the book is divided into three basic sections. These sections roughly progress in knowledge level from intermediate user through advanced programmer. The sections are Introductory Illuminations, Arcana of Programming, and Esoterica of Implementation.

Most papers are presented as tutorials. The introductory section of the book covers the origin and development of UNIX, communicating and using the USENET network, UNIX mailers, comparing UNIX shells, and power applications with awk. The programming section teaches the new C++ language; writing UNIX and XENIX device drivers; SVR3's remote file system (RFS), streams, and the Transport Level Interface (TLI); designing an Ethernet network; and using UNIX in real time. The implementation section covers porting and using UNIX on the new 80286, 80386, and 68030 microprocessors and the state of the art in loosely and tightly coupled multiprocessor UNIX systems. The final paper discusses the future of UNIX and open system standards, such as the IEEE POSIX and ANSI C standards; the paper also projects where UNIX is headed.

We hope you are pleased with the result. If you have any questions or suggestions about this book, would like to contribute to a future revision, or would like to know more about what we do, please contact The Waite Group, 3220 Sacramento Street, San Francisco, CA 94115, (415) 929–7088 and ask for our author brochure. Or send me an email on USENET at {hplabs, lll-lcc, glacier, ptsfa} on The WELL (415–332–6106) to Mitch, or on BIX to mwaite.

Mitchell Waite
The Waite Group

Acknowledgments

First, we would like to thank the individual UNIX Papers contributors for their extreme attention to detail and their dedication to this project. Each is a tribute to the professionalism in the UNIX industry. We personally found it delightful to work with each of you.

We would also like to extend our sincere appreciation to Harry Henderson, who quietly accepted manuscripts delivered electronically in 15 different word processing formats; put up with complaining email daemons; diligently edited supertechnical papers; calmly asked authors for more clarity, for more illustrations, and for more information; and did this all while authors changed addresses, went through divorces, and had babies.

We would also like to thank The WELL computer conferencing system in Sausalito, California, and the entire UNIX community for creating the uucp network in the first place. It was really uucp and the USENET news system that allowed an intellectual concert such as this book to be arranged and executed almost completely electronically.

Finally, we give our sincere thanks to the people behind the scenes at Howard W. Sams & Company who took our manuscript and turned it into a smooth, marketable product we are all proud of: Jim Hill for seeing the vision and taking the risk of acquiring *UNIX Papers* in the first place; Wendy Ford and Katherine Ewing for managing the book's production and putting up with a potential logistic nightmare; Lynn Brown for her diligent editing and patience with dealing with 15 authors; Kevin Caddell for his wonderful cover painting (resemblance between any of the figures in the cover and the actual authors is strictly coincidental); and all the other people at Howard W. Sams & Company who one way or another were involved with making *UNIX Papers* a success.

Mitchell Waite
The Waite Group

Trademarks

All terms mentioned in this book that are known to be trademarks or service marks have been appropriately capitalized. Neither The Waite Group nor Howard W. Sams & Company can attest to the accuracy of this information. Use of a term in this book should not be regarded as affecting the validity or any trademark or service mark.

Ada is a registered trademark of the U.S. Government Ada Joint Program Office.

Amiga is a registered trademark of Commodore Amiga, Inc.

Appletalk is a registered trademark of Apple Computer, Inc.

AT&T—C++ Translator, AT&T—Mail, AT&T—Toolchest, Programmer's Workbench, Remote File System, and STARLAN NETWORK are registered trademarks of American Telephone and Telegraph.

ATARI ST is a registered trademark of Atari, Inc.

COMPAQ 386 is a registered trademark of COMPAQ Computer Corporation.

CompuServe is a registered trademark of CompuServe Information Services, an H & R Block Company.

CRAY 1 and CRAY XMP are registered trademarks of Cray Computer, Inc.

D-Nix is a registered trademark of Databoard, Inc.

DECconnect, ThinWire, ULTRIX 1.2, and VAX are registered trademarks of Digital Equipment, Inc.

Ethernet is a registered trademark of the Xerox Corporation.

EtherSeries is a registered trademark of 3 COM Corporation.

FastPath is a trademark of Kinetics, Inc.

4341 and IX/370 are trademarks and IBM PC/AT, Operating System/2, PC-DOS, Personal System/2, RT PC, 3B, 3081K, and Topview are registered trademarks of International Business Machines, Inc.

HP-VX is a registered trademark of Hewlett-Packard.

IDRIS is a registered trademark of Whitesmiths, Ltd.

Intel 80286 and 80386 are trademarks of Intel Corporation.

LaserWriter is a trademark of Apple Computer, Inc.

Lotus 1-2-3 is a registered trademark of Lotus Development Corporation.

Macintosh is a registered trademark of Macintosh Laboratory, Inc., licensed by Apple Computers, Inc.

MazeWars is a registered trademark of MacroMind.

MC68030 is a registered trademark of Motorola, Inc.

Microport V/At, Microsoft Windows, MS-DOS, and XENIX are registered trademarks of Microsoft Corporation.

Motorola MC68010 and MC68020 are registered trademarks of Motorola Inc.

National Semiconductor 32016 and 32032 are registered trademarks of National Semiconductor, Inc.

Network File System, Network Window System (NEWS), Sun, and Sun/3 are registered trademarks of Sun Microsystems.

PC/IX is a registered trademark of Interactive Systems Corporation.

PostScript is a registered trademark of Adobe Systems, Inc.

Printer Control Language and ThinLAN are registered trademarks of Hewlett-Packard.

Regulus is a registered trademark of the Alcyon Corp.

RTV is a registered trademark of Masscomp Corp.

The Source is a registered trademark of Source Telecomputing Corporation.

TRS-80 is a registered trademark of Radio Shack, a Tandy Corporation.

UNOS is a registered trademark of Charles River Data Systems.

WE 32100 Microprocessor is a registered trademark of AT&T Technologies, Inc.

XENIX/86 Operation is a registered trademark of the Santa Cruz Corporation.

Introduction

UNIX Papers is a collection of papers about UNIX topics that are on the cutting edge of technology and not well known outside the UNIX community. The subjects chosen for this book are presented in a tutorial manner, are aimed at an intermediate to advanced UNIX user, and are chosen to be of practical value. Each essay was written especially for this book and has never been in print before.

UNIX Papers Selection Criteria

The topics for this book were chosen by The Waite Group editors if they met a majority of the following criteria:

- The topic was one that was not yet written about in the general UNIX trade in a major way, that is, no book or long-running magazine series was available to the public, or if material existed, it was in obscure, "guru intensive" journals.

- The topic had to be one that was "new" in some way, meaning either the subject was new because it was just announced (like RFS, streams, or C++), or it was new because it was in vogue right now (like anything having to do with UNIX communications, multiprocessing, and the 80386 chip).

- The topic had to be capable of being explained in a 40- to 50-page straightforward tutorial, in a style characteristic of other books from The Waite Group. We did not want to choose topics that honestly took an entire book to explain adequately.

- The subject had to be generally interesting to a group with a wide range of technical skills, and not so narrow in focus that only a few percent of potential readers would be interested. This allowed us to skip the "Josephson Junction-Based Paged Memory Management Unit for Increased UNIX Whetstones" type of essay.
- The topics had to be a balanced mix between hardware and software for the UNIX market with the weighting in the direction of software.

These were our basic selection criteria. The result is that UNIX Papers describes a fairly broad range of topics while covering a broad range of reader skills.

What You Should Know to Read UNIX Papers

This book contains essays that cover a broad swath of topics that are suitable for intermediate and advanced UNIX users. UNIX beginners will also find a variety of techniques, tips, and perspectives that will improve their skills and understanding of the UNIX operating system. People who are new to UNIX but have some background in other operating systems (such as MS-DOS) will find this book to be a good introduction to the application of the UNIX philosophy. Intermediate UNIX "power users" will find that several essays reveal hard-to-find information and techniques that had been poorly documented. Intermediate level programmers will find essays on writing programs for UNIX, such as device drivers, while advanced programmers will find essays on porting UNIX to various 16 and 32 bit microprocessors.

We perceive *UNIX Papers* to be a book for everyone who wants to keep up to date about this increasingly popular operating system.

Organization of the Book

The following explains how *UNIX Papers* is organized and the subjects covered.

Part One: Introductory Illuminations

The first part contains topics suitable for beginning and intermediate UNIX users and programmers.

1. UNIX: Rights and Wrongs

The keynote paper for the book, "UNIX: Rights and Wrongs," describes the philosophy behind the design of the UNIX operating system interface (at both the user and system levels) and documents UNIX's history and divergent evolution. It can help you appreciate why UNIX is the way it is and from where it derived its strengths and weaknesses.

2. The USENET System

The power of UNIX communications and the UNIX network (USENET), with an estimated 200,000 users, is explained in this paper. You are shown how to use the readnews and postnews programs and given examples of many kinds of exciting information that can be obtained from USENET.

3. All About UNIX Mailers

The multitude of UNIX mail programs with dozens of different features is revealed in "All about UNIX Mailers," which describes the variety of electronic mail systems, how they work, their features, and a description of David Taylor's new Elm mailer. Elm is the first UNIX email program that provides a modern, user friendly screen-oriented interface.

4. Comparing UNIX Shells

The next paper explores the differences among the three most popular UNIX shells: Bourne, Korn, and C. It describes the differences from the point of view of both the interactive user and the shell script programmer and concludes with a look at some experimental and future shells.

5. awk Power Plays

The final paper in this part reveals version-specific problems in the powerful text-oriented programming language, awk. It shows the proper process for developing awk scripts and provides examples of tips, tricks, and traps to watch out for when you use awk.

Part Two: Arcana of Programming

This set of papers explores new developments related to UNIX software and programming. The papers are suitable for intermediate level to advanced UNIX programmers.

6. C++ Under UNIX

The first paper, "C++ under UNIX", provides an introduction to this new language, revealing the powerful ideas of modular data structures and of object-oriented programming a la Smalltalk. This essay is based on the AT&T UNIX System V C++ compiler.

7. Device Drivers Under UNIX

This paper reveals all the secrets of writing, testing, and debugging device drivers for UNIX and XENIX. Device drivers are the software that connects UNIX to the computer's peripheral devices. Anytime a new device is added, a device driver must be written for it. This essay provides examples of various types of drivers, and examples of C code that follow the driver function from the user level into the kernel's data structures.

8. Remote File Systems, Streams, and the Transport Level Interface

One of the most important new features of UNIX System V release 3 is its shared file system and interprocess communications features. This essay describes in detail how remote file systems operate and how they are used in programming. Also covered is the new standard for writing communications and network programs using streams and the TLI.

9. Ethernet: A UNIX LAN

Networks is the buzzword of the 1980s, and UNIX computers are being connected together for increased performance and communications. In "Ethernet: A UNIX LAN," Charles Spurgeon tells all that is needed to design an Ethernet LAN for a network of UNIX computer systems. Ethernet is one of the most popular LAN architectures in the UNIX community and is known for its highly reliable carrier detect multiple access (CSMA) methodology and its respectable greater than one megabit data rates. This essay demystifies network terminology and provides sources for further information.

10. Real-Time UNIX

Geoff Kuenning describes an excellent way to control physical devices and processes, such as the machines on a factory floor or test equipment in a laboratory. Most often these devices require that the computer controlling it respond almost instantly, in what is called "real time." UNIX is capable of making a practical real time system, but there are important factors to consider. This paper discusses alternatives for achieving real-time performance with standard UNIX, "enhanced" UNIX, and UNIX clones.

Part Three: Esoterica of Implementation

This last set of essays discusses how UNIX has been ported to, or implemented on, the most popular 16 and 32 bit microprocessors and the use of UNIX in the multiprocessor mode. The essays are suitable for the advanced UNIX programmer and system implementor, and will also be of interest to the programmer with non-UNIX operating system experience.

11. A UNIX Port to the 80286

This first paper explores running UNIX on the Intel 80286 processor and shows the difficulties that processor's segmentation scheme makes for such a UNIX port.

12. A UNIX Port to the 80386

UNIX runs much better on the 80386 microprocessor, because it has full 32 bit addressing and a hardware based memory management unit (MMU). In this essay, David Robboy, who has ported UNIX SVR3 to the Intel 80386, points out the way it was done and the methods that make the 80386 such a great choice for a UNIX port.

13. A UNIX Port to the MC68030

The Motorola MC68030 presents a rich platform for running the UNIX kernel. This paper describes the features of the 68030 and what gives it so much potential for a UNIX port.

14. Multiprocessor UNIX

A new growth area for UNIX is in multiprocessing: computers that allow UNIX processes to run in parallel at full speed. This paper explores the current UNIX multiprocessor market and defines the different types of multiprocessor architectures that exist.

15. The Future of UNIX and Open System Standards

This final essay describes the new standards that are driving UNIX toward becoming an "open" system, including the new public domain POSIX (a version of UNIX defined by the IEEE) and the new ANSI C standard. The essay takes a look at where UNIX is heading in light of the new IBM Personal System/2 and OS/2 standard and the new Macintosh II UNIX card.

Onward

Now you know more about the contents of *UNIX Papers*. As you can see, the book is designed so you can begin reading at any essay; there is no need to read from beginning to end. Instructors may want to assign certain essays corresponding to their individual courses. Independent readers may want simply to open it anywhere and start reading. Whatever technique you use, we hope you find *UNIX Papers* enlightening and rewarding.

## Part One

INTRODUCTORY ILLUMINATIONS

There is a large body of knowledge about UNIX that just never seems to make it out of the back rooms of software houses or beyond the expensive and hard-to-find UNIX technical journals. Why? Many would argue that it is because UNIX had its roots in Bell Labs and in academia, has never been supported by AT&T as a profit-oriented product, and as a result it has remained outside the main realm of the business community. Some would say that UNIX is technically excellent at the expense of user friendliness. Others would argue that it is the sheer complexity of UNIX—its over 100 commands, its ideas of standard input and output, redirection and pipes, regular expressions, one tool for one job—that has given UNIX its somewhat exclusive, mathematical, overly pedantic reputation. This first part of *UNIX Papers* attempts to illuminate some obscure but interesting facts and features of UNIX that are important to the average user and programmer—facts not well-documented in books or popular magazines.

Much success in using UNIX depends on the user's mental sharpness: the ability to manipulate and remember an extensive command set is paramount for taking advantage of this operating system. With a system that depends on memory rather than intuition, features that seem to be a boon to the technically oriented programmer are often at odds with the desires of the average application user who just wants to type a letter. So the first paper explores this issue, along with the philosophy behind the UNIX operating system. Also, you'll find a paper on the 200,000 strong USENET online network and how to access its vast amount of free technical and social information, followed by a paper on the UNIX mailers—how to use them, the addressing scheme, and how the most popular mailers work. These illuminations are concluded with two papers for the programming-oriented user.

KEYWORDS

▶ Consistency

▶ Portability

▶ Standards

▶ Pipe and Redirection

▶ Ritchie, Dennis M.

▶ B and C Languages

Paper Synopsis: The keynote paper looks at the development of UNIX in perspective. We see how UNIX made popular the powerful ideas of tools as building blocks, modularity, and portability. But divergent evolution, inconsistency, and certain design decisions have hampered the development of UNIX. This paper shows how UNIX can overcome these weaknesses in its future development and how programmers handle current UNIX inconsistencies.

Dan Franklin holds a master's degree from the Massachusetts Institute of Technology in computer science and he has been using UNIX since 1975. He worked at Bolt, Beranek and Newman, Inc., where he made many enhancements to the UNIX kernel (including an improved terminal driver) and worked at Interactive Systems Corp., where he worked on Interactive's port of UNIX to the IBM RT PC. Dan is now working on the Prophet II project at BBN, a UNIX-based reimplementation of a PDP-10-based support system for pharmacological research.

UNIX: Rights and Wrongs

Dan Franklin

The UNIX family of operating systems has proven to be enormously popular with computer programmers. The basic ideas of UNIX are over 15 years old, yet UNIX is still regarded as the operating system of preference by many professional programmers, and it continues to attract a wide following in universities from computer science researchers and programmers-to-be. UNIX is widely used in companies involved in engineering and research. Clearly, UNIX is meeting some peoples' needs. What is it about UNIX that programmers find so attractive, even after over a decade of further operating system development? This paper will provide some answers to that question.

On the other hand, many people dislike UNIX or feel intimidated by it. Its user interface is generally not well-suited to business applications— or to almost any application involving nonprogrammers. For example, UNIX error messages usually do not provide enough information about what the user did wrong. Many feel that UNIX is "guru-friendly," but "user-intimidating."

Another aspect of the difficulty of UNIX lies in the sheer number and variety of tools UNIX provides, some of which actually provide small programming languages. Certainly, with over 200 commands with no apparent organization, it is hard to get started with UNIX, especially if you simply want to get something done rather than spend months mastering the ins and outs of the system.

Both programmers and users agree that while UNIX has advantages over other operating systems, it is showing its age. UNIX compares favorably with other text-based operat-

RELATED PAPERS

4 Comparing UNIX Shells

6 C++ Under UNIX

8 Remote File Systems,
   Streams, and Transport
   Level Interface

10 Real-Time UNIX

ing systems such as VM/CMS, because UNIX uses powerful ideas such as redirection and pipes, which this paper discusses later. These ideas make possible a "building-block" approach using simple tools. But "standard UNIX" lacks windows, mouse control, and other modern user-interface improvements exemplified by the Macintosh and GEM interfaces in the microcomputer world. And the existing UNIX user interface using command lines seems inconsistent, hard to learn, and quite clumsy in places. Is UNIX really a programmer's dream? Can it avoid being a user's nightmare?

This paper examines the principles that distinguish UNIX from more traditional operating systems and shows why it has gathered such a following. It also examines the ways in which UNIX falls short of the ideal system, both for ordinary users and for programmers, and whether its problems might be fixed.

Paper Topics

Specifically, this paper examines the following areas:

Fundamental Ideas

- Pipes and the "building-block" philosophy of UNIX

User Interface Issues

- Error handling and users' needs
- Difficulties with "wildcard" filename expansion
- Command options and their readability and consistency

Portability Issues

- UNIX, C, and portability
- Divergent evolutions: BSD versus System V
- Portability and the search for standards

UNIX Internals

- Kernel size and modularity
- The UNIX terminal driver: a design issue

Some parts of the discussions that follow, such as the comparison of different versions of UNIX and the discussion of the kernel and terminal driver, are unavoidably rather technical. However, you can skip over these sections if you prefer and still understand the fundamental issues raised in this paper.

The UNIX Philosophy

The developers of UNIX were very clever people who in their efforts to devise their own easy-to-use computer system came up with a number of remarkably powerful ideas. The most important of these ideas, generally referred to as the "UNIX philosophy," is the notion of meeting a need by adding a small number of simple, general capabilities.

How does this contrast with traditional programming? When any program, or collection of programs, is found to be unable to perform some function, the first impulse of many programmers is to add a "feature" to perform exactly that function. The new feature is usually not very general; it meets the current need, and little more. As the programs are used by more and more people, the code grows more and more features in response to user requests and the natural desire of programmers to be creative. Every new feature adds to the complexity of the program and makes it harder to maintain. As time goes on, it becomes impossible to add new features without introducing bugs in old ones, or making the program too slow. And users (and developers!) find it increasingly hard to remember all the different features and to keep track of the ways they interact.

A better way for a programmer to meet a user need is to analyze it to determine what functions are needed to implement it. Those functions that are not already available can be written as a set of simple, flexible capabilities or "software tools." These tools can then be used in the application program or set of programs to provide the desired functions. Programmers using this methodology always keep in mind the environment in which a program "lives" and try to use, and build on, the facilities already available rather than duplicating them unnecessarily.

Thus, the programmer meets a given need by combining the individual tools in a specific way. Meeting later needs often requires no more than recombining the same facilities in a new way.

To understand this idea, look at a concrete example: handling messages in an electronic mail program. There is an obvious need in a mail system for the user to print messages (especially long ones) on paper so they can be read more easily than on the CRT screen. One way to meet this need would be to add a command that does just that: prints a message. But soon after this feature was added, people would probably request that the mail system put a header on the message, perhaps starting each page of a long message with the message number, and adding page numbers as well. Or users might want to print many messages at once. In that case, it would be desirable for the program output to start with a page summarizing the messages in the listing (giving the author, date, and subject of each one). And what about telling the printer to use a different font, or indenting the text of each message? Could spelling errors be corrected before the permanent copy is made? Clearly there is no end to the number of options the print-a-message command could provide.

But the operating system running the electronic mail program probably already has a command to print out files. The system can probably print files with headers, page numbers, different fonts, and so on. The computer system may also have a spell checker, which again works on files. Rather than provide a print command that performs all of these functions, it would make much more sense to provide a command that puts a selected set of messages in a file. With messages stored in a standard, widely understood file format, the user can run separate programs that operate with this format to perform the desired functions. Besides just printing the messages, the user can feed them to a spell checker or even an indexing program. Another new mail-system command might put a summary of the messages in a file; the two files could be combined before printing. Making this command separate from the command to put messages in a file permits the user to get a printed summary alone. (See Dave Taylor's paper for a detailed consideration of mailer functions.)

By using a file as the interface between the mail system and the rest of the system's software, much needless programming effort can be saved. The mail system programmer just provides a basic set of functions, including the "put message-into-file" and "put summary-into-file" commands, and a very simple "macro" or "script" that will run first those commands and then an existing UNIX command for printing files, such as lpr. As other programmers find new uses for messages, they don't have to wait for the original developer to add them; they can implement them by using the message-into-file command in conjunction with UNIX commands and other programs that manipulate files. For example, a simple scheme for searching messages by keyword could be implemented by using the UNIX grep command on the message files.

In other words, having a way to get messages into files means that you can now use the many other UNIX commands that work with files to have your messages perform more functions. The message-into-file command is thus a simple tool that really does only one thing, but that thing helps you build many new functions.

UNIX relies very heavily on coupling programs in this way. In fact, the technique of coupling programs was clearly so worthwhile that the designers of UNIX provided a facility just to make that coupling easy: the pipe.

HOWARD W. SAMS & COMPANY
Excellence In Publishing

DEAR VALUED CUSTOMER:

Howard W. Sams & Company is dedicated to bringing you timely and authoritative books for your personal and professional library. Our goal is to provide you with excellent technical books written by the most qualified authors. You can assist us in this endeavor by checking the box next to your particular areas of interest.

We appreciate your comments and will use the information to provide you with a more comprehensive selection of titles.

Thank you,

Vice President, Book Publishing
Howard W. Sams & Company

SUBJECT AREAS:

Computer Titles:
- ☐ Apple/Macintosh
- ☐ Commodore
- ☐ IBM & Compatibles
- ☐ Business Applications
- ☐ Communications
- ☐ Operating Systems
- ☐ Programming Languages

Electronics Titles:
- ☐ Amateur Radio
- ☐ Audio
- ☐ Basic Electronics
- ☐ Electronic Design
- ☐ Electronic Projects
- ☐ Satellites
- ☐ Troubleshooting & Repair

Other interests or comments:

_____

_____

Name_____
Title_____
Company_____
Address_____
City_____
State/Zip_____
Daytime Telephone No._____

A Division of Macmillan, Inc.
4300 West 62nd Street
Indianapolis, Indiana 46268 USA

22578

Book Mark

HOWARD W. SAMS & COMPANY

Book Mark

fff

HOWARD W. SAMS
& COMPANY

The Pipe: Keystone of the UNIX Philosophy

The UNIX *pipe*, which couples the output of one command to the input of another, is the single best example of the UNIX philosophy of providing one tool for many functions.

The notion that one program's output should be able to become another program's input is a major innovation in computer system design. By making it possible to link any two (or more) programs in this way, the UNIX pipe makes it possible to construct programs from available parts at a very high level. Because the individual parts can be combined flexibly, no one part needs to be overly complex. Thus this "tinker-toy approach" made it possible for UNIX to apply its second powerful idea: *one program, one function*. "Make each program do one thing well," UNIX developers said.[1]

Pipes have many uses, but perhaps the best way to understand their power is to consider their application to the problem of handling lists.

There is a large class of computer programs that produce lists: lists of files, people logged in, processes, and so on. For each such program, users generally want to:

- select classes of items to display (or not display)
- sort the items on some key
- produce "reports" based on the information in the list (counting the number of items in each class, summing columns, and so forth)

The non-UNIX way to solve this problem is to provide options to each of the list-producing commands to control output processing. A sort command in some operating systems may be provided with many options that select which lines will be sorted and displayed.

With UNIX pipes, such options are not necessary; the user can easily feed the output of a command that displays a file (such as cat) into another command (such as the grep pattern-matching command) to select which lines of output to process, sort the selected lines (using sort), or perform more complicated processing using a "report generator" such as awk. The result of this processing can be fed into yet another command, such as pr to get printed output, and this can go on and on. The following examples of the flexibility of pipes are my favorites; Brian Kernighan used them to introduce me to pipes when I started using UNIX at Bell Labs.

---

[1] In the foreword to the original *Bell System Technical Journal* special issue on UNIX (volume 57, no. 6, part 2, p. 1902) by M. D. McIlroy, E. N. Pinson, and B. A. Tague.

Most time-sharing systems have a command to print out the names of all the users currently logged in. In UNIX, this command is called who. Now, suppose you want to know whether "fred," a friend of yours, is currently logged in. You could just type the who command, but if there are a lot of people logged in, the listing would be quite long and would scroll off the screen; it would be hard to spot "fred," and you might miss him entirely. Traditional time-sharing systems don't usually provide an option to the who command to select particular people. But with UNIX, you don't need one. Thanks to pipes, you can use the list provided by the who command with the grep command to isolate just those lines containing Fred:

```
who ! grep fred
```

The output of the who command doesn't appear on your screen; it's fed as input to the grep command, which will discard all lines of input except those containing "fred." Those are the lines that will appear on the screen.

What if you just want to know how many people are logged in? Some, but not all, time-sharing systems provide an option that just counts the number of logged-in users, but with UNIX, you don't need one. You just use wc (word count) with the -1 (number of lines) option, and a pipe:

```
who ! wc -1
```

Here the wc -1 command counts the number of lines in the output of the who command: since who uses one line to list each user, this is equivalent to counting the total number of logged-in users.

In both these cases the pipe serves as the coupling between the output of one program and the input of the other. You are able to combine two general commands to do a very specific job.

These examples are pretty conventional; where UNIX excels is in handling the unconventional. Suppose you've been using UNIX from several different terminals, and you're not sure whether you've logged out of all of the others. What you want to know is how many times you're logged in. There are no time-sharing systems that provide an option to do *that*, but on UNIX it's no harder than anything else you've done so far. This example assumes your name is Dan:

```
who ! grep dan ! wc -1
```

As before, grep selects only the lines from who that contain your name; then wc counts them up.

Note that the way the grep and wc commands are used almost makes them look like options to the who command. But because they're separate commands, they can be applied to other list-producing commands, such as ls (which lists files) or ps (which lists *processes*—currently running programs). Thus, commands like grep and its cousins give all list-producing commands the ability to manipulate their output in many ways. And since the same commands are used to work with all lists, the syntax is always consistent.

But the UNIX philosophy isn't a panacea. It has its disadvantages, too, though many UNIX proponents hate to admit them (and some aren't even aware of them).

Not a Perfect World

Extracting common list-manipulating operations—or any other set of operations—from programs that produce lists and making them general programs in their own right, certainly permits them to be used in many more places. But the usefulness of these commands for particular purposes may be diminished as a result.

For example, suppose your main UNIX directory contains a mixture of files and directories, and you want to list just the directories. The UNIX ls command has no option to list directories without listing regular files. How could you get such a list on your screen?

If you've never done it before, you'll find it more work than you might expect. It goes without saying that you won't find it in the UNIX manual anywhere; the manual almost never discusses the results you can get by combining commands. But you might expect that, since selection is involved, you could use grep somehow to select the lines giving the names of directories.

All you need to know is what distinguishes ls output lines naming directories from those naming individual files. The default format for ls just gives the file or directory names, without labeling them as files or directories, so it is not useful for this purpose. The long format, however, provides much more information:

```
ls -l
total 7
drwxrwxrwx  2      dan.sys     512 Oct 24  1985 bg
drwxrwxr-x  2      dan.sys     512 Jan 24 16:35 bin
drwxrwxr-x  2      dan.hacks   512 Jan 24 18:13 hacks
-rw-rw-r--  1      dan.sys    2528 Jan 24 15:16 profile1
-rw-rw-r--  1      dan.sys     139 Jan 24 15:51 term.alias
```

There's a lot of extraneous information here, but notice that the difference between directories and files is that the line for a directory (such as bg) begins with a *d*, while lines for files (such as profile1) begin with a dash (-). This is a difference we can take advantage of by using grep:

```
ls -l | grep '^d'
```

This command pipes the output of ls into a grep command that specifies lines beginning with *d* (the ˆ character stands for the beginning of the line). Given the ls output from before, you would get:

```
drwxrwxrwx  2      dan.sys      512 Oct 24   1985 bg
drwxrwxr-x  2      dan.sys      512 Jan 24  16:35 bin
drwxrwxr-x  2      dan.hacks    512 Jan 24  18:13 hacks
```

That's fine if you wanted to see the long form of the output. But what if you only wanted a list of directories, in the same form that plain old ls produces, without all the other information that the -l option provides? When grep selects a line, it always prints the whole thing; it provides no way to trim down the line. But you can use sed (the "stream editor") to edit the lines produced by grep:

```
ls -l | grep '^d' | sed 's/.* //'
```

This command produces the lines shown above and feeds them as input to sed, which will substitute (*s*) "nothing" for all the characters up to and including the last space (blank) in the line. In other words, everything but the last word in the line (the directory name itself) will be removed, and sed will output just the name. Now you've got the output the way you want it.

Figuring the sed command out was a lot of work for a seemingly simple task. It took some mental effort to realize that you could extract the filename field of each line by removing all of the line up to the last blank. This trick relies on the fact that the filename (usually) has no blanks in or after it.

Each serious UNIX user develops a personal collection of "tricks" and a personal toolkit. UNIX gurus take delight in refining such tools. For example, the example of extracting a filename could be made more compact by having sed select the lines as well as trim them down:

```
ls -l | sed -n '/^d/s/.* //p'
```

This command line instructs sed to perform the substitution only on lines beginning with *d*. You also have to tell it not to print lines by default (the -n flag) and add an explicit print command on the end of the substitute command (the p on the end) to print the selected lines. This version is more efficient, but it's also more cryptic. The nonguru is liable to simply walk off in a bemused, bewildered daze.

The price you pay for the approach of combining simple tools is that you have to provide most of the functionality yourself. The result is that UNIX is far more powerful than most other operating systems, but does les...

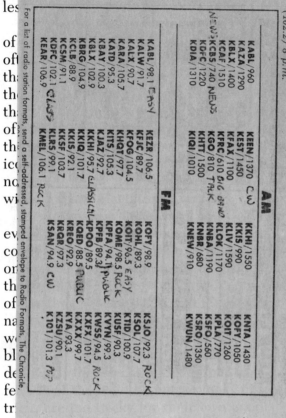

...n option to their equivalent
...want; the UNIX philosophy
...ems when it comes to tasks
...stems have anticipated. On
...always possible to do things
...his is not the case with most
...s. The operating system for
...ys to arrange file and folder
...e size of each folder. It has
...ere is no way you can do it

...ling-block philosophy is that
...mmer. After all, the sample
...ittle programs. In miniature,
...-test-debug. There is always
...s expected or only work most
...be blanks in your directory
...ur hard-won command line
...f each filename after its last
...s that sed doesn't really "un-
...ou're just using an incidental
...the entries you want.[2] Some

...ften in UNIX tools. To see it
...us), which displays processes
on the system, to make a list of all the processes having some common characteristic, such as being "niced down" (running at a lower priority than normal). The "nice value" is one of many numeric columns of output produced by ps; you can select the lines for which that column is nonzero using awk (once you count out the columns to make sure you have the right one). However, your command line will give very misleading results when some of the numeric fields of ps's output overflow and the spaces between the columns disappear! It is an odd fact of life under UNIX that some of its commands are not well-designed for use with pipes. Of course it is difficult when one designs a UNIX command to anticipate all the ways people might want to use the command with other commands.

---

[2]If you have access to a UNIX system, you might try to solve the embedded-blank problem. Some possible approaches are to beef up the sed expression, use awk instead of sed, or use find instead of ls.

To summarize, the UNIX tinker-toy philosophy is somewhat of a mixed blessing. On the one hand:

- You can solve almost any problem and meet almost any requirement by combining existing UNIX programs. This means you can perform a wide variety of tasks with UNIX in much less time than with other systems that would force you to write a program in a traditional language, with all the work that entails.

- Using separate programs connected by pipes through which ordinary text passes makes debugging easy: to find out whether each stage in the pipeline is performing correctly, you just display the output of that stage on your screen.

- UNIX provides a framework in which new programs gain a great deal of power just because of the potential ways they can be "connected" to other programs through pipes. For example, suppose you wanted to see how well-commented your UNIX C code was. Once you write a C program to count lines of comments in source files, you can now also find out the average percentage of lines commented, just by using awk to manipulate the line counts that your program produces.

- Pipes and filters can be used very widely, once you understand them.

On the other hand:

- Simple, obvious problems sometimes require time and effort out of all proportion to their apparent simplicity.

- Sometimes, after a lot of work, you find that you can't do what you want at all, or that it would have been easier to write a "real" program in the first place.

- It's a lot of effort to remember all the tricks once you expend the effort to work them out in the first place.

- Building a pipeline can be a real distraction from getting your work done, particularly if you're not a programmer.

- The tinker-toy philosophy makes building new commands so easy for UNIX programmers that it hardly seems to matter to them that some obvious commands and options aren't there. To nonprogrammers, of course, it matters a lot.

One might almost say that UNIX programmers, like theoretical mathematicians, feel that it is not necessary for UNIX to provide a solution to a problem; it is sufficient that a solution (in the form of a pipeline) is known to exist. The exercise of developing the solution is left to the user. Occasionally, as with tar or lorder, a starting point will appear in the manual. Many useful pipelines and shell scripts may be found in the book *The UNIX Programming Environment,* by Brian Kernighan and Rob Pike. Don't look for them to appear in a standard UNIX release, though; the fact that they appear in the book will be considered good enough by most UNIX developers.

Error Handling

There are other ways in which the UNIX system may be regarded as incomplete when compared to operating systems designed for the non-programmer. UNIX not only assumes you will be willing to write your own programs; it also assumes that you are willing to do some debugging whenever you issue a command that goes wrong.

Most commercial operating systems make some effort to provide complete, consistent, systematic error messages. The Honeywell Multics operating system is a particularly good example, because it was well-known to the developers of UNIX. In fact, as will be mentioned later, some of UNIX's good ideas came from Multics, which was originally a joint effort of MIT, Bell Labs, and GE; some of the same people worked on both systems. In the Multics operating system, virtually all error messages gave the name of the command issuing the error, a complete English sentence describing the error, and another sentence giving the context of the error. For example, suppose you are using UNIX and want to look at a file in a subdirectory, but (unknown to you) you do not have permission to look inside that directory. You might try using ls:

```
ls book/chapter
```

and you would get:

```
cannot find book/chapter
```

From this vague message, you might assume that the file doesn't exist; but that is not necessarily the case. It could take you a while to discover the real problem—lack of the appropriate permissions.

If the ls command were written to Multics standards, then the error message might say:

```
ls: The file "book/chapter" could not be found.  You do not have search
access to the directory.
```

The Multics messages tended to be quite wordy, but they also provided more information than typical UNIX error messages. To give another example, it can be very frustrating to keep trying to write into a file and only get the message can't open when the file is obviously there. You must stop and think about the possible reasons the system might not be able to open a file for writing—when with a little extra effort, the author of the program could have told you why the operating system kernel wasn't opening it, in a short message such as "Permission denied" or "Read-only file system" or even "Too many files open system-wide." You would not need to know very much about UNIX files in order to figure out that you were being denied permission, but figuring out the other possibilities takes a lot more knowledge about UNIX than most UNIX users possess or want to possess. The authors of all UNIX programs could have saved far more effort on the part of users than it would have cost if they had consistently provided this additional information.

The current versions of the UNIX system give much better error messages than earlier ones, however. In one early version of UNIX (the "Version 6"), the frequently used cat command gave no error message at all if the files you specified could not be opened. The pr command, which formatted a file for printing, said only "Very funny" if you specified too large a number for multicolumn output! Most modern UNIX commands at least print the name of the command and something about what actually went wrong. Some, like the cat command, give the error message generated by the UNIX kernel itself when the "system call" it makes on your behalf fails.

But there is still work to be done to bring UNIX up to anything like commercial standards of friendliness. When a UNIX program does give the operating system's error message, it usually leaves out other useful information like the name of the program running at the time (extremely useful if you are running several programs at once, or running a shell script containing several commands in a row) or the name of the file that generates the problem (very useful when you're processing a list of files). For example, cat (in the BSD version of UNIX) leaves out its own name. The reason is that the UNIX standard library routine for printing out the kernel error message, perror, takes a single string argument; the manual recommends that this be the name of the program, but some developers recognized that the name of the file was usually more useful and provided that instead. Both are useful, and both should be provided—but perror only takes one argument.

In my UNIX programs, I use a routine I wrote called ecmderr to handle these situations. This single routine combines all the operations usually needed when an error happens; it prints out the name of the program (which it gets from a global variable progname the programmer must set once, when the program starts), a user-specified error message (which need not be a single string, but a formatted string after the manner of the system routine printf), optionally appends the error message corresponding to the most recent error signaled from the kernel, and exits. This routine suffices for 90 percent of all error handling. A variation, cmderr, does all that without exiting, in case the command must delete files or clean up in other ways.

Both routines call another routine, errmsg, to get the string for the kernel error message; this routine simply looks up the kernel error number in the system-supplied table of possible kernel errors, being careful to check that the number is valid. The result of having these tools is that any UNIX program can be given a reasonable degree of error handling with little effort on the programmer's part.

AT&T has indicated that in future releases of UNIX it plans to have a standard error message format that not only includes all the information mentioned so far, but adds a short tag that you will be able to use to look up the message (for a lengthier explanation) or to refer to it in bug reports. This, too, is often provided in more mature commercial operating systems. Perhaps other UNIX vendors will follow AT&T in this attempt to make UNIX more usable for nonprogrammers (and programmers too!).

UNIX Wildcard Processing: Too Much Too Soon

Another odd aspect of the UNIX user interface is the way it handles wildcard expansion in filenames. In many computer systems, when you specify a group of files to be operated on, as in:

```
rename *.c *.x
```

the program that "knows" how to expand *.c into a list of all the files ending with .c is the rename command itself. That is, when you type this line, the command line reading software divides the line into three parts ("rename", "*.c", and "*.x"), looks at the first part—the command name (rename in this case)—and invokes the code that implements the rename function. The rename code then expands *.c into a list of filenames and renames each filename to end in .x instead. (This is true whether the rename command is part of the same program that reads your typed lines, as in MS-DOS, or a separate program.)

This would seem to be the only logical way to perform wildcard expansion: only the rename command itself really "knows" whether an argument is actually intended to be a list of files or not. In this example, the rename command knows that the second wildcard, *.x, is not intended to be expanded into a list of all the files whose names ended in .x, but is rather a specification or pattern for how the renamed names should look.

UNIX doesn't do it this way. Instead, in UNIX, the expansion of these abbreviations is done in the shell (command processor), rather than in the individual commands. That is, when you type the UNIX command:

```
mv *.c /usr/sources
```

(which moves a group of files whose names end in .c to another directory), and the mv command starts running, the command line has already been expanded. To the mv command, it might look like:

```
mv main.c subr.c utils.c /usr/sources
```

This division of labor has several undesirable effects. First, UNIX cannot provide a rename command that works on a group of files. You can rename a single file by using mv:

```
mv main.c prog.c
```

but you cannot say:

```
mv *.c *.x
```

as in the earlier example. One of several things might happen if you try; most likely, you will get an error message from mv because it expected a directory called *.x to exist, and it doesn't. If you want to rename a group of files, you have to write a small program in the UNIX command processor's language that loops through the list of files. To do the job of the previous command, you have to say:

```
for f in *.c
do
    mv $f `basename $f .c`.x
done
```

This loop says that for each file in the list (of files ending in .c), call the mv command with two arguments. The first argument is the name of the file; the second argument is constructed by taking the name of the file, removing the .c suffix, and putting a .x suffix on it. So, given the files listed here, this loop would execute three mv commands:

```
mv main.c main.x
mv subr.c subr.x
mv utils.c utils.x
```

There are other disadvantages to the way UNIX handles filename expansion. Whenever you want to use the wildcard characters (asterisk, question mark, and open square bracket, [) in a nonfilename context, you must usually enclose them in single quotes to ensure that they are not expanded by the command processor.

Also, it is impossible for a command to check for dangerous arguments. The UNIX rm command cannot check whether you are removing all the files in your directory (the infamous rm * command) and ask you whether you really intended that, because it doesn't see the *, only a list of files that looks just like any other. (There are some ways around this problem that we won't go into here, since they don't change our basic point.)

These observations are not new; they have been made over and over again since UNIX first became generally available. In response, UNIX defenders generally offer the following:

- Having the shell perform the expansion saves individual command developers the trouble of doing it themselves.

- Consistency in wildcard handling among commands is ensured without having to force individual command developers to follow standards.

- If the expansion syntax or implementation is changed, only the shell itself must be changed; all commands in the system do not need to be recompiled.

- The filename expansion code need not be loaded with every command.

One may argue with these justifications on the grounds of consistency:

- Wildcard expansion was in the shell long before library routines existed to perform many other frequently needed operations, such as string manipulation; the philosophy of "saving developers the trouble of doing it themselves" was clearly not widely applied.

- Other aspects of the UNIX user interface, such as the interpretation of option arguments, also clearly required a mechanism to enforce, or at least encourage, consistency; a routine for processing options (getopt) did not appear in any standard UNIX version until relatively recently.

- Having to recompile every command was not usually regarded by UNIX developers as an impediment to change; total recompilation was one of many headaches that those who upgraded from one early version of UNIX to another (Version 6 to 7) had to deal with, and sometimes it has been required by more recent UNIX upgrades as well. (As it happens, the wildcard expansion syntax has remained unchanged for at least a decade.)

- The space taken up by wildcard expansion code would not have been excessive compared with the space currently taken up in every program by standard I/O library routines, such as printf. This objection, in any case, remains a problem with **UNIX** that more traditional operating systems (as well as the latest **UNIX** release from AT&T) have solved by providing "shared libraries" of common code so that every executable program on the system need not have its own copy of the most commonly used routines.

But the primary problem with these justifications is that they are programmer-oriented answers to user interface problems. They assume that the convenience of **UNIX** developers takes precedence over the convenience of **UNIX** users. But there are many more users than developers, and it is users who justify the existence of developers, rather than the other way around. Instead of putting wildcard expansion in the shell, **UNIX** should have provided support library routines for wildcard expansion (not to mention other aspects of command line processing); user pressure would have provided the incentive for developers to remember to call these routines when their commands processed filenames. This was the experience of the Multics operating system project.

The result of putting filename expansion in a library routine rather than embedding it in the command processor (shell) would be that each **UNIX** command could use these routines to "look at" the command line in the way most appropriate for its intended operation. There would also be the advantage of keeping the command processor smaller.

Unfortunately, this aspect of **UNIX**'s user interface is one that is very unlikely to change; it is too firmly embedded in the current implementations. Once made, the decision to include wildcard expansion in the shell is hard to undo, because the code for nearly every **UNIX** command would have to be revised to call the new library routine. Only when that entire user interface is replaced with something better will there be an opportunity to correct this problem. Until then, new users will continue to be "initiated" into **UNIX** use by removing all of their files when they accidentally insert a space in an rm command. Many of them will learn the small, but tricky, shell loop that renames files. And some of them will come to believe, along with most **UNIX** developers, that this is the only way wildcard expansion should ever be done.

UNIX Command Options: Brief or Cryptic?

Another facet of the **UNIX** user interface that has been criticized is the way it handles command line options. Most other operating systems use short words or multicharacter abbreviations; UNIX uses single characters. Usually the character has a certain mnemonic value. For instance, the egrep command takes a "regular expression" argument that specifies the pattern input lines should match in order to be printed on the output. This regular expression can get so complicated that it is useful to be able to put it in a file. Hence egrep takes a -f option to specify that the next argument is not the regular expression itself, but the name of a file to be opened to get the regular expression. The commands fgrep, sed, and awk also accept a -f flag that means "file."

Unfortunately, not all UNIX commands use the same character to mean the same thing. Both the rm and mv commands use the -f flag to mean "force" the action (that is, skip asking the question these commands sometimes ask).

Also, a single character is hard to remember, even when there is some mnemonic value, if you don't use the option very often. Unfortunately some options used infrequently have odd names, such as the cc -E option, which passes your C source files through only the C preprocessor without recompiling them, or the make -k option, which asks make to continue running even in the face of errors, but not to use the results of any command that got an error. This makes the more unusual options hard to remember. A command's more recently added options, in particular, often have no mnemonic value at all, because the obvious candidates were used up.

Single-character options do save typing, though. Before I started working with UNIX, I used Multics for several years. The Multics command set was similar to UNIX in some ways, but had longer option names. The -f option mentioned earlier would have been -file (for egrep) or -force (for rm). Though the options all had abbreviations, none consisted of fewer than two characters (-fi and -fc, respectively). Multics required so much typing that over the course of my Multics work I just about doubled my typing speed! I know others who also worked extensively with Multics who had the same experience. Single-character options save more typing than you might expect, because they can be combined. For example, I can type:

```
ls -ltug *.c
```

combining the -l (long form) -t (sort by time), -u (use last-time-referenced), and -g (give group name) options. Most UNIX commands accept "bunched" options like this. A system that uses options that can be either a whole word or an abbreviation would have a much harder time allowing "bunching" without creating ambiguity.

Single-character options, then, represent a classic trade-off: easier to type, harder to remember. UNIX was definitely designed for people who use it all the time, and who are not touch-typists. For them, the trade-off is probably not unreasonable. For novice UNIX users, it is unfortunately just one more obstacle in their path.

There is also a philosophical justification for making all options be single characters. In the UNIX philosophy, a command should only do one thing. If it's only doing one thing, how many different ways can it do it? If, as you code or modify a UNIX command, you find yourself wishing that ASCII had more characters, you are probably trying to combine two or more functions in one command. Certainly that is true of the ls command, which has a long list of options. It doesn't just produce a list of files; it can also sort them in several different ways and even list them in a line across the screen or in columns across the screen instead of in a single column. Rob Pike has argued eloquently[3] that the ls multicolumn format option was a mistake: it should have been provided in a separate command, since files are not the only things one can imagine being printed in a multicolumn format. He points out that the pr command could already print files in a multicolumn format, so that adding it as an option to ls was quite unnecessary. There is always the question of how far to break down the functional elements when commands are being designed.

Philosophy aside, problems with learning UNIX command options are not hard to fix. In the future you can probably expect to see user interfaces that provide pop-up windows listing command options (in fact, someone has probably already done it). It is unfortunate, from the novice's point of view, that "raw UNIX" is not very accommodating in this respect, but it is hardly fatal. Thus, you can expect improvement in this area as more UNIX developers and vendors strive to make UNIX acceptable in the business world.

UNIX and Command Consistency

There is another problem with UNIX command syntax: it is not very consistent. For example, from the previous discussion you might have gotten the impression that all UNIX commands have only single-character options. They don't: the find, stty, and dd commands all take multicharacter option names. (This is probably fortunate, since most users employ these commands rarely enough that the extra wordiness is more helpful than otherwise.)

You might also have gotten the impression that if a UNIX command took single-character options, then those options could always be given

---

[3]In Pike's address, "cat -v Considered Harmful," at the June 1983 USENIX Conference.

either individually (for example, -l -t -u -g) or "bunched up," as shown earlier for ls. Again, you would be wrong; though the degree of consistency depends on the brand of UNIX involved, some commands take their options only bunched up in the first argument, treating remaining arguments as files (ar, tar), while a few others must have all options be separate (cat, at least in BSD UNIX).

There are other little inconsistencies among groups of functionally related commands. The grep, egrep, and fgrep commands all have different subsets of options, generally for no apparent reason. (For example, grep, unlike the other two commands, does not accept a -f option, indicating that the actual pattern to be matched will be found in a file instead of on the command line.) Worse, ed, grep, egrep, and lex all have pattern-matching facilities, but the syntax they accept for specifying patterns (called "regular expressions") is slightly different for each one.

These inconsistencies arose because of the environment in which UNIX development took place: a research environment in which each researcher who needed a command just wrote it. There were no standards committees or formal reviews before a command could be installed on the system. UNIX was not regarded as a commercial product, but rather as a home-grown tool to use in performing computer-related research. As a result, the commands available are sometimes very advanced: yacc, a parser generator, and lint, a program consistency checker, are two examples of programs never found in purely commercial systems when UNIX was being developed. But there are also rough edges.

Now that AT&T views UNIX as a commercial product, it is introducing consistency in these matters. AT&T UNIX provides a library routine called getopt, which standardizes the use of single-character options. It not only ensures that they can be bunched together or appear separately on the command line, but also provides a common notation (--) to indicate the end of the list of options; this replaces older, ad hoc methods for specifying a file or pattern-match beginning with a - in such a way that it would not be taken as an option name. The same routine produces a standard error message when an unknown option name is given and requires that any option names in the command line appear to the left of any filenames.

To help resolve the pattern-matching problem, AT&T has provided regular-expression parsing code as an independent library module. In AT&T's UNIX, the ed, grep, and egrep commands now accept a more similar regular expression syntax.

Over time, UNIX will thus become more consistent—at least when it comes from AT&T. Unfortunately, there are multiple flavors of UNIX (as you will see), so this problem may take some time to be completely resolved.

The Little Languages

Some UNIX commands are complicated enough that they may be said to define small computer languages of their very own, designed for specialized tasks. The term *little languages* has been coined to describe them.

Since text files are the fundamental form in which much UNIX data is expressed, most of these languages deal with text processing in some form or another. The grep command defines a tiny "language" in which you can describe the characteristics of the lines of text you would like it to display. The sed command describes a more complicated language for text processing, including a test primitive and a transfer of control (goto) statement. The awk command describes a still more sophisticated language for text processing; its language includes variables, expressions, loops, and built-in subroutines. Its language is similar to, but not identical with, the C language in which it and most other UNIX commands are written. Together, these commands constitute a powerful arsenal of text-manipulating tools.

However, each of these commands was designed by a different individual or group for a need not met by earlier commands in its genre. The result sometimes appears to be a hodgepodge of programs with overlapping and indistinctly defined functionalities.

For example, the awk command was written after sed and is generally more powerful. Anything you can do using sed you can also do using awk. Well, almost: using awk alone, you cannot transliterate one set of characters to another (such as for changing uppercase to lowercase). A built-in transliteration function would have been quite useful. Also, sed can divide each line it reads in almost completely arbitrary ways: you can specify that the line's first field be separated from the second by a single tab, while the third field comes after either a colon or semicolon, and the fourth is found after one or more combinations of asterisks and hyphens. But awk can only understand lines whose fields are separated by white space (blanks and tabs) or by a single kind of character. The ability to begin an awk program with a regular expression in the manner of sed—which predefined the meaning of "first field," "second field," and so on—plus a few other minor improvements, would have made awk essentially a replacement for sed; the older command would still have been useful for certain occasions, but it would have been unnecessary for every good UNIX guru to know the subtle details of both commands.

As these commands stand, the choice between sed and awk often depends on subtle aspects of the task and the tools. The awk command is generally better when each line of the input to be processed can be considered to be divided up into fields separated by the same character, or by blanks and tabs. More intricate field separation requires sed, but then you cannot hold much information from one line to the next. Also, awk becomes unsuitable if you want to extract a field that looks like, but isn't, a floating-point number; awk will treat it as one and "round it off" for you as it copies it. Choosing between both commands often requires trying to accomplish the task in each one, using successively more baroque language in each, and then deciding which little language comes closest to being able to do the job you had wanted done. Perhaps future versions of UNIX will remedy this situation by rewriting these little languages, perhaps under new names so the old versions can be kept in place for compatibility with existing shell scripts.

Fortunately, if you know your task requires writing a real program, you don't have to make a choice. UNIX provides only one standard programming language: C.

UNIX, C, and Portability

The development of the C language was an important innovation of UNIX. C is the premier *practical* systems-programming language. It is much easier to use (and much more portable) than assembler, yet provides much of the same "control over the machine" that often drives programmers to use assembler. It is also a relatively simple language to compile and thus is practical to implement for a wide class of machines. C may someday be eclipsed by other languages, such as Modula-2 or Ada (though there are those who doubt it), but it will always occupy a unique position in the pantheon of programming languages. C has been criticized elsewhere as a difficult language to learn and use (for example, its declaration syntax is opaque),[1] but all programming languages have their weak points. Instead, we will focus on one of its strongest advantages: its portability. The issue of portability is important in assessing the strengths and weaknesses of UNIX.

C's combination of efficiency and portability has led to its near-universal use on systems ranging from mainframes down to PCs. Many more machines can now run UNIX, and for most users that means running C. Unfortunately, C was not designed with portability in mind. Just because your C program compiles and runs perfectly on one machine doesn't mean it will run on another. To put it another way, the C compiler won't refuse to compile a program just because it's nonportable. This is sometimes a virtue, since it means that you can write nonportable code when you need to, but it is also a nuisance. Nonportable constructs that the C compiler

---

[1] "Type Syntax in the Language C: An Object Lesson in Syntactic Innovation," by Bruce Anderson, reprinted in *Comparing and Assessing Programming Languages*, Alan Feuer and Narain Gehani, eds. (Englewood Cliffs, N.J.: Prentice-Hall, 1984).

will pass include attempting to store pointers into integers (and vice versa), using a pointer to point to another kind of object than the one it was declared to point to, and even generating and using an arbitrary address that has no relationship to any data in the program!

In all of these cases, the C compiler will at least provide a warning that you are doing something dubious, until you silence it by adding a "cast" to convert a value from one type to another. There are other, more subtle nonportabilities, such as attempting to point to the data with an uninitialized pointer, which can arise very easily and not be caught by the compiler or when the program runs. The C compiler also can't usually tell if you write code that depends on the order in which bytes occur within an integer or pointer, or on the number of bytes in an integer.

And finally, the C compiler is incapable of catching you if you call a routine in another file with arguments of the wrong type or expect a return value of the wrong type—problems that often don't show up on machines for which the two types are the same size, but that cause disaster on machines for which they differ.

That last class of error—inconsistencies across source files—is the main reason for the existence of the lint program. It examines all the source files that compose a program in one sweep, and compares subroutine calls and variable uses to their respective definitions. The lint program makes other portability checks as well. But it is not much help at identifying byte-ordering problems, accidental misuse of the NULL pointer, or most of the other portability issues mentioned earlier, so the programmer must still be very careful.

With all its problems, though, the C language is still eminently usable. You can achieve any degree of portability and trade off efficiency for portability, or vice versa, as you deem fit, given skill and attention. A large application can even be written in a very portable form and then "optimized" by providing less portable C versions of critical routines that run very quickly on particular kinds of machines. The result is a program that will run on any UNIX computer, but will run faster on the most vital computers.

Even very large applications can be written in a relatively portable way—even, in fact, entire operating systems.

UNIX: The Portable Operating System

An important demonstration of the portability of C code (in the right hands) occurred about 12 years ago, when the developers of UNIX attempted to make UNIX a portable operating system. At that time, UNIX ran on the DEC PDP-11 series of minicomputers. Their initial target was the Interdata

8/32—another minicomputer, but one with a very different instruction set, addressing scheme, and I/O structure than DEC's. The results of this work became available in the next version (the "Version 7") of the UNIX system:

- enhancements to the C language itself to support more portable code, such as casts and unions, and tighter type checking
- a new C compiler, pcc (for "portable C compiler"), intended to be easier to adapt to new architectures than the original PDP-11 compiler
- a program, lint, to check for portability problems
- new versions of the standard UNIX system programs, including the UNIX kernel itself, which were recoded to be more portable and adaptable to new machines

Although a skilled compiler wizard was still required to make the C compiler produce code for a new machine, and a trained UNIX kernel programmer was still needed to adapt the kernel to a new hardware architecture, most Version 7 UNIX programs worked on new machines without too much effort.

When Version 7 UNIX was released to the outside world, other groups started putting UNIX on different machines, even IBM mainframes. Today UNIX runs on a wider range of mini- and mainframe computers than any other operating system, and even microcomputer versions are now available. Many UNIX programs need only recompiling to work on a new machine with a completely different instruction set, I/O devices, and so on. In retrospect, it is hard to imagine a more unique development in the history of computers. Before UNIX came along, operating systems were developed by the manufacturers of the hardware; they had (and still have) virtually no incentive to make their operating systems portable. While the *idea* of portability may have been in the air, and such operating systems as Multics possibly could have evolved into portable operating systems, it took a company that manufactured no computer hardware—Bell Labs—to achieve this breakthrough and bring such an operating system into widespread use.

Unfortunately from the point of view of portability, more than one version of UNIX was developed. The presence of different flavors of UNIX has produced a new problem and a new kind of nonportability: programs depending on a particular version of the UNIX operating system.

BSD and System V: Two Families and Their Children

The fact that UNIX runs on a machine unfortunately doesn't mean all the UNIX programs you've written will run on that machine, no matter how much care you've taken to avoid depending on the size of an integer or byte ordering. For one thing, different vendors have "ported" UNIX to various machines with different degrees of care. For another, subtle differences may exist in the contents of system *header files*, which define kernel data structures or the data types passed across the interface between the kernel and your program. But the major source of problems a developer—or a user—will encounter when trying to move from one flavor of UNIX to another are the differences between the two major lines of UNIX development.

Figure 1–1 gives an overview of UNIX genealogy. Briefly, the initial versions of the system came from the group that originally developed UNIX, the Computer Science Research Center at Bell Labs in Murray Hill, New Jersey. Their Version 6 UNIX was the first to be made available to the general public (including commercial firms). It also became popular within Bell Labs itself. It was the last version of UNIX before the split.

The Murray Hill group produced a Version 7 of UNIX. Another group within Bell Labs produced their own enhanced Version 6 UNIX, which later became the Programmer's Workbench (PWB), partially because the original Bell Labs group was not interested in providing UNIX support and maintenance to the entire Bell System. PWB and the Version 7 were somewhat incompatible. Though most of the differences were ironed out, other groups within Bell also started modifying UNIX.

It was the UNIX support groups' work that eventually became the AT&T System V series of UNIX operating systems, and one major variant of UNIX. This variant gained a wide following within AT&T for its support of telephone switching system development and related activities.

Meanwhile, Digital Equipment Corporation developed a new, more powerful computer as a successor to their popular PDP-11 (the computer upon which the Version 7 and PWB ran). Among many other new capabilities, the new computer, called the VAX (for Virtual Address eXtension) could support *virtual memory*, permitting programs to run without all of their instructions and data being in main memory at once (and without the use of overlays).

Another Bell Labs group in Holmdel, New Jersey, "ported" Version 7 UNIX (or something very close to it) to the VAX. The group members did not, however, use the virtual memory mechanism; their version of UNIX still swapped entire programs in and out of main memory. This was UNIX 32V.

At the University of California at Berkeley, it was felt that a version of UNIX for the VAX that didn't take advantage of its virtual memory hardware was definitely deficient. In their Computer Science Research Group, Berkeley programmers modified UNIX to provide virtual memory. While they were at it, they threw in a few other enhancements. This was

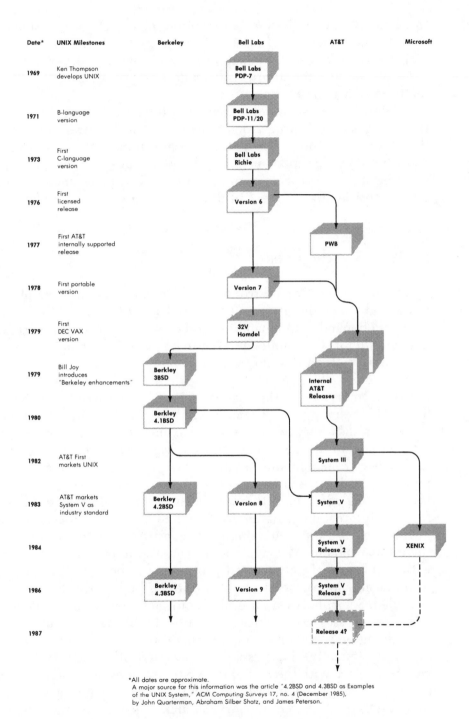

Date*	UNIX Milestones	Berkeley	Bell Labs	AT&T	Microsoft
1969	Ken Thompson develops UNIX		Bell Labs PDP-7		
1971	B-language version		Bell Labs PDP-11/20		
1973	First C-language version		Bell Labs Richie		
1976	First licensed release		Version 6		
1977	First AT&T internally supported release			PWB	
1978	First portable version		Version 7		
1979	First DEC VAX version		32V Homdel		
1979	Bill Joy introduces "Berkeley enhancements"	Berkley 3BSD		Internal AT&T Releases	
1980		Berkley 4.1BSD			
1982	AT&T First markets UNIX			System III	
1983	AT&T markets System V as industry standard	Berkley 4.2BSD	Version 8	System V	
1984				System V Release 2	XENIX
1986		Berkley 4.3BSD	Version 9	System V Release 3	
1987				Release 4?	

*All dates are approximate.
A major source for this information was the article "4.2BSD and 4.3BSD as Examples
of the UNIX System," ACM *Computing Surveys* 17, no. 4 (December 1985),
by John Quarterman, Abraham Silber Shatz, and James Peterson.

Figure 1–1   Major Lines of UNIX Development   *(SOURCE: "4.2BSD and 4.3BSD as Examples of the UNIX System,"* ACM Computing Surveys 17, no. 4 (December 1985) by John Quarterman, Abraham Silbershatz, and James Peterson.)

the Third Berkeley System Distribution, or 3BSD.[5] It was soon followed by 4.1BSD, 4.2BSD, and (as of this writing) 4.3BSD. It became the other major variant of UNIX; its support for virtual memory drew many sites initially, and its later addition of standard networking protocols and other features kept people using it.

How do the two systems compare? In broad outline, they are similar, though most UNIX programmers express a strong preference for one or the other. Unfortunately, neither system is universally superior. Each has taken its own direction in meeting today's needs in areas such as networking and interprocess communications. This paper mentions just some of the most important areas of difference.

System V Advances

System V from AT&T is stronger on "commercial" aspects of UNIX. As has already been discussed, AT&T is polishing UNIX's rough edges in the area of command option handling and error messages. Some programmers also consider its C compiler and lint to be more robust and to have a better user interface than the BSD versions.

System V also features a way for two processes to share a common area of memory. Using this facility, AT&T is now able to provide "shared libraries," helping to overcome UNIX's reputation in the microcomputer world as a disk hog. System V also has *message queues*, which provide a way for several processes to send messages to a common receiver with each message maintaining its integrity. Message queues are better than pipes because if several processes write to a single pipe, the messages may be intermingled. Even if they are not intermingled, there will be no way for the pipe-reading program to tell when one message ends and the next begins, because pipes are simple streams of characters. Message queues solve this problem. Message queues can also have permissions associated with them, so that only trusted processes can be permitted to use them. Another new interprocess communications facility, the *semaphore*, is also provided. Semaphores are useful in conjunction with shared memory, permitting processes to coordinate their updates of shared-memory data without relying on special machine instructions.

Unfortunately, the message queues and other new features are not well-integrated with the rest of the system. A message queue is not a pipe, and you cannot hand an ordinary UNIX program a message queue for its standard output. Shared memory, similarly, is not integrated with the file

---

[5]Berkeley programmers had been modifying UNIX even before the VAX implementation. Their PDP-11 versions were the first and second Berkeley System Distributions.

system; you cannot map a file into shared memory, though you can (of course) read it in yourself. Mapping a file into shared memory would permit it to be accessed like memory, with only the parts of the file that need to be read actually loaded from the disk. It would also permit the file to be changed like memory; merely storing into a shared memory location associated with the file would cause the file to be changed. (The IBM RT PC version of UNIX, AIX, does permit files to be mapped in using the shared-memory facility.) Also, naming message queues and shared-memory segments is done using numeric identifiers; only the crudest provision is made for avoiding collisions among independent users of these facilities. It would have been better to associate each of these entities with a file system entry. (A routine exists to generate a numeric identifier from a filename, but it cannot guarantee that a collision will not occur even when independent filenames are used.)

Berkeley (BSD) Advances

Berkeley UNIX is generally stronger on educational, technical, and research-related features. Universities appreciate its *disk quotas*, which prevent an errant student program (or student) from filling up an entire file system. Its support for standard networking protocols, particularly TCP/IP over Ethernet, makes it the preferred system in environments using those protocols to tie their machines together. Researchers in communications can access the networking facilities in various ways using *sockets*, which are essentially a generalization of pipes. Sockets can carry data in two directions (pipes are unidirectional) and can connect programs on two different machines. Communications work is facilitated by the select system call, with which a single process can wait for input from more than one source, such as either a terminal or a network connection. (AT&T System V does provide the ability to await input from more than one message queue at a time, but terminals are not message queues.) For some networking jobs, such as "remote login," a way to have a process "type" on a pseudoterminal is mandatory; BSD provides pseudoterminals.

BSD UNIX also improves on the original (and System V) UNIX signaling mechanism. The System V signaling mechanism is less robust than the BSD mechanism; the latter is modeled after hardware interrupts and permits a program to catch a signal at any time, perform an arbitrary series of actions, and resume precisely where it was interrupted. With System V, a signal can disrupt certain system calls, such as terminal read calls. Also, when a System V process is catching a signal, if it receives the signal twice in a row, very quickly, it may not be able to field the second occurrence of the signal and may terminate as a consequence.

But BSD UNIX is not always better than System V UNIX. BSD sockets are like pipes; they do not provide dividing lines between messages, nor can you associate permissions with a socket. And BSD signals, though better than AT&T's for many purposes, are subtly incompatible with the mechanism of earlier UNIX systems.

BSD also provides a facility called *job control*, by which individual commands ("jobs") may be started and stopped, and their access to the terminal controlled. Thus, if a command needs to read a few lines of input from you, but will thereafter run for a long time before finishing, you could use job control to start it, tell it what it wants to know, then move it to the "background," where it will continue running while you issue other commands. You can also stop and start background commands. System V provides a similar, but different facility; it manages terminal access like BSD job control, but does not permit commands to be started and stopped. It is a more elegant facility, but incomplete.

There are also many less important differences, For example, each brand of UNIX also provides its own set of handy library routines and commands. To programmers, these often make less difference in choosing a UNIX version than the kinds of differences detailed here, because they can always be rewritten from their documentation; the differences in kernel capabilities (and, to a lesser extent, C language support) are what really matter. The facilities already described are some of the most important inherent, unchangeable differences between the two implementations.

The Search for Portability and Standards

Despite the many differences between BSD and System V, it is quite practical to write large, complex programs that work on both kinds of UNIX systems—though not without having a sample of each kind of system on hand! In the future, it will become easier to write portable UNIX programs, because the Institute of Electrical and Electronics Engineers (IEEE) is working on a standard operating system (called POSE, for Portable Operating System Environment, but usually referred to as POSIX) modeled after both UNIX System V and BSD. POSIX defines a rich set of system calls and library routines that can be used from any C program running on a conforming system. When the POSIX effort is complete, it is expected that many UNIX vendors will rush to comply with it—especially because the U.S. government and large corporations such as General Motors strongly support it. With the arrival of POSIX, the need to handle variants of UNIX will all but disappear. The separate universes of BSD and System V UNIX will at last be merged.

Even as POSIX merges BSD and System V UNIX, other variants of UNIX are springing up. The "Version 8" and "Version 9" of UNIX, as the names imply, are the latest versions of the UNIX system from the original UNIX developers at Bell Labs. They are much-modified versions of Berkeley UNIX. They include many novel and interesting ideas, some of which will be mentioned later in this paper. Unfortunately, they are not generally available, and so most UNIX users outside Bell Labs can only admire them from afar.

There are also two interesting rewrites of UNIX. MINIX is a low-cost but complete implementation of Version 7 UNIX that was written from scratch, so it uses no AT&T code and requires no source license. GNU, a collective project led by Richard M. Stallman, is a free, public-domain UNIX look-alike. Both of these will be discussed further in Eric Raymond's paper at the end of this book.

UNIX Modularity

Thus far this paper has been looking primarily at the UNIX user interface and command processor. Additionally, any operating system also provides an interface that programs can use to request that various system-level functions be performed—the operating system interface. Without going into this interface in much detail, the paper looks at one key idea: the relationship of the core of the operating system (the "kernel") to the bulk of commands, utilities, and functions, and to the file system.

The basic idea in UNIX is to keep the kernel small and simple, and to provide most needed services with replaceable modules rather than hard-wiring them into the kernel. (UNIX inherited many of these ideas about modularity from the Multics project mentioned earlier.)

What are the advantages of a small kernel? One is that it puts most of the system software "outside the kernel," where it is easier to debug, test, and maintain. This is especially important because you cannot test a new kernel without taking over the whole machine to run it. Another advantage is that it permits a user to change more aspects of the behavior of the system. Said Ken Thompson, an originator of UNIX (in "UNIX Implementation," *Bell Systems Technical Journal* 57, no. 6, Part 2, July–August 1978, pages 1931 and 1945):

> The kernel is the only UNIX code that cannot be substituted by a user to his own liking. For this reason, the kernel should make as few real decisions as possible. This does not mean to allow the user a million options to do the same thing. Rather, it means to allow only one way to do one thing, but have that way be the least-common divisor of all the options that might have been provided. . . . The UNIX kernel is an I/O multiplexer more than a complete operating system.

Following this strategy produced what is probably the simplest time-sharing system kernel, considering its capabilities, that the world has ever seen. The UNIX kernel once contained less than 10,000 lines of code.

A good illustration of this practice is the UNIX command processor. The command processor, or *shell*, is what processes each command you type, splitting the line of characters into a command name and its arguments, then running the command. Because it's just an ordinary program, new versions can be debugged like any other program and replaced by the user if necessary or desirable. (Indeed, three different UNIX shells are generally available: the Bourne shell, C shell, and the newer Korn shell, each with its own emphases and strengths.) In other operating systems of the time, the command processor generally played a very special role; it was unthinkable, for instance, to allow a user to replace the standard IBM job control language (JCL) interpreter with a custom version!

UNIX also follows Multics tradition in providing a "logical" rather than "physical" file system. Most operating systems use the physical configuration of the system as the starting point for their file system. For instance, the first component of a full MS-DOS filename is the name of the disk drive, or pseudodisk drive, containing the file. The same is true of filenames under many other operating systems, such as the Digital Equipment Corporation's operating systems (VAX VMS, PDP-10 TOPS-10, and PDP-20 TOPS-20), as well as most microcomputer operating systems.

But UNIX separates the physical configuration of the system from the logical filenames seen by users. Even though your home directory and your friend Fred's may be on different disk drives, you can refer to both of them (if the system is configured appropriately) by using the common /usr prefix: /usr/dan and /usr/fred. Thus users are spared having to remember anything more than another user's name in order to find that user's files— and the filenames don't change if the system is reorganized to use a new disk drive.[6]

Other operating systems also tend to use a plethora of separator characters to indicate the device name, user name, and filename. For example, a complete **VAX VMS** pathname looks like this:

```
nodename::device:<dir1.dir2>file.suffix;version
```

Many other operating systems similarly use a different separator character for each of the components of the name. UNIX's ancestors made file system names easy to work with by recognizing that a hierarchical file system is just a tree. All you need is one special character to separate the

---

[6]This is much more practical to achieve with BSD than with System V, due to BSD's "symbolic links."

components of the tree (which in UNIX is the slash). Working with such simplified names is much easier than manipulating traditional filenames.

The uniform logical hierarchy provided by UNIX has encouraged novel ways to provide new capabilities, such as a distributed file system (DFS) in which users and programs can use files on another machine as easily as those on their own machine. An obvious way to provide a DFS is to put the name of the other machine at the front of the pathname, as in the VMS pathname just shown. But because UNIX already provided filenames that didn't have to name the disk drive containing the file, UNIX DFS developers (of which there have been several) were generally led to the idea that you shouldn't need to name the machine a file was on, either. For instance, a list of books by author might be referenced as /usr/books/authors. A user naming this file would not need to know, or care, whether the file was located on the user's own machine or another one in another building. Both Sun Microsystems' Network File System (NFS) and AT&T's new Remote File System (RFS) work in this way.

UNIX also reduces file contents, like filenames, to their simplest form: a collection of bytes. This is another idea from Multics: the designers of Multics saw no reason to have the operating system manage different file types, or divide a file into records. All any operating system really needs to do is associate a filename with a list of disk blocks (as microcomputer operating systems often do). UNIX does go one step further: it provides a *byte count* for each file, which is just the total number of bytes in the file. Providing this count means that user programs do not have to invent their own methods for indicating when data ends in the middle of a disk block (such as the CTRL-Z of some minicomputer and microcomputer operating systems) and in general don't need to know the size of disk blocks on their machine.

Unfortunately, not everything in the kernel is as simple as it could have been. The philosophy of the "least common denominator" was not carried out consistently.

The UNIX Terminal Driver: The Worst Mistake?

There is one particularly unfortunate violation of the notion that the kernel should be kept small by not having it make any policy decisions: the UNIX terminal driver. The UNIX terminal driver not only moves characters between your terminal and a program; it processes them too. It reads a "line" of characters at a time, and implements a small (but growing) line editor to permit users to correct their typing mistakes, replay what they've typed, and finally submit their lines to the currently running program.

Though the circumstances are entirely understandable, the decision to put the terminal driver entirely in the kernel was possibly the worst mistake made by the designers of UNIX. It was contrary to the "just an I/O multiplexer" philosophy that UNIX developers applied so successfully elsewhere in the kernel to have the kernel perform any kind of interpretation of the characters coming in—line delimiters, editing characters, signaling characters, and so on.

Once the decision was made to put these functions in the kernel, the Pandora's box was opened and would never be shut again. The first serious enhancements to the UNIX terminal driver were made almost as soon as the first systems were released outside Bell Labs. For a time, writing a new terminal driver became a kind of fad (in which I participated). Each new terminal driver was larger than the last, for there were always new ways of saving a few characters' worth of typing. The only limitation was the size of the PDP-11 address space, and with the advent of the VAX, even that limitation was removed. The terminal driver is the only part of the UNIX kernel that now resembles, in its complexity, traditional operating systems such as VAX/VMS.

But it wasn't just the terminal driver's tendency to grow without bounds that was bad. When UNIX began to be applied to networking, implementing "remote login" made it necessary to provide access to these complex terminal functions through a network connection. So the UNIX kernel gained the pseudoterminal (PT or PTY). The PT is a bidirectional communications mechanism that "looks like" a software keyboard and printer. The network software writes on the "keyboard" and its characters are seen by UNIX programs as though a person had typed them; what the programs write as output can be read by the network software on the "printer." The PT is essentially an entry point into the kernel solely to get access to the terminal driver code, divorced from an attachment to any particular hardware. It would have been completely unnecessary if the kernel terminal driver had not implemented so many policy decisions about handling user input.

There are also applications where the opposite effect is desired: access to the terminal hardware without the intervening terminal driver software. For example, a low-cost way to link two computers together is via their serial ports. Although ways have been provided to turn off all the special functions of the terminal driver, what was really wanted was a way to avoid the terminal driver code entirely, especially when one was trying to receive data from another computer at 9600 baud (960 characters per second), which most UNIX systems cannot do without some form of flow control. If the kernel had implemented only the most fundamental access to terminals, as it did for other devices, "raw" mode, "tandem" mode, and so on, would have been unnecessary, and fast character reception would have been much easier.

"More" Is Less (Than Perfect)

When UNIX users started switching from printing terminals to CRT screens, they quickly found that they needed a way to stop their output before it rushed off the screen. But by that time, it seems, people didn't want to add yet another function to the terminal driver, so instead they created a program to perform this function, called more (or in System V, page). The more program does a lot more than stop at the end of a screenful of output and wait for you to ask for more, but that was its reason for existence.

The trouble is that more doesn't work very well. It's not bad for displaying text files sequentially on the screen. But having to add a little pipeline that invokes more at the end of any command line you think might produce more than 24 lines of output is clumsy. Few other operating systems put you through such an operation. In the second place, more is inadequate for many purposes; you cannot, for instance, satisfactorily use it with an interactive program such as a debugger, so that you could pause after every 24 lines worth of long output (such as a stack backtrace). This is because more needs to read your answer to its question (more?) from the terminal directly, rather than from its standard input as most UNIX programs do. Its standard input contains the data to be parceled out to the screen. But the debugger is also reading from the terminal to get your commands. So what the debugger reads from the terminal and what more reads can get intermixed. You may think you're typing a command to the debugger, but more will read it, or vice versa. And more can't determine when the debugger has to pause anyway in order to wait for more commands; a smart screen-paging program would recognize these natural pauses and reset its internal line counter. But more cannot get this information. All of these problems are not merely bugs in the more command; there is no way to fix them merely by modifying more. Rather, the problems result from trying to perform this function in the wrong way.

In addition to these problems, UNIX now has many programs that insist on being connected to a terminal and behave peculiarly if they are not, sometimes to the point of refusing to function. Some mail systems have a send command that cannot be properly invoked from a shell file, but only from the terminal, no matter how hard you try. Using some versions of the Berkeley file transfer program (FTP) from a shell file can also be a real challenge. If terminals were not so different from files and pipes, these programs would not be so prevalent.

All these problems fundamentally stem from the decision to put the policy functions of the terminal driver into the kernel, rather than devising a way to let users provide their own terminal code, just as users can provide their own command processor. There were several obstacles to providing terminal drivers as ordinary programs.

The first obstacle was that pipes are not powerful enough to connect to a terminal driver. Pipes are unidirectional, but a terminal is fundamentally a bidirectional device. Assuming the use of two pipes, a user's terminal driver would have to be ready to receive either typing from the terminal, to be fed to the program, or output from the program, to be fed to the terminal. Since there would be no way to tell which might happen next, the driver would have to be prepared for either. But UNIX programs could only accept input from one source at a time.

A more subtle problem was hinted at earlier. A good terminal screen-paging algorithm should recognize when natural pauses occur and reset its internal line counter. Otherwise, a user would have to tell the pager to continue every 24 lines even when the user was issuing a series of commands that all gave one-line responses. Obviously, by the time a user issues a new command, he or she has read the output of the previous one; it is only a stream of uninterrupted output that must be parceled out. This requires a terminal pager that is able to determine when a program issues a read to the terminal, and to pause for the user to type an answer. But a terminal driver at one end of a pipe cannot tell when the other end is waiting for more input.

Finally, almost any terminal driver is probably going to have different modes of operation, such as edited or nonedited input, or paged or non-paged output (nonedited input and nonpaged output are necessary for screen editors). A program must be able to pass orders to the terminal driver to make the driver change modes. But pipes pass only data; there is no notion of special control information.

Another obstacle is that the program would have been too slow. Any kind of terminal driver user program would have been unacceptable to most users, because there would have been appreciable and unpredictable delays between the time you typed a character and the time the program was finally awakened to echo it; a user program under UNIX used to be a pretty major affair, before demand paging was implemented. Unpredictable echoing—particularly echoing that cannot keep up with a fast typist, but puts out characters in bursts—is extremely annoying.

There were several reasons for this problem; the primary one was probably the inefficient use UNIX made of main memory. UNIX systems divided programs into only two parts as they were kept in main memory: the "text" (instructions) were one part, and the "data" and stack were the other. When a large program needed to run, the entire program had to be "swapped in," which meant that two large empty pieces of main memory—one for the program's text, and one for the program's stack and data—had to be found. To find them, the scheduler might have to swap out a lot of smaller programs. It didn't help matters any that the scheduler wasn't very intelligent about choosing programs to swap out. The result was that main memory was not used very efficiently.

While demand paging would have been difficult to add to UNIX in those days (on the PDP-11), it would probably have been reasonable to at least break up programs into smaller pieces, so that memory could be used more efficiently. Also, a way could have been provided to lock the program into memory, and to ask the scheduler to give it high priority. Several UNIX sites (and later, System V UNIX) implemented kernel extensions to perform these simple operations. A user's terminal driver would have been an excellent candidate to lock into memory and run as soon as the user typed any character. After all, the kernel code to perform terminal driver functions was effectively locked into memory and run instantly anyway; it was just hidden away where users couldn't change it. Running it at a higher priority would similarly be reasonable, because the terminal driver code normally ran at interrupt-level priority anyway. (With this priority it could potentially interfere with the system's ability to respond to other interrupts. The terminal driver is one of the reasons UNIX systems often have difficulty responding to interrupts with a guaranteed maximum response time.)

Still another obstacle is that it would have been very inefficient. All the characters appearing on your screen would have to be copied an extra time: from the program that generated them to the terminal driver program and thence to the kernel. (The other direction is not much of a problem, since most people can't type faster than about 10 bytes per second.) It would have been particularly inefficient to use a pipe-like mechanism to do the copying, since pipes were (and still are, in System V UNIX) implemented as unnamed disk files! At the very least, a communications mechanism that kept data only in memory was needed. It might also have been worthwhile to provide a special shared address space between the terminal driver and the kernel to facilitate transferring characters out quickly.

These major obstacles stood in the way of providing user terminal driver programs. Every one of these problems was worth solving in its own right, but merely because a problem is worth solving doesn't mean it must be solved; other problems can be more pressing. It would have been hard to justify the effort involved in solving all these problems just to provide a more elegant way to correct some typing errors.

Solving the Problem

Now that UNIX has advanced, many of these problems *have* been solved:

- BSD provides the ability to wait for input from more than one source.

- BSD's sockets are a memory-resident communications mechanism rather than disk-based.

- Both BSD and AT&T System V are demand-paged, and BSD also provides a way to lock a process into memory.

Unfortunately, in the meantime the terminal driver has grown, and there is still no communications mechanism other than the pseudoterminal that really "looks like a terminal" to UNIX programs. The pseudoterminal is not a complete solution; it cannot be used, for example, to implement a clever screen-paging algorithm, because the program on the "keyboard/screen" side has no way to tell when the application is doing a read. It is also difficult to have the pseudoterminal provide new features, such as screen paging, because there is no way an ordinary user program can ask for it to be turned on or off through the PT.[7]

There is help on the horizon. Dennis Ritchie has designed and implemented a new communications mechanism called a *stream*, which appears to provide enough power to permit a user to install a personal terminal driver. A stream module is a bidirectional communications mechanism that implements some processing of the data as it goes through the module. Stream modules can be attached together in much the same way that UNIX programs can be attached in pipelines. But the module is bidirectional, and the data flows through in explicit read and write requests rather than as a homogenous stream. Thus, a stream module could implement screen paging, and this module could be inserted between a stream module that implemented the traditional UNIX terminal driver functions and user programs. The result would function exactly like a terminal with user programs.

Stream modules are an internal kernel mechanism, mainly used to connect parts of the kernel to one another, but one kind of stream module permits a user program to be inserted, by providing the program with the actual read and write requests being made by other stream modules (or applications). Thus streams finally permit the terminal driver to be moved out of the kernel entirely.

Unfortunately, streams are currently implemented only in Versions 8 and 9 UNIX and in AT&T System V release 3, not in any readily available UNIX version. One can hope that System V release 3 will soon be readily available, and that some enterprising student may reimplement them for BSD; perhaps they may become a future extension to POSIX. Now that a

---

[7]There are ways to solve these problems for screen paging, but they do not generalize.

solution has been developed, surely its widespread availability cannot be far off.

The Future of UNIX

Even though the developers of UNIX may have made some mistakes, they have still provided a very good operating system that has withstood radical changes over time. Network communications were added relatively easily to UNIX, in part because of the simplicity of UNIX's interface with the rest of the world. Modern notions such as distributed file systems, diskless workstations, windowing systems, and mouse control have been fitted into UNIX by various vendors without undue strain, and standards for them are starting to appear.

Facilities for support of commercial applications such as file record locking and file synchronization have also been added. It is a tribute to UNIX that so many people have found it so easy to adapt to their needs. Its user interface, though imperfect, can be replaced, and in fact several companies offer new kinds of command processors that are much easier for nonprogrammers to use.

As a basis for operating system development, the UNIX kernel has grown somewhat large and unwieldy (at least by UNIX standards), and it might be thought that UNIX system evolution would become more difficult, as new ideas need to be fitted into the old system. Fortunately, the complexity of the kernel has been recognized as a problem. In one recent effort at recoding the entire kernel, MINIX, UNIX returns to its roots: the kernel is indeed nothing more than an I/O multiplexer. The only functions that the kernel provides are process creation, interprocess communication, and controlled access to peripheral devices and the central processing unit (CPU). All other activities, including file system management, terminal drivers, network protocols, and so on, are done as nonkernel system programs that send and receive messages from applications. The result is a new kind of simplicity and modularity that could easily engender an entire generation of UNIX system evolution, particularly because the sources to MINIX are so readily available, unlike UNIX sources.

As a foundation for applications, UNIX's portability and relative simplicity remain strong advantages. Corporations that have long been captive to a single vendor because of the effort involved in converting their programs from one proprietary operating system to another will find liberation in UNIX. The IEEE standards effort will greatly accelerate the trend away from single-vendor solutions. The availability of low-cost versions of UNIX (such as MINIX) may cause UNIX to become a more widespread and portable operating system for microcomputers—possibly even supplanting MS-DOS, for example.

The future of UNIX, then, is bright. With so much progress on the commercial front, with a truly inexpensive and adaptable microcomputer version of the system, and with a fundamental structure that makes extensive change practical, there is every reason to believe that UNIX will continue to be used more and more widely. In the future, though it may then be almost unrecognizable to current UNIX aficionados, UNIX may become the primary operating system of the world.

KEYWORDS

▶ USENET

▶ Netnews

▶ .newsrc

▶ postnews

▶ readnews

▶ Netiquette

▶ Backbone sites

▶ Flooding algorithm

Paper Synopsis: Did you know that your UNIX system can be part of a worldwide news network/bulletin board? This paper provides a complete tutorial on using the readnews and postnews programs, a brief look at alternative news programs, plus descriptions of the most popular and informative newsgroups. It describes how to tap into a wealth of free expert advice, program source code, and many more features of this network with more than 200,000 members.

Harry Henderson is a freelance technical writer and editor. He has edited and contributed to computer books for The Waite Group, Atari, Blackwell Scientific, Benjamin/Cummings, Wadsworth, and other publishers. He has a special interest in the UNIX operating system and is the series editor for Howard W. Sams's and The Waite Group's *Tricks of the UNIX Masters, UNIX Bible, UNIX Communications,* and *UNIX Papers.*

## 2

The USENET System

Harry Henderson

$\mathbf{M}$any UNIX users are not aware that they have virtually free access to USENET, a sort of super bulletin board on which an estimated 150,000 UNIX users at 5,000 sites exchange news and views on over 250 different topics. (The name USENET comes from the USENIX Association, a professional group for UNIX users.) For just the cost of your normal connect time, you can, among other things:

- express opinions on controversial issues
- make announcements
- advertise or find jobs
- get help on hardware problems and software bugs
- explore the frontiers of artificial intelligence
- obtain public domain source code
- play games
- publish newsletters

One reason why more people don't know about this significant resource is that the software used to read and post news articles on USENET is public domain, and not part of the standard UNIX distributions. It is not described in the standard AT&T or Berkeley System Distribution (BSD) UNIX manuals. While systems that offer USENET usually have *online* (computer-based) manuals for the news software, tutorials actually explaining how to use USE-

NET are hard to come by. (There are some useful articles on various aspects of USENET available online, but you have to know how to access USENET before you can read them. We'll look at some of them later.)

This paper offers an introduction to the resources available on USE-NET and follows that with an easy to use tutorial that will show you how to read and reply to news articles, as well how to as post original articles of your own. It closes with some advice on how to learn more about USE-NET. Even if you already are familiar with USENET, you may find our observations and tips helpful in your exploration of the net world.

When you have finished reading this paper, you will be ready to take part in a fascinating and informative exchange with thousands of interesting people. You will be ready to explore the more sophisticated features offered by the USENET software. I look forward to seeing you in the news!

A USENET Sampler

Before you delve further into the workings of USENET, take a look at the following potpourri of sample articles. It is not easy to make a representative selection out of the thousands of articles and subjects available on the net at any given time, but this selection will at least suggest the range of possibilities. By the way, in this paper parts of the article headers and much of the text is omitted in order to save space.

This paper includes a variety of actual USENET messages. In some cases the names of message authors have been changed, especially for ephemeral material. Parts of message headers and text have also been omitted to save space. Some editing for grammar and consistency was done to the articles.

As you read USENET messages, you'll encounter words with asterisks around them, like *this*. This is a convention users interpret as emphasized text (as you would see underline, boldface, or italics in printed text). Other conventions of USE-NET messages are described later.

USENET can provide a timely way to announce conferences or other programs that might be of interest to your colleagues. Not only does USE-NET beat the long lead time of print journals, it is also easy, as you'll see later, for interested users to ask for more information by email (electronic mail). For example:

```
From: Marcella.Zaragoza@ISL1.RI.CMU.EDU
Newsgroups: comp.ai
Subject: Seminar - Understanding How Devices Work (CMU)
Date: 30 Jan 87 15:45:09 GMT
```

AI SEMINAR

TOPIC: Understanding How Devices Work: Functional Representation
         of Devices and Compilation of Diagnostic Knowledge

SPEAKER: B. Chandrasekaran
          Department of Computer & Information Science
          The Ohio State University
          Columbus, OH 43210

PLACE: Wean Hall 4605

DATE: Wednesday, February 4, 1987

TIME: 10:00 a.m.

ABSTRACT:

Where does diagnostic knowledge--knowledge about malfunctions and their
relation to observations--come from? One source of it is an agent's
understanding of how devices work, what has been called a "deep model."
We distinguish between deep models in the sense of scientific first
principles and deep cognitive models where the problem solver has a
qualitative symbolic representation of the system or device that accounts
qualitatively for how the system "works." We provide a topology of
different knowledge structures and reasoning processes that play a role in
qualitative or functional reasoning. We indicate where the work of Kuipers,
de Kleer and Brown, Davis, Forbus, Bylander, Sembugamoorthy, and
Chandrasekaran fit in this topology and what types of information each of
them can produce. We elaborate on functional representations as deep
cognitive models for some aspects of causal reasoning in medicine.

If you want information on the reliability of a vendor or product, or
hardware or software recommendations, USENET can also be of help. The
user in the following example wants to know what experience other users
have had with a particular mail-order PC clone vendor. By sharing such
information, you and your colleagues can help each other save money and
avoid hassles.

From: ku@intelca.UUCP (Roger Ku)
Newsgroups: ca.wanted,misc.wanted
Subject: Questions about a mail order company called PC Network

```
Date: 4 Feb 87 20:16:10 GMT

I have some questions about the reputability about a mail order
house called PC Network.  This company advertises in CP Magazine.
The prices are fairly low for the products advertised. It is
based in Chicago.

I would like to know if anybody has ordered anything from this firm.  Did
you get what you ordered?  How long does it take an order to travel to
its destination--did you have to wait long for your order to arrive?
Did you have any problems with the product after you received it?
And any other experiences, opinions or advice that you may have on this
company would be greatly appreciated.
```

USENET is a great place to share bug fixes and software revisions, and to ask for other users' help in tracking down all sorts of software and hardware problems, not just on UNIX systems, but on nearly every microcomputer, minicomputer, or mainframe in existence! Here's an example of how a terminal problem was solved:

```
From: jeff@voder.UUCP (Jeff Gilliam)
Newsgroups: comp.unix.wizards
Subject: termcap entry for tvi925 is wrong +FIX
Date: 21 Nov 86 21:41:26 GMT


Index: etc/termcap/termcap.src 4.3BSD

Description:
        The termcap entry for the Televideo 925 specifies the 'fs'
        capability incorrectly.  Running sysline will cause the cursor
        to jump to column 1 of the screen every time sysline updates
        the status line.
Repeat-By:
        Obvious.
Fix:

Index: termcap.src
diff -c -r1.3 -r1.4
*** /tmp/,RCSt1022496     Fri Nov 21 13:39:46 1986
--- /tmp/,RCSt2022496     Fri Nov 21 13:39:52 1986
***************
*** 2078,2084 ****
        :up=^K:do=^V:kb=^H:ku=^K:kd=^V:kl=^H:kr=^L:kh=^^:ma=^V^J^L :\
        :k1=^A@\r:k2=^AA\r:k3=^AB\r:k4=^AC\r:k5=^AD\r:k6=^AE\r:k7=^AF\r:\
```

```
    :k8=^AG\r:k9=^AH\r:kO=^AI\r:ko=ic,dc,al,dl,cl,ce,cd,bt:\
!      :ts=\Ef:fs=^M\Eg:ds=\Eh:sr=\Ej:vj!tvi925vb!925vb!
televideo model 925 visual bells:\
```

This article may look a little cryptic. Basically, the user is reporting an error in the termcap (terminal capability file) for the Televideo 925. *Termcaps* contain the cursor and screen definitions for various terminals that may be connected to UNIX. He is showing how to fix it by using the diff command to show just where his revised termcap and the current one differ. (Showing just differences is a common practice; it saves space, especially with long binary files.) There are many people on the network who are happy to share their knowledge and work with you. Often cooperative efforts develop in which several users work together to fix bugs or add news features to a program.

We are all engaged in a lifelong battle to keep up with the knowledge explosion, particularly in a field that changes as rapidly as does the computer field. In the next example, a user is asking for recommendations of books and other training materials on the C++ language. This object-oriented offshoot of C was new enough that at the time this message was posted that it was still hard to find good materials for learning it. (At the time you are reading this, of course, you have Keith Gorlen's excellent paper on C++ included in this book.) USENET is a good resource for pointers to knowledge you need to keep your career moving.

```
Subject: c++ reading list
Keywords: c++, reading
From: pjdevries@watrose.UUCP (P. DeVries)
Newsgroups: comp.lang.c++
Date: 30 Jan 87 14:55:16 GMT


--------
Can anyone recommend good books on the C++ language?
I'm particularly interested in primers or tutorials that go
beyond a very elementary level. Does anyone know of a computer
based training package for C++ ?

Thanks.
```

USENET also provides a forum for the discussion of political, social, philosophical, and religious issues:

```
From: nelson_p@apollo.uucp
Subject: what's fair
Date: 8 Feb 87 00:30:00 GMT
```

To: soc.women@news

Adrienne Regard notes that:

> It is grossly unfair for society as a whole to make one half of it's
> members pay more for an act that the entire society benefits from and
> that the other half cannot perform anyway. Which is why it is unfair for
> insurance companies to charge women more for medical insurance based
> on maternity costs.

It is true that women did not choose to be the ones to have to
bear the children but, for the most part, an individual woman
may choose whether or not to have a baby. My wife and I, for
instance, decided not to have children. Any 'fair' system of
insurance would charge extra for maternity coverage, though I
agree that there is no particular reason to just charge the woman
extra. Incidentally, many forms of group insurance *do* charge
extra for maternity coverage and pediatric care and this strikes
me as perfectly reasonable.

It is not clear that the entire society benefits from people having
babies in the general case. The world is grossly overpopulated
and the U.S. is proportionately overpopulated. By that I mean that
amount of energy and resources consumed, and the amount of pol-
lution generated by the average American is quite a bit higher than
that accounted for by, say, the average Nigerian. Personally, I
am in favor of economic disincentives for having children.

Insurance companies care not a whit for what is 'fair' or in the
best interest of society. They are businesses and operate on that
basis. If society's interests were a factor in running businesses
then cigarettes would be banned. I suspect there would also be big
changes in network TV, children's toys, breakfast cereal, and a lot
of other things.

                              --Peter Nelson

There is no point of view that does not have its ardent supporters on
the net. The last example was one of the more thoughtful contributions.
(The > symbols lines indicate material quoted from another article.) Unfortunately, the network's more controversial topics are often prone to
epic bouts of name-calling and near-slander, called "flames" in net slang.
(You don't need an example here. You will run into one soon enough when

you start reading news articles, particularly in the "talk" groups.) But some provocative but courteous discussion is possible.

Life isn't always serious, though. USENET has lively newsgroups devoted to many recreational activities, including computer games and traditional games like chess and go. You can even set up email games with kindred souls. And if you've been stumped by a computer game, chances are excellent that someone on the net can help:

```
From: boston@tc.fluke.COM (George Boston)
Newsgroups: comp.sys.cbm,rec.games.misc
Subject: Bard's Tale Help Needed (this means YOU)
Keywords: on bended knee
Date: 30 Jan 87 16:39:07 GMT


HHHHEEEEELLLLLPPPPP!!!!!  Ok, here I am in the first tower,
after knocking off the crystal statue in the castle, walking
around like crazy looking in every corner for the
door/stair/teleport square, to the next level. I don't know the
answer to the question of "who's name is spoken of twice,"
or even if it matters.

So, what's next? How do I get to the next level Hmmmm? Do I slash
my wrists now or later? How come I feel so dumb? What am I
missing?

Do YOU know? PPPLLLEEEAAASSEEE!!!!!!


Lost George
```

The next sample is on one of the net's most popular subjects, the net itself. There are numerous discussions on the appropriate use of existing topics (newsgroups) and the desirability of creating new ones. (You will see how topics are organized into newsgroups later.)

```
From: gam@amdahl.UUCP (Gordon A. Moffett)
Newsgroups: ca.unix,ca.news
Subject: ca.unix, three months later
Summary: the experiment worked
Date: 21 Feb 87 03:31:54 GMT
Reply-To: gam@amdahl.UUCP (Gordon A. Moffett)


After three months, I'd say the ca.unix experiment has been a success.
It has a good audience of technical people, and now I see regular
traffic in it on an almost daily basis. It is not crowded with
```

repetitive questions or the even more repetitive responses as found
in the comp.unix.* newsgroups. It is a comfortable-sized newsgroup.

This is an example of what the future of USENET might be. When some
worldwide newsgroups become burdened because of the *hundreds* of
participants, perhaps the People can be better served by regional
newsgroups, which are of course smaller in size and volume, and
readers are more willing to review those articles rather than a
nearly automatic pressing of the "n" key. And the total cost of such
regional newsgroups is cheaper, of course.

Before you ask: no, I don't have any new candidates for regional
newsgroups, such as ca.unix is. But it is something to think about.

I do have one question: how many readers of ca.unix have given up on
the comp.unix.* newsgroups completely?

[follow-ups to this article are directed to ca.news only]
--
Gordon A. Moffett   gam@amdahl.amdahl.com

This example contains a report on the success of the newsgroup ca.unix,
which was formed to provide a group of a more manageable size for the
discussion of UNIX questions. (The ca. prefix means "California," as opposed to comp.unix, which is netwide. Naming of newsgroups is discussed
later.)

Now that you've whetted your appetite a bit, look more closely at
how USENET developed and how it is organized.

What Is USENET?

A Bit of Background

The story of USENET begins in 1979 in North Carolina, with two programmers at Duke University, Tom Truscott and James Ellis. At that time
UNIX already had the capability of moving files from one UNIX site to
another over the phone lines, using cu to make connections and uucp to
manage the transfer. Most users also had access to mail in one form or
another, often with remote mail capability. Thus, a user could send a
message or a batch of files to another user, provided the other user's uucp
address was known and the two users' software was compatible. While this

capability is fine for personal messages, it is not very useful for announcing a meeting, debating a ballot proposition, or trying to find out if anyone can help you with a new C compiler. Many mail programs can maintain lists of addresses, and a given message can be sent to everyone on the list. But sending a hundred copies of an article to another UNIX site wastes both disk space and processing time. It would be far better to send one copy of the message that anyone at the destination UNIX site could read. And if that message were systematically distributed, every UNIX site that wanted one would get a copy. Users at a given site could then access a directory containing all the messages that had been received, hopefully organized by topic in some fashion. To respond to this need, programs (collectively called *Netnews* software) were written to make this kind of distribution possible.

The earliest Netnews software was simply a set of shell scripts that moved files back and forth between Duke University and the University of North Carolina. The programs were rewritten in C and released to the public in 1980 by Tom Truscott and Steve Daniel. This set of programs was known as Netnews Release A.

These first Netnews programs were described at the 1980 USENIX conference. As word of what Duke and UNC were up to spread, the idea quickly caught on at other UNIX sites. From its original two sites, USENET began to spread. On the West Coast, Mark Horton and Matt Glickman at U.C. Berkeley revised the Netnews programs to create the "B" version. These changes added new features, including a better organization of topics (newsgroups), as well as being able to accommodate the growing number of sites. USENET was adopted by the influential people at Bell Labs, and it continued to spread throughout North America as well as Australia, parts of Asia, and Europe. There are now estimated to be over 5,000 academic, research, and commercial sites on the net, as shown in net readership surveys.

Talented individuals continued to contribute to the Netnews software in response to user needs and problems. As the news volume became still larger, many newsgroups became glutted with articles, many of which seemed at best marginally appropriate. In response to this, Version 2.10.2 of Netnews B set up a collection of "moderated" newsgroups. In a moderated newsgroup, articles are submitted to the moderator rather than posted directly. This allows some filtering and control over the appropriateness of submissions. Some topics continue to have both moderated and unmoderated newsgroups.

At the time of writing (Spring 1987), the latest version of Netnews is 2.11. It incorporates a more logical system for naming newsgroups, using a scheme of topics and subtopics discussed later. It also allows moderated groups to be handled automatically. Other efforts are underway to allow USENET to use emerging standard Internet network protocols (such as

TCP/IP) instead of uucp, allowing articles to be exchanged between different networks at the network level. Access to USENET is spreading beyond its traditional domain. For example, some microcomputer bulletin board systems using FidoNet now send and forward selected newsgroups downloaded from USENET. There are also some public access USENET nodes, such as Whole Earth's Well in Sausalito, California. The Netnews software is now mature, but it is also flexible and still growing.

USENET: Structure Through Cooperation

USENET is organized a little differently from other information services. Generally speaking, there are two common kinds of information systems that allow users to share news. Commercial information services such as CompuServe or The Source provide a wide range of services, including discussion forums, public domain software distribution, electronic shopping, and so on. They are privately run and charge by the "connect minute" or hour and, as anyone who has become addicted to them can tell you, they can run up a big bill of access and telephone charges for you amazingly quickly.

The other common kind of information service is the local computer bulletin board system (BBS). These normally have no charges other than the phone cost. While many of them are interesting, they usually have only a limited variety of messages, which are often not well organized by topic, and they lack depth and capacity. They are also pretty much limited to news in their local area due to phone costs.

USENET in a way combines the best of both these kinds of systems. Like the commercial information systems, it has a great variety of discussions organized by topic and is national (indeed international) in scope. Like the local BBS, it is generally free. What's even more remarkable is how USENET is actually run.

USENET is in fact not administered in the sense that a commercial service or local BBS is, and in fact has been referred to as a kind of "organized anarchy." To see what this means, imagine that your UNIX site at work does not belong to USENET, but your boss becomes enthusiastic about joining after you have explained USENET's many virtues to her.

To join USENET, you ask around until you find a local UNIX site that already participates in USENET. You arrange for them to give or send your company a copy of the Netnews software, the set of programs that are used to distribute and read news. You install the software on your machine. (This can be a bit tricky, and this paper won't go into it. Some helpful references appear at the end of the paper, however.) You then arrange for that site or another one to provide you with a *news feed*, which is simply the stream of articles being distributed along the network. The

Netnews software at your site and the other site uses batch files (and usually the at facility) together with low-level news programs and uucp to arrange automatic transfer of articles between the machines. Now you can read articles as they come in and send your own articles out into the world.

The key thing to understand about all this is that you didn't have to fill out a membership application. No USENET administrator or committee had to approve your participation in the net. The net is a voluntary association of people who commit some of their own time and computing resources to the free exchange of news.

This lack of centralization has both strengths and weaknesses. Its biggest strength is that it is (except for the moderated newsgroups) completely uncensored and free of political pressure. Its main weaknesses are two: it is hard to agree on desirable changes with so many people participating, and there is little to stop people from abusing the net by posting inflammatory or inappropriate articles. The efficiency of the network and its value to its users depends in large part on how responsibly each user handles its resources. This is why some guidelines on when and how to post news appear later.

Newsgroups and Their Organization

As mentioned earlier, articles in USENET are organized by newsgroups. Newsgroups names follow a convention that, when you learn to interpret it, tells you

- what geographical area is covered by the newsgroup
- the major topic or type of newsgroup
- subtopics or specific topics

The most common prefix for newsgroup names is one of five indicating general areas of interest:

comp.	computer systems and technology
news.	discussions of USENET itself
rec.	recreational activities (the arts, games, entertainment)
sci.	science and technology (excluding computer science, which is in comp.)
soc.	society and culture, social issues, sexuality

Newsgroups can also have prefixes indicating the type of group or the nature of the discussion:

misc.	topics that don't fit under one of the five broad areas above, such as items for sale, jobs, and legal issues
talk.	free-wheeling, often heated discussions on philosophy, politics, religion, and so on

The talk group was actually created to isolate discussions that some users and site administrators feel are not worth the disk space and processing time. The commitment of a site to USENET is flexible; sites can choose which newsgroups they will actually subscribe to, so your site may or may not necessarily have a given group or class of groups.

Finally, there are geographical prefixes. These indicate the area of distribution for articles:

ba.   San Francisco Bay Area (other regions have similar prefixes)
ca.   California (other states may have their own prefixes)
att.   AT&T (other companies and sites may have similar institution or site-specific prefixes)

Figure 2–1 shows some sample newsgroup names and what their components mean. Note that the first component of a newsgroup name is always one (and only one) of the following: a geographical prefix, a type of group (such as talk.) or a general topic area (comp., rec., and so on). If the first component is a general topic area, the second will be a subtopic, and the third (if present) will be a specific topic (such as a model of computer). If the first component is a geographical area or a type of group, then the second component will be a general topic and the third a specific topic.

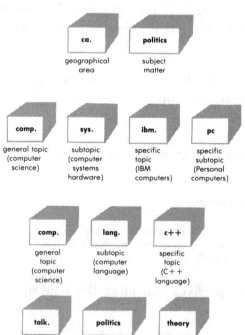

Figure 2–1   Components of Newsgroup Names

The net. prefix is being phased out. Netwide distribution is now the default, unless one of the listed prefixes is used. Thus all the comp., soc., misc., talk groups, and others, are netwide.

Table 2–1 lists all the newsgroups that were active in Spring 1987, with brief descriptions of their contents. You might want to browse through them and note any that are of particular interest. If your site is part of USENET, you will find a similar file in your system's news directory (usually /usr/lib/news) with the filename newsgroups. The regional groups at the head of the list will probably be different for your site.

Table 2–1   Newsgroups for UNIX Users, Spring 1987

Newsgroup	Description
comp.ai	Artificial intelligence discussions.
comp.ai.digest	Digest on artificial intelligence.
comp.arch	Computer architecture.
comp.binaries.amiga	Binary-only postings for the Commodore Amiga.
comp.binaries.atari.st	Binary-only postings for the Atari ST. (Moderated)
comp.binaries.mac	Binary-only postings for the Apple Macintosh.
comp.bugs.2bsd	Reports of UNIX version 2 BSD related bugs.
comp.bugs.4bsd.ucb-fixes	Bug reports/fixes for BSD Unix. (Moderated)
comp.bugs.4bsd	Reports of UNIX version 4 BSD related bugs.
comp.bugs.misc	General bug reports and fixes (includes V7 and uucp).
comp.bugs.sys5	Reports of USG (System III, V, and so on) bugs.
comp.cog-eng	Cognitive engineering.
comp.compilers	Discussion about compiler construction, theory, and so on.
comp.databases	Database and data management issues and theory.
comp.dcom.lans	Local area network hardware and software.
comp.dcom.telecom	Telecommunications.
comp.dcom.modems	Data communications hardware and software.
comp.doc	Archived public-domain documentation.
comp.doc.techreports	Announcements and lists of technical reports.
comp.edu	Computer science education.
comp.emacs	EMACS editors of different flavors.
comp.graphics	Computer graphics, art, animation, image processing.
comp.lang.ada	Discussion about Ada*.
comp.lang.apl	Discussion about APL.
comp.lang.c	Discussion about C.
comp.lang.c++	The object-oriented C++ language.
comp.lang.forth	Discussion about Forth.
comp.lang.fortran	Discussion about FORTRAN.
comp.lang.lisp	Discussion about LISP.
comp.lang.misc	Different computer languages not specifically listed.
comp.lang.modula2	Discussion about Modula-2.
comp.lang.pascal	Discussion about Pascal.
comp.lang.prolog	Discussion about PROLOG.
comp.lang.smalltalk	Discussion about Smalltalk 80.
comp.laser-printers	Laser printers.
comp.lsi	Large scale integrated circuits.
comp.mail.headers	Gatewayed from the ARPA header-people list.
comp.mail.maps	Various maps, including uucp maps.
comp.mail.misc	General discussions about computer mail.

comp.mail.uucp	Mail in the uucp network environment.
comp.misc	General topics about computers not covered elsewhere.
comp.newprod	Announcements of new products of interest to readers.
comp.org.decus	DEC* Users' Society newsgroup.
comp.org.usenix	USENIX Association events and announcements.
comp.os.cpm	Discussion about the CP/M operating system.
comp.os.eunice	The SRI Eunice system.
comp.os.fidonet	FidoNew digest, official newsletter of FidoNet Assoc.
comp.os.minix	Discussion of Tanenbaum's MINIX system.
comp.os.misc	General OS-oriented discussion not carried elsewhere.
comp.os.os9	The OS9 operating system.
comp.os.research	Operating system theory and issues.
comp.periphs	Peripheral devices.
comp.protocols	Computer communication protocols.
comp.protocols.appletalk	The Appletalk protocol.
comp.protocols.kermit	The Kermit protocol and Kermit programs.
comp.protocols.tcp-ip	The TCP-IP protocol.
comp.risks	Risks to the public from computers and users.
comp.soc	Discussions of computers and society.
comp.sources	For the posting of software packages and documentation.
comp.sources.amiga	Source code-only postings for the Amiga. (Moderated)
comp.sources.atari.st	Source code-only postings for the Atari ST. (Moderated)
comp.sources.bugs	For bug fixes and features discussion pertaining to items in comp.sources.
comp.sources.d	For any discussion of source postings.
comp.sources.games	Postings of recreational software.
comp.sources.mac	Software for the Apple Macintosh.
comp.sources.misc	Source code that fits in no other category.
comp.sources.unix	Source code for UNIX systems.
comp.sources.wanted	Requests for software and fixes.
comp.std.c	C language standards.
comp.std.internat	Discussion about international standards.
comp.std.misc	Standards that don't fit in other groups.
comp.std.mumps	Discussion for the X11.1 committee on Mumps.
comp.std.unix	Discussion for the P1003 committee on UNIX.
comp.sys.amiga	Discussion about the Amiga micro.
comp.sys.apollo	Discussion about Apollo computers.
comp.sys.apple	Discussion about Apple micros.
comp.sys.atari.8bit	Discussion about 8 bit Atari micros.
comp.sys.atari.st	Discussion about 16 bit Atari micros.
comp.sys.att	Discussions about AT&T microcomputers.
comp.sys.cbm	Discussion about Commodore micros.
comp.sys.dec	Discussions about DEC computer systems.
comp.sys.hp	Discussion about Hewlett-Packard equipment.
comp.sys.ibm.pc	Discussion about IBM personal computers.
comp.sys.ibm.pc.digest	Digest on IBM personal computers.
comp.sys.intel	Discussions about Intel systems and parts.
comp.sys.m6809	Discussion about 6809's.
comp.sys.m68k	Discussion about 68k's.
comp.sys.mac	Discussions about the Apple Macintosh and Lisa.
comp.sys.mac.digest	Macintosh digest.
comp.sys.masscomp	Discussion of the Masscomp line of computers.
comp.sys.misc	Micro computers of all kinds.
comp.sys.nsc.32k	National Semiconductor 32000 series chips.
comp.sys.pyramid	Pyramid 90X computers.
comp.sys.ridge	Ridge 32 computers and ROS.
comp.sys.sequent	Sequent systems, especially Balance 8000.

comp.sys.sun	Sun "workstation" computers.
comp.sys.tandy	Discussion about TRS-80s.
comp.sys.ti	Discussion about Texas Instruments.
comp.sys.vax	DEC's VAX line of computers.
comp.sys.workstations	Workstations (general).
comp.terminals	All sorts of terminals.
comp.text	Text processing.
comp.unix	General UNIX discussions. (Moderated)
comp.unix.questions	UNIX neophytes group.
comp.unix.wizards	Discussions, bug reports, and fixes on and for UNIX.
comp.unix.xenix	Discussion about the XENIX OS.
comp.windows.misc	Discussion of windowing software.
comp.windows.news	News and reports on windowing software.
comp.windows.x	Discussion about the X Window System.
misc.consumers	Consumer interests, product reviews, and so on.
misc.consumers.house	Discussion about owning and maintaining a house.
misc.forsale	Short, tasteful postings about items for sale.
misc.handicap	Items of interest for/about the handicapped. (Moderated)
misc.headlines	Current interest: drug testing, terrorism, and so on.
misc.invest	Investments and the handling of money.
misc.jobs	Job announcements, requests, and so on.
misc.kids	Children, their behavior and activities.
misc.legal	Legalities and the ethics of law.
misc.misc	Various discussions not fitting in any other group.
misc.psi	Discussion of paranormal abilities and experiences.
misc.taxes	Tax laws and advice.
misc.test	For testing of network software. Very boring.
misc.wanted	Requests for things that are needed (*not* software).
news.admin	Comments directed to news administrators.
news.announce.conferences	Calls for papers and conference announcements.
news.announce.important	General announcements of interest to all.
news.announce.newusers	Explanatory postings for new users.
news.config	Postings of system down times and interruptions.
news.groups	Discussions and lists of newsgroups.
news.lists	News-related statistics and lists. (Moderated)
news.misc	Discussions of USENET itself.
news.newsites	Postings of new site announcements.
news.software.b	Discussion about B news software.
news.software.notes	Notesfile software from the University of Illinois.
news.stargate	Discussion about satellite transmission of news.
news.sysadmin	Comments directed to system administrators.
rec.arts.books	Books of all genres, shapes, and sizes.
rec.arts.comics	The funnies, old and new.
rec.arts.drwho	Discussion about "Dr. Who."
rec.arts.movies	Discussions of movies and movie making.
rec.arts.movies.reviews	Reviews of movies. (Moderated)
rec.arts.poems	For the posting of poems.
rec.arts.sf-lovers	Science fiction lovers' newsgroup.
rec.arts.startrek	"Star Trek," the TV show and the movies.
rec.arts.tv	The boob tube, its history, and past and current shows.
rec.arts.tv.soaps	Postings about soap operas.
rec.arts.wobegon	"A Prairie Home Companion" radio show discussion.
rec.audio	High fidelity audio.
rec.autos	Automobiles, automotive products and laws.

`rec.autos.tech`	Technical aspects of automobiles, et al.
`rec.aviation`	Aviation rules, means, and methods.
`rec.bicycles`	Bicycles, related products and laws.
`rec.birds`	Hobbyists interested in bird watching.
`rec.boats`	Hobbyists interested in boating.
`rec.food.cooking`	Food, cooking, cookbooks, and recipes.
`rec.food.drink`	Wines and spirits.
`rec.food.recipes`	Recipes from the USENET Cookbook (troff and text).
`rec.food.veg`	Vegetarians.
`rec.games.board`	Discussion and hints on board games.
`rec.games.bridge`	Hobbyists interested in bridge.
`rec.games.chess`	Chess and computer chess.
`rec.games.empire`	Discussion and hints about Empire.
`rec.games.frp`	Discussion about fantasy role playing games.
`rec.games.go`	Discussion about Go.
`rec.games.hack`	Discussion, hints, and so on, about the Hack game.
`rec.games.misc`	Games and computer games.
`rec.games.pbm`	Discussion about Play by Mail games.
`rec.games.rogue`	Discussion and hints about Rogue.
`rec.games.trivia`	Discussion about trivia.
`rec.games.video`	Discussion about video games.
`rec.gardens`	Gardening, methods and results.
`rec.guns`	Firearms
`rec.ham-radio`	Amateur radio practices, contests, events, rules, and so on.
`rec.ham-radio.packet`	Discussion about packet radio setups.
`rec.humor`	Jokes and the like. May be somewhat offensive.
`rec.humor.d`	Discussions on the content of rec.humor articles.
`rec.mag`	Magazine summaries, tables of contents, and so on.
`rec.mag.otherrealms`	*Otherrealms* science fiction/fantasy magazine.
`rec.misc`	General topics about recreational/participant sports.
`rec.motorcycles`	Motorcycles and related products and laws.
`rec.music.classical`	Discussion about classical music.
`rec.music.folk`	Folks discussing folk music of various sorts.
`rec.music.gaffa`	Progressive music discussions (such as Kate Bush).
`rec.music.gdead`	A group for (Grateful) Dead-heads.
`rec.music.makers`	For performers and their discussions.
`rec.music.misc`	Music lovers' group.
`rec.music.synth`	Synthesizers and computer music.
`rec.nude`	Hobbyists interested in naturist/nudist activities.
`rec.pets`	Pets, pet care, and household animals in general.
`rec.photo`	Hobbyists interested in photography.
`rec.puzzles`	Puzzles, problems, and quizzes.
`rec.railroad`	Real and model train fans' newsgroup.
`rec.scuba`	Hobbyists interested in SCUBA diving.
`rec.skiing`	Hobbyists interested in skiing.
`rec.skydiving`	Hobbyists interested in skydiving.
`rec.sport.baseball`	Discussion about baseball.
`rec.sport.basketball`	Discussion about basketball.
`rec.sport.football`	Discussion about football.
`rec.sport.hockey`	Discussion about hockey.
`rec.sport.misc`	Spectator sports.
`rec.travel`	Traveling all over the world.
`rec.video`	Video and video components.
`rec.woodworking`	Hobbyists interested in woodworking.
`sci.astro`	Astronomy discussions and information.

sci.bio	Biology and related sciences.
sci.crypt	Different methods of data en/decryption.
sci.electronics	Circuits, theory, electrons and discussions.
sci.lang	Natural languages, communication, and so on.
sci.math	Mathematical discussions and pursuits.
sci.math.stat	Statistics discussion.
sci.math.symbolic	Symbolic algebra discussion.
sci.med	Medicine and its related products and regulations.
sci.misc	Short-lived discussions on subjects in the sciences.
sci.philosophy.tech	Technical philosophy, math, logic, and so on.
sci.physics	Physical laws, properties, and so on.
sci.research	Research methods, funding, ethics, and whatever.
sci.space	Space, space programs, space related research, and so on.
sci.space.shuttle	The space shuttle and the STS program.
soc.college	College, college activities, campus life, and so on.
soc.culture.african	Discussions about Africa and things African.
soc.culture.celtic	Group about Celtics (*not* basketball!).
soc.culture.greek	Group about Greeks.
soc.culture.indian	Group for discussion about India and things Indian.
soc.culture.jewish	Group for discussion about Jewish culture and religion.
soc.culture.misc	Group for discussion about other cultures.
soc.human-nets	Computer-aided communications digest.
soc.misc	Socially oriented topics not in other groups.
soc.motss	Issues pertaining to homosexuality.
soc.net-people	Announcements, requests, and so on about people on the net.
soc.religion.christian	Discussions on Christianity and related topics.
soc.roots	Genealogical matters.
soc.singles	Newsgroup for single people, their activities, and so on.
soc.women	Women's rights, discrimination, and so on.
talk.abortion	All sorts of discussions and arguments about abortion.
talk.bizarre	The unusual, bizarre, curious, and often stupid.
talk.origins	Evolution versus creationism (sometimes hot!).
talk.philosophy.misc	Philosophical musings on all topics.
talk.politics.arms-d	Disarmament issues.
talk.politics.misc	Political discussions and ravings of all kinds.
talk.politics.theory	Theory of politics and political systems.
talk.religion.misc	Religious, ethical, and moral implications.
talk.religion.newage	Esoteric and minority religions and philosophies.
talk.rumors	For the posting of rumors.

Note: some groups are moderated or have moderated versions. Netnews version 2.11 handles this automatically.

How News Is Written

Now that you have seen how articles are organized into newsgroups, let's look briefly at how the news gets to you. How do news articles get written? Say that a user sitting at a terminal at U.C. Berkeley is running the Netnews software and reading some news articles. The user can:

- send mail to the author of a particular article
- post a reply article in response to a particular article
- post an original article

The Netnews news reading programs have commands you can use to write mail and send it directly to the author of an article, without having to leave the Netnews program. The mail address is provided automatically: all you have to do is write your message, using one of the UNIX editors if you wish. (You'll see later, in this paper's tutorial, how to do everything discussed here.)

You can use *follow-up commands* to post a follow-up article. Unlike mail, which is a private message to the author of an article, a follow-up article is a regular news article posted to the net. It is linked by the Netnews software to the original article, and with some Netnews news reading

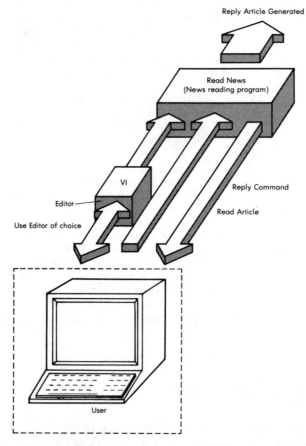

A. Reading and Replying to Articles

Figure 2–2   Reading and Posting News Articles

software you can follow a whole "thread" of responses to a given article. This is a very natural way to keep up with an ongoing discussion.

The other way to write a news article is to run a news posting program called postnews. This results in an "original" article: one that is not based on another article. Figure 2–2 shows schematically the ways users can interact with the news they read, creating mail and news articles.

Assume the Berkeley user has generated a news article. How does it get from that user's site to you? News articles are usually transferred via uucp. (You can read more about uucp and other UNIX communications programs in *UNIX Communications* by The Waite Group (Indianapolis, Ind.: Howard W. Sams, 1987.) As you probably know, any site with a modem can reach virtually any other such site given a phone number and uucp. Of course, some paths between sites can go through a dozen intermediate sites or more, using a "hop and skip" approach.

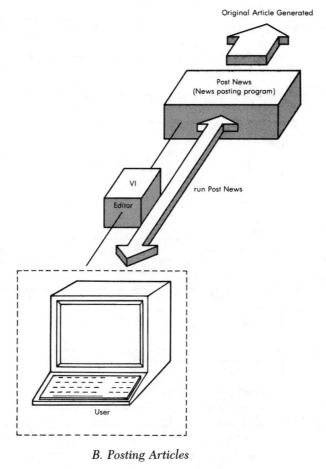

B. Posting Articles

Figure 2–2 *(continued)*

The Netnews software has access to a map showing nodes connected to the site on which it is installed. Figure 2–3 shows a schematic map of major sites that exchange USENET news. (These are called *backbone sites;* more on them later.) The map is actually stored in the UNIX system as a data file rather than a tree diagram, of course.

You might think that each site simply sends the news articles written by its users along all the available uucp paths. If each machine that received an article forwarded a copy through its local paths, the article would indeed get widely distributed. The main problem is that machines A and B might have a dozen valid uucp paths connecting them. Machine C might also be

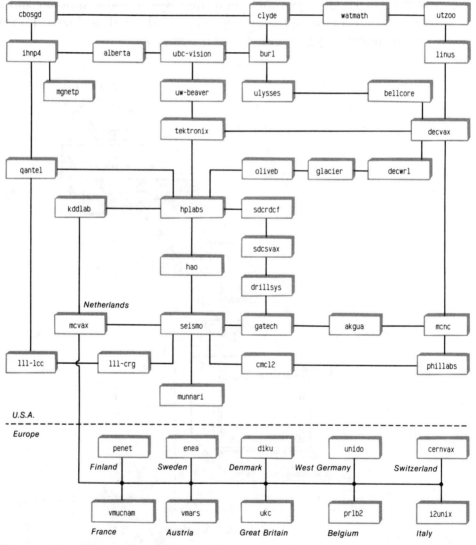

Figure 2–3   Major uucp Nodes (Backbone Sites)

connected to both A and B, so that when A sends an article to C, C sends a copy to B (which has already received a copy from A). The result would be vast amount of duplication and a huge uucp workload.

Instead, when a user has posted an article, it is sent by the user's site normally to one other site—the site from which it gets its "news feed." That site in turn passes the article along to a site that has agreed to serve as a sort of regional USENET clearinghouse, a backbone site. Thus, the backbone is receiving news from many local sites, either directly or via an intermediate "feeder" site. Since all of this is arranged informally, the number of sites the news passes through on its way to the backbone varies. Figure 2–4 shows how this works.

The backbone site essentially does two things. It collects all the news articles generated in its region (an arbitrary area that is only roughly geographical) and sends them on to other backbone sites serving other regions (usually at least two). At the same time, the backbone site receives a packet of news from other backbone sites and distributes it back "upstream" to its regional news feed sites, which in turn feed it to their local "client" sites. Thus, the article from the hypothetical user in Berkeley reaches your backbone site and later arrives in your site's news feed.

You will recall that Figure 2–3 showed a map of backbone sites. Refer to it again; note that it covers many areas (ubc-vision, for example, is at the University of British Columbia, while gatech is Georgia Tech). Remember that this is a map of connectivity, not geography.

Figure 2–5 shows how the news spreads through the net via the backbone sites. This method of distribution is called the "flooding" algorithm.

People who benefit from USENET owe a debt of gratitude to the backbone sites. While an ordinary site usually only needs to make a local

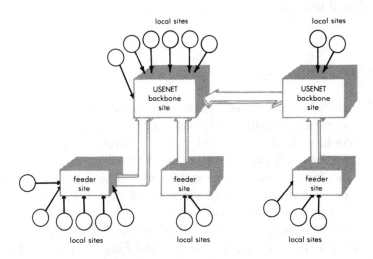

Figure 2–4   From Local Site to Backbone Site

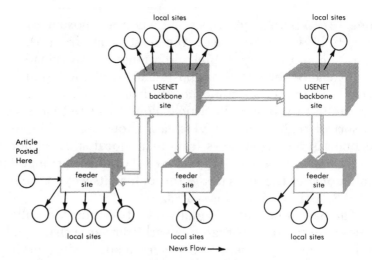

Figure 2–5   The "Flooding Algorithm" for News Distribution

phone call to get its news feed, the backbone site must usually call long distance to exchange news with other backbones. It also has to store and process articles in over 250 newsgroups. (A local site can choose which newsgroups it will "subscribe" to, depending on resources and local interest.) Because the backbone site administrators are committed to making USENET work, they have an interest in preventing waste and abuse of the net (such as cases where people who post an article in two dozen different newsgroups, none of which fit the group's topic). Thus, the backbone administrators are the closest thing USENET has to a governing body; if they decide a newsgroup is not useful, they can simply refuse to process it. No vote is taken; if the newsgroup is rejected at enough important sites, its distribution diminishes and it dies.

News Programs

When news articles reach your site, various low-level Netnews programs go to work. Duplicate articles and expired articles (usually ones more than two weeks old) are discarded. Special articles called *control messages* tell the Netnews software at your site if a new newsgroup has been created or if an existing one is no longer valid. The news is then stored in your site's news directory (often via a spool directory). The question is now: how do you read the news?

Actually, you don't need the Netnews software to read news. News is simply a set of UNIX directories and files. You could do something like this to read news articles (entries are indicated in boldface):

```
cd /well/news
$ ls
ba       ca      control junk    maps    news    sci     src
batch    comp    etc     lib     mi      rec     soc     talk
```

Here the user is in the directory where news is stored (the path will be different on your machine, so you might have to explore a bit.) Do you recognize some of these subdirectories? Some of them are the same as newsgroup prefixes, such as comp, news, sci, soc, and talk. Others correspond to the geographical distribution areas and special types of newsgroups such as mod for moderated groups.

```
$ cd comp
$ ls
ai              dcom            lsi             periphs         terminals
arch            edu             mail            protocols       text
bugs            emacs           misc            sources         unix
cog-eng         graphics        org             std             windows
databases       lang            os              sys
```

Here the user changes to the comp directory, in which all the newsgroups starting with comp. (comp.ai, comp.sys, and so on are stored as subdirectories. Now the user can change to the sys subdirectory of the comp. directory:

```
$ cd sys
$ ls
amiga           cbm             intel           masscomp        tandy
apple           dec             m6809           misc            ti
atari           hp              m68k            nsc
att             ibm             mac             sun
```

Here are all the subdirectories of the sys directory. They correspond to the newsgroups for the various computer systems: comp.sys.amiga, comp.sys.ibm, and so on.)

```
$ cd ibm
$ ls
pc
$ cd pc

$ ls
1410    1469    1529    1588    1648    1707    1766    1825    1884    1946
1411    1470    1530    1589    1649    1708    1767    1826    1885    1947
```

1412	1471	1531	1590	1650	1709	1768	1827	1886	1948
1413	1472	1532	1591	1651	1710	1769	1828	1887	1949
1414	1473	1533	1592	1652	1711	1770	1829	1888	1950
1415	1474	1534	1593	1653	1712	1771	1830	1889	1951
1416	1475	1535							

There's one subdirectory in comp/sys/ibm, called pc. The user has reached the directory for the newsgroup comp.sys.ibm.pc. Instead of more topic names, the user sees a bunch of numbered files. What is in them?

```
cat 1504
Path: well!lll-lcc!styx!ames!oliveb!intelca!mipos3!pinkas
From: pinkas@mipos3.UUCP (Israel Pinkas)
Newsgroups: comp.sys.ibm.pc
Subject: Re: patches to DOS v 3.1
Message-ID: <418@mipos3.UUCP>
Date: 5 Feb 87 20:30:41 GMT
References: <108@nikhefk.UUCP> <1438@tekigm2.TEK.COM>
Reply-To: pinkas@mipos3.UUCP (Israel Pinkas)
Organization: Intel, Santa Clara, CA
Lines: 46


In article <1438@tekigm2.TEK.COM> jimb@tekigm2.UUCP (Jim Boland) writes:
>In article <108@nikhefk.UUCP> keeshu@nikhefk.UUCP (Kees Huyser) writes:
> >     COMMAND.COM--SOME UNDOCUMENTED FEATURES
> >          /E:NN      Set size of Environment area to NN paragraphs. Range
> >                     is 10 to 62  Numbers outside that range are ignored.
> >                     The default is /E:10.
```

The answer is that the numbers are filenames, and the files actually are news articles in the newsgroup comp.sys.ibm.pc. The whole point of this example is to show that the Netnews software, like most other UNIX software, is not really magic. It uses the existing UNIX file hierarchy to store and manipulate the news articles. To summarize, the newsgroup structure and the UNIX file system structure correspond like this, using the example of the newsgroup comp.sys.ibm.pc, as shown in Table 2–2.

The Netnews User Interface

The previous example shows that you could explore news articles simply by using cat or a pager such as more to read the news articles. This would not be very practical, however. Not only would you have to type a lot of UNIX commands, you would also have to keep track of which articles you

Table 2–2   Correspondence of the Newsgroup Structure and File System Structure

Newsgroup Name	Pathname
comp.	/news/comp
comp.sys	/news/comp/sys
comp.sys.ibm	/news/comp/sys/ibm
comp.sys.ibm.pc	/news/comp/sys/ibm/pc

have read. If you wanted to reply to an article by mail, you would have to type in the author's pathname from the article header. To create a more practical approach to reading news, the Netnews software provides a user interface, or, rather, a choice of several different interfaces suitable for different levels of sophistication and different styles of interaction. The interface consists of three news reading programs: readnews, rn, and vnews, plus postnews, which is used to post original news articles.

The tutorial uses readnews and postnews, although this paper will talk a bit about the other programs later. While not the most powerful news reading program, readnews is easy to learn and to use, and it is the one guaranteed to be on any system that supports USENET. Let's learn how to read and post news.

Reading Articles

Like most UNIX programs, readnews has an assortment of command line options. You can ignore them for now and just type readnews. It is a simple line-oriented program that requires no special terminal characteristics. When you first run it, allow a few moments for it to create and initialize the file it uses to keep track of what news you have read. This file is called .newsrc, and we'll look at it later.

readnews

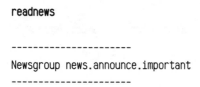

```
----------------------
Newsgroup news.announce.important
----------------------


Article 14 of 14, Feb  8 20:11.
Subject: CHI+GI 1987 Conference - Student Volunteers needed
Keywords: student volunteers, graphics, human factors, free conference
Path: ..!cbosgd!samackay (Stephen MacKay @ National Research Council, Canada)
(13 lines) More? [ynq] y
```

Notice that the name of the first newsgroup readnews finds is printed, followed by the header of the first article found. You can see that this is the last article of 14 articles in the news.announce.important newsgroup. (The others had either been read previously or are no longer available.) You are then asked whether you want to see more of this article. In responding to the More? [ynq] prompt, y means "yes, I want to see more" (in this case, the body of the article). The n means "no, don't show me any more, show me the next article." The q means "quit readnews." There are a number of other commands you can use while viewing an article header; you'll see more of them shortly.

You can type y to view the rest of the article. (Note that you must also press RETURN after commands given at this prompt in readnews.)

```
Student volunteers are needed to assist with the CHI+GI 1987
conference to be held April 5-9 in Toronto, Canada.  CHI+GI 1987
integrates the annual ACM SIGCHI CHI conference and the annual CMCCS
Graphics Interface (GI) conference for 1987.


Student volunteers will be expected to work between 16 and 24 hours over a six-day
period in exchange for free conference attendance.
For more information, please see the detailed posting in comp.graphics
or comp.cog-eng or contact the CHI+GI 1987 Student Volunteer Coordinators:


George Mace                 or            Fred Douglas
(633) 943-6553                            (436) 979-5100
Email: mace@nrcctis.UUCP




--------------------------------
Newsgroup news.announce.newusers
--------------------------------


Article 93 of 109, Jan 31 21:16.
Subject: Introduction to news.announce.important (Last changed: 29 October 1986)
Path: ..!gatech!usenet
(47 lines) More? [ynq] y
```

The rest of the article is displayed. Since there are no more articles in the news.announce.important newsgroup, readnews moves on to the next newsgroup, which happens to be news.announce.newusers. The header of the first available article in that group is displayed, and again you would see the More? prompt. Again, you type y to see the rest of the header and the beginning of the article text:

```
Original-from: mark@cbosgd.UUCP (Mark Horton)
[Most recent change: 29 October 1986 by spaf@gatech.edu]

"news.announce.important" is a newsgroup for important announcements.  It is
intended to be read by everyone on USENET, although nobody is forced to
subscribe.  To post to news.announce.important, send mail to the moderator at
"announce@cbosgd.att.com".  Some netnews implementations will
automatically mail to the moderator anything posted instead of
attempting to post it directly.  If the message is appropriate, it will
be posted by the moderator; if not, the moderator will suggest a more
appropriate place to post it or a better way to go about the same
goal.

Discussions in news.announce.important are explicitly forbidden, and the volume of
traffic will be kept low enough to keep people from feeling a need to
unsubscribe.  USENET administrators for each site should make a point
of reading news.announce.important.

Some messages will be repeated every month, in order to reach all
newcomers.  These messages will be placed in news.announce.newusers,
which is also moderated.  This makes it safe for experienced users who
have already read these messages to unsubscribe to news.announce.newusers

--More--
```

Unlike the previous one, this article is too long to be concluded on one screen. You see a new readnews prompt, --More--.

While this looks similar to the More? [ynq] prompt you received at the start of the article, it is in fact the pager prompt. A pager is a program such as more in BSD systems and pg in System V and XENIX. Its purpose is to allow text to be displayed one screen at a time. The Netnews software again embodies the typical UNIX approach of using existing tools: rather than writing a new program to display text, the existing UNIX command is used. (The system here happens to be BSD, so it uses more as its default pager.)

Depending on what pager your system uses, there are a number of commands you could type at this point. You can refer to your UNIX manual or type h for a list of commands. For example, more will give you a help display like this:

```
Most commands optionally preceded by integer argument k.  Defaults in brackets.
Star (*) indicates argument becomes new default.
-----------------------------------------------------------------------------
<space>                  Display next k lines of text [current screen size]
```

```
z                        Display next k lines of text [current screen size]*
<return>                 Display next k lines of text [1]*
d or ctrl-D              Scroll k lines [current scroll size, initially 11]*
q or Q or <interrupt>    Exit from more
s                        Skip forward k lines of text [1]
f                        Skip forward k screenfuls of text [1]
'                        Go to place where previous search started
=                        Display current line number
/<regular expression>    Search for kth occurrence of regular expression [1]
n                        Search for kth occurrence of last r.e [1]
!<cmd> or :!<cmd>        Execute <cmd> in a subshell
v                        Start up /usr/ucb/vi at current line
h                        Display this message
ctrl-L                   Redraw screen
:n                       Go to kth next file [1]
:p                       Go to kth previous file [1]
:f                       Display current file name and line number
.                        Repeat previous command
-------------------------------------------------------------------------------
```

Of the commands listed, by far the most commonly used are typing a space to see the next screenful, or typing q to quit the pager. (When the latter happens, readnews moves on to the next article.) The command ctrl-L is useful for redrawing the screen when dealing with a noisy phone line. The other commands are usually not that useful in dealing with news articles, but are provided by the pager for looking through long files.

In the previous example, you just typed a space. (Note that you do not press RETURN at the pager prompt.) The next screen of text is displayed:

```
without missing anything new in news.announce.  If you aren't familiar
with the netnews guidelines in news.announce.newusers, please read them
carefully.  Your understanding of these rules will assure that you don't
annoy the 10,000+ members of the net community by unintentionally abusing
the net, and will help you get more value from the net.

The current policy is that news.announce.important submissions
must be:

(a) short - preferably they should fit on one crt screen, including headers.
(b) important enough to at least have their header shown to everyone on the
      net.  The posting should be more of benefit to the net than to the poster.
(c) not posted to any other newsgroup - news.announce.important by itself
      is supposed to be sufficient to reach everybody, and nobody should have to
```

```
      read an announcement more than once.
(d) signed - the author should be clearly evident.
(e) not commercial, political, or religious in nature.

The moderation mechanism is working. You would not believe how many people
have posted a follow-up to news.announce.important, including an entire article,
followed by only "REPLACE THIS LINE WITH YOUR MESSAGE."  These get mailed
to the moderator instead of being posted to the net.

--More--
```

Reading a Series of Articles

As you can see, the author of this message is telling users of the net how to work with the moderated "announce" newsgroups.

It is unlikely that you will want to read through every article in a newsgroup. Some newsgroups can have hundreds of new articles posted every day, and you probably wouldn't be interested in reading all of them even if you had hours to spend at the terminal. To skip over an article header and see the next article, you would type n (think of it as "next"). To go back one article, you would type b ("back").

```
Article 95 of 109: <11057@gatech.EDU>
Subject: A Primer on How to Work With the USENET Community (Last changed:
7 December 1986)
Path: lll-lcc!mordor!sri-spam!rutgers!clyde!cuae2!gatech!usenet
(274 lines) More? [ynq] n


Article 96 of 109, Jan 31 21:17.
Subject: Hints on writing style for USENET (Last changed: 2 March 1985)
Path: ..!gatech!usenet
(75 lines) More? [ynq] n


Article 97 of 109, Jan 31 21:18.
Subject: Answers to Frequently Asked Questions (Last changed: 31 January 1987)
Path: ..!gatech!usenet
(261 lines) More? [ynq] b
```

You would type n twice to get from article 95 to 96 to 97. (These numbers are merely the sequential order in which the article arrived at the local site. The unique article ID is a separate field not shown here.) At article 97, you would type b—if you wanted to go back to article 96.

Note how the article headers usually give you enough information for you to decide whether to type y and read the article. There are many other possible article header fields, including keywords, the newsgroups to which the article is posted, and so on. You'll see some of these fields later.

The p ("previous") command may seem a little confusing at first. Most of the time, it seems to get you the previous article number, but not always:

```
Article 96 of 109, Jan 31 21:17.
Subject: Hints on writing style for USENET (Last changed: 2 March 1985)
Path: ..!gatech!usenet
(75 lines) More? [ynq] b

Article 95 of 109, Jan 31 21:17.
Subject: A Primer on How to Work With the USENET Community (Last changed: 7
December 1986)
Path: ..!gatech!usenet
(274 lines) More? [ynq] p

Article 96 of 109, Jan 31 21:17.
Subject: Hints on writing style for USENET (Last changed: 2 March 1985)
Path: ..!gatech!usenet
(75 lines) More? [ynq]
```

The reason is that p actually means "the previously displayed article." Since you went back from article 96 to 95, when you type p you get 96, the previously displayed article, rather than 94, the previously numbered article.

Filing and Saving Articles

There may be times when you are reading news and come across some interesting articles, but you don't want to take the time to read through them right then. Typing e at the article prompt marks the current article (the one whose header is shown) as "unread." Normally, once an article is displayed, readnews marks the article as "read" so that you will not see it the next time you enter the newsgroup. Because readnews always offers you the new (unread) articles in each newsgroup, marking the article as unread means that it will turn up again.

```
Article 94 of 109, Jan 31 21:16.
Subject: Rules for posting to USENET (Last changed: 29 November 1986)
Path: ..!gatech!usenet
```

```
(108 lines) More? [ynq] e
Holding article 94
```

After you typed e you would be informed that article 94 is being "held" as unread.

Note that if you have already seen the whole article (or quit the pager by typing q), readnews will be now be showing you the next article. In order to mark the previously displayed article as unread (or give another command concerning it), you can type p (for "previous") first to get back to the article you want to work with, and then type e. But an even faster way (that works with many other readnews commands that affect articles) is to follow the command with a minus sign; e- also marks the previously displayed article as unread.

Since articles usually expire after having been at your site for two weeks, an article marked as unread may be lost before you get back to it. A safer way to make sure that you can refer to an article is to save it in a file.

To save an article to a file for permanent reference, use the s command. If you just type s, a file called Articles will be created in a subdirectory of your home directory called News, and the current article will be saved in it:

```
Article 95 of 109: <11057@gatech.EDU>
Subject: A Primer on How to Work With the Usenet Community (Last changed: 7
December 1986)
Path: lll-lcc!mordor!sri-spam!rutgers!clyde!cuae2!gatech!usenet
(274 lines) More? [ynq] s
./Articles: New file
```

If the file already exists, the new material will be appended:

```
Article 96 of 109, Jan 31 21:17.
Subject: Hints on writing style for Usenet (Last changed: 2 March 1985)
Path: ..!gatech!usenet
(75 lines) More? [ynq] s
./Articles: Appended
```

Finally, you can specify a filename in which to save the article. Again, if the file already exists, the new material will be appended.

```
Article 95 of 109, Jan 31 21:17.
Subject: A Primer on How to Work With the Usenet Community (Last changed:
7 December 1986)
Path: ..!gatech!usenet
```

```
(274 lines) More? [ynq] s usenet.primer.how
./usenet.primer.how: New file
```

Replying to an Article

Since USENET contains much that is interesting and more than a little controversial, you may soon tire of passive reading and want to express your own opinion on a subject, or reply to articles you are reading. While the mechanics of this are very simple, the why and how of it requires some thought. In a way, you are standing in front of an open microphone with 150,000 people who may be listening. This is not meant to be intimidating, but just to indicate the need for responsibility in using the network.

The last few examples have been some articles from the newsgroup news.announce.newusers. You may have noticed that this is a special newsgroup devoted to helping new USENET users become oriented. Material written by various net luminaries that will help new USENET users is kept permanently for reference (of course the article numbers will vary). Before replying to or writing news articles, you will find it useful to read the article "A Primer on How to Work with the Usenet Community," described fully at the end of this paper. (You may also want to read the chapter on "Writing News with Postnews" in the Sams *UNIX Communications* book cited earlier.) Just a brief summary of the most important points is given here.

Reply by Mail or Article?

There are two ways you can reply to an article that you have just read: by email, which is a private message to the author, or by posting a reply article for all the network world to see. Which should you use? It depends on mainly on two factors: whether your reply is of general interest and whether there are likely to be many similar replies.

If the article is a "for sale" ad, it benefits no one to have 50 reply articles saying that so and so is interested in that particular used car, or asking the author what kind of mileage it gets. Remember that each of these articles has to be transmitted, stored, and processed at thousands of sites. If this happens often enough, site administrators are liable to drop or curtail their support for USENET at their site. Send an email message to the article's author instead. (This is very easy to do, as you'll see.)

Common sense offers other examples of when private email replies are appropriate. If you just want to tell an article's author "I agree with you," that is not of particular interest to other users. If someone is asking for information that is readily available (such as where to obtain a particular product), it's again better to mail the answer. Even though this material may be of general interest, it helps no one to have 20 such articles posted. As a courtesy, the author of the original query should summarize the responses received by email in a single follow-up article to his or her original article. Something like: "I have received several dozen replies to this article. They basically say that . . ."

If you don't like someone and absolutely have to pick a personal quarrel with him or her, again, do it by email. A reasoned disagreement as part of a discussion of a controversial topic is a different matter, of course. The test should be whether one is disagreeing with what someone has said and giving the reason(s) why, or attacking him or her as a person (an "ad hominem").

"Spelling flames," where a poorly written article (or just one with a single typo in it) is pounced upon by dozens of would-be copy editors, is another bane of the net. Again, if you *have* to do it, do it by mail. The general rule is: when in doubt, use email. Many articles will remind readers to use email for replies; such requests should be honored.

Replying by Mail

While using readnews, you can reply to the currently displayed article by email, rather than making a public response, by typing rd ("reply direct"):

```
Article 108 of 138, Jan 30 06:55.
Subject: c++ reading list
Keywords: c++, reading
Path: ..!watrose!pjdevries (P. DeVries @ U of Waterloo, Ontario)
(7 lines) More? [ynq] rd


To: lll-lcc!mordor!styx!ames!Think!mit-ed-
die!bacchus!husc6!rutgers!clyde!watmath!watnot!watrose!pjdevries
Subject: C++ books
   By early summer 1987 a book called *UNIX Papers* by various authors will
be out. It will be published by The Waite Group and Howard W. Sams. It will
have an excellent paper by Keith Gorlen of the National Institutes of Health
that includes a tutorial on C++ (I'm the editor for the book, but I can
still be objective about its value, I think.)
^D
Article 108 of 138, Jan 30 06:55.
Subject: c++ reading list
Keywords: c++, reading
Path: ..!watrose!pjdevries (P. DeVries @ U of Waterloo, Ontario)
(7 lines) More? [ynq]
```

Typing rd puts you directly in whatever UNIX mail program your system has set up for use with Netnews. (You can override this and "customize" readnews to give you a mailer, editor, or pager of your own preference. You'll see how to do that later.) Notice that when you do an rd the address and subject are provided for you from the original article. You just type your message and end it with [control]-D as usual in mail. When you do that, the mail is sent, you exit mail, and readnews redisplays the screen where you left off.

An alternative command for mailing replies is r. This works the same as rd, but it runs your default editor to compose your message, rather than running mail directly. You just write the message and quit the editor (using wq in vi, for example) as usual, and the message you have written is mailed. This command is probably better for long messages, although most mailers let you use some sort of escape command to run an editor, anyway. With UNIX the question usually is not "Can you do it?" but "Which way do you want it?"

Posting Reply Articles

If you have something of general interest to say, and it is unlikely to be known by many people, posting a public reply article is appropriate. After telling the author of the original article that *UNIX Papers* has a paper on C++ that he might be interested in, it occurred to the sender that other people might want to know about this. After all, there is a shortage of good material on this new language. So the sender typed f ("follow-up") to begin writing a reply article:

```
Article 108 of 138: <8422@watrose.UUCP>
Subject: c++ reading list
Path: lll-lcc!mordor!styx!ames!Think!mit-
eddie!bacchus!husc6!rutgers!clyde!watmath!watnot!watrose!pjdevries
(7 lines) More? [ynq] fd
Please enter a short summary of your contribution to the discussion
Just one or two lines ...   (end with a blank line)
>     Forthcoming UNIX book to discuss C++
>
```

First enter a summary of your article. The summary is optional, but useful, as it will help others decide whether they want to read the article. (This is even more useful for longer articles.)

```
Do you want to include a copy of the article? y
OK, but please edit it to suppress unnecessary verbiage, signatures, etc.
```

```
No lines in the buffer
No lines in the buffer
"/tmp/post014160" 17 lines, 555 characters
> I would appreciate any titles, along with the publisher and date if possible.
> Of special interest are primers, tutorials on using C++ that go beyond a very
> elementary level.
> Does anyone know of a computer based training package for C++?
>
> Thanks.

"/tmp/post014160" 17 lines, 555 characters

The Waite Group and Sams Publications will be publishing a collection
called *UNIX Papers* in summer 1987. This includes an excellent
tutorial on C++ by Keith Gorlen, which includes a discussion of data
structures with built in operators and functions, and a look at
object-oriented programming with C++. Other papers cover a variety of
topics of interest to serious UNIX users and developers. (Caveat: I
am the editor of this book, but it's good anyway :-)
:wq
"/tmp/post014160" 23 lines, 1017 characters
```

You are then asked by readnews if you want to include a copy of the article you are replying to in your reply article. Note the several lines beginning with brackets (>) at the start of many articles. This "quoting" mechanism is useful because many unrelated articles usually arrive in a newsgroup between an original article and replies to it. The quoted material helps readers see what is being commented on without having to go back and find the original article (which may have expired and thus be no longer available). However, excessive quoting wastes space. If the quoted material that readnews puts in your editor buffer is more than a few lines, try to edit it down to just what is needed to provide context. Here you would edit out the reference to the training manuals, and the "thanks."

As you can see, readnews put the material in your edit buffer, and you could go ahead and type in your text. (The editor happens to be vi.) When you have exited the editor, you would be asked:

```
What now?  [send, edit, list, quit, write] s
Posting article...
Article posted successfully.
(7 lines) More? [ynq]
```

You would enter s for send, which means to post the reply article. For the other options, edit means restart the editor to allow revision, and list simply displays the text of the article. The quit option aborts the procedure without posting the article, while write saves a copy of the article in your home directory.

Creative Punctuation . . . a USENET Tradition

Were you puzzled by the strange punctuation mark at the end of the article, ":-)"? This is a USENET tradition called the "smiley face" (to see how it got that name, rotate this page clockwise 90 degrees). Since body language is not available (yet) in electronic communications, (although "face" icons and attributes have been used in some experimental systems to accompany text), the smiley face is used to indicate that the remark is not meant to be taken seriously. It's also just a bit of fun.

One other bit of unusual punctuation is in the way the *UNIX Papers* title is represented in the article. Normally this would be underlined or italicized, but there is no way to actually underline something or use italics in a message. So asterisks or single underscores (_UNIX Papers_) are usually used to indicate underlining. The asterisks can also serve the purpose of an alternate font (such as bold or italic) to indicate emphasis. Someday USENET may support full graphics capabilities. Whether this will be a blessing remains to be seen.

Moving Between Newsgroups

So far you have been reading, filing, and replying to articles in the same newsgroup, except where you have reached the end of a newsgroup and have thus been automatically moved to the next one. Chances are good that you don't have the time or interest to read the more than 250 newsgroups. One way to browse through the newsgroups without seeing more than the header of the first article in each group is to use the N and P commands (note the uppercase):

```
----------------------
Newsgroup news.announce.important
----------------------


Article 14 of 14, Feb  8 20:11.
Subject: CHI+GI 1987 Conference - Student Volunteers needed
Keywords: student volunteers, graphics, human factors, free conference
Path: ..!cbosgd!samackay (Stephen MacKay @ National Research Council, Canada)
(13 lines) More? [ynq] N


------------------------------
Newsgroup news.announce.newusers
------------------------------
```

```
Article 93 of 109, Jan 31 21:16.
Subject: Introduction to news.announce.important (Last changed: 29 October
1986)
Path: ..!gatech!usenet
(47 lines) More? [ynq] N


-----------------
Newsgroup comp.ai
-----------------


Article 577 of 1200, Jul 14 09:42.
Subject: Re: common sense
Path: ..!XEROX.COM!Newman.pasa (Newman.pasa @ The ARPA Internet)
(22 lines) More? [ynq] P


------------------------------
Newsgroup news.announce.newusers
------------------------------


Article 93 of 109, Jan 31 21:16.
Subject: Introduction to news.announce.important (Last changed: 29 October
1986)
Path: ..!gatech!usenet
(47 lines) More? [ynq] N
```

You can see that this works the same way as the commands for moving between articles within a newsgroup. N gets you the next newsgroup, and P gets you the previous one. Remember to use uppercase: the lowercase n and p are, as you've seen, for articles within the newsgroup.

It would still take a long time to go through all the available newsgroups this way. You can, however, use the name of a newsgroup with N to jump directly to the desired group:

```
----------------------
Newsgroup comp.compilers
----------------------


Article 93 of 161, Jul 12 16:01.
Subject: George Logothetis' compiler book
Path: ..!ima!johnl (Compilers mailing list)
(18 lines) More? [ynq] N comp.sys.apollo


----------------------------
Newsgroup comp.sys.apollo
----------------------------
```

```
Article 176 of 350, Jul 13 12:31.
Subject: Please add me to your mailing list
Path: ..!MITRE-BEDFORD.ARPA!tom (McCarthy @ The MITRE
Corporation, Bedford, MA.)
(7 lines) More? [ynq]
```

Here you moved from comp.compilers to comp.sys.apollo by specifying the latter group with an N command.

Finally, when you are currently looking at a newsgroup that is of no interest to you, you can "unsubscribe" to the newsgroup. This means that you will no longer be shown that newsgroup or any articles in it:

```
--------------------
Newsgroup rec.humor
--------------------


Article 850 of 1258, Feb  1 15:10.
Subject: "What Managers Can Learn from Manager Reagan"
Path: ..!violet.berkeley.edu!potency (Jim Davis [408-496-5954] @ dis)
Newsgroups: rec.humor,talk.politics.misc
(8 lines) More? [ynq] U
Unsubscribing to newsgroup: rec.humor
```

Editing Your Subscription List

At this point readnews is still going to show you more newsgroups than you probably care to see. There are three approaches to getting readnews to show you just those groups you are interested in. The first, unsubscribing to the current newsgroup with the U command, you have already seen. The other two involve a special file used by readnews.

The .newsrc File

You may have been wondering how readnews keeps track of what articles you have read and how it knows which newsgroup to show you next. When you first run readnews, a file is created in your home directory with the name .newsrc. Here is what the beginning of such a file looks like:

```
$head .newsrc
ca.wanted: 1-147,283
comp.ai: 1-577,1044,1059
comp.sys.amiga:
comp.sys.binaries.amiga: 1-1
```

```
comp.sources.amiga: 1-12
news.announce: 1-12
news.announce.newusers: 1-86
comp-society: 1-72
comp.compilers: 1-92
```

When readnews is run, it compares the active file in the /news directory with a default "subscription list" for your site. (A given site need not carry every newsgroup.) The result is a list containing every newsgroup subscribed to by your site. As you read articles, the article numbers following the newsgroup names are updated to show which articles have already been read. Thus in the newsgroup ca.wanted, articles 1 through 147 and 283 have been read, and will not be shown again. There are no numbers following comp.sys.amiga, so no articles in that group have been read. (You could make those earlier articles that are still available appear by editing your .newsrc to remove the numbers following the newsgroup.)

You have already seen that you can jump to specified newsgroups within readnews, and you can use the U command to unsubscribe to the current newsgroup. If you use the U command with comp.sys.amiga, for example, and look at the .newsrc file again, the entry for comp.sys.amiga will look like this:

```
comp.sys.amiga!
```

The exclamation point indicates that the newsgroup is unsubscribed. The group (and its articles) will no longer be automatically presented to you as you move through the list of newsgroups to read news. If you wish, you can go into your favorite editor and edit the .newsrc file, putting exclamation points after all the names of groups you are not interested in. This is a quick way to prune USENET down to a more manageable size.

Using the Options Line

Thus far you have just learned to type readnews to start up the program. There are a number of command line options that you can use, however, and you can read more about them in the manual entry. One of the most useful is -n:

```
readnews -n comp.unix.questions
```

will start readnews and take you directly to the comp.unix.questions newsgroup. You can also use all, which works like the UNIX * metacharacter:

```
readnews -n comp.sys.all
```

This entry will restrict your session to all newsgroups that start with `comp.sys`, such as `comp.sys.amiga` and `comp.sys.ibm.pc`.

It may happen that after you've been reading news for a few weeks, you can come up with a list of a dozen or so newsgroups that you are interested in reading regularly. One way to see these groups (and only these groups) automatically is to put an *options line* in your `.newsrc`. Edit `.newsrc` and insert a line at the beginning, such as this:

```
options -n news.announce.all,comp.unix.all,comp.sys.all
```

This means that in each session, `readnews` will first show you all `news.announce.important` groups, all `comp.` groups relating to UNIX, and then all groups relating to computer systems. If you ever want to see other groups, you can always use the `N` command with the group name within `readnews` to get to the desired group.

Posting Original Articles

An *original article* is one that is not a reply to any specific article. The considerations for posting original articles are similar to those for posting reply articles: appropriateness and general interest. There are a few other things to think about as well, though, as you'll see in a moment.

The `postnews` program is used to post original articles:

```
postnews
Is this message in response to some other message? n
```

You are first asked if the article is a response to another article. If you say yes, you are asked for the article identification number (`Article-Id`), which is given in a field of that name in the complete article header. These numbers aren't easy to work with (for example: 8611102040.A0936@ucbvax.Berkeley.EDU), so it is usually much easier to post the follow-up from within `readnews`, as you saw earlier.

Because this is an original article, you say "no."

```
Subject: B- C compiler Ver. 1.0 bug report, pointer size problem
Keywords: B- compiler bugs pointers allocation
```

The subject and keywords help people who are browsing decide whether to read your article. More sophisticated news reading programs such as `rn` can scan the articles in a newsgroup by subject and follow a "subject thread," or group of articles with the same subject. Thus it is useful to provide good descriptive subjects and keywords. Here you are asking for help with a (fortunately imaginary) C compiler that has been giving you problems. Postnews then asks you what newsgroups(s) to which you want to post:

```
Newsgroups (enter one at a time, end with a blank line):

The most relevant newsgroup should be the first, you should
add others only if your article really MUST be read by people
who choose not to read the appropriate group for your article.
But DO use multiple newsgroups rather than posting many times.

For a list of newsgroups, type ?
```

You are given some good advice by postnews here. Most articles will fit in a single newsgroup. The newsgroups have arisen from a consensus about what the most useful topic divisions are. While this scheme is far from perfect, try to find the one most appropriate newsgroup. If the subject matter legitimately concerns two (or rarely three) newsgroups, list all of them. This is preferable to posting several times. When you post to several newsgroups at once (called "cross posting"), the overhead is less than if you make separate postings. Because this issue is C, you'll try comp.lang.c. (If it were about a problem with the interaction of the compiler with UNIX, you might have also added comp.unix.wizards, the advanced group for UNIX-related questions.)

```
> comp.lang.c
>
Distribution (default='comp', '?' for help) : ?

How widely should your article be distributed?

local   Local to this site
ba      Everywhere in the San Francisco Bay Area
ca      Everywhere in California
usa     Everywhere in the USA
na      Everywhere in North America
net     Everywhere on USENET in the world
mi      Everywhere in the state of Michigan

Enter the word that specifies the distribution that you require.

Distribution (default='comp', '?' for help) :
```

Here you are being asked how widely your article is to be distributed. Note that some newsgroups (such as ca.unix) are already restricted to a certain geographical area. But you can also restrict your posting to a normally netwide group (such as comp.unix so that it only goes to California), by typing ca when asked for the distribution. You might want to do this if you suspect a fair number of people will be able to help you, and you don't want 400 messages to flood your mailbox! (It *can* happen!) Here you would type ? to get a list of available distributions, and then accepted the default, comp. for netwide, by pressing RETURN. Now you are running the editor and are ready to write the article:

```
No lines in the buffer
No lines in the buffer
"/tmp/post002967" 5 lines, 132 characters
Subject: B- C compiler ver. 1.0 bug report pointer problems
Newsgroups: comp.lang.c
Keywords: B- C compiler bugs pointer problems
~
~
"/tmp/post002967" 5 lines, 132 characters
    I have discovered that the behavior of the B- C compiler is erratic.
It does not handle pointers consistently. For example, when I
declare a pointer to long int., it actually fetches the value as
though it were a double. This caused a "mysterious" loss of
precision on some engineering calculations we did recently!
:wq
"/tmp/post002967" 10 lines, 446 characters
```

After exiting the editor, you are asked what to do with the article:

```
What now?  [send, edit, list, quit, write] send
Posting article...
Article posted successfully.
```

These are the same options that appear after you write a follow-up article from within readnews. You type send to post the article.

Posting to Moderated Newsgroups

As was mentioned earlier, some newsgroups do not accept postings directly. Postings for such groups are submitted to a moderator who reviews them for appropriateness. The advantage of such a group is that it considerably reduces the amount of irrelevant material that you must sift through.

If you are using the 2.11 version of the Netnews software with the vnews or rn news reading programs (described briefly later), the word *moderated* will appear in the group readings to inform you that it is a moderated group. Your posting will be sent to the moderator automatically. If you are running readnews or other older software, you may need to find the name and uucp address of the moderator for the group you are interested in. A list of moderators is usually kept in the newsgroup news.announce or news.lists. You would then email your submission to the moderator.

Other readnews Options

This paper cannot cover all of the readnews options. It will just note a few things here that will give you some idea of how you can "customize" your news environment.

Environmental Variables: Specifying Editor, Mailer, and Pager

Like many UNIX programs, readnews lets you set a number of "environmental variables" that control aspects of the program's behavior.

The variables, EDITOR, MAILER, and PAGER, can be set so you can use a different editor, a different program for mailing reply articles, and a different program for displaying article text. They are set by giving the pathname of the program or file to be used. The defaults are usually /usr/ucb/vi, /bin/mail, and /usr/ucb/more, for EDITOR, MAILER, and PAGER, at least on BSD systems. If you wanted to use emacs for your editor instead, you could use this statement (if you are using the C shell, csh):

```
setenv EDITOR "/usr/ucb/emacs"
```

assuming that is the correct pathname on your system. You would put this in your .login file. If you use the Bourne shell (sh), you would set the variables this way:

```
EDITOR="/usr/ucb/emacs" ; export EDITOR
```

and put the line in your .profile file.

There are other environmental variables given in the readnews manual entry.

Command Line Options

Previously it was noted that readnews has command line options and that the -n option can be used to specify newsgroups when you run readnews. There are several other options. Here are just a few examples, with explanations of what they do.

```
readnews -n comp.unix -t vi
```

This line tells USENET to show all articles in the moderated UNIX discussion group (comp.unix) that mention vi. The -t option means "title string." (Note that phrases must be quoted so they will not be treated as separate strings, and strings containing symbols special to the shell should also be quoted.)

```
readnews -n sci.space -a last thursday
```

This tells the system to display only articles submitted since last Thursday to sci.space. readnews is smart enough to know about days of the week, as well as "last" week.

```
readnews -x -n comp.lang.lisp
```

This line tells USENET to read all articles on the Lisp language, regardless of whether you've seen them before. (-x overrides the information about what articles have been read.)

```
readnews -M -n comp.lang.c++
```

This one is interesting. It takes all the unread articles in comp.lang.c++ and treats them like mail. Your mailer is invoked, and you can read the articles just as though they were mail messages, as well as reply to them or save them using the normal mail commands:

```
"/tmp/M1018363": 30 messages 30 new
& headers
>N  1 rosie!richard Fri Jan 30 16:42  17/634  "c++ vendors"
 N  2 alice!bs Sun Feb  1 19:27  91/2266 "Re: Problem with asm()s in in"
 N  3 alice!bs Mon Feb  2 07:04  51/1304 "Scope of class name bug fix f"
 N  4 hplabsc!kempf Fri Feb  6 08:48  56/1746 "Some Questions"
 N  5 hplabsc!rodrique Fri Feb  6 08:58  10/261 "testing,sorry"
 N  6 alice!bs Sun Feb  8 18:58  89/2896 "static member initialization,"
 N  7 otc!mikem Sun Feb  8 19:17  147/4727 "Re: Some Questions (1) - Also"
 N  8 otc!mikem Sun Feb  8 19:43  98/2632 "Re: Some Questions (2 & 3)"
```

```
N  9 rochester!sher Tue Feb 10 10:22  49/1062 "A couple of bugs with cin in "
N 10 uwmcsd1!dave Thu Feb 12 12:20  21/740 "c++ ordering info needed"
&
```

Here you can use the headers command in the mail program to display the sender, date, size, and subject of the first 10 messages.

Using checknews

Finally, you can put a line like this in your .profile or .login file:

```
checknews -e N comp.sys.ibm.pc,comp.os.unix
```

Note that checknews is a separate program that is part of the Netnews software. Here, checknews will check after you log on to see if there is any news waiting for you in the specified newsgroups. If there is, readnews will be run automatically.

Where Do You Go from Here?

You now know enough to use USENET effectively to read, reply to, and post news. There are two areas where you might want to explore further: the use of more advanced Netnews interfaces, and good news writing.

Alternative Netnews Interfaces

In addition to readnews, there are two other commonly available news reading programs, vnews and rn. The vnews program has nearly the same set of commands as readnews, so you can pick it up quickly. Its main distinction is that it is screen-oriented rather than line-oriented. This means that instead of simply displaying text that scrolls continuously up the screen, as readnews does, vnews displays the current article header or text in the center of the screen and updates this display as necessary. It also maintains status lines that show you where you are in the newsgroup. Figure 2–6 shows a typical vnews screen.

The vnews program works best at high speeds (4800 baud or higher), but works tolerably well at 1200 baud if the system is not heavily loaded. To use vnews you must have suitable terminal settings similar to those that work with vi.

The rn program is a different sort of beast, complex and powerful. (Its manual entry is more than 30 pages long.) It attempts to be more efficient

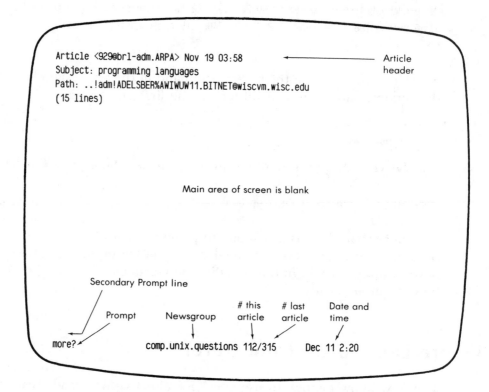

Figure 2–6   The vnews Display at Beginning of an Article

in displaying information than is readnews, and at the same time it offers an incredible array of features. For example, you can scan articles by subject or other header fields, apply commands to articles that match regular expressions, automatically kill articles, define key macros, and feed articles to shell scripts for further processing. People who graduate to rn usually say they would never go back, but the program does require work to master its many features.

If your system has vnews or rn, there will be a manual available somewhere online, perhaps in the /news directory (but you may have to ask where it is kept; it is not part of the regular online or printed manual).

If you decide that you are happy using readnews, you may want to read its online manual entry as well, because this paper has not been able to cover everything you can do even with this relatively simple program.

Finding Out More About USENET

In addition to the manual mentioned earlier, there are a number of places you can read more about specific programs and about USENET in general.

One place already mentioned is the `news.announce.newusers` newsgroup. Here are some items that are normally available in that newsgroup, with a brief description of each:

- "A Primer on How to Work with the USENET Community" (by Chuq von Rospach)
  This is the single most important guide to USENET in general and to courteous use of the net ("netiquette").

- "Rules for Posting to USENET" (by Mark Horton)
  Guidelines for judging when posting is appropriate, and what kinds of postings to avoid.

- "Introduction to news.announce.important" (by Mark Horton)
  There are rules about posting to certain newsgroups. This describes how to use announcements properly.

- "Hints on Writing Style for USENET" (by A. Jeff Offutt VI)
  Combines some generally-applicable points of writing style with considerations that are specific to the medium of USENET.

- "Answers to Frequently-Asked Questions" (by Jerry Schwarz)
  If everyone read this, the net wouldn't be subjected to an endless supply of articles asking questions like "what does UNIX stand for?" It also answers many common nontrivial questions about USENET and how to go about doing various things on the net.

- "List of Active Newsgroups"
  A list of the currently functioning newsgroups.

- "List of Publicly Accessible Mailing Lists"
  Topics that are of specialized interest often have mailing lists rather than newsgroups. In a mailing list, everything submitted by each member is sent to every other member by email.

- "USENET Software: History and Sources" (by Gene Spafford)
  Gives some information on the history of the development of the Netnews software, and the status of various releases.

- "Procedure for Creating New Newsgroups" (by Dave Taylor)
  If you have a topic that you feel really deserves its own newsgroup, here's how you can test the waters without upsetting people.

In addition to these articles, check the newsgroups whose names start with `news.` for a variety of lists, statistics, and discussions that might be of interest to the truly avid "news hound."

Two books that have some good material on using and managing USENET are: *Using uucp and USENET* by Grace Todino and Tim O'Reilly, *A Nutshell Handbook* by O'Reilly & Associates.

The most complete introduction and tutorial on USENET that I have known of is found in several chapters of the book *UNIX Communications* by Bart Anderson, Bryan Costales, and Harry Henderson, The Waite Group. This book also covers many other aspects of UNIX communications that are related to USENET, such as electronic mail and the use of uucp. An appendix shows you how to download special kinds of files (shar, binary format, and so on) from USENET.

Setting Up Netnews on Your System

As was mentioned earlier, installing Netnews is too complex a topic to describe in detail here. It is best to get the help of an experienced USENET administrator. For background, however, you can obtain the manuals for the various Netnews programs from a nearby USENET site, including a document called *USENET Version B Installation*, by Matt Glickman. Additionally, the magazine *UNIX World* contains a two-part series on installing the Netnews software, in its November and December 1986 issues.

Summary

USENET is a significant resource for the professional, social, and recreational needs of UNIX users. It is easy to learn how to read, reply to, and post news, although there are advanced programs that can take quite a while to master. This paper presented both background material to help you understand the "why" of the USENET community, and a practical tutorial to get you started with the "how."

KEYWORDS

▶ Electronic mail

▶ User interfaces

▶ AT&T Mail

▶ Berkeley Mail

▶ Binmail

▶ Elm

▶ MH

▶ Alias

Paper Synopsis: "All About UNIX Mailers" presents a survey of the most popular email programs found on UNIX systems, tracing their roots and explaining how they differ in operation. A discussion of what an "ideal" mailer should do, and an introduction to the author's own Elm mailer. Elm is the first UNIX email program to provide a consistent user-friendly, screen-oriented interface. This paper is a must if you will be using any kind of UNIX mail system.

Dave Taylor is a research scientist in multimedia communications systems at Hewlett-Packard's Palo Alto Research Labs. He has over six years of industry programming experience with UNIX and other operating systems, and is the author of the publicly available, license-free Elm Mail System, and moderator of the *Computers and Society Digest.*

## 3

All About UNIX Mailers

Dave Taylor

One of the most revolutionary and exciting areas in which computers are now being used is for interpersonal communication. Many thousands of people now use computers to help them communicate with their peers, be it the desk next door or halfway around the world.

Where there are raw capabilities, polished products eventually emerge, and UNIX is no different. Once people began using the new electronic mail facilities, they realized that there was a dire need for more sophisticated software. This paper discusses the results of this electronic mail software explosion, to help you decide which mail program is best for you.

A significant amount of credit for the popularity of electronic mail on UNIX is due to the particular type of network communications software that UNIX has: uucp. With this program, users "on the network" merely need to have a computer, phone line, and a modem. They can then automatically telephone other sites and exchange various types of information. In this way, information can be rapidly disseminated throughout a large user community in a short period of time, and with little cost, using the "hop-to-hop" approach. Most important to this approach is having a machine accept and transmit information that was neither destined for it, nor originated at that site—that is, "relay" the message. It is this spirit of cooperation throughout the network that makes it so successful.

With this veritable flood of bits flying through the world, though, it was only natural that some software would be written to help users deal with it intelligently—and thus not only was one mailer written, but dozens were.

RELATED PAPERS

2 The USENET System

15 The Future of UNIX and Open System Standards

Of those, this paper discusses the most representative ones, shown in Table 3–1.

The paper concludes with a short discussion of some other mailers that are available, and also mentions some nagging problems that none of the mailers has solved.

Format for This Paper's Mailer Descriptions

This paper discusses each mailer using the following set of topics:

- An introduction and some history and comments on the system
- The availability of the system
- An exemplary section demonstrating some typical user tasks
- General characteristics of the interface

The sample section for each mailer shows a typical user trying to perform the following functions:

- receiving new mail
- reading a specific message
- sending mail to a friend
- saving a message into a folder

Table 3–1   Representative UNIX Mail Programs

Program Name	Description
binmail	The "original" mailer from Bell Labs, this was part of the very first UNIX release.
Berkeley Mail	(Also known as mailx on System V machines and CapMail, both names are to distinguish it from binmail.) This is the Berkeley rewrite of the binmail program and adds many functions.
MH	A public domain mail system from Rand Corporation designed to integrate with the day-to-day commands issued to the system (that is, MH commands can be interspersed with standard UNIX commands like ls, who, and so on).
Elm	A relatively new, publicly available mail system that presents a new and easier to understand interface to aid in the reception and transmission of mail.
AT&T Mail	Another new mail system, offered by AT&T. It's really much more than just a user interface program, but that is discussed later. It's the only one of those listed here that actually costs money, but that is discussed later, too.

- searching for a specific message

- printing a message

The discussion of system characteristics centers on how the system interacts with the user, whether it offers quick and simple ways to accomplish various tasks, how well it hides the internal workings of the UNIX system from the user, and how flexible it is.

Before you actually begin to examine the various mail systems, however, consider what the characteristics of a mail system are and why each is important. The primary characteristic is the system's ability to present a consistent "illusion"—the typical computer user isn't really interested in the actual bits flying through the chips or the protocols being handed back and forth on the phone line. Rather, the user's concern is the delivery of the mail, especially that the message has been given to a reliable delivery service.

By analogy, when you drop a letter into the mailbox you don't expect to have to stand at the street corner to make sure that the mail carrier really shows up to pick your letter up, and then follow the letter to the local post office, then the central post office, and so on.

The concept of a user illusion is an important one, and having a good understanding of it will certainly help make this paper clearer.

Because of the desirability of this illusion, the areas most vital to examine in mail systems are those that "hide" the system by creating and maintaining an illusion of a postal service where the user need merely know the name of the person and where to drop the letter off. The rest should be done without user intervention. In fact, on most of the systems discussed here the mail system is more akin to having a personal assistant who keeps the addresses for you—you simply say to whom you wish to send the message.

In an electronic mail system the areas that are ideal for this approach are user addresses (due to the complexity of the vast number of networks and different addressing styles on each), the routing and system information in each message (not readable by humans, usually), and the folder storage mechanism.

The following is a reference point you can use to compare the various mailers, because you'll feed the same material to all of them. The mailbox you'll use is:

```
From hplabs!hpl-opus!joey Wed Oct 30 14:03:36 1985
Date: Wed, 30 Oct 85 01:55:05 pst
Received: by HP-VENUS id AA26352; Wed, 30 Oct 85 01:55:05 pst
Message-Id: <8510300955.AA26352@HP-VENUS>
To: hplabs!taylor
```

```
Subject: What's new in your life?

Now that you've gone and created a new universe to populate, what's
left?

joey

From smith Wed Oct 30 14:03:39 1985
From: Richard Smith <hplabs!smith>
Received: by HP-VENUS id AA12562; Wed, 30 Oct 85 12:57:11 pst
Message-Id: <8510302057.AA12562@HP-VENUS>
To: mail-men@rochester
Subject: Another test of the new mail software
References: <36700044@hpcnof.UUCP>
Priority: Most Urgent

Is this working?
```

Don't worry about not being able to understand it all! You shouldn't have
to—that's the whole point of having mailers.

binmail

This is the "original" mail system from the earliest days of Bell UNIX. It
is the quintessential low-level mail system. Compared to the other mailers
you'll learn about, this one is primitive, but when originally written, it was
very innovative.

The commands available from the interactive mode are quite few, and
are listed in Table 3–2.

Table 3–2   Interactive Commands for binmail

Command	Meaning
q	Quit
x	Exit without changing mail
p	Print
s [file]	Save (the default file is mbox)
w [file]	Save without header
-	Print previous
d	Delete
+	Next (no delete)
m user	Mail to user
! cmd	Execute cmd

Notice that even this primitive program can save messages without headers. Note also the inappropriately named command p, which actually displays the message on the screen and doesn't have anything to do with printing. (As you compare the different mail systems you'll find that inappropriately named commands are a widespread problem.)

For the most part, this mailer is used at sites as a lower-level program users run either simply to check whether they've received mail in a mailbox or to transport mail to or from other systems. The most typical usage is either:

```
if test mail -e
then
     echo You have mail, $LOGNAME
fi
```

from within the /etc/profile file for all users logging onto the system, or as a less powerful alternative to sendmail (in which case a link called rmail normally is used).

The binmail program is usually shipped with standard Bell UNIX as the default system mailer. The Berkeley systems have a slightly rewritten version of this program that fixes some of this strange behavior, but is still far less powerful than the "real" Berkeley Mail, discussed later.

Sample Session

Throughout this session, please keep in mind the historical background of binmail as you compare it with the more recent, advanced systems.

Receiving New Mail

The system is started quite simply by typing the following (your entry is shown in bold):

```
% mail
From smith Wed Oct 30 14:03:39 1985
From: Richard Smith <hplabs!smith>
Received: by HP-VENUS id AA12562; Wed, 30 Oct 85 12:57:11 pst
Message-Id: <8510302057.AA12562 HP-VENUS>
To: mail-men@rochester
Subject: Another test of the new mail software
References: <36700044 hpcnof.UUCP>
Priority: Most Urgent
```

```
Is this working?
?
```

When you start up the mailer it's hard not to notice that it immediately dumps the first message on the screen, then presents the first prompt. This is quite an assumption to make of the user's intentions, and usually is not what the user wants. Many people want to browse their mail by subject and sender, and then select what to read.

Reading a Specific Message

To read a specific message, you need to move through the file using the + and − keys to move to the desired message. Unfortunately, each time you move, the new message is displayed. This can be merely annoying on high-speed terminals, but is unacceptable if you're using slower baud rates. Once you find the message to display, you can use the print command to display it:[1]

```
? print

From hplabs!hpl-opus!joey Wed Oct 30 14:03:36 1985
Dave: Wed, 30 Oct 85 01:55:05 pst
Received: by HP-VENUS id AA26352; Wed, 30 Oct 85 01:55:05 pst
Message-Id: <8510300995.AA26352 HP-VENUS>
To: hplabs!taylor
Subject: What's new in your life?

Now that you've gone and created a new universe to populate, what's
left?

joey

?
```

Sending Mail to a Friend

Because binmail has no aliases (that is, shorthand for the addresses of friends) available, you must type in the entire address and send the message accordingly:

```
? m hplabs!hpl-opus!joey
```

---

[1]Interestingly, binmail accepts full-word commands, but doesn't list them on the command menu. This is because the program only checks the first character, so *peach* and *pathetique* would also work in this context.

```
This is a test
.
?
```

(The period on a line by itself signifies the end of the message. Also notice that this system lacks a message subject line.)

Saving a Message into a Folder

This particular message can be saved in a folder, called "joey," by entering:

```
? s joey

%
```

While there was no explicit onscreen feedback, it turned out that the message was indeed added to the requested folder. For some reason not immediately apparent, because you worked with the last message in your mailbox binmail was exited under the mistaken assumption that you were actually done with the program.

Characteristics of the Interface

By virtue of its simplicity, you would expect binmail to be fairly easy to use, but also not very powerful. Indeed, that turns out to be the case, so the program doesn't really achieve the goal of hiding the system from the user.

There are no aliases, no internal knowledge of routing or headers, no ability to reply to a group (or even to reply at all), no facility for filtering messages through other programs, no searching capabilities, and other such features. There really isn't any user *illusion* at all.

Berkeley Mail

Of the mail systems that come with the standard UNIX operating system distributions, the Berkeley mailer, originally written by Kurt Schoens, is certainly the most powerful. Originally started as a simple rewrite of binmail the system soon took on a life of its own, and now has many dozens of options and flags. It has paved the way for some very interesting mail systems. Among its innovative features are the ability to have aliases for commonly used addresses, permanently toggled flags to modify the behavior of the program (also known humorously as the '.rc' syndrome, in which files that begin with a period and end with the letters *rc* proliferate), and operations based on strings rather than just message numbers.

The mailer is overall still line-oriented, and the syntax, to quote the author, Schoens, is "reminiscent of ed(1)," a simple line editor. The system is easy to use once the user masters its particular usage of English. As with binmail, this program uses English in strange ways, such as a print command to *display* a message on the screen and a file command to *list folders* rather than save a message. There is a lot of power available, however, especially embodied in the idea that almost any command that you apply to a single message can also apply to a list of messages. So, for example, you could reply to all the messages from Joey with a single command:

```
reply "joey"
```

The alias feature is very similar to the alias function of the C shell. The program also has a large number of options that can be set from either within the program or within the automatically read startup file (HOME/.mailrc), including those that will give you a saved copy of each message sent and those that tell you what directory to use for folders.

Sample Session

This session assumes that you have no aliases and no special options set. The process described can be changed by judicious use of the startup file, but what is shown is a more straightforward interaction (and is also more typical of an average user).

Receiving New Mail

Entering Berkeley Mail with new/pending mail is quite simple:

```
% Mail

Mail version mailx 23.2 4/23/84.  Type ? for help.

"/usr/mail/mailuser": 2 messages 2 new

>N  1 hpl-opus!joey Wed Oct 30 14:03  12/323 "What's new in your life?"
 N  2 smith    Wed Oct 30 14:03  10/320 "Another test of the new mail"

&
```

You now have headers of messages, rather than simply having the message fly by, as with `binmail`. This is a large step toward a useful model of how a mail system should work. Also, the > symbol indicates the current message.

Reading a Specific Message

To read a specific message, you can get the number of the message from the header page by:

```
& headers

>N  1 hpl-opus!joey Wed Oct 30 14:03  12/323 "What's new in your life?"
 N  2 smith     Wed Oct 30 14:03  10/320 "Another test of the new mail "


&
```

and then either use the `print` or `type` command:

```
& type 1

Message  1:
From hplabs!hpl-opus!joey Wed Oct 30 14:03:36 1985
Date: Wed, 30 Oct 85 01:55:05 pst
Received: by HP-VENUS id AA26352; Wed, 30 Oct 85 01:55:05 pst
Message-Id: <8510300955.AA26352 HP-VENUS>
To: hplabs!taylor
Subject: What's new in your life?
Status: R

Now that you've gone and created a new universe to populate, what's
left?

joey

&
```

One of the more questionable features of Berkeley Mail is that it actually changes the message by reading it—notice the `Status:` header that wasn't part of the original message. Once this mailer has processed the message, it will permanently have this affixed to it. Perhaps it's a personal bias, but I don't agree with the philosophy of a reader altering the item being read.

Sending Mail to a Friend

As has been already mentioned, Berkeley Mail has aliases available, so you can send mail by creating an appropriate alias and then specifying joey, but since this discussion assumes a neophyte user who hasn't yet learned the ins and outs of the various mailers, the following specifies the entire address:

```
& mail hpbals!hpl-opus!joey²
Subject: Just testing


Just a test, kiddo!


EOT³


&
```

One of the problems with this particular form of mailing a message is that the user is left hanging after the program prompts for the subject line. All of a sudden nothing happens, and it's not obvious that the message should be directly typed in following the subject line.

Consider how much easier it would be if the previous example were altered slightly to be:

```
& mail hplabs!joey
Subject: Just testing


Please enter your message, ending with a . by itself on a line:


Just a test, kiddo!


EOT
.
&
```

Saving a Message into a Folder

To save a message or set of messages to a folder is quite simple:

---

²This is indeed a typo. Notice that the mailer isn't even aware of the problem.

³EOT, cryptically enough, stands for end of text or end of transmission.

```
& save 2 "joey"
"joey" [appended] 10/320


&
```

where the last two numbers are the number of lines and number of characters saved, respectively. The word *appended* in brackets indicates that
the file already existed and you added message 2 to the existing file. If
the file hadn't existed, it would have said saved instead.

Searching a Folder for a Specific Message

Unfortunately, there doesn't seem to be any facility to search a folder for
a specific message in Berkeley Mail. Finding a folder with a specified
message would be fairly easy—a UNIX command like:

```
% grep -l PATTERN FOLDER-DIRECTORY/*
```

would tell us what folder or folders the pattern occurs in, but to find the
specific message is far less simple.

Printing a Message

To print a message, you're forced to pipe the specified message or messages
to the line-printer program via:

```
& save 2 !lpr -Pbonsai3u
"lpr -Pbonsai3u" [Piped] 10/320
```

This isn't particularly satisfying, interface-wise, because the print command
should do this, but it's functional.

Characteristics of the Interface

Notice the complete breakdown of the user illusion when you try to print
a message out. You had to use a very cryptic and obscure syntax to achieve
a printout.

There are some other drawbacks, too—Berkeley Mail isn't much better at hiding the underlying system than binmail is. The program has aliases,
which is a useful addition, but there is no way short of writing-down-and-
adding-by-hand to add new aliases to the "database" included in the program (that is, your .mailrc file). Likewise, the system doesn't verify addresses that you type in and doesn't have any knowledge of mail routing.

MH

The Rand Corporation, when it first started working with the Advanced Research and Projects Agency (ARPA), a division of the U.S. Department of Defense, found that the available electronic mail software was rather poor. Consequently, Bruce Borden, using some suggestions from Stockton Gaines and Norman Shapiro, wrote the MH mail system. MH stands for "mail handler." Later, Marshall Rose and John Romine, from The University of California at Irvine, ported the programs to a number of new machines.

Most interestingly, this mail system consists of a set of discrete commands rather than a monolithic program. For example, to read a specific message, the user would, from the UNIX command line, type:

```
% show 4
```

The core of the MH package consists of the 16 programs shown in Table 3–3.

The basic design of the system is that of a set of interacting programs, each of which depends on the state of the system as created and altered by the other commands. The system appears to have been designed for a sophisticated class of users. Certainly it is not immediately obvious how to perform any of the operations usually associated with reading and writing mail.

It's also line-oriented and quite functional as a lower-level mail system that other programs or UNIX shell scripts could use to present different

Table 3–3   MH Programs and Their Functions

Program Name	Function of the Program
comp	Compose a message
dist	Redistribute a message
file	Move messages between folders
folder	Select/list status of folders
forw	Forward a message
inc	Incorporate new mail
next	Show the next message
pick	Select a set of messages by context
prev	Show the previous message
prompter	Friendly editor front end for composing messages
repl	Reply to a message
rmf	Remove a folder
rmm	Remove messages
scan	Produce a scan listing of selected messages
send	Send a previously composed message
show	Show messages

user interfaces. You'll see a few examples of this later, when you look at some other mailers.

MH is available through the Berkeley 4.3 distribution tapes, which can be ordered directly from the University of California at Berkeley or through various public bulletin boards including the USENET.

Failing these outlets, there are inevitably some local UNIX systems that can supply you with the system.

Sample Session

This sample session uses the same mailbox as before.

Receiving New Mail

While you are using the shell you'll see a message like:

```
%
You have new mail.
%
```

To incorporate this into your existing mailbox, merely issue the inc—incorporate new mail into my inbox—command:

```
% inc

#      Date    From     Subject
1+     10/30   joey     What's new in your life?
2      10/30   smith    Another test of the new mail software
%
```

The + indicates that this is the new current message.

Reading a Specific Message

Try to read the message from joey, next (note that it is defaulting to the current message indicated by the + above):

```
% show

From hplabs!hpl-opus!joey Wed Oct 30 14:03:36 1985
Date: Wed, 30 Oct 85 01:55:05 pst
Received: by HP-VENUS id AA26352; Wed, 30 Oct 85 01:55:05 pst
Message-Id: <8510300955.AA26352 HP-VENUS>
```

```
To: hplabs!taylor
Subject: What's new in your life?

Now that you've gone and created a new universe to populate, what's
left?

joey


%
```

Regular MH users will immediately point out that there is in fact a way to "teach" MH what headers you're interested in and which you aren't, but to avoid clashing with the various local versions, merely note that a possible display would have been something far more succinct, like:

```
From: hplabs!hpl-opus!joey
Subject: What's new in your life?
To: hplabs!taylor


[message body]
```

Sending Mail to a Friend

The first step is to compose the message:

```
% comp
```

which runs your favorite editor and displays the following template:

```
To:
cc:
Subject:
------------
```

You could fill it in with something like this:

```
To: hplabs!hpl-opus!joey
cc:
Subject: Missive of the day
------------
And what are today's words of wisdom?
            -- Dave --
```

Once you're done, you leave the editor and are asked What Now? The valid responses at this point are:

list, to list the draft of the message

quit, to leave and keep the draft

quit delete, to leave and remove the message

send, to send the message

edit to enter the editor again to continue composing

Here you would choose send, and the message would be sent.

Saving a Message into a Folder

Now that you've read this message from joey, you want to file it in a folder that bears his name (to organize your old mail by who sent it). The MH command to do this is:

```
% file cur +joey
```

Again, cur is short for current and can be omitted—MH will default to the current message.

Searching a Folder for a Specific Message

Next, look for another message Joey sent you a while ago, discussing the metaphysical ramifications of planet creation. To accomplish this, you can use:

```
% pick metaphysic +joey
```

```
[1 hit]
```

```
% scan
#       Date    From    Subject
5+      8/14    joey    Creating planets and other games...
```

```
% show
```

```
From hplabs!hpl-opus!joey Sun Aug 14 14:38:27 1985
Subject: Creating planets and other games...
To: hplabs!taylor
```

```
But have you considered the metaphysical ramifications of
```

```
creating a new planet?  Who would be 'in charge'??
```

```
joey
```

```
% folder +inbox
```

Notice a few features about this: first off, a + sign as a command argument always delimits a folder filename, as opposed to its use as the current message indicator in scan listings. Secondly, the pick command created a different folder for the selected messages and then made that the current folder selected. As a consequence, the following commands act on that folder, rather than on the incoming mailbox.

Printing a Message

As discussed previously, MH tends to neatly sidestep issues of this nature, preferring to let the user figure out how to print messages. There are two methods for printing a message, neither of which are particularly intuitive:

```
% show 5 -pr
```

```
% show 5 ¦ lpr -Pprinter
```

Further Notes

As can be seen, MH gives the user a lot of power, but at the price of a more awkward, UNIX-command style interface. There are some neat tricks you can do with the system, however, such as:

```
% show 'pick -from joey +contracts +stuff' ¦ lpr
```

This prints all messages from joey in either the "contracts" or "stuff" folder.

An ingenious way that some people use to get around the explicit inc call that is required to read new mail is to have an entry in their crontab similar to:

```
0,15,30,45 * * * * su joey -c /usr/bin/mh/inc > /dev/null
```

which tells cron (a program that executes jobs based on time-of-day) to check for new mail every 15 minutes and to include it if present in the new mailbox, throwing the rest of MH's output into the "bit bucket."

The portability of the folder format is another story entirely, however. The MH implementors chose to exploit the hierarchical directory structure of the UNIX system and designed the system to use folders that are really directories, and individual messages that are really individual files. This leads, as mentioned previously, to some substantial gains in the speed of various operations, but is very nonstandard. It is impossible, for example, to read an MH folder by using binmail or Berkeley Mail. This is a considerable drawback unless you're willing to use MH exclusively.[4]

On the other hand, it has some nice side-effects; for example, you can search for mail in *all* your folders and find the specific message you want by using the UNIX grep utility.

Characteristics of the Interface

For all its power, MH is still not very good at hiding the underlying system. This mailer, as do most mailers, suffers mostly because its creators didn't realize that the typical user doesn't want to know the details of the system. One example is the process of sending mail to a friend. There is no alias feature in MH to handle this, and, indeed, the user must type in the entire routing address each time the program is invoked to send a message.[5] This is okay for people who like to learn about the various addressing and routing schemes, or who don't mind having "template" files for each person to mail to, but for the average user this is a real problem.

Also worth noting is that the program tends to be slow, even with the extensive performance improvements that Van Jacobsen of the University of California Berkeley has added.

The Elm Mail System

While all the mailers you've looked at so far assume that the user is using a line-oriented system (such as a teletype), the Elm mail system, which I

---

[4]As it turns out, there is an easy-to-use UNIX command you can use to build a more standard mailbox from an MH one:

```
for each file (MH Folder Directory)
  cat $file >> New folder name
end
```

(this is a csh script).

[5]Two notes on this: first, a user of MH swears that there is an alias facility, but since it's not mentioned in any of the documentation it apparently isn't used at all, and second, on some systems a lower-level program, sendmail, has an alias facility that is used instead. The inherent problem with this, though, is that the user has no idea if the address (or alias) he or she chose is the correct one or even a valid one.

Table 3–4 Elm Programs and Their Functions

Program Name	Function of the Program
answer	Transcribes phone messages using email.
autoreply	Automatically answers mail.
checkalias	Verifies personal and system user aliases.
elm	The main mailer software.
fastmail	A low level interface for programmatic mailing.
filtev	Automatically process incoming mail using user-defined rules.
from	Summarizes the from and subject lines of mail or folders.
messages	Counts messages pending or in a folder.
newalias	Installs new user or system aliases.
newmail	Monitors and informs you of newly arrived mail.
printmail	Prints mail or folders in a readable format.
readmsg	Reads a specified message or messages.
trim-headers	Removes extraneous headers from mail.
wnewmail	Same as "newmail" but for window systems.

designed and wrote, uses a fast, screen-oriented display. The program has been evolving considerably in the past year or so and is now a suitable replacement for any of the other mailers discussed here. (Versions 1.3 and above support AT&T Mail style "forms," too.)

The Elm mail system consists of a set of programs, with elm as the main program, which can be used for reading, writing, and filing messages. The package comes with the programs listed in Table 3–4.

The Elm mail system is available from a number of public bulletin board systems, including the USENET, and also from a number of large UNIX sites in various geographic areas.

Sample Session

This session uses the same default mailbox as did the preceding mailers. Notice that the default for this system is a bit more user-friendly than that of the other mailers. As with the other examples in this section, this example is based purely on the default action of the system.

Receiving New Mail

The newmail daemon (a program that is always running in background) would notify you of new mail by sending a message such as the following to the screen:

```
%

>> New mail from hpl-opus!joey - What's new in your life
>> New mail from Richard Smith - Another test of the new mailer

%
```

The mailer can then be started by:

```
% elm
```

which causes a display like this:

```
    Mailbox is '/usr/mail/mailuser' with 2 messages.  [Elm 1.4]

->   1      Oct 30  hpl-opus!joey   (12)    What's new in your life?
     2      Oct 30  Richard Smith   (10)    Another test of the new mail




    !=pipe, !=shell, ?=help, <n>=set current to n, /=search pattern
   A)lias, C)hange mailbox, D)elete, E)dit, F)orward, G)roup reply, M)ail,
   N)ext, O)ptions, P)rint, R)eply, S)ave, T)ag, Q)uit, U)ndelete, or eX)it

Elm : @
```

Reading a Specific Message

To read a specific message, you merely press RETURN. Something like the following is displayed:

```
Message #1 from hpl-opus!joey           Mailed October 30, 1986 at 1:55 am

Date: Wed, 30 Oct 85 01:55:05 pst
To: hplabs!taylor
Subject: What's new in your life?

Now that you've gone and created a new universe to populate, what's
left?

joey

Please press <return> to return:
```

Sending Mail to a Friend

Of all the mailers discussed in this paper, only Elm confirms the aliases as they are typed in; also, only Elm allows the user to add new aliases from within the program. For example, you could alias the return address of the current message by choosing the A)lias menu option, then the A)lias Current Message option from the alias submenu.

Once the alias is installed, you can then mail a message to Joey with:

```
Command: m
```

This is immediately altered to:

```
Command: Mail
To: joey
```

which is *then* immediately translated to the equivalent alias:

```
Command: Mail                     To: hplabs!hpl-opus!joey (Joey Matthews)
Subject: testing
Copies To: <return>
```

An editor screen now displays so you can compose the message. When you're done, you're prompted:

```
Please choose: E)dit msg, edit H)eaders, S)end or F)orget: s
```

and choosing S sends the mail off.

Without an alias, however, you can still type in a minimal subset of the address, `hpl-opus!joey`, and the system will figure out the appropriate route and display the expanded address, or it will warn you that you cannot get to the requested system. This is done through a file created by the `pathalias` program, or created by hand.

Saving a Message into a Folder

To save a message, you simply press S to invoke the `save` command, and you see the prompt:

```
Save message to : =joey
```

with the cursor sitting on the equals sign. Pressing RETURN gives you this as the default folder, or typing any other character will clear the buffer, and you can enter whatever folder you want.

Searching a Folder for a Specific Message

To search a folder, you can either look just at the `from` and `subject` lines, or you can consider every line of the messages. These two different searches are done by:

```
/pattern
//pattern
```

respectively.

Printing a Message

Printing is also simple: selecting P)rint will do the trick. For this option, however, you must have a default value for printing set up in your `.elmrc` file. Something of the form:

```
print = lpr -Plineprinter3
```

would suffice. Note that this is a UNIX command, so you could invoke anything, even

```
print = cat ->/dev/lp
```

Characteristics of the Interface

Unlike the other mailers discussed here, with Elm you wouldn't be stuck if you didn't have documentation. Elm was designed specifically not to need any documentation and to require simply someone to tell the new user how to bring up the main program. From this point, everything is self-documenting and relatively intuitive. Aliases, for example, can be checked and added without leaving the program. Indeed, you can say "alias the return address of the current message to x" (that is, A)lias Current Msg to: x) without any problem at all. The user illusion is preserved throughout.

For the more sophisticated user and for someone on a slow terminal line (1200 baud or slower), the interface is a bit slow, since it's screen-oriented, but it seems to be a small price to pay for a system where the user doesn't need to remember sequences of arcane commands.

AT&T Mail

As you have seen, there are a plethora of mail systems available of varying levels of sophistication, as either part of the standard UNIX system or available for free from various distribution channels. With this, then, you might well ask why AT&T introduced yet another mail system—one that costs money—to the marketplace.

The answer is that AT&T Mail is considerably more than just a user interface to the existing UNIX mail transport scheme. In fact, the AT&T Mail system is part of the Unified Electronic Messaging Facility that AT&T is offering.

This facility includes an amazing number of features, including the ability to check your electronic mail on a pushbutton phone; the ability to move from a PC to a UNIX machine and back without any transition pains, due to a consistent user interface; and, perhaps most importantly, a message transportation system that is far more reliable than the existing UNIX point-to-point network. You're interested here in the user interface to AT&T Mail on UNIX systems, however, so the other systems and features aren't discussed here.

There are really three ways to read messages from AT&T Mail—one way is to use an existing mail program (people use both Berkeley Mail and Elm to read mail from the AT&T Mail system) or to use the PMX/TERM system.[6] The third alternative is to connect to one of the AT&T Mail Service machines and use the command line system found there. This discussion describes AT&T Mail running with PMX/TERM.

The PMX/TERM system is a single program that offers a very familiar style of interface for those people used to a PC environment. Indeed, the PMX/TERM system is an emulation of the Access I and Access II software on the PC.

The system presents a screen broken into four windows: the function key menu, the in box, the out box, and a small display that indicates the status of the current outbound message (either pending transmission or sent).

Sample Session

This session uses a mailbox with some slightly different headers. But there's nothing to worry about!

Receiving New Mail

Similar to most of the other systems discussed here, PMX/TERM assumes you'll know when mail arrives. This is typically through notification at login; you have mail, <username>; or between user commands; you have new mail. . . .

The mailer can then be started by:

---

[6]Private Message eXchange/TERMinal system.

```
% pmxterm
```

after which you'll see a screen display like this:

```
Aug 24 1986  11:24

1        2           # Addressee     Subject        Date    Type Len   Status
CREATE   REVISE
3        4           1 F:...!pmxhelp  Welcome        8/1     T    709   New
READ     DELETE      2 F:...!pmxhelp  User Comments  8/1     F    547   New
5        6
SEND     RECEIVE
7        8
FOLDERS QUIT


                     # Addressee     Subject         Date  Type Len    Status
    -- PMX/TERM --


          0          --------------------- Empty  --------------------
    -  -  -  -
    -  -  -  -


      Copyright (c) 1986 by AT&T Information Systems

(SP) More Functions      (Top, Btm,^,v) Select Message   (Up) Select Folder
```

Reading a Specific Message

To read a specific message, you use the arrow keys to move the current message indicator up and down or use CTRL-X (move up) and CTRL-C (move down) keys instead. When the desired message is highlighted you can press RETURN to read it. You see something like this:

```
Subject: Hello there!                          Date: Aug 14, 1986
To: !dave
From: Richard Anderson


From what I understand, you're the same person who wrote the section in
"UNIX Papers" about mailers?  Is this the case?  If so, I'd just like to say
that I enjoyed it, and also found it to be the first viable presentation of
the PMX/TERM package from AT&T.  Most of the discussions I've seen have
compared it to a square wheel (haha).

I'm a marketing representative for AT&T and have to admit to a touch of deja
```

vu knowing that the message I'm sending you has already appeared in the book. There's something very odd about the whole affair.

I wonder if Rod Serling has anything to do with this...

```
1->BEG   2->END   3->NW   4->DW   5->IL   6->DL   7->QUIT   8->SAVE
```

Pressing 7[7] (done) exits back to the main screen.

Sending Mail to a Friend

To send a message, you press the 5 key (function key 5 selects the Create Message option), which then runs the PMX/TERM editor with a template as listed next. You then fill the fields in accordingly, compose the message, and press 8 to send it. Notice the software's ability to use full names and to have copies of the mail go to people as printed messages sent by U.S. mail:

```
Subject: The 1987 Email Conference              Date: Sep 5, 1986
To: !joey
Cc: John Richardson


Paper-To:  [Dave Taylor          ]USMAIL
           [c/o Company X         ]
           [1234 A Road Court     ]
           [Somewhere, CA         ]
           [90043                 ]
           Phone: [(415) 555-1212 ]
```

Just a short note to confirm that you are all penciled in as keynote speakers for the conference. If you have any questions please give me a call at 555-0943.

                                        Larry

```
1->BEG   2->END   3->NW   4->DW   5->IL   6->DL   7->QUIT   8->SAVE
```

---

[7]Assume here a terminal that doesn't have the appropriate function keys available. If it did, you would actually press programmable function key 7 for this function.

Saving a Message to a Folder

To save a message to a folder, you need to display the alternate menu screen. Press the SPACEBAR. The menu display on the top left of the main screen will be changed to display functions for: STATUS, CONFIG, COPY, PRINT, ATTACH, DETACH, UNIX, and FORM. Now you want to COPY the message, so press 3. The system then displays a list of all the available folders, so you can leaf through them as desired. Then press 8 to save the message to the folder selected.

Searching a Folder for a Specific Message

There is currently no facility available for searching through folders for specific messages.

Printing a Message

To print a message, you need to move the current message indicator to the desired message, get the alternate menu screen by pressing the SPACE-BAR, then press 4 to print the message.

Characteristics of the Interface

There are a few other points worth noting about AT&T Mail, perhaps the most important being that the PMX/TERM is not suitable for high-volume mail throughput. You can have a maximum of 99 messages in a folder, for example, which you'll easily exceed if you become actively involved in electronic mail.

Also, note that it is a bit awkward for more advanced users to leaf through menu screens to get to the function desired (a limit of 10 functions per "menu" is imposed). When composing a message, the user is required to use the PMX editor, one unlike any other available on UNIX—yet there are a vast number of different editing systems available.

There are some really wonderful features, though, including sending a printed copy of the message.

Other Mailers

The mailers presented herein are not by any means an exhaustive list of all the mailers available on the UNIX system. Among the other mailers, those of interest include:

Rmail

Unlike the rmail link to binmail, this program is actually a powerful mail system that runs from within the emacs editor environment. It is essentially a line-oriented program running in a screen-oriented environment, but it has been smoothly integrated into the overall environment of emacs. This system is available with either Gosling emacs or GNU emacs.

MH-Rmail

This is an interface to the MH program from within the emacs environment.

MM

This is a simulation of the popular mm mailer that was available on the TOPS-20 operating system. It was written by David Kashtan of SRI International and is reputed to be slow and missing some of the key features of the original.

snd/msg

This pair of programs was originally written for the Tenex Operating System by Rand and has undergone at least two major rewrites—one from the MMDF[a] group, and one from the University of California at San Diego. It is a pair of line-oriented programs with a style of interaction similar to Elm. The various versions are available by either contacting the CSNET administration group or by contacting the university.

VuMail

This is the only mailer in this list for which there is a charge, rather than being public domain or part of another system. Not much is known about it other than that it is full-screen, supports the MH style of interface (indeed it uses some of the MH commands for low-level functions), and has been written and is being marketed by Jim Guyton of MIT.

IMS

This is another variation of the MH program in an early stage of development by Brandon Allberry of Tridelta Industries, in Mentor Ohio.

uumail

A mailer for pure uucp sites, this is really a complex shell script that invokes binmail for transmission of messages.

nmail

A mailer for pure local area network sites, this is also really a shell script, but this one performs fast delivery in a LAN-based envi-

---

[a]Multi-Channel Memo Distribution Facility.

ronment by opening a port on the remote side at transmission time
and sending the message straight through.

dmail
This is another public access mail reader, from Matt Dillon of the
University of California at Berkeley.

fmail
This mail system is part of the AT&T Toolchest distribution
package and is a subset of the Elm mailer.

As you can see, there are a lot of mail systems available!

What Mailers Should Do

The final topic of this paper is a brief discussion of an ideal interface for
a mail system, with the hope of perhaps stimulating some enthusiastic
software engineer out there to go ahead and implement it.

The best way to illustrate the style is through interaction, so you can
try another sample session. As usual, the user input is in **boldface**. (This
is the MH style of interaction, taken to its logical extreme.) It wouldn't be
unreasonable for this to actually be a dialog between user and computer
via voice synthesizer and a speech recognition system if you consider
"terminals" to have been obsoleted:

```
> do I have any new mail?
```

```
Yes.  Two messages:
    One from Joey asking 'what's new in your life?'
    and one from Richard Smith testing new mail software.
```

```
> show me the message from Richrad Smith
```

```
I'll assume you really mean "Richard Smith...."
```

```
  Message from Richard Smith of HP Labs, mailed to 'mail-men at
  rochester' at 2:03 pm today:
```

```
  Is this working?
```

```
> I'd like to send a short message to joey
```

```
Do you mean "Joey Wu" or "Joey Heatherton," Dave ? wu
I'll remember that...

Please enter your message to Joey Wu, end by pressing [END]:

how goes it?  Interested in lunch?

[END]

Shall I tag this as "important" or "urgent?" urgent

Urgent message sent to Joey Wu.

> Please show me all messages that are from joey and contain
  the phrase "such is life" or similar

I'll assume you are referring to "Joey Wu...."

Looking...

I found three messages:
  One dated Tuesday 7/6/84 and entitled "raises at XYZ Co.,"
  one dated Friday 9/23/84 and entitled "Another downer date,"
  and one from yesterday entitled "So you wanna dance...."

> print all three messages

Spooling...done
```

There are a number of things to notice about this example, not the least of which is that the system is accepting some very complex commands. Other points of interest are that the system not only corrected the misspelling of *Richard*, but it also remembered that you're referring to *Joey Wu* when you say *joey*. Also, the indirect reference "all three messages" was accepted and acted upon, too.

There is no concept of mailboxes and folders, either. These are in fact rather anachronistic and will gradually go away as mail systems move towards a more powerful database structure. Also, there are no aliases (or, perhaps there are, but they're so smoothly integrated into the system that it's painless for the user) since, again, they're not really necessary.

At this point, consider the user illusion and go and reread the example. The concept of mailers as electronic postal systems will become clear from this sample session. Compare it to the various existing systems you saw earlier in the paper and consider the vast difference in ease of use.

There are other visions of the future certainly, including "intelligent agents" that filter the mail before you even see it, so that it can remember what meetings you're being asked to attend, what files you backed up, and so on.

Another vision is that of each message being an "icon" and folders being "stacks of message" that can be shuffled through. This is very much a model of the way people deal with paper mail. It seems like a waste of the abilities of the computer, though—why model an existing, inefficient system when newer, more powerful ones can be created? (Have you ever wished for commands like "find me all the relevant news in all the world newspapers"?)

Conclusion

You've spent a lot of time looking at various electronic mail systems in great detail. While there certainly is a lot of information in this paper, I hope that you will come away with a feeling of having experienced a part of the world of electronic mail on the UNIX system and will be better able to decide which of the systems is the appropriate one for your use!

KEYWORDS

▶ Bourne shell

▶ Korn shell

▶ C shell

▶ Shell script

▶ Functions

▶ History

▶ Aliasing

▶ Job control

Paper Synopsis: *Shells* are the user interface that surrounds the UNIX kernel. The shell programming language is thus a critical part of any UNIX user's understanding. This paper takes a close look at three UNIX shells (sh, csh, and ksh), identifying the important features of each. The relative merits of each shell's ease of use and programming power are presented. While individual needs of users differ, the new ksh (Korn shell) turns out to be the best for most applications. The paper concludes with a look at some experimental shells and ones currently under development.

John Sebes received a bachelor's degree in philosophy from Yale in 1984. Since then he has been employed by Intermetrics, Inc., a Cambridge-based high technology systems company that specializes in developing software development tools and high-order programming languages for major industrial and federal customers.

## 4

Comparing UNIX Shells

John Sebes

A UNIX *shell* is a program that people use to communicate with the UNIX operating system. Most UNIX users spend much of their time using a shell, so it makes sense for people to choose a shell that best suits their needs. This paper compares different shells in a variety of ways, in order to determine which shell is the best match for given requirements.

There are several different ways to look at what a shell is and what it does, and each view corresponds to a way to compare shells. The most obvious way to look at a shell is as a command interpreter—you type commands to a shell, and it performs whatever operating system functions are necessary to execute each command. Command execution is the heart of daily interactive use. Since the primary way most people use shells is interactively, one way to compare shells is to compare their interactive features—comparing how powerful, convenient, or efficient various shells are for everyday use.

Many UNIX users also spend a fair amount of time writing *shell scripts*, which are files of shell commands that a shell interprets by reading the file as if it were a terminal at which a person sat, entering the commands. Shell scripts are essentially programs written in the language of shell commands. The features of shells that are useful in writing shell scripts tend to be different from the features important for interactive use. So, another way to compare shells is to compare how useful, convenient, or powerful these programming features are.

Besides specific features useful in writing any shell script, a shell language also has an overall structure that can be important as well, especially when you write large or sophisti-

RELATED PAPERS

1 UNIX: Rights and Wrongs

5 awk Power Plays

15 The Future of UNIX and Open System Standards

cated shell scripts. UNIX users who write such scripts generally have to view a shell as an interpreted programming language. What makes a shell language special is that the operations it is best suited to perform mostly relate to the UNIX operating system. Therefore, another way to compare shells, aside from the specific programming features, is comparing how good shells are as programming languages.

The most widely available UNIX shells are the Bourne shell (sh— available with almost all versions of UNIX), the C shell (csh—available with BSD releases), and the Korn shell (ksh—available from the AT&T Toolkit to run on either AT&T or BSD versions of UNIX). The Bourne shell was the first widely available UNIX shell and is in many ways still the standard UNIX shell. The C shell was written after the Bourne shell, and it was developed primarily to create a shell that was much more easy to use interactively than the Bourne shell. On systems where the C shell is available, it tends to be the shell of choice for most interactive users. The Korn shell is a recent addition. It is a superset of the Bourne shell; that is, anything that works with the Bourne shell will work with the Korn shell, and any scripts that the Bourne shell will run, the Korn shell will run as well. But the Korn shell also has many additional features that are like many of the advances of the C shell over the Bourne shell. Thus, ksh combines the conveniences of the C shell with features of the standard Bourne shell.

These three are the most popular shells and are the ones compared in this paper. First, the paper spells out in a slightly greater detail what shells do. Then it compares the three shells, first on the basis of their interactive features, and then on their programming features. After that, you should be able to decide under which circumstances one of the three is best because of its features. Next, the paper evaluates how good the shells are as programming languages, and how this might be significant when you choose a shell. Finally, the paper compares how these three standard shells compare to new, developing shells.

Overview of Shell Features

Before you see how the three shells differ, you first should see what they have in common and what sorts of things shells do in general.

Command Execution

The first and simplest thing that shells do is execute commands—a program that doesn't do this isn't a shell. When you give a command such as cat foo to a shell, it looks in the file system for a program named cat and executes it with the argument foo. Most shells also have some commands built-in, such as cd (change directory). When you give a shell a command that is built-in, the shell performs the necessary actions itself, rather than starting up another program to do it. Also, because much of the time arguments to commands are the names of files, most shells provide a shorthand for filenames. For example, each of the three shells will interpret the word fo* to mean all the files in the current working directory whose names begin with fo.

When a shell executes a program, it usually waits for the program to finish before it does anything else. One useful thing most shells can do is enable you to execute more than one command at the same time. A shell does this simply by not waiting for a newly started program to end. This program is said to be running in the *background*. While it is doing so, you are free to do other things, which of course include running another program normally (in the foreground), or backgrounding other programs. An example of when this might be useful is when you have a task that you know will take a bit of time (perhaps compiling a C source file you've just finished writing) and you'd like to do something else (perhaps read your electronic mail) while the first task is going on.

Input/Output Control and Redirection

Another important thing that most shells do is to control the input/output of a program. Many programs take input from a keyboard and expect to write to a screen or terminal. When a program does so, it is said to be reading from the standard input, and writing to the standard output. It can also write to the standard error output, which usually also goes to a screen. Shells can control a program's I/O by changing the destination of the standard input, output, or error. By telling the shell to change the input to a file, you can have a program that normally reads from the terminal read instead from a file. For example,

```
mail fred < fred.txt
```

runs the mail program in such a way that it reads the file fred.txt as is if you were typing on the terminal and then mails it to Fred. This is called *input redirection*. Similarly, *output redirection* of a command causes the program to run in such a way that what would normally be displayed on the screen of the terminal is instead written to a file. For example:

```
wc fred.txt > fred.count
```

125

counts the words in the file fred.txt and saves the count in the file fred.count. Finally, the shell can create *pipes* by piping, or connecting, the output of one command to the input of another, as in

```
nroff fred.nr ¦ mail fred
```

Here, the file fred.nr is formatted, and the formatted text is used as the input to mail, just as fred.txt was before.

Features for Shell Scripts

Most shells also have a set of features that are useful when you write shell scripts. Most shells provide variables, or *parameters,* as they are called in the Bourne shell. These are referenced by means of some special notation (usually preceding the name of the variable by a $) and set with some built-in function (the set built in the C shell, and an assignment operator = in the Bourne and Korn shells). For example:

```
x=hello
```

assigns hello to the variable x, and:

```
echo $x
```

gets its value so that echo can print it.

Also, most shells provide some kind of control structuring, with built-in primitives like if and while, which are familiar features of many programming languages. An example of the Bourne shell's if structure is:

```
if diff fred.txt bob.txt > fredbob.out
    then echo "Fred is different from Bob"
fi
```

Here, two files are compared, their differences saved in a third file, and a message is printed if there are any differences.

A final feature provided by most shells is the ability to use the output of commands as text to be used for other commands or for setting variables. This is called *command substitution.* For example:

```
x=`date`
```

takes the output from the program date, replaces the back-quoted command, and saves the result in a variable.

All of these features taken together compose the basic repertoire of a UNIX shell. These features are summarized in Table 4–1, which also summarizes the main additional features discussed in this paper. Each shell is shown with the features it provides. When you compare shells, evaluate them both by how well they provide these basic features and by how these features are related to the additional features a shell may provide. This is what we'll do next.

C Shell Interactive Features

Given the choice of the Bourne shell or the C shell, most people choose the C shell to be their *default shell*, the shell that they use to actually do most of their work. The reason is simple: of the features that the C shell has that the Bourne shell lacks, the most important ones are the ones that make interactive use easier. Of these features, three—history, aliasing, and job control—are really major advances over the Bourne shell, while others, though useful, are of a more miscellaneous nature.

History

Of these three major features, the one with perhaps the most immediately obvious use, is the *history*. The C shell keeps a list of the commands you have given it (and you can specify the number of command lines kept).

Table 4–1 Summary of Basic Shell Features

Feature	sh	csh	ksh
Command execution	•	•	•
Output redirection	•	•	•
Input redirection	•	•	•
Piping	•	•	•
Background execution	•	•	•
Control structure	•	•	•
Filename expansion	•	•	•
Command substitution	•	•	•
Variables	•	•	•
Tilde substitution		•	•
Tests and expressions built in		•	•
History		•	•
Job control		•	•
Aliasing		•	•
Functions			•

These saved commands are called the *history list;* an item on the list is called an *event*, and it has an event number. This chronologically numbered list may be displayed using the built-in command history.

The main function of the history mechanism is to correct or re-enter commands easily. The C shell also provides a variety of ways to refer to events and use them in constructing new commands—the process of *history substitution.* When you enter a command that has in it a reference to an event (a previous command), the reference is replaced by the text of the event, and the resulting command is evaluated and executed. When the C shell evaluates a command in which there is a history substitution, it echoes the command after the substitution before executing the command. This enables you to understand what went wrong if the result is not what you expected. Events can be referred to in three ways, each beginning with the special character !. For examples, refer to this transcript of a C shell session:

```
% history
    12  mail fred < fred.txt
    13  print fred.txt
    14  make -s myprog
    15  cat myprog.c
% !m
make -s myprog
% !mai
mail fred < fred.txt
% !?myprog
make -s myprog
% vi fred.txt
% !-3
mail fred < fred.txt
% !15
cat myprog.c
```

One way to refer to an event is by prefix: !m refers to the last event beginning with m. Note that !mai in this example refers to a different command, because it matches mail, not make. Similarly, you can refer to an event by a substring of its text: !?myprog refers to the last command with myprog in its text. Another method is referring to an event by event number; so !15 is simply the fifteenth command. Finally, an event can be described by its relative position from the end of the history list. For example, !-2 refers to the second to last command. !-1 may be used to refer to the last command, but an abbreviation is also provided: !!.

Simply redoing commands, especially the last one (!!), turns out to be the most common use of the history mechanism. Another simple use is composing new commands from old ones by embedding event references in new commands, as in the first command in Figure 4–1.

The real power of the history mechanism, however, lies in the rich set of operations provided to select and modify individual portions of events and use them in constructing new commands. All the selectors follow a colon after an event specification. For example, a number, n, which follows the colon denotes the n'th arguments of the event; that is, !!:2 would denote the second argument in the previous command. The second example in Figure 4–1 shows that a range of words (:0-1) can be selected. There are several other selectors as well, and some convenient abbreviations, like !$ for the last word of the last command. Then, following this "word specification," you can add modifiers to change the selected word. The second example in Figure 4–1 also shows a modifier, :r, which removes the extension from a filename; in this case, it changes m2.c.bak to m2.c. Other modifications include string substitution, prefix or suffix deletion, repetition of the last modification, and making the last modification global.

Of this plethora of ways of picking apart, modifying, and assembling pieces of old commands, few are used with any frequency by most users. It is quite convenient, however, to be able to fix up a laboriously written command with some mistake in it, instead of retyping it. In fact, an additional quick fix method is provided to substitute a string in the last com-

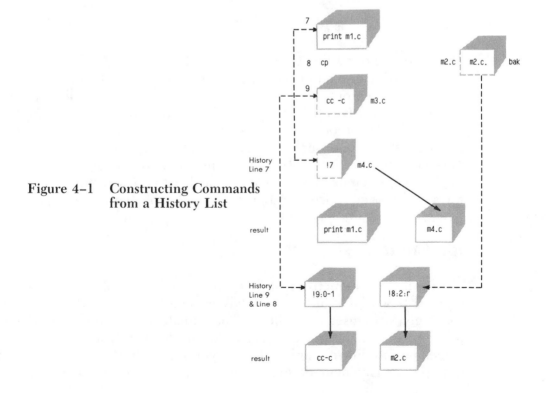

Figure 4–1   Constructing Commands from a History List

mand. By typing `ˆoldˆnew` the first occurrence of `old` in the last command will be replaced by `new`. In fact, most users get by quite happily by using the quick fix, by simply referring to events as a whole, and by using `!$` as the only frequently used word specification. But just this list of ways to use history shows how useful it can be, even though it is small subset of the whole system.

Aliasing

The second new interactive feature of the C shell is called *aliasing*. The built-in `alias` command provides users with the ability to define their own commands. The simplest kind of alias is one in which a more apt (or easy to remember) name is given to an existing command, as in `alias copy cp`, which makes `copy` do the same thing as `cp`. A slightly more useful example is the common `alias rm rm -i`, which makes all invocations of the common file removal utility take the `-i` option, which prompts the user for each file before it is removed.

Aliasing can also be used to define a kind of shell macro. That is, you can define aliases that can reference their argument list. The notation for the arguments is the same as the word specification of the history mechanism. A common alias is:

```
alias print 'pr \!* ¦ lpr'
```

The `\!*` refers to all the arguments (the `\` is to quote the `!`), so that using this alias will cause all of the arguments to be given as arguments to the formatter `pr`, the output of which is sent to `lpr`. (`lpr` is usually a program or device that drives the line printer.) The alias is enclosed in quotes to prevent the `¦` from being immediately interpreted. As seen earlier in discussing history, more sophisticated use can be made of the argument list. This, combined with the ability to define an alias with several commands (separated by semicolons), provides a facility to create simple and flexible ways of referring to frequently used but complicated commands.

Job Control

The third new interactive feature of the C shell is simpler in notation, but is just as powerful as history and aliasing. This feature is called *job control*, and it gives the user the ability to manipulate several processes at once. Job control is made up of a few built-in commands and the ability to suspend a job. For example, suppose you are editing a file and you want to stop it for a moment, do something else, and resume editing. By pressing

CTRL-Z, you can suspend the editor and return to the C shell. After doing whatever else you wanted to do, you can restart the editor with the built-in `fg` command.

This is especially useful for jobs that would take a long time to restart if you simply quit. Another built-in command is `bg`, which switches a process to the background. Suppose you started a long job, then decided that you want to run it in the background. You could quit and re-enter the command with `&` at the end to background it, or you could suspend the job using CTRL-Z and then use `bg`. Conversely, you may have started a job in the background, and now want it to run in the foreground, typically to do I/O. To do this you may use `fg` to bring it into the foreground.

These two built-in commands operate by default on the most recently started job, but you can in fact manage more than a couple of processes and refer to them. The built-in `jobs` command gives you a list of all the jobs that the C shell is running for you, with a number for each job. So if you want to do something with some job on the list, you can use the job number to refer to it, as in `fg %4` (the % denotes a job number). You can also use `stop` to halt running jobs in the same way. Also provided is the built-in `kill` command, which terminates a process and which can be given a job number as argument. Just using these few commands to manage processes, you have much of the control of a windowing environment, if not the attractive windowed display.

Additional Interactive Features

In addition to history, aliasing, and job control, the C shell has a few other features that the Bourne shell lacks and that make interactive use a bit more convenient. For instance, the C shell has an option that provides for automatically presenting timing statistics on jobs that run for more than a specifiable amount of time. Also, the filename patterns used by the C shell are a bit more flexible because of the addition of {, }, and ~ as meta-characters. For example, `my.{spc,bdy}` denotes `my.spc my.bdy`; a ~ by itself denotes your home directory; and a ~ followed by a name denotes the home directory of the user of that name. While the Bourne shell is more flexible for handling file descriptors, the C shell at least makes it simple to redirect standard out and standard error to the same place by using `>&` and `|&` instead of `>` and `|`. Finally, the C shell has a feature called "noclobber," which may be turned on or off. When it is on, the C shell will not redirect output to an existing file, so that there is no danger of accidentally clobbering a file, as in the classic example:

```
some-cmd file1 > file1
```

which would result in file1 being empty. This is also useful for when several people share a directory, so that they do not destroy each other's temporary files. The C shell also provides a mechanism for overriding no-clobber in a given command, if necessary.

Korn Shell Interactive Features

After you've learned about the various interactive features of the C shell, it is pretty easy to see why it is generally preferred over the Bourne shell for interactive use. But the Korn shell has many useful interactive features as well. In fact, one reason the Korn shell was developed was to remain compatible with the Bourne shell while adding many of the C shell's innovative features. Another reason was to implement those features better. For example, the Korn shell has a job control facility that is practically identical with the C shell's. (There are some versions of UNIX that do not support job control, such as System V; on such systems, neither shell would offer job control). Other C shell features that the Korn shell improves upon are aliasing and history; and the Korn shell also adds new built-ins and features.

The Korn shell's built-in alias command is similar to the C shell's. It is different, however, in that the Korn shell alias fixes an admitted shortcoming of the C shell—that aliases are often used as a clumsy way of writing shell subroutines. The Korn shell alias is more like the simple renaming use of the C shell alias; that is, Korn shell aliases do not have arguments. For more complex purposes, the Korn shell has a more general feature—the function. A Korn shell function is a real shell subroutine with arbitrarily long bodies, which aliases are not. So, you can view the Korn shell's alias and function features as doing what C shell's alias does, but in a better way. Furthermore, by implementing the functionality of the C shell's alias in two separate features, the Korn shell conveniently separates the simple use of aliasing—used most commonly in interactive shell use—from the more complicated use of functions, which are more useful when you write shell scripts. This paper later returns to the topic of functions as part of the discussion of Korn shell scripts.

The Korn shell also improves on the history mechanism of the C shell; like the C shell, the Korn shell keeps a history list. You saw that the C shell history mechanism was powerful, but rather complicated—many people find all those special characters a bit forbidding. Most people don't use the full expressive power of history because the notation is too strange and unfamiliar. The method of accessing the history list in the Korn shell is quite different, however. Instead of using an obscure notation to reference, select, and delete previous commands or parts thereof, you can actually edit the history list inline, with commands that look just like those of familiar UNIX editors. You simply delete, insert, or change whatever you want in a familiar fashion.

This is how it works. There are two inline command editing modes, named for the UNIX file editors that they resemble—emacs mode and vi mode. In either of them, the command line is like a one-line window onto a file whose contents are the history list. There are commands to move, search, and edit this file. For example, in emacs mode, the previous command is CTRL-P; it steps back one line in the history file. So, CTRL-P followed by a RETURN will redo your last command. In vi mode, you must first type the escape character to finish inserting; then the vi previous line command (the minus character) will get your last command. So, pressing ESC, −, then RETURN will redo your last command. Each mode has more than 40 commands that mimic the editor of the same name. Because you probably already know one of these editors, you already know how to use most of the history editing feature.

The useful quick-fix substitution provided by the C shell is also contained in the Korn shell, but is implemented not with a special character, but with a built-in command, fc. There is a predefined alias, r, in the Korn shell that aliases one way of using fc. The command r simply redoes the last command. If it is followed by old=new, the command is redone after making the substitution of new for old. For example, if you just entered the command echo foobar, then r foob=g would cause the command echo gar to be executed.

Another form of the fc built-in command can be used when you want to do rather complicated tasks, such as wanting to type a command from within the C shell that combines elements of several old commands in tricky ways, thus using more of the power of the history expressions. The fc command will actually start up a real editor (that you can specify) on a real file constructed from the history list. When you exit the editor, the commands in the file are executed. Thus, you can create a new command by using your favorite editor's text manipulation commands.

There are other options to fc as well, including one that simply prints out the history list, as the C shell command history does. In fact, the Korn shell has a built-in alias, history, that does this.

The Korn shell also has many built-in commands, some taken from the C shell, some altogether new. In addition, ksh has some predefined aliases as well (like r, described earlier) that gloss over some of the details of some built-in commands, or that implement some Bourne shell built-ins in terms of more general Korn shell built-ins. With all these features and built-ins (all of the Bourne shell's, and many of the C shell's, plus new ones), one problem with the Korn shell is that it can be difficult to know what a given command will actually do.

A Korn shell built-in that addresses this problem is whence, a kind of built-in dictionary. It is a bit like the UNIX utility whereis, which will report where in your path a utility may be found; but since it is a built-in command, whence can give information about functions, aliases, and built-ins. If you are wondering just what a certain word really means, you can use it as an argument to whence, and the Korn shell will tell you what it is.

For instance whence cd will tell you that cd means the built-in command cd; whence r will tell you that r means fc -e -. Whence also has a verbose option, which will tell you in greater detail what something is.

The Korn shell has other added features as well, but most are additions that are useful in shell scripts, discussed later. One feature worth mentioning here is that the Korn shell interprets the character ˜ as the C shell does, as referring to home directories. Another miscellaneous feature may be of interest to system administrators: the Korn shell can be configured to read a system-wide startup file that could contain, for instance, system-wide functions or aliases. To finish examining the interactive features of the Korn shell, note that the only interactive feature of the C shell that the Korn shell lacks is the noclobber option. The C shell's means of overriding noclobber doesn't seem to fit in with the Korn shell, but since other C shell options are present in the Korn shell, one could wish for noclobber as well.

Bourne Shell Programming Features

While the C shell is generally favored over the Bourne shell for everyday interactive use, the reverse is true for use in writing shell scripts, although to a lesser degree. The reason it's true to a lesser degree is that people who use the C shell and who don't know the Bourne shell usually find it easier simply to write C shell scripts than to learn the Bourne shell. But there are many who advocate the Bourne shell as a command programming language, and some of them are interactive C shell users as well. Also, some standard UNIX utilities are implemented as Bourne shell scripts for portability and efficiency. This fact shows two of the simplest advantages of the Bourne shell: first, it is available at almost all UNIX installations, unlike the C shell; and second, the Bourne shell is more efficient than the C shell, for reasons examined shortly. There are also other features of the Bourne shell that are useful in writing shell scripts, discussed after an explanation of the Bourne shell's efficiency and speed.

Generally speaking, the Bourne shell is smaller, faster starting, faster running, and more efficient than the C shell. This isn't really surprising, since it lacks all the interactive features of the C shell discussed before; there is simply less of the Bourne shell, and less to start up. And because the Bourne shell does less, it interprets commands more simply and so tends to run faster. Because it is simpler than the C shell, the Bourne shell can parse control structures more efficiently and better execute scripts with control structuring. However, the Bourne shell's speed and efficiency are hampered because it lacks certain built-ins that are useful in writing control structured scripts; as a result, it must execute UNIX utilities to perform some tasks.

Another important feature of the Bourne shell is its built-in trap command, which you can use to write shell scripts that can trap signals. (Signals are one of the means by which you can change the state of a process, for example changing it from a running process to a suspended process, as with job control.) The C shell has a built-in, onintr, which traps the interrupt signal, but trap enables you to trap any signal, and to perform different actions for different signals. Thus, Bourne shell scripts can do relatively sophisticated exception handling.

The Bourne shell also provides greater control of I/O than the C shell. With the C shell you can redirect or pipe the standard output of a simple command, or redirect or pipe the standard output and error output together. While the latter is simple and useful in an interactive setting, when you write sophisticated scripts it is useful to have direct control of the file descriptors that control I/O. There are a variety of reasons for this, but the most common use is to redirect standard output and standard errors separately. The actual method of doing so is powerful, but somewhat complicated and confusing to a shell programmer who is not also a UNIX systems programmer. An additional convenience related to I/O is the fact that output can be redirected or piped from a whole control structure, which is not possible with the C shell. The Bourne shell fragment

```
for i in *.txt do
  diff file1 $i
done : spell > spellsort.out
```

compares favorably with the C shell fragment

```
foreach i (*.txt)
  diff file1 $i >> tmpfile
end
spell tmpfile > spellsort.out
```

because in order to do the same thing with the C shell, you must repeatedly append a temporary file.

Besides efficiency (with some trade-offs), signal handling, and better I/O control, the Bourne shell also has a few other features worth mentioning that are more conveniences or matters of taste. First, the Bourne shell allows new lines to be embedded in quoted strings without preceding them by a backslash. Second, the shell includes an input built-in command, read; it seems more normal than the C shell's input, $<, which looks like a variable or even some input redirection. Third, the Bourne shell's control structure syntax is bit more flexible because of its better parsing. In general, one has to do less quoting in the Bourne shell simply because there are fewer features, and hence fewer metacharacters. These conveniences, however, are just extra benefits that further confirm the opinion of many people that the Bourne shell is superior to the C shell for writing scripts.

C Shell Programming Features

Although the Bourne shell has some distinct advantages over the C shell for writing shell scripts, there are some advantages to the C shell, as well. For some C shell programmers, the fact that the C shell resembles the C programming language rather than Algol is itself a major convenience. But most of the advantages are functional; for instance, the C shell has arrays of a sort, as illustrated here:

```
% set foo = `date`
% echo $#foo
6
% echo $foo
Tue Nov 18 16:22:35 EST 1986
 % echo $foo[2]
Nov
```

The $#foo denotes the number of elements in foo. As you can see, the elements may be referenced with the usual subscript notation. (Actually, in the Bourne shell there is one array; you can use the script's argument list like an array, but with obscure syntax.)

But the main advantage of the C shell over the Bourne shell is the drawback of the Bourne shell mentioned before—it lacks some important built-ins. This can be more important than any of the features discussed previously.

The drawback of lacking these built-ins is that when you write a script with some control structure, you usually want to test conditions. That is, if you write an if command, you have to have something after the if. Most frequently, when the condition of the if is not the value of a variable or the return value of a command, it is either an expression (of strings, and/ or numbers represented as strings), or a test of some condition(s) of file(s). There are two UNIX utilities, expr and test, respectively, that perform these functions; and in order to do anything like expressions or file tests in a Bourne shell control structure, you have to use these utilities. So frequently the Bourne shell must execute a separate program simply to evaluate a control structure. This is especially telling in scripts that do a lot of looping.

For example, this is a typical Bourne shell if command:

```
if test -r $file
   then print $file
fi
```

This prints the file named by the contents of the variable file if the file is readable. In order to decide this, test must be executed. With the C shell, you could use test to do the same thing if you wished, but you don't actually have to; you may instead use an operator built in to the C shell. The same example for the C shell would be:

```
if (-r $file) then
   print $file
endif
```

The important thing to note is that -r is part of the C shell, which goes and checks the file itself without executing any other program.

The functionality of expr is similarly built in and extended to include the whole range of C operators. These expressions may appear within the parentheses of the if, while, and exit commands, and in the built-in @ command used to make assignments from expressions to variables. The following Bourne shell fragment illustrates the somewhat odd method one must use to increment an integer variable.

```
i=`expr $i + 1`
```

The following C shell fragment illustrates both the expression and the @ built-in:

```
set i = 1
while ( $i < 4 )
   @ i = i + 1
end
```

The other useful feature of C shell expressions is the pattern matching capability. In both the C shell switch and the comparable Bourne shell case commands, the case labels are patterns of the same sort that match file-names in ordinary circumstances, except that they match the switch or case expression. One shortcoming of the Bourne shell is that there is no such pattern matching in if or while statements. In the C shell, however, there is an expression operator =~, which is true if the left-hand side matches the pattern on the right-hand side, as in:

```
if ( $file =~ *.txt)
  then echo Found a text file: $file
endif
```

(There is also !~, which serves as a pattern not-equals.) In order to do this with the Bourne shell, a single-case switch statement would have to do:

```
case $file in
  *.txt) echo Found a text file: $file ;;
esac
```

This is somewhat strange, but not awful; and fortunately the need to do this sort of match in while or assignment commands (which would be a bit uglier) is seldom necessary. However, this pattern-matching capability would be useful in Bourne shell scripts with many case commands of this sort, or nested ones.

Korn Shell Programming Features

Just as the Korn shell incorporates most of the interactive features of the C shell that are advantages in comparison to the Bourne shell, so the Korn shell also incorporates the programming features of the C shell just mentioned (for example, arrays). Furthermore, the Korn shell has a host of new features that are significant improvements over both the C shell and Bourne shell.

Built-In Commands for Expressions and File Tests

The most significant feature the Korn shell shares with the C shell is that it has built-in functions that permit evaluation of file tests and expressions. As a result, the Korn shell does not suffer from the performance problems of the Bourne shell. Furthermore, the Korn shell is faster and more efficient than the C shell, because the Korn shell is implemented in a well-organized fashion that prevents the extra features from slowing the whole shell down. In addition, the Korn shell also does command substitution more efficiently than either of the other shells, has real memory management, and optimizes it own I/O buffering. As a result of these implementation details and the new built-in commands, the Korn shell tends to be faster than either of the other two shells.

As mentioned, the Korn shell has the test built-in. But unlike the C shell, which simply has as part of its expressions about half of the file tests provided by test, the Korn shell actually implements the full capability of test, plus a few extra file tests. The built-in test is implemented with the same syntax as the UNIX utility used in writing Bourne shell scripts. While this provides for backward compatibility with Bourne shell scripts, some may find the resulting control structure syntax a bit odd. Therefore, the Korn shell also has a built-in function, [, which is like the not-so-common UNIX utility of that name. This utility is like test in all respects except that it expects its last argument to be]. This utility is sometimes provided so that Bourne shell scripts can be a bit more attractive; and having it built-in, the Korn shell provides this as well. So, instead of writing the odd-looking:

```
if test -r foo
   then echo foo is readable
fi
```

you can write instead:

```
if [ -r foo ]
   then echo foo is readable
fi
```

which in fact looks somewhat similar to the C shell.

As mentioned, the Korn shell also has built-ins to do expressions. This is one case where backward compatibility to the Bourne shell was ignored in favor of developing a better feature. To be sure, Bourne shell scripts with fragments like:

```
if expr "$i < $j" then
   i=`expr $i + 1`
fi
```

will run under the Korn shell, but the expr UNIX utility will be executed just as with the Bourne shell, with the same performance penalty. Rather than having expr built in, like test, the Korn shell has a new built-in, let, for expression evaluation. Used by itself, it is virtually syntactically identical with the C shell built-in @, and a bit more aptly named. However, let does not implement the same set of operations as either expr or the C shell's expressions. While the syntax of let is the same as the C-style expressions of the C shell, only the arithmetic and relational operators, and the simple assignment operator, are implemented; so let only operates on numbers.

The numbers that let manipulates are not, however, strings representing the value of numbers. With both the C shell and the Bourne shell, the values of variables are strings, and when arithmetic operations are performed, the values must be converted from a string to an integer (for example, three characters, one for each character in *142*, to one number, 142) before the operation is performed; and the result of the operation is converted back to string form.

Of course, the C shell does the conversions itself, while the Bourne user would have expr do the conversion of the command line arguments given it. But the Korn shell can store variables as actual integers, and let can use these to perform integer arithmetic directly, and much more efficiently.

As with the C shell, Korn shell expressions may be used in control structures as well; but while the C shell has the expressions grouped in parentheses as part of the syntax of the control structures, the Korn shell does not. As a result, one must use the let built-in in the control structure, and quote any characters that have other meaning to the shell. So, just as in the Bourne shell you write:

```
if expr "$i < $j" then
```

in the Korn shell you write:

```
if let "i < j" then
```

Again, this is a bit cumbersome, but just as with test, the Korn shell has an alternate syntax for expressions, only instead of using square brackets, double parentheses are used. So the previous fragment could also be:

```
if (( i < j )) then
```

This is similar to the C shell fragment:

```
if ( $i < $j ) then
```

By using this form in the Korn shell, you gain the benefit that you don't have to escape special characters; like the C shell, the parentheses establish a special scope where just expressions are evaluated.

Given the similarity of forms between the last two fragments, one might wonder why the double parentheses are used by the Korn shell. The reason is that single parentheses denote a command list to be run in a subshell. But this is so in the C shell as well; the difference is in the syntax, as mentioned earlier. The syntactic role of the expression is different in the two shells in an important way. In the C shell, an expression is a series of characters that is formed according to a syntax different from the rest of the shell, and that appears in the if, while, exit, and @ commands. Furthermore, the syntax of if and while have the expression enclosed in parentheses. So, in the C shell parentheses have a separate meaning for the if and while commands. But in the Korn shell, the syntax for if and while is like all the other control structures that have commands in them—there is simply a command list as part of the structure, for example after the word if or while. And an expression is simply a particular command: let for arithmetic expressions, or test for file tests. That let and test can be dressed up or made more convenient doesn't change this.

So, the Korn shell's method of implementing expressions and file tests has two important characteristics: first, special syntax is not necessary for these tests (in that test and let may be used as any other command); second, these tests are better conceptually organized (in that different kinds of operations are done by different commands). In contrast to this, the C shell puts everything in a big grab-bag kind of expression, which must be used in special contexts. But it should not be overlooked that you can execute commands in C shell expressions. In typical C shell style, command execution is given a bit of extra syntax and thrown in the grab bag. For example, in the Korn shell you would write:

```
if diff file1 file2 then
    echo file1 and file2 are different
fi
```

whereas in the C shell you would write:

```
if ( ! { diff file1 file2 } ) then
    echo file1 and file2 are different
endif
```

where the braces are the special syntax that denote command execution, and the ! is needed because the two shells make opposite interpretations of the command's return code.

Note, however, that in keeping the Bourne shell control structure and implementing different kinds of expressions in different built-in commands, the Korn shell has three shortcomings. First, the compartmentalization is not complete; while let is a laudable achievement, test is almost as much a grab bag as C shell expressions, and with an odder syntax. Second, some functionality is left out of the Korn shell's scheme; the string manipulations of expr are not built-in to the Korn shell (although string equality is part of test). The most powerful string operation, pattern matching, is available in the C shell with the =~ and !~ operators. So, in the Korn shell some things must still be done using expr, just as in the Bourne shell. Third, some organization got lost in the shuffle; one cannot combine integer expressions and file tests and string manipulations nearly as conveniently in the Korn shell as one can in the C shell where everything is in the same grab bag.

With all this discussion of which kinds of operations are available in which UNIX utility or which built-in of which shell, a table and diagram should be useful; Figure 4–2 breaks up the various operations into various classes and shows which UNIX utilities and shell features implement the operations.

New Programming Features

In addition to sharing the features of C shell that were lacking in the Bourne shell, the Korn shell has several new features that are convenient for writing shell scripts. There are some new features for shell variables, and there are new built-ins, new options, a new control structure, and—perhaps most importantly—there is the shell function.

The new control structure is select, which makes it easier to write interactive, menu-driven shell scripts. The syntax is: select choice in list. The result is that each word in the list is printed on standard error on a line by itself, with a number; a response is prompted for and saved in the special variable REPLY. If the response was one of the numbers next to

Op class	expr	test	ksh-test	ksh-let	csh
Arithmetic + − * /% logical not	•			•	•
Bit << >> | ~					•
Relational <> <= >= == !=	•	•	•	•	•
Logical-or logical-and	•	•	•		•
String equality	•	•	•		•
String pattern match	•				•
Other string operations	•				
Basic file test		•	•		•
Other file tests		•	•		
File data tests			•		

Figure 4–2   Shell File Test and Expression Operators

one of the choices, the variable named after select is set to the choice with that number. The following example should illustrate (>? is the prompt):

```
$ cat party.script
select action in eat drink be-merry
case "$action" in
   eat)      echo "Wonderful--have some crumpet" ;;
   drink)    echo "Mahvellous--have a spot of tea" ;;
   be-merry) echo "Oh goodie. Do sing a song with the dormouse" ;          ;
   *)        echo "Dear me; I don't think we do that
                  at a Wonderland tea party" ;;
esac
$ party.script
1) eat
2) drink
3) be-merry
>? 1
Wonderful--have some crumpet
$
```

Korn shell options are controlled via the built-in set command, as in the Bourne shell, and all Bourne shell options are supported. The C shell built-in set sets the values of both variables and options; options are in fact predefined shell variables. So, for example in the Bourne shell, you could disable filename generation with set -f; in the C shell it would be set noglob. In the Korn shell the former method works, as well as set -o noglob. Most of the flag-style Bourne options have been given such C shell-like names in the Korn shell. Also, new options have been added, such as options to control which command line editing mode you are using.

The new features for variables are of two sorts: new predefined variables and new ways to reference the values of variables. Of the latter, there are, as was mentioned before, arrays just as in the C shell; and there are new pattern matching primitives as well. These are best explained by example.

Assume $var represents the value of the variable var. But ${var#pattern} is the value of var with first part of the value deleted that matches the pattern. For example:

```
$ x=hello
$ echo $x
hello
$ echo ${x#hel}
lo
```

143

```
$ echo ${x%llo}
he
```

The latter example shows that % may be used instead of # to delete from the end of the string. Both of these delete the smallest matching pattern. Also provided are ## and %%, which delete the largest matching pattern.

In addition to these pattern features, there are also some useful new predefined variables. For example, PS3 is the prompt used in select statements; its initial value, as you saw, is #?. The previous example could have set it to a more friendly value, like:

```
PS3='would you prefer?'
```

Others of the several new variables are RANDOM, the value of which is a random number that changes every time it is used, and OLDPWD, the last working directory.

Of the new or improved built-ins, the most flexible are read and print, which are the Korn shell's I/O routines. The read command is like the Bourne shell's read, but has flags added that provide greater flexibility. The output routine, print, is new. Besides echoing its arguments like the Bourne and C shells' output echo, it has many options that include what terminal mode to use and what file descriptor to write to. For backward compatibility with the Bourne shell, echo is a predefined alias for print -v.

The other important new built-in is typeset. It is used to change attributes of shell variables. This statement alone shows great advances over the other two shells. In both shells, variables are simply strings, and their values can be used as such. But Korn shell variables have several properties: for instance, a variable can be a string or an integer. Also, as in the Bourne shell, variables can be read-only. But in addition to supporting the Bourne shell built-in readonly, the read-only attribute is managed like others in typeset. So, for example, you may write either readonly x or typeset -r x. But with typeset you may also remove attributes by using + instead of -. To "unread only" the variable x, you would typeset +r x. Other attributes include upper- or lowercase for strings, length, and right or left justification by filling within a length. The ability to change attributes provides a handy method for changing the value of a variable. For instance, typesetting a string variable that already exists so that it has the uppercase attribute causes its value to be changed into uppercase.

The typeset command may be used to set values of variables as well, as in:

```
$ typeset -u str=hello
$ echo $str
HELLO
```

which creates a variable named str that is uppercase. The value is converted to match the specified attributes. If the =value part is not present, the command acts as a simple declaration. In fact, there is a predefined alias, integer, which is just typeset -i; it declares a variable as an integer.

Functions

The most versatile new programming feature of the Korn shell is the shell function, or subroutine, mentioned a few times before. It is essentially like a subroutine definition in a block-structured programming language such as Pascal. There is an outermost routine, which in Pascal would be the program; in ksh this is simply the shell input, or the text of the script, which is initially not within the definition of any shell function. Within this outermost level or scope, there may be definitions of functions, each of which is another scope; and there can be functions defined within functions. Within each scope you can access the variables defined in that scope or the scopes that enclose it, just as in Pascal. The ksh function definition consists of the function name and the body, which is just ksh commands such as those anywhere else in a script. A very simple function is the following, which simply prints the current directory that is stored in a predefined variable that the Korn shell maintains.

```
function whereami {
  echo $PWD
}
```

The way functions use variables depends in great measure on the fact that each function body is a separate scope. Any variable used in the scope where a function is defined can be used in the function body; and when the function is called, the function can change the variables in the enclosing scope. Conversely, there may be variables that are not used in the enclosing scope until after the function is called; the function may set these variables, and the enclosing scope may use them as well. In other words, functions normally share their variables with the enclosing scope, and vice versa. Another way to say this is that the variables of a function are normally exported to the enclosing scope. But if variables are initially set or declared with typeset, they are local, or private, to the body of the function. That is, the enclosing scope cannot use local variables of the function. Furthermore, there can be in the enclosing scope a variable of the same name as a local variable, which is not affected by changing the value of the local variable. To explicitly export a local variable, it may be declared with typeset -x. A variable that is not typeset is automatically exported. The ability to declare variables as local or global provides a clean way to write shell subroutines so that they don't have unexpected side effects; it is also essential to writing recursive shell functions.

Within the body of a function may be references to the arguments of the function call. Unlike Pascal, however, ksh functions do not have parameter lists. In the body of a ksh function, $1 is used to refer the first actual parameter, $2 for second, and so on. These are called the *positional parameters*, and in the outermost scope of a ksh script they are the arguments to the invocation of the script. So, ksh functions are just like smaller scripts within a script. If the call of a function or script did not have a particular argument, then the corresponding positional parameter will not be set. The positional parameters of a function are all local variables. For example, the following script echoes a greeting given to it as an argument, or echoes a default greeting if none was given:

```
function greeting {
  typeset message
  if [ $1 ]
    then
      message=$1
    else
      message='how are you today?'
  fi
  echo  Hello--$message
}
```

The variable message is defined with typeset, so it is a local variable and does not affect anything in the scope enclosing the function definition.

Once a ksh function is defined—in a script or in an interactive session—its name is a valid command just like a built-in command. So, to use a function, you just treat it like any other command; the command greeting hi would result in an echo of Hello--hi.

The general usefulness of functions in Korn shell programming is the same as programming in any language. When there is a task that must be done in more than one place or in more than one way, a subroutine can be made to do the task; and it may be called in all the places where the task needs to be done, and called with arguments that specify exactly how or with what to perform the task.

Furthermore, once a ksh function body has been evaluated (and the shell then knows how to do a call of the function), it is efficient to use. In some complicated Bourne or C shell scripts, the equivalent of subroutines are done by simply calling another shell script. This gets the job done: the called script can share variables with the calling script through the environment, and the called script can have its own private variables as well.

However, starting up a new shell every time a subroutine call is needed can be quite expensive. Another way subroutine calls are done is by including a file of shell commands by using the source built-in command. Using source causes the shell go off and execute commands from the included file before doing anything else. (The source command is a C shell built-in; the Korn and Bourne shell command is a period.) This is much less expensive than putting the commands in another script, but the shell does have to evaluate the commands every time a particular file is sourced, so sourcing is not as efficient as functions. Furthermore, the execution of the sourced file shares all the variables of the script, and there is no way to have a sourced file have private variables.

Besides being a great aid in writing shell scripts, functions can also be used to customize the shell environment by defining new commands to use interactively. This way, the full power of the shell programming features can be used to encapsulate into one convenient command a series of commonly done tasks or an idea for a new command. This same kind of customizing can be done with aliasing as well, but the since aliases are more limited, much more can be done with a function. The way most ksh users customize their shell environments is by including alias definitions and function definitions in their .profile file, which the Korn shell reads when it starts up. The Korn shell thus evaluates these functions when it starts, and they can be used just like built-ins.

Function Examples

An example of this kind of customization is the implementation in the Korn shell of three C shell built-ins that the Korn shell lacks. These are pushd, popd, and dirs, which keep a stack of directories. For instance, you may be using one directory and want to do something in another directory, and then return to the first one; perhaps you also want to use a third directory briefly and come back to the second. Instead of remembering the pathnames of the directories in question and changing directories with cd, you can use pushd. The C shell remembers the directories, and you can use popd to return to the previous directory. The command dirs prints the stack of directories so you can know where you have been and where you can easily return. The Korn shell does not have these built-in routines, but with functions, you can write your own versions of them, or use those written by someone else. A Korn shell implementation is:

```
alias dirs='echo ${PWD}:$DS'

function pushd {
    DS=$PWD:$DS
```

```
    cd $1
    echo ${PWD}:$DS
}


function popd {
  if [ $DS ]
  then
    cd ${DS%%:*}
    DS=${DS#*:}
    dirs
    echo ${PWD}:$DS
  else
    echo "popd: Directory stack is empty"
  fi
}
```

The directory stack is kept in a shared variable DS. Dirs is implemented as an alias, because it is simple to just print the current directory and the stack. The function pushd shows that the stack is just a string in which the directories are separated by a colon. Pushing a directory on the stack is simply prepending the name of the directory and a colon to the list. Popping a directory from the stack involves two changes to the stack. First, you get the directory on the front of the stack to which you'll change directories with cd. This is done by deleting everything after the first colon with the %% operator on variable values. Second, you delete this directory from the front of the stack using the # operator to set the stack so everything before the first colon is deleted.

To use such function interactively, you must first have ksh evaluate them. This is usually done by including the function definitions in your .profile file. However, the evaluation of a function body takes some time. In a shell script this time is small compared to the time saved by using the function, but for interactive use, it can be annoying to have to wait for the Korn shell to evaluate all your functions, especially if you end up not using some of the functions in a particular session. This startup time can be spread out by means of the following stratagem (which I heard from a colleague, Eric Leo). Instead of defining a function in your .profile, for example a function doit, you may instead alias doit to source a file that has the definition of the function doit, in this way:

```
alias doit='. ~/doit.func'
```

Then, the file doit.func in your home directory (or whatever file you choose to keep this in) should contain:

```
unalias doit
function doit {
  : the body of doit
}
doit
```

The first time you call doit, the alias is evaluated, and the file is sourced; this removes the alias doit, defines the function doit, and calls the new function doit. The next time you call doit, the function will be called. This way, the evaluation of the function is delayed until the first time it is actually used, rather than at the startup of the shell.

Choosing the Shell for Your Needs

Now that you have compared the features of the three shells fairly completely, you should be able to compare the shells and decide in what circumstances one is preferable to another. It should be pretty clear by now that the Korn shell is clearly superior to the Bourne shell. The ksh shell does everything sh does, but without performance penalties, and the Korn has many other features besides. The comparison between the C shell and the Korn shell isn't quite as simple, but here, too, ksh is the more powerful and easy to use. For interactive use, the Korn shell is a pretty clear choice, if only for the much more convenient means of history editing. Almost every interactive feature the C shell has, the Korn shell has with improvements. For writing shell scripts, the Korn shell is again a pretty clear choice. The greater efficiency and speed, and the ability to write real shell functions are big deciding factors by themselves. The only C shell features that the Korn shell lacks are the noclobber option, pattern matching expressions, and bit arithmetic expressions. With the qualification that these might be desirable to some users, the conclusion is inevitable that the Korn shell is preferable to the C shell for most users. Even most C shell users should consider switching to the Korn shell if they can, because the slowness of C shell scripts and the arcana of the history substitution are two frequent gripes about the C shell.

Lacking the Korn shell, the choice is clear between the other two shells this paper has evaluated: for interactive features, the C shell wins hands down. The only reasons you would not use the C shell interactively are that you already know the Bourne shell and don't want to learn another, or that you have decided to use the Bourne shell for programming and don't want to bother with two shells.

For programming, the choice between the C shell and the Bourne shell depends on what kind of scripts you tend to write. For frequently used, relatively simple scripts the Bourne shell runs a lot faster. But for scripts with while loops, the fact that the Bourne shell has to execute test and expr as separate programs will end up slowing things down to the point where the C shell is faster. Also, for large and complicated scripts, the relative cost of the C shell's startup time becomes less important and may be balanced out by uses of nonbuilt-in test or expr in a corresponding Bourne shell script. And of course there are the other programming features of the two shells; your relative preference for arrays, pattern matching expression, fine I/O control, signal trapping, and the like, will influence where you will want to draw the line on efficiency. But for almost all users there is such a line that, when crossed, means that the C shell is more efficient. To summarize, the Bourne shell is preferable for programming only if you are very concerned with a particular feature like trapping or with the speed of smaller scripts; otherwise, the C shell is preferable.

The choice of the Korn shell tends to be strengthened when the shells are considered as programming languages. Unfortunately, none of these shells is really a good programming language, because all of them suffer in various degrees from a syntax that is a bit arcane. It is difficult enough at times to keep track of the substitutions of the Bourne shell (command, variable, and filename), and the three ways of preventing the substitution (with single quotes, double quotes, and backslashes). The added complexities of the C shell, while useful, allow the construction of commands that are rather bewildering collections of quotes and special characters. The Korn shell adds more substitutions to the Bourne shell, but it does so a way that is cleaner and easier to understand than the C shell, especially in the areas of aliasing and history. Furthermore, most of the Korn shell's additions to the Bourne shell are via built-in commands rather than expressions with special characters; and the whence built-in command is provided to sort out UNIX commands from various Korn shell features.

Besides having a relatively simpler syntax, the Korn shell is better as a programming language because it has real subroutines, and some data typing. The Bourne shell has little typing at all: just string variables and boolean command return codes. However, most Bourne shell scripts use UNIX utilities (such as test and expr) that interpret their arguments as data of a certain type: numbers, strings, or file attributes. The C shell provides expressions that combine various of these types, but all in one kind of expression, as has been explained; so figuring out what operators should be used on what kinds of operands can be a bit confusing. The Korn shell at least separates some kinds of operations from others. Although the integer data type is the only one that is really well defined, it is at least a step in the right direction. At the least, the Korn shell test and let expressions are no more potentially confusing than C shell expressions.

One hope for development of future shells is better syntax and more data typing. Other trends include windowing, editor, and graphics interfaces to shells rather simple line I/O. (The Korn shell fc history editing built-in, while not frequently useful, anticipates this.) For example, using the Bourne shell in the kind of windowing environment available on UNIX workstations provides many of the interactive features of the Korn and C shells.

Another new direction is better process management; future shells may provide features with which users can specify how UNIX processes might communicate with one other in other ways besides pipes. One example of this might be synchronizing processes in real time; another is a clearer conception of file descriptors so that more complex I/O connections than pipes become possible. There are many experimental shells that implement some of these new ideas, and perhaps in the future a widely available UNIX shell may incorporate some the features being explored.

Conclusions

A UNIX shell is an interactive command interpreter, and it can usually also be considered as a command programming language. In addition to sharing these two basic roles, most shells (including the three featured standard shells—the Bourne, Korn, and C shells) share many features. They have many important distinctions as well; some shells lack certain interactive features another has, or one has more facilities for shell programming than another.

In comparing shells, the main considerations are first, how the shell will be used—primarily interactively, writing simple scripts, writing complicated scripts, or any combination; and second, how well the features of each shell match the use in terms of convenience, simplicity, expressive power, and efficiency. On most points and in most situations, the Korn shell seems preferable. Lacking the Korn shell, the C shell is preferable to the Bourne shell in many situations, but not all.

The Bourne shell can be viewed as the first, basic shell, and the C shell as the first standardized attempt to extend shell functionality beyond the basics. The Korn shell, then, is a second such attempt, in which prominent goals were compatibility with the Bourne shell and implementation of C shell extensions in a better framework. The Korn shell's better organization and framework indicate both the beginnings of solutions to some of the three shells' common problems, and also some of the directions in which future standard shells are developing.

KEYWORDS

▶ Action

▶ awk

▶ Regular
expression

▶ Pattern

▶ Field

▶ Separator

▶ Control structures

Paper Synopsis: Did you know that a powerful data manipulation tool comes with every UNIX system? The awk utility is in fact a complete text-oriented programming language. This utility is powerful, but the manuals make it appear quite forbidding. The paper starts with an introduction and then gives tips, tricks, and traps to watch out for when you use awk. The examples illustrate interesting tools and applications that awk can create.

David Huelsbeck is studying computer science, mathematics, and philosophy at New Mexico State University. He is also a computer programmer working at Los Alamos National Laboratory and has used most flavors of UNIX.

5

awk Power Plays

David Huelsbeck

This paper explores techniques for using the UNIX awk utility to its fullest potential. It assumes you are an experienced UNIX user with some previous exposure to awk, but not necessarily familiar with the details of awk programming. What follows is intended to be both a tutorial in the basic principles of awk and a guide to ways in which awk can be used to solve common problems that might otherwise require tedious calculation or editing.

If you find that you are unfamiliar with the UNIX commands and concepts mentioned here, you may wish to explore them on your own before going further. You will also find it helpful to read the programming sections as you sit at your terminal, so you can execute the commands and programs as you go along.

Introduction to awk

The awk utility is a powerful and flexible feature of UNIX. Named for its creators—Alfred Aho, Peter Weinberger, and Brian Kernighan—awk is more similar to high-level programming languages like C and FORTRAN than to the smaller, more specialized filters such as grep and tr. A paper describing the utility was given the title *A Pattern Scanning and Processing Language*[1] by its authors. The high-level pro-

---

[1] Alfred V. Aho, Brian W. Kernighan, and Peter J. Weinberger, *awk—A Pattern Scanning and Processing Language*, 2nd ed. Murray Hill, N. J. Bell Laboratories.

gramming capabilities of awk make it useful for both simple and complex text manipulations, and certain types of data processing. This paper shows not only the basics of the awk language, but also demonstrates how awk can be used to solve complex problems.

Features of awk

In deciding what sorts of problems to tackle with awk, you should first identify where and when awk is useful and appropriate. You've already been given a clue about awk's two major features:

- Like egrep, awk incorporates the ability to scan for occurrences of regular expressions.
- As with most programming languages, you can use awk with numerical and textual variables and functions.
- An ability nearly unique to awk is the facility for breaking its input into fields and records.

Applications of awk

Its unique combination of features makes awk suitable for three basic types of applications:

- filtering, using awk as a more powerful and flexible egrep
- numerical processing on rows and columns of numerical data
- text processing, using awk to perform repetitive editing tasks

Of course, there are other possible uses for awk and not all applications will fit exactly into one of these three categories. This paper gives examples of the last two types of applications. After a review of the basics of awk, you will begin by constructing the basis for a general purpose spreadsheet calculator using one of awk's less documented features and a few of its numerical functions. Next, you will see how awk can save you time and effort when you perform repetitive editing on large text files. Finally, the paper provides some warnings and tips about how to avoid problems and discusses the use of awk's less documented features.

Basics of awk

Before you learn about the more powerful applications of awk, you need a firm grasp of the basics. If you feel you are already knowledgeable about the basics, you may wish to skip ahead to the next section. If you are at all unsure, please follow this section closely. At the ends of several subsections, summary tables have been included. These tables are intended to encapsulate briefly information covered in those subsections. Due to space considerations, specific examples of all the information found in the tables cannot be provided in the text. The information in the tables has been organized in this form to allow it to be used as a quick reference. You may find it helpful to glance back at the tables periodically. Knowing this information well is essential to using awk effectively. The topics covered in the basics review are:

- an overview of an awk program
- the calling sequence
- patterns
- regular expressions
- actions
- built-in functions
- complex actions
- control structures

The awk Program

An awk program consists of one or more pattern-action pairs. awk scans its input for the pattern(s) and takes the associated action when one is found. If you have had experience with ed, sed, or any of the grep filters, this idea of pattern scanning should be a familiar one. However, if most of your experience has been with other more general-purpose programming languages, pattern-action pairs may seem strange at first. It is in fact a very natural way of describing many algorithms. It is quite similar to the method you would use to give strangers directions in a city they had never visited before. For instance if you were asked "How do I get to the nearest phone?" You might respond by telling the person:

"At the stop sign, turn left."
"At the next intersection, turn right."
"At the gas station on the left, you will find a phone."

In each case you have provided a pattern and an associated action to be taken when the pattern is found. In two cases you provided extra information about the basic pattern to make your instructions clear. You

stipulated the "next" intersection and the gas station "on the left." This
is very much like the pattern-action pairs of an awk program.

In awk, however, the language used to specify the patterns and actions
is far more terse, formal, and descriptive. The general format is:

```
/pattern1/ { action1 }
/pattern2/ { action2 }
...
/patternN/ { actionN }
```

If the pattern portion of the pair is omitted, awk defaults to a pattern
that matches every line of the input. If the action portion is missing, awk
will execute the default action of copying the input line in which the
pattern was found to the standard output. To illustrate this, look at a few
examples.

The awk program /xyz/ will copy all lines containing the string "xyz"
to the standard output.

The awk program { print $3 } will print the third column of each line
of the input.

The awk program /Dollars/ { sum = sum + $2; print sum } will output the run-
ning total of the value of the second field in each line containing the string
"Dollars."

At this point it may not be clear just how the last two examples work.
That's exactly what this section is intended to explain. You can start by
looking at how the user calls awk and what options awk provides for the
command line. Then you'll see how patterns and actions work in greater
detail. This will prepare you to understand how the "awk power plays" in
the rest of the paper work.

Calling awk

The general format for calling awk is:

```
awk [-Fc] [-f scriptfile] [script] [initializations] [file...]
```

All of the arguments to awk are optional. The script option is actually
an awk program. Since the length and complexity of the programs you can
input from the command line are limited, you can use the -f option to
specify a text file whose name is given as the *scriptfile*, the file containing
your awk program.

The file arguments specify the names of text files for your awk program
to use as input. If no file arguments are given, awk will process the standard
input. To explicitly specify the standard input, you can use the file spec-

ification - (hyphen). This feature is useful when an awk program is used as a filter in a sequence of commands and pipes. If this seems a little abstract, don't worry. Several examples of the various options are given later.

Before looking at how the awk options are used, note how the basic elements of an awk program (or script) work. We'll start by looking more closely at patterns and how they are specified.

Patterns

Patterns in their simplest form are just sequences of characters enclosed by slashes. They are matched whenever awk reads a line that contains a sequence of characters that exactly corresponds to those within the slashes. Remembering that the default action is to copy the matched line to the standard output, note that the command awk '/Albuquerque/' cities is equivalent to grep Albuquerque cities. Both will copy each line of the file cities that contains the word *Albuquerque* to the standard output.

However, awk is more like egrep than grep, because the pattern is a regular expression. *Regular expression* is the name given to a standard technique for describing sequences of characters. It is very likely that you have used regular expressions before. In your work here with awk you will need to use them to their fullest extent, so look now at how they are used.

Regular Expressions in awk

You have already seen an example of the simplest form of a regular expression—a simple sequence of characters that matches itself. Often, though, expressions of this type are either too ambiguous or not general enough. For example the command awk '/cat/' file will not only print lines containing the word *cat* but also lines containing words like *catch* and *concatenate*. However, lines containing the words *Cat* and *CAT* will not be matched unless a word like those in the previous list is also a part of the line. This is where regular expressions are useful.

If you want to skip words like *catch* and *concatenate*, you could put spaces in your pattern before and after *cat*. awk '/ cat /' file. This will eliminate the unwanted matches. However, it will also eliminate the case where *cat* is preceded or followed by a tab character. To avoid this, change your expression to match the case where *cat* is preceded and followed by either of the two white space characters:

```
awk '/[ tab]cat[ tab]/' file
```

Here the word tab refers to the actual ASCII 9 character, which you should type here, to stand for an otherwise invisible tab character. This is not a special feature of awk. If you find the need to make the distinction between a tab character and several spaces in your own awk scripts, you can use the octal values for space and tab. (See Table 5–1.)

The square brackets are an important construct in regular expressions. A string of characters enclosed in these brackets stands for (matches) any single character in the string. Unfortunately, the brackets also cause many special characters to be interpreted differently. In particular, the \ddd construct no longer stands for that single octal character. Within the brackets, this stands for any of the three digits, d, d, or d. To use this octal notation in an equivalent expression, use the ¦ (or) operator. This can also be used to allow an or interpretation of the beginning-of-line and end-of-line characters, ˆ and $. This section gives an example of how to use the octal notation.

You can also use the brackets feature of regular expressions to allow for the cases of *Cat* and *CAT*:

```
awk '/[ tab][Cc][Aa][Tt][ tab]/' file
```

Table 5–1   Regular Expressions

Expression	Meaning	Example
c	Matches the character c when c is not a special character	/A/ matches *A* but does not match *B*
\c	Matches the character c even if c is a special character	/\\/ matches \°
\oct	When oct is a three digit octal number, matches the character (byte) having the octal value oct	\011 matches the tab character
ˆ	Matches the beginning of a line or string	/ˆA/ matches the line *All UNIX users:* /ˆson/ matches the strings "son" and "song", but not "Johnson."
$	Matches the end of a line or string.	
[list]	Matches any character in the string list. Ranges such as A–Z can be used to match any character in the range	/[0-9]/ matches any digit†
[ˆlist]	Matches any character not in list	
r°	Matches zero or more occurrences of the regular expression r	[a-zA-Z]° matches zero or more alphabetic characters
r+	Matches one or more occurrences of the regular expression r	
r?	Matches zero or one occurrence of the regular expression r	Matches r1 or r2
r1¦r2	Matches r1 or r2	
r1r2	Matches the string matched by r1 followed by the string matched by r2	

°/\t/ matches *t*, not the tab character.
†The hyphen, -, may be a character in list if placed at the beginning or end, such as /[ACB-]/.

You may have realized by now that this leaves out at least two cases. What if a line begins or ends with one of your desired words? You could include the beginning-of-line symbols using the "or" technique mentioned earlier:

```
awk '/(^¦[ tab])[Cc][Aa][Tt]($¦[ tab])/' file
```

This is very close, but it still does not cover all cases. What is really needed is a way to tell awk to match only cases in which any form of the word *cat* is not preceded or followed by another letter. That is, the match occurs whenever the word is preceded and followed by nonletters. There is a simple way to show this. You can use the not-in-list notation and list all alphabetic characters. So finally, you have this:

```
awk '/(^¦[^a-zA-Z])[Cc][Aa][Tt]($¦[^a-Za-Z])/' file
```

Try a few examples on your own to convince yourself this works. While this notation may seem very cryptic at this point, after a little practice and experience, regular expressions of this sort will become mundane.

Logical Expressions

Now suppose that you want awk to print only lines in which forms of both *cat* and *dog* appear together. You can build from the expression for *cat* and combine the two resulting expression with a logical operator, &&. First, you see the counterpart of the *cat* expression for *dog*:

```
(^¦[^a-zA-Z])[Dd][Oo][Gg]($¦[^a-zA-Z])
```

Now you can combine the two into a single awk command:

```
awk '/(^¦[^a-zA-Z])[Dd][Oo][Gg]($¦[^a-zA-Z])/ && \
    /(^¦[^a-zA-Z])[Cc][Aa][Tt]($¦[^a-zA-Z])/' file
```

The awk utility in fact provides a number of logical operators for combining or modifying expressions, as shown in Table 5–2.

Special Patterns

In addition to the default pattern and those patterns you can define using regular expressions and logical operators, there are two others. These are the special patterns BEGIN and END. These are the only patterns not enclosed in slashes. The actions associated with BEGIN will be executed before the first line of input is read. This pattern is useful for performing initialization actions. The actions associated with END will be executed

Table 5-2 Logical Expressions

Expression	Meaning
pattern1 ¦¦ pattern2	Matches if pattern1, pattern2, or both match
pattern1 && pattern2	Matches only if both pattern1 and pattern2 match
!pattern	Matches all strings not matched by pattern
var ~ pattern	True only if pattern matches the value of var
var !~ pattern	True only if pattern does not match the value of var
> < <= >= != ==	Used to test for lexical greater than, less than, less than or equal, greater than or equal, not equal, and equal

after the last line of input has been read and parsed. It is useful for manipulating summary data. Next you will see what sorts of actions you can perform when a pattern is matched.

Actions

All of the examples you've looked at so far would have been better accomplished by egrep. Because egrep is a special-purpose filter it is more efficient than awk. However, with the introduction of specific actions, you leave the realm of what egrep can do.

In conjunction with the coverage of actions you will learn two new ideas. The previous examples dealt with lines of input. It would have been more correct to say "input records." The awk program reads its input file(s) a record at a time. Each record is then divided into a number of fields. The default record separator is a new line. The default field separator is a sequence of white space characters. So input is read a line at a time and sequences of nonwhite space characters are parsed into fields. Fields are referenced in much the same way as arguments passed to shell scripts. The field $1 refers to the first sequence of nonwhite space characters in the input record, $2 to the second, and $n to the nth. The construct $int (where int is the name of an integer-valued variable) may also be used. You will see an example of this later. The command:

```
ls -l ¦ awk '{ print $4 }'
```

will copy a list of the file sizes of the files in the current directory to the standard output.[2]

The field $0 refers to the current record itself. The command:

```
awk '{print $0}' file
```

---

[2]This assumes the Berkeley form of the ls command. System V users should replace this with ls -o.

is equivalent to the default command, awk file. Figure 5–1 shows some sample field references.

Unlike arguments passed to shell scripts, $0 and $n can be assigned values as well as referenced. Except in BSD version 4.2 and Ultrix 1.2, assignments to $n will change the value of $0 accordingly. This bug, introduced in BSD version 4.2, has been fixed in BSD 4.3. However, under Ultrix 1.2, a BSD compatible, the same bug is also present.

Basic Actions with Fields

At this stage you have been introduced only a few relational operators and the field variables. It turns out that both may be used in patterns as well as in actions. The patterns you have seen so far have been a shorthand notation for the expression "$0 ~ pattern." If you wanted to find all lines in the file "mbox" that began with capitol letters you would use:

```
awk '/[^A-Z]/' mbox
```

If you wished to find all lines in the file mbox whose second field began with a capital letter, you could use the command:

```
awk '/^[ tab]*[^ tab]+[ tab]+[A-Z]/' mbox
```

or you could use the equivalent command:

```
awk '$2 ~ /^[A-Z]/' mbox
```

If you were looking for all lines in the file mbox where the first field is lexicographically greater than the second, you could use:

```
awk '$1 > $2' mbox
```

However, you are left with the default action of copying the matched record to the standard output. It is time to broaden your horizons.

Mathematical Operators and Functions

Surprisingly enough awk, a string-oriented utility, provides quite a range of mathematical operators and functions (listed in Table 5–3). In combi-

Figure 5–1   Field References

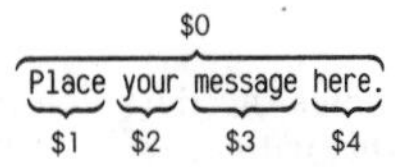

$0
Place your message here.
$1 $2 $3 $4

Table 5-3   Mathematical Operators and Functions

Operator/Function	Meaning
++ --	Increment or decrement
° / %	Multiply, divide, and remainder°
+ -	Addition and subtraction
> < <=	Relational operators: greater than, less than, less than or equal,
>= != ==	greater than or equal, not equal, and equal
cos(expr)	Cosine of expr
exp(expr)	Exponential of expr (e raised to the expr power)
int(expr)	Value of expr truncated to an integer
log(expr)	Natural log of expr
sin(expr)	Sine of expr
sqrt(expr)	Square root of expr

°These are real valued operators.

nation with the field referencing capability, these enable you to perform many spreadsheet like functions with awk.

The most common example is summing a column of numbers. Going back to a previous example, if you wanted to know the sum of the sizes of the files in the current directory, you could use this command:[3]

```
ls -l ¦ awk '{sum = sum + $4}; END { print sum };'
```

You may be wondering where the variable SUM came from. In awk to declare a variable you need only mention it. In this way awk is similar to the shell. It differs from the shell in that the special variables $0, $1, ..., are the only variables that are preceded by a $.

When a variable is first used, its value is guaranteed to be 0 or null. Variables in awk have no true type. When two variables containing numeric values are compared or operated on by a numeric operator, they are taken to be numbers. When a variable containing a numeric value is compared with or operated on by a string function, its value is taken to be a string of digits that may contain a decimal point.

String Functions

As you might expect, awk also provides a full set of string operations and functions (listed in Table 5-4). With the single exception of concatenation, all of the string operators have already been introduced. The comparison operators (~, !~, >, <, <=, >=, ==, and !=) may be used to perform comparisons on strings within the action. The functions provide character-level manip-

---

[3]This assumes the Berkeley form of the ls command. System V users should replace this with ls -o.

Table 5–4   String Operators and Functions

Operator/Function	Meaning
string1 string2	The concatenation of string1 and string2; for example, var = string1 string2
getline	Reads the next record; returns 0 if end of file, 1 if not
index(str1,str2)	Returns the integer index of str2 in str1; returns 0 if str2 is not contained in str1
length(str)	Returns the number of characters in str
print [args]	Copies the strings args to the standard output; copies $0 to the standard output if args are not given
printf "fmt", args	Copies args to the standard output using the format defined by fmt; this is equivalent to the C library function printf
split(str,array,c)	Divides string str into array[1]..array[n] on each occurrence of character c and returns n
sprintf(fmt,args)	Formats args according to fmt and returns the resulting string
substr(str,index,len)	Returns the substring of str beginning at character index with length len

Table 5–5   Built-In Variables

Variable	Meaning
FILENAME	Name of the input file. Assignments to input file will not change the contents of the file being read
FS	Field separator. Defaults to match a sequence of blanks and tabs (white space), but may only be assigned the value of a single character. The assignment FS = " " will result in the default value (white space)
RS	Record separator. Defaults to newline. The assignment RS = "" will cause RS to match blank lines and FS to match newlines at the end of input lines
NR	Number of input records read
OFMT	Output format for numbers. Defaults to %g
OFS	Output field separator
ORS	Output record separator

ulation of the input and a great degree of control over output formats. This combination of input and output control enables awk to perform nearly any text manipulation possible.

Built-In Variables

In addition to $0 through $n, awk has a number of other built-in variables (listed in Table 5–5). These variables provide a convenient method for accessing information about the input and for changing the default parameters affecting the output.

All of the built-in variables in ask may be assigned values as well as referenced. Assigning values to certain built-in variables will change the way in which awk reads and writes information. Some of the built-in variables, however, are provided only for your information. An example of this is the FILENAME variable. This variable contains the name of the file being read. If you wanted to list all of the files in the current directory followed by the number of lines in each file, you could use the shell to execute this command:

```
$for file in *
>do
>awk 'END { printf "%s: %d\n", FILENAME, NR }' $file
>done
```

Complex Actions and the -f Option

With the exception of the last example, your uses of awk so far have been simple one-liners. It was mentioned earlier that awk enables you to do much more than these primitive searching and printing actions. To facilitate complex actions, awk provides the -f option. When the -f option is used in calling awk, it must be immediately followed by a *scriptfile*. The scriptfile must be the name of a text file containing one or more valid awk pattern { action } pairs. Using the -f option gives you much more freedom than before. Actions contained in the scriptfile may span many lines of text. With it you can specify a number of commands to be executed in conjunction with each pattern. A simple example is the awk script used to swap the first and second columns of a text file:

```
        #awk script to swap the first and second
        # columns of any file
{   temp = $1
    $1 = $2
    $2 = temp
    print     # same as "print $0"
}
```

If the scriptfile were named swap.awk you would invoke it with:

```
awk -f swap.awk file
```

Note that a # is used to tell awk that the rest of the line is a comment.

If you wanted to swap the items in the first and second columns only when the first item was greater than the second, you could modify swap.awk to look like this:

```
        # awk script to swap the first and second columns
    # of any file when the item in the first column is
    # greater than the item in the second column


$1 > $2 { temp = $1          # swap the first and second items
            $1 = $2
            $2 = temp
            print
            next          # read the next record and begin processing
                          # at the top of the script

        }
{ print }                     # no swap needed,
                          # copy the line to the standard output
```

Notice the use of the next command to cause awk to start over with the next record. If this command had been omitted, awk would have gone on to compare the original $0 with the default pattern. Since the default pattern matches in every case, awk would have printed all lines twice in which $1 was greater than $2. The first time the items would be swapped, and the second time they would not. The next command differs from getline in that it causes awk to start processing at the top of the script. This is the simplest form of control flow available in awk. The awk program provides nearly all the control flow capabilities found in most high-level programming languages. The syntax is most similar to that of the C language. This means that techniques used to solve problems with awk can generally be converted to C if necessary. It is this capability for control flow that makes awk the powerful tool it is.

Control Structures

The most interesting and powerful control flow is handled by the various control structures. You use them to make decisions about the contents of the records you manipulate and take action accordingly. Table 5–6 summarizes flow control commands.

A previous example used the shell to provide a control structure for awk. This meant you could call awk on one file at a time and list the number of lines in each. At that stage you had no control structure internal to awk to help you. Now that you do, try rewriting that function without using the shell:

Table 5-6   Control Flow

Control Structure	Meaning
`next`	Read the next input record and begin processing at the top of the script.

`if ( expr ) {`
`      cmd1`
`}`
	If expr evaluates to TRUE execute the command(s) cmd

`else   {`
`      cmd2`
`}`
	If expr evaluates to FALSE execute the command(s) cmd.

`for (init; expr; inc) {`
`      cmd`
`}`
	Execute the command init once. Until expr evaluates to FALSE continue executing inc and cmd.

`while ( expr ) {`
`      cmd`
`}`
	Execute the command(s) cmd until expr evaluates to FALSE.

`exit(expr)`	Immediately terminate processing as though the end of input had been reached. If expr is given return its value as the script's exit value.
`print args ¦ "cmd"`	Copy args to the standard input of the command or program cmd. Example: `print $0 ¦ "tr [a-z] [A-Z]"` The `printf` command may also be used with "¦."
`print args > file`	Redirect the output of print to file (equivalent to output redirection in the shell).
`print args >> file`	Append the output of print to file.

```
# an awk script to count the number of lines in each
# of a stream of files and output the file name and
# line count to the standard output


         # first file
cf == ""    { cf = FILENAME }  # initialize current file
                         # current file not current and
                         # this is not the first file
FILENAME != cf && cf != "" {
        printf "%s: %d\n" cf, NR -1  # print the number of
                                  # lines in the last file
        cf = FILENAME # update current file
        NR = 1          # reset number of records
}
```

Finally, to execute it, use the command:

```
awk -f lines.awk *
```

Basics Summary

At this point you've seen in one form or another everything you'll need to make your awk power plays. What you haven't seen yet is how to put it all together to solve large problems. The next two sections will illustrate some important techniques and methods by building solutions to two sample problems. Though the idea is to demonstrate method, please give careful attention to the "nuts and bolts." Close attention to each line of each script will help you further your understanding of the basics introduced in the last section as well as ensure that you understand how the script works. Once again, it's best for you to go through the paper in front of your terminal, entering the scripts and commands as you go along.

A General-Purpose Spreadsheet Calculator

Jump right in and start building your calculator. Start with the most basic function of the calculator and add features and complexity as you go. While the result will not be Lotus 1-2-3, you will have constructed a useful tool and learned more about awk in the process.

Spreadsheets, or *worksheets,* are primarily rows and columns of numerical data used to prepare "what-if" projections. The rows and columns correspond to awk's default records and fields. Each line of input is considered a row. Each sequence of nonwhite space characters is considered to be in a column. The most common function your calculator should perform is summing a column of numbers and outputting the result. For example, to calculate the sum of sizes of all of the files in the current directory, you could use the now-familiar awk command:[1]

```
$ls -al | awk '{ sum = sum + $4 }; END { print sum }'
```

To save the trouble of typing this simple program over again the next time you use it, store the awk portion in a text file. At the same time you can enhance it slightly and add some internal documentation. The resulting file will be called scalc.awk, and its contents will look like this:

```
# scalc.awk - A General-Purpose Spreadsheet Calculator
{ sum = sum + $4 }   # Increment the variable sum by the value of

                # column four of each line read
```

---

[1]This assumes the Berkeley form of the ls command. System V users should replace this with ls -o.

```
                    # When the end of input is reached
                    # output the sum
END { printf "The sum of column 4 = %d\n", sum }
```

Now to find the sum of the size of the files in your current directory, you would enter the command:

```
$ls -al ¦ awk -f scalc.awk
```

Generalizing the Calculator

Because it's likely that some time in the future you might wish to sum a column of numbers other than column four, it would be desirable to put your calculator into a more general form. In doing this you'll have made your first true awk power play. The feature of awk that you will use now is one that is almost totally unmentioned in the standard UNIX documentation: awk, like C or FORTRAN, provides the facility to pass arguments to your awk programs from the command line. Some details and caveats related to this will be discussed later, but for now you'll learn how to use a simple example. You first change your calculator to look like this:

```
# scalc.awk - A General-Purpose Spreadsheet Calculator

{ sum = sum + $(col) }  # Increment the variable sum by the value of
                        # the col'th column of each line read

                        # When the end of input is reached
                        # output the sum
END { printf "The sum of column %d = %d\n", col, sum }
```

Now to perform your file size calculation, enter the command:

```
$ls -al ¦ awk -f scalc.awk col=4 -
```

Note here the use of the explicit specification of standard input as the file to be processed (as indicated by the hyphen at the end of the command). On many systems this is necessary to prevent awk from trying to process the nonexistent file col=4.

So far you've greatly increased the complexity of your original one-line command without gaining much in return. However you will soon see the payoff of this approach as you add more relatively simple features to your calculator. As well as summing columns of input, you may also desire to sum rows of input. If you could count on your input containing a fixed number of columns, this feature would be trivial to add. You could just print each line followed by the sum of all of its columns.

```
$awk '{ printf "%s = %d\n", $0,
$1+$2+$3...$n }' input
```

However it's far more likely that you will want to find the sums of rows of numbers with various lengths. To do this you will need to make use of another of awk's features that you introduced in the last section: control structures. The particular structure you will be using is the for loop. Using one of awk's built-in variables and this looping structure, you can reliably sum a row of numbers without knowing ahead of time how many numbers it contains. You will also need a way to decide whether you are summing a row or a column. You can accomplish that by using different patterns to decide which action to take and by using a pair of if statements in your end block. The resulting awk program will look like this:

```
li # scalc.awk - A General-Purpose Spreadsheet Calculator

col != 0 {                    # If a value has been set for the variable col
   sum = sum + $(col)         # increment the variable sum by the value of
   }                          # the col'th column of each input line.
row!=0 && NR==row {           # If a value has been set for the variable row
                              # and the row'th input line has been read.

   for (i=1; i<=NF; i++) {
         sum = sum + $(i)     # For each field (1 to the number of fields)
         }                    # increment the value of sum by the value of
   }                          # the i'th field.


END {                         # When the end of input is reached
   if (col != 0) {
         printf "The sum of column %d = %d\n", col, sum
         }
   if (row != 0) {
         printf "The sum of row %d = %d\n", row, sum
         }
   }
```

To use the new function just written as before, use the command:

```
$awk -f scalc.awk row=n input
```

Adding More Features

Your calculator has now grown to be rather complex. While there are probably an almost infinite number of features left to add, you'll add just two more. After you have seen how these final two features work, adding more will become quite repetitive. However, you may want to try to add one or two on your own as an exercise.

   The two features you'll be adding are the ability to find the square root of a given cell of your spreadsheet and the ability to truncate the decimal portion of each of a column of numbers. The result looks like this:

```
# scalc.awk - A General-Purpose Spreadsheet Calculator

op=="sc" {                 # If the sum-column function was specified:
   sum = sum + $(col)      # Increment the variable sum by the value of
   }                       # the col'th column of each input line.


op=="sr" && NR==row {      # If the sum-row function was selected
                           # and the row'th input line has been read:
   for (i=1; i<=NF; i++) {
           sum = sum + $(i) # For each field (1 to the number of fields)
           }               # increment the value of sum by the value of
   }                       # the i'th field.


op=="tc" {                 # If the truncate-column function was specified:
   print int($(col))       # Output the truncated value of the col'th field
   }                       # of each line.


op=="rc" && NR==row {      # If the root-of-cell function was selected and
                           # the row'th input line has been read:
   sum = sqrt($(col))      # Assign sum the value of the square root of
   }                       # the col'th field.

END {                      # When the end of input is reached
   if (op == "sc") {
           printf "The sum of column %d = %d\n", col, sum
           }
   if (op == "sr") {
           printf "The sum of row %d = %d\n", row, sum
           }
   if (op == "rc") {
           printf "The square root of cell (%d,%d) = %f\n", col, row, sum
           }
   }
```

Now the use of the calculator always requires that two variables be set on the command line. In the case of the square root function, three variables must be set. To find the square root of the size of the fifth file in the current directory you use the command:

```
$ls -al ¦ awk -f scalc op="rc" row=5 col=4 -
```

There are two final modifications that will make your tool much more useful. Often your data includes text. To avoid trying to process this text as numerical data, you can add a regular expression to your calculator in a few key places. Also, an advantage of using a tool like this one over using a commercial product is that it operates on standard text files and its output may be piped to another program or another use of itself. To make this easier, you'll remove the text from out output.

```awk
# scalc.awk - A General-Purpose Spreadsheet Calculator

op=="sc" {                     # If the sum-column function was specified:
   if ($(col) ~ /^[0-9\.]+$/) {
                               # If the col'th field contains only a number:
         sum = sum + $(col)
                               # Increment the variable sum by the value of
   }                           # the col'th column of each input line.


op=="sr" && NR==row {          # If the sum-row function was selected
                               # and the row'th input line has been read:
   for (i=1; i<=NF; i++) {     # For each field (1 to the number of fields)
         if ($(i) ~ /^[0-9\.]+$/) {
                               # If the i'th field contains only a number:
            sum = sum + $(i)
         }                     # increment the value of sum by the value of
                               # the i'th field.

      }
   print sum                   # Output the sum
   }


op=="tc" {                     # If the truncate-column function was specified:
   if ($(col) ~ /^[0-9\.]+$/) {
                               # If the col'th field contains only a number:
         print int($(col))
                               # Output the truncated value of the col'th field
      }                        # of each line.
   }
```

```
op=="rc" && NR==row {        #If the root-of-cell function was selected and
                             # the row'th input line has been read:
    if ($(col) ~ /^[0-9\.]+$/) {
                             # If the col'th field contains only a number:
        sum = sqrt($(col))
                             # Assign sum the value of the square root of
                             # the col'th field...
        print sum           # and output sum.
    }
}

END && op="sc" {             # If the end of input has been reached and
                             # the sum-column function was specified:
    print sum                # Output the result
}
```

Text Processing Power Plays

In the last section you used awk to build a general-purpose tool. In this section, the tool you construct will not be general-purpose. In fact, the type of tool you will be building might only be used once. This doesn't make it any less useful. Often, when a great deal of tedious, repetitious text editing is needed, skillful use of awk and the other UNIX filters will not only reduce editing time but will have more accurate results.

In the last section you learned an important technique without even knowing it. The technique was one of incremental building and testing. You started with a very simple one-line command and progressed to a complex multifunction program. You somehow avoided making mistakes along the way, but that is the exception and not the rule. It's probable that a very experienced awk programmer would have bungled if asked to produce the final product without going through the intermediate steps. In text processing you need to be extra careful. You should be safe if you hold strictly to the following rules.

- Never replace the original file.
- Never destroy intermediate files.
- Never proceed without double checking your intermediate output.
- Build a debugging feature into your tools the *first* time.

Each of these cardinal rules of automated text processing deserves some additional explanation.

Why not replace the original? As long as the original file still exists, you can always undo an error—no matter how serious.

Then why not destroy intermediate files? One reason is if that intermediate files are kept until the task has been completed and results have been confirmed to be correct, errors introduced along the way only set you back to the step where the error was introduced. Second, without these intermediate files it is often difficult to tell just which step was done incorrectly.

Then why not just charge ahead and find out at the end if something went wrong? Not only will all the steps following an error be wasted time, but they may serve to disguise an error that would have been obvious at an earlier stage.

Why spend the time to build in debugging when what you're writing may be correct? There are generally a finite number of ways to do something correctly and an infinite number of ways to do it wrong. In some very large files, subtle errors can be introduced and later missed by a human inspection. Since most often errors arise as the result of special cases, the one or two minutes it takes to input the a few print statements to flag exceptions may save hours later.

You still may be wondering what sort of editing task could be so enormous and repetitive that it makes useful—or even requires—the use of a custom program to do it. The easy answer is "fortunately, not many." However, on occasion you may find that you need to index a very large document, change all occurrences of one subroutine call in a large source file to another, reformat and merge two heterogeneous mailing lists, or some other task of this sort. The things that each of these tasks have in common are:

- The input can be relied upon to be in a standard format.
- The files concerned will be so large as to make the task difficult for a human, even using a sophisticated screen editor.
- A high degree of accuracy is required; "almost" just won't do.

An Example: Merging Mailing Lists

The specific problem that you will address is how to merge two heterogeneous mailing lists—a problem most suited to awk and perhaps the most instructional. Looking back on your criterion for what makes this a good problem to solve with awk, you can start filling in the details.

First, what are the formats of the two lists? The first list is in machine readable form. It consists of a nroff or troff file that uses a special set of macros. You will ignore the details of the macros. The general format of this file is a sequential list of records. There is no text that is not a part of some record. Each record begins with the begin-record macro, .BR, and ends with the end-record macro, .ER. Each record contains four fields, each one beginning with its own unique macro. Now here's a short sample list containing just two records:

```
.BR
.NM "Waite Group" "The"
.ST "3220" "Sacramento Street"
.CT "San Francisco" "CA"
.ZC "94115"
.ER
.BR
.NM "Public" "John" "Q"
.ST "4567" "Main" "#10"
.CT "Cactus" "NM"
.ZC "12345"
.ER
```

The second list is a human-readable list. Perhaps it was being maintained as a temporary list and has grown so large that it needs to be merged into the main mailing list. Luckily, the person maintaining it always put extraneous information like titles on lines that begin and end with asterisks. While in real life you are not always this fortunate, it is generally possible to find a regular expression sufficient for extracting what is needed from what is not. Once again, your sample list is short.

```
******* Sample Mailing List ************

        Howard W. Sams & Company
        4300 West 62nd Street
        Indianapolis, IN
        46268

        John Doe
        123 Any Street
        Tinytown, IA
        50310

********* Extraneous Information Line ********
```

Obviously, it would be trivial to merge the two lists by hand, even with a rather poor-quality line editor. You have to assume that the lists are in reality hundreds of records long.

Reformatting a List

Two factors point to what to do next. The first is that you want both lists in one list, and you want to use the format of the first list. The second is just common sense. It's easier to merge two lists if they are both in the same format first. So the obvious place to start is with the second list. You will make your job easier by first removing the extraneous text from the file. You do this with a few calls to some of your favorite filters. Remember your rules. You will do tasks one step at a time, retaining all intermediate files.

```
$grep -v \* list.2 > list.2.tmp1
$uniq list.2.tmp1 > list.2.tmp2
$sed 's/^[ tab]+//g' list.2.tmp2 > list.2.tmp3
$sed 's/[ tab]+$//g' list.3.tmp3 > list.2.tmp4
$sed 's/[ tab]+/ /g' list.2.tmp4 > list.2.tmp5
$sed 's/.$/&\@/g' list.2.tmp5 > list.2.tmp6
$sed '1d' list.2.tmp6 > list.2.clean
```

What you've just done in sequence was:

1. copied all lines in list.2 that do not contain asterisks to the file list.2.tmp1
2. reduced all sequential multiply occurring lines, in this case sets of blank lines, to a single occurrence, one blank line
3. removed all leading white space (blanks and tabs)
4. removed all trailing white space
5. reduced all sequences of white space to a single space character
6. placed an "@" at the end of each line of text.
7. removed the first line (a blank line)

The result is now in the file list.2.clean. Now you can use awk to process this file into the other format. As you will see shortly, this will not be trivial. To write a single awk script to do the reformatting would be at best difficult. If you examine the problem closely, though, you see that it's actually several smaller problems. You'll start by solving the easiest and work your way up to the most difficult.

The easiest problem by far is will be to extract the zip codes and put them into the proper macro form. While finding them with a regular expression would be simple, don't forget that this is only part of the larger problem. Also, the preprocessing you did earlier lets you make use of two more features of awk to simplify the overall task. You'll use the -F option to set your field separator to the "@" that you have already placed at the end of each text line. In your script you'll use the begin block to set the record separator to the null string, RS="". If you consider this carefully you'll realize that by normal interpretation of the RS variable, this makes no sense. It is really a special value that tells awk to consider a blank line the record separator and to use not only white space to separate fields but also new lines at the end of text lines. However, the -F option will override the use of white space as a field separator. In effect, you have made each of your mailing list entries into a single awk record with each line representing a field. However, awk sees each entry as seven fields rather than four. It sees the null string between each "@" and the new line as a field also even though it does not actually contain text. It is impossible to cause awk to create fields that span line boundaries, though as you have seen multiline records are possible. You will simply note the existence of these null fields and take care to avoid them. For example, the zip code field is $7 rather than $4. The awk script you'll use to extract the zip codes follows.

```
BEGIN { RS="" }

{   if ($7 !~ /^[0-9]+\-?[0-9]*/) {  # Don't forget the new 9 digit zips!
            printf "          WARNING: Strange zip code in record %d\n", NR
            }
    printf ".ZC \"%s\"\n", $7
    }
```

Now you enter the command:

```
$awk -F\ @ -f zips.awk list.2.clean > zips.txt
```

Because you were careful to include error detection facilities the first time, you can quickly scan the output file with more, or if you prefer, an editor. A more precise way of checking the results would be to use egrep. Working with your awk script as a guide, it should be clear what the correct regular expression would be. Executing egrep with the -v option should then show up any exceptions. This will be left as an exercise for you.

The next problem in order of ascending difficulty is extracting the city and state information and putting it into macro form. So that you don't grow weary of using the -F option, you'll include this action in your initialization. You also have the opportunity to make use of two of awk's string functions. You'll use the split function to divide your line into city and state. Using the substr function, you avoid including an extra blank in the state portion of the macro. This is another reason for the preprocessing you did earlier. The following awk program will extract and reformat the city and state information:

```
BEGIN {    RS=""
           FS="@"   # Replaces the use of -F\@
           }

{   n = split($5, city, ",")
    if (n < 1) {
           printf "ERROR: no city, record %d\n", NR
           }
    else {
           printf ".CT \"%s\"", city[1]
           if (n == 1) {
                   printf "        WARNING: only 1 city field."
                   }
           else {
                   if (n > 2) {
                           printf "WARNING: more than 2 city fields."
                           }
                   printf " \"%s\"", substr(city[2], 2, length(city[2])-1)
                   }
           printf "\n"
           }
    }
```

By now it's clear why you didn't set out to do this in one script. You still have two more sets of information to extract—and they're the tough ones! Before you move on, execute your last script, check the results, and store your results for later. You do it again with:

```
$awk -f cities.awk list.2.clean > cities.txt
```

Don't forget to verify your results.

Moving up one more notch of difficulty, you find the last of the easy problems, the street addresses. Because you will be preserving the order of the street address, this ought to be relatively simple. Keep in mind the need to watch out for exceptions. The only possible valid variant is when the street address includes an apartment number. In a real-life situation, the apartment number could also be a suite number, a letter, or an internal mail stop, but you won't worry about that here. That would only add complexity to the regular expression you check against to look for the occurrence of apartment numbers. Although skilled use of regular expressions is integral to using awk effectively, you will not concentrate on this here. You may, however, wish to try improving this script on your own as an exercise to test your skill with regular expressions. You put this awk program into the file streets.awk. It looks like this when you are through:

```
BEGIN {     RS=""; FS="@"}

{   n = split($3, street, " ")          # This time you use a blank as
                                        # the separator
    if ( n < 1) {
            printf "ERROR: no street, record %d\n", NR
            }
    else {
            printf ".ST \"%s\"", street[1]
            if (n == 1) {
                    printf "         WARNING: only 1 street field."
                    }
            else {
                    printf " \""
                    for (i=2; i < n; i++) {
                            printf "%s\"", street[i]
                            }
                    if ( street[n] !~ /\#[0-9]+/) {
                            printf "%s\"", street[n]
                            }
                    else {
                            printf "\" \"%s\"", street[n]
                            }
                    }
            printf "\n"
            }
}
```

Now execute it:

```
$awk -f streets.awk list.2.clean > streets.txt
```

Did it work?

Now you are left with just one more tiny problem to solve and you'll be nearly ready to merge the two lists. Unfortunately, this is the rough one. Not only do you need to swap the positions of the first and last names while you insert the macro names and the quotation marks, you also need to move the middle initial to the end of the line (if there is a middle initial). This will require only slight variation on your established theme and is a good example of how the incremental approach makes your task easier. You've already seen how to divide each line into separate words. You know how to include checks for any exceptions you might find. You've seen how to build each output line one printf statement at a time. You won't be doing anything totally new to solve this problem; you just need to be careful how you put the pieces together. You will put the following awk script into the file names.awk, execute it, and your task will be nearly complete.

```
BEGIN {      RS=""
             FS="@"
             }


{   n = split($1, name, " ")
    if (n < 1) {
           printf "ERROR: no name, record %d\n", NR
           }
    else {
           if (n == 1) {
                  printf ".NM \"%s\"\n", name[1]  #Only 1 name field is OK
                  }
           else {
                  if (name[2] ~ /[A-Z]\./) {  # If field 2 is a middle initial
                         firstlast = 3
                         }
                  else {
                         firstlast = 2
                         }

                  printf ".NM \""
                  for (i=firstlast; i < n; i++) {  # Fill in the last name
                         printf "%s ", name[i]
                         }
                  printf "%s\"", name[n]            # Finish the last name

                  printf " \"%s\"", name[1]         # Add the first name

                  if (firstlast == 3) {  # If there was a middle initial
                         printf " \"%s\"", name[2]  # tack it on
                         }
                  printf "\n"
                  }
           }
}
```

Now you can test it and store your results.

```
$awk -f names.awk list.2.clean > names.txt
```

After you have checked the results, you see that it's all downhill from here. You have two choices at this point. You could use a text editor to put all of the awk scripts you've just written into one enormous awk script and then process your text file again with it. This is not a bad solution. If there were a chance that you'd be using this script again in the foreseeable future, you might want to do that to cut down the number of files you need to maintain. If you did that, it would be a good idea to comment the file very heavily. While your individual scripts could be deciphered, even if not well commented, one giant, lightly commented script would be mind boggling.

Reassembling the List

You do have another choice. All along you have been following the rules and saving your intermediate results. You now have all the information from the second list in the form you want. The fact that it is in four separate files should not present much of a problem. You can collate your lists with a C program, a shell script, or even by hand. By now, though, you are an awk veteran. This is not only a good problem to solve with awk, but it will also serve as a good warm-up for your final step of merging the two lists.

You will use some additional awk features: arrays, the FILENAME variable, and the END block. This is perhaps the simplest program you've written yet. The real trick here is using another variable to tell you when the input file has changed so you can reset the NR variable. This approach depends on all of your files having an equal number of lines. If you've done the previous steps correctly, they should. If you'd like a quick way to check this, try using the wc command. Now look at the script merge.awk:

```
# If the input file name is not equal to the value of "infile"
# then this is the first file read or the input file has just
# changed to the next file. In either case set the Number of
# Record variable back to one.

infile != FILENAME {       NR = 1
                           infile = FILENAME
                           }
    # Store the lines into their appropriate arrays in order.

infile == "names.txt" {    name[NR] = $0   }

infile == "streets.txt" {  street[NR] = $0 }

infile == "cities.txt" {   city[NR] = $0   }
```

```
infile == "zips.txt" {       zip[NR] = $0     }
END {   for (i=1; i <= NR; i++) {
               printf ".BR\n%s\n%s\n%s\n%s\n.ER\n", name, street, city, zip
                    }
          }
```

Now you merge your existing files with:

```
$awk -f merge.awk *.txt > list.2.new
```

Be sure not to forget to check the output. This time you did not include any exception handling. If you had made an error in this program, it would have been obvious in the output.

To conclude your task, you will need to use a the UNIX sort command. You can make this a bit easier by packaging it in a shell script. The shell script will be called sort.list.

```
cat list.1 list.2.new > big.list
awk '/^\.NM/ { print substr($0, 5, length-4) }'big.list > msrt.tmp sort -df msrt.tmp >
  keys.sorted
awk -f msrt.awk keys.sorted big.list > big.list.sorted
```

The shell script combines both of your lists into one, big.list. Then it extracts the name portion of each record. In truth, there's no need to trim off the macro portion. Since it will be identical for each record, it should not adversely affect the alphabetic sorting you'll do later. Next, the script alphabetically sorts the keys and stores the new list in the file keys.sorted.

The final awk script will use this list of sorted keys to sort the list of records itself. You'll use the FILENAME trick again as well as the array technique to sort the list.

```
FILENAME == "keys.sorted" { key[++j] = $0 }

FILENAME != "keys.sorted" && /^\.BR/ {
      getline; found=0; j=i    # Read the next line and initialize the variables
      while ((found != 1) && (j <= i)) {
             if (key[j] == subsrt($0, 5, length-4)) {
                    found = 1
                    }
             else {
                    j++
                    }
                }
      if (found != 1) {
```

```
                        printf "EXCEPTION: %s\n", $0
                        }
            else {
                    name[j] = $0
                    getline; street]j] = $0 # Get the next line and store it.
                    getline; city]j] = $0
                    getline; zip[j] = $0
                    }
            }

END {       for(j=1; j <= i; j++) {
                    printf ".BR\n%s\n%s\n%s\n%s\n.ER\n", name[j],
street[j], city[j], zip[j]
                    }
            }
```

So, with one last command your job is done.

```
$sort.list
```

Now that wasn't so bad was it?

Important Notes

If You're Still Unsure

If any of the features of awk or the rest of the UNIX system that you used
were unfamiliar, you may need to go back and look at some more introductory material. I would suggest *Advanced UNIX: A Programmer's Guide*
by Stephen Prata with The Waite Group (Indianapolis, Ind.: Howard W.
Sams, 1985), for a good tutorial on awk and other parts of the UNIX system.

Undocumented Features of awk

Several of awk's features are not well-documented. An example of an almost
totally undocumented feature is argument passing from the command line.
The *UNIX System User's Manual* from AT&T and Prentice-Hall mentions
it briefly, while the *UNIX User's Manual* for BSD versions 4.2 and 4.3
doesn't mention it at all. For that reason you may want to take the time
to read about it here.

Though you've already used this feature, there are several limitations and rules about its use you've not seen yet here. Since you didn't make use of it with an awk program that had a BEGIN block, you never saw that these values are not available until the first record has been read and divided into fields. If for some reason you need to perform initialization using these values, use the pattern NR==1 as your first pattern and put the initializations in the corresponding action. If this is your first pattern, it will ensure that the initializations are done before any further processing is performed. Also, awk does not distinguish between strings and numbers. To force awk to treat the value as a string, enclose it in quotes.

Another option that is not documented but is available is the -d option for producing debugging output. Though this option is standard with most UNIX commands, it generally requires that the command be compiled with the -DDEBUG option. And awk is no exception. This is usually not done, mainly because the debugging output produced is designed for debugging awk itself, not the individual script. It may however prove useful in debugging extremely large or complex scripts. Note, though, that the important routine yyparse will never produce debugging output unless modifications are made to the source code. This is at least true for the three versions of awk source code that I have worked with.

Bugs

In the Berkeley 4.2 version of awk, assignments to fields (such as $1 = xyz) will not result in any change to the record $0. That causes simple scripts not to perform as would be expected and makes it greatly more complicated to make them work. Perhaps the best example is the script to swap the members of the first two columns of input:

```
{  temp = $1
   $1 = $2
   $2 = temp
   print
   }
```

This script will do nothing more than copy the standard input to the standard output under BSD 4.2. If you have the need to swap two fields under BSD 4.2 or Ultrix 1.2, you'll need to use a for loop or its equivalent. For example, the previous script can be changed to this under BSD 4.2:

```
{  temp = $1
   $1 = $2
   $2 = temp
```

```
for (i=1; i<=NF; i++) {
        printf "%s ", $(i)
        }
printf "\n"
}
```

This solution, however, does not preserve the field separators. I know of no solution to this problem that does preserve the field separators without doing large amounts of extra processing.

If you at some point discover that even simple awk scripts cause awk to dump core, it is likely that this is caused by debugging being turned on in the standard library. When debugging is turned on, particularly in malloc, awk scripts that use regular expressions will generally cause awk to terminate and dump core with a message like ASSERT(testbusy(p->ptr)). It seems that somewhere in the code that handles regular expressions, awk attempts to free pointers that are not busy. Turning off debugging in the library when awk is compiled should fix this problem.

More References

If you are fortunate enough to have access to source code, recommended reading is the README file from awk's source code. Whether or not you have access to source code, I would suggest getting a copy of *A Supplemental Document for awk* by John W. Pierce of the Department of Chemistry, University of California, San Diego. This paper does an excellent job covering material of interest to the serious awk user. One topic covered there is awk script compilation, and some of the topics covered in this paper are discussed as well.

ARCANA OF PROGRAMMING

O pen a conversation with any UNIX user and see how quickly it ends up on the subject of programming. UNIX is the programmer's dream operating system—one containing every conceivable type of programming tool, compiler, batch language, pattern scanner, make utility, parsers, lint checker—you name it. UNIX offers sophisticated device driver facilities, interprocess communications, and extremely powerful networking. Yet much of this programming information remains as baffling topics that only experienced UNIX hackers understand. This second part of *UNIX Papers* presents some of these more arcane subjects for the intermediate to advanced level programmer. We chose topics that are fairly new, important for the future, and that few people have written about.

The first paper looks at one of the latest offerings in programming languages, a new Bell Labs "translator" for the C language called C++. With this language you can write object-oriented programs that provide a new model particularly suitable to multitasking, interprocess communications, device drivers, and other modern programming needs. The paper then moves on to the nuts and bolts of device drivers, those essential workhorses of computing input and output. Device drivers serve to communicate between the application program and the hardware device, but we'll find that in their UNIX multitasking and multiuser incarnations, device drivers are more complex to use and write than their single-tasking cousins. Next, there are two papers on networks, one on the new Remote File System features of System V, release 3, including streams and the Transport Level Interface, and another on designing and installing your own UNIX based Ethernet system. Finally, a paper describes the rare but important instance of using UNIX for real-time processes, including examples of running a factory floor and laboratory test equipment using a UNIX system.

KEYWORDS

▶ Data abstraction

▶ Classes

▶ Object-oriented programming

▶ Encapsulation

▶ Dynamic binding

Paper Synopsis: The new C++ language has caught the attention of the C programming community. It remedies the weaknesses of C and offers powerful new ways to build and manipulate data structures. It also provides C programmers with the ability to use object-oriented program (OOP) techniques. This paper is an introduction and tutorial to C++, with many examples, all of which compile with the AT&T C++ translator. C programmers will find this material vital.

Keith Gorlen is an electronics engineer with the Computer Systems Laboratory, Division of Computer Research and Technology, at the National Institutes of Health. He earned a bachelor's degree in electrical engineering from Northwestern University in 1970 and a master's in electrical engineering from New York University in 1973.

Currently he is involved with the development of an advanced network of 32 bit UNIX workstations for scientific computation and laboratory automation. He became interested in C++ while looking for a more productive method for programming these workstations.

C++ Under UNIX

Keith Gorlen

The C++ programming language was designed and implemented by Bjarne Stroustrup of AT&T Bell Laboratories as a successor to C. It retains compatibility with existing C programs and the efficiency of C; it also adds powerful new capabilities, making it suitable for a wide range of applications from device drivers to artificial intelligence. C++ will be of interest to UNIX users because of its intimate relation to C and its potential use for building graphic user interfaces to UNIX, for UNIX systems programming, and for supporting large-scale software development under UNIX.

C++ evolved from a dialect of C known as "C with Classes," which was invented in 1980 as a language for writing efficient event-driven simulations. Several key ideas were borrowed from the Simula67 and ALGOL 68 programming languages. Figure 6–1 shows the heritage of C++.

The definitive book on C++ is Bjarne Stroustrup's *The C++ Programming Language,*[1] published by Addison-Wesley. It gives a detailed description of the language and contains many examples and exercises. It also includes the C++ reference manual, which is a concise, more formal definition of the language.

This paper shows how C++ corrects most of the deficiencies of C by offering improved compile-time type checking and support for modular programming. It also introduces many of the new features of C++:

RELATED PAPERS

1 UNIX: Rights and Wrongs

15 The Future of UNIX and Open System Standards

- classes
- operator and function name overloading
- free store management

---

[1]Reading, Mass.: Addison-Wesley, 1986.

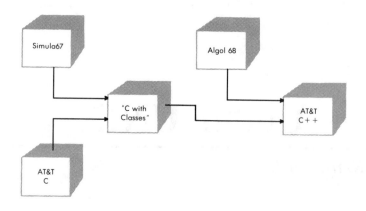

Figure 6-1   The Heritage of C++

- constant types
- references
- inline functions
- derived classes
- virtual functions

The paper presents these features in the context of a nontrivial example so that you'll understand the motivation behind them and see how they are typically used.

By the end of the paper, you'll see how proper use of C++ can dramatically increase a programmer's productivity. C++ programs are shorter, clearer, and more likely to be correct from the outset. As a result, they are also easier to debug and to maintain.

The paper concludes by discussing the current status and future of C++.

A C++ Example

The best way to learn about C++ is to write a program in it, starting in familiar territory with a simple program written in plain old C:

```
main()
{
```

```
    int a = 193;
    int b = 456;
    int c = a + b + 47;
    printf("%d\n",c);
}
```

This program declares three integer variables named a, b, and c, initializing a and b to the values 193 and 456, respectively. The integer c is initialized to the result of adding a and b and the constant 47. Finally, the standard C library function printf() is called to print out the value of c. The quoted string "%d\n" tells how to print the result: %d prints c as a decimal number, and \n adds a new line character. If this program is compiled and executed, it prints out the number 696 and exits.

Now suppose the program were to perform a similar calculation, but this time a and b were big numbers, like the U.S. national debt expressed in dollars. Such numbers are too big to be stored as ints on most computers, so if the code included int a = 25123654789456 the C compiler (one would hope) would return an error message and fail to compile the program. There are many practical applications for big integers, such as cryptography, symbolic algebra, and number theory, where it can be necessary to perform arithmetic on numbers with hundreds or even thousands of digits.

It isn't easy to write a program to deal with these big numbers in ordinary C. Coding and debugging the algorithms that perform arithmetic operations on big integers in C involves a significant amount of work, so programmers usually make them general-purpose. A programmer wouldn't be able to predict how big the numbers might become in advance, so a dynamic memory allocator would be used to manage their storage at execution time. The programmer would need to write a C library of functions for creating, destroying, reading, printing, assigning, and performing basic arithmetic on big integers. These functions would have to have distinctive names such as create_bigint, print_bigint, and add_bigints to avoid confusion with other kinds of data that might be created, printed, or added in the same program.

Worst of all, programmers wishing to use big integers would have to know the names of these functions and the rules for calling them. They would have to remember to create and initialize big integers when they needed to use them and to destroy them when they were finished. Even simple arithmetic expressions would be awkard to write; c = a + b would have to be coded as:

```
assign_bigint(&c,add_bigints(a,b))
```

and there might be problems with handling temporary results calculated during the evaluation of a complex expression. Also, programmers would have to be careful when they combined big integers with other data types such as int. They would need to call a function to convert ints to big integers before adding them, for example. Any C program using big integers would be both difficult to write and difficult to read.

C++ programs still must include code to manage the storage of big integers and functions to perform the same operations on them. The difference is that in C++ a programmer can "package" this code so that using big integers is as convenient as using the int data type that is built into C. Programmers can, in effect, extend the C++ language by adding custom data types. This tutorial will discuss a custom data type called BigInt. Notice how similar the sample C program is to this C++ program that performs a similar calculation using BigInts instead of ints:

```
#include "BigInt.h"
main()
{
    BigInt a = "25123654789456";
    BigInt b = "456023398798362";
    BigInt c = a + b + 47;
    c.print();      /* print the result, c */
    printf("\n");
}
```

Data Abstraction

This technique of defining new data types that are well-suited to the application to be programmed is known as *data abstraction,* and a data type such as BigInt is called an *abstract data type.* Data abstraction is a powerful, general-purpose technique that, when properly used, can result in shorter, more readable, more flexible programs.

Data abstraction is supported by several other modern programming languages such as Ada.

In these languages, and in C++ as well, a programmer can define a new abstract data type by specifying a data structure together with the operations permissible on that data structure, as shown in Figure 6–2.

It is difficult or impossible to practice data abstraction in most other programming languages currently in widespread use, such as BASIC, C, COBOL, FORTRAN, Pascal, or Modula-2.[2] This is because data abstraction

---

[2]Proponents of Modula-2 claim that this language supports data abstraction. The following papers discuss some of the difficulties with Modula-2's support for abstract data types:

Jon Bondy, "Uninitialized Modula-2 Abstract Object Instances, Yet

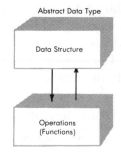

Figure 6–2   An Abstract Data Type

requires special language features not available in these languages. An analysis of the sample C++ program shows what these features do.

The first three statements in the body of the `main()` program declare three type `BigInt` variables, `a`, `b`, and `c`. The C++ compiler needs to know how to create them—how much space to allocate for them and how to initialize them.

The first and second statements are similar—they initialize the `BigInt` variables `a` and `b` with big integer constants written as character strings containing only digits. To do this the C++ compiler must be able to convert character strings into `BigInt`s.

The third statement is the most complicated. It adds `a`, `b`, and the integer constant 47 and stores the result in `c`. The C++ compiler must create a temporary `BigInt` variable to hold the sum of `a` and `b`. Then it must convert the `int` constant 47 into a `BigInt` and add this to the temporary variable. Finally, it must initialize `c` from this temporary `BigInt` variable.

The fourth statement prints `c` on the standard output, and the last statement calls the C library function `printf()` to print a new line character. C programmers are probably familiar with `printf()`, but `c.print()` probably looks a bit strange. It is a call on a special kind of function available in C++ called a *member function*. You'll learn more about this later, but for now just think of it as a function that prints out a variable of type `BigInt`.

Even though there are no more statements in the body of `main()`, the compiler isn't finished yet. It must destroy the `BigInt` variables `a`, `b`, and `c`

Again," *SIGPLAN Notices* 22, no. 5 (1987), pp. 58–63.

John Leeson and Michele Spear, "Type Independent Modules: The Preferred Approach to Generic ADTs in Modula-2," *SIGPLAN Notices* 22, no. 3 (1987), pp. 65–70.

Jeffrey Savit, "Uninitialized Modula-2 Abstract Objects, Revisited," *SIGPLAN Notices* 22, no. 2 (1987), pp. 78-84.

Michael Torbett, "A Note on 'Protecting Against Uninitialized Abstract Objects in Modula-2,' " *SIGPLAN Notices* 22, no. 5 (1987), pp. 8–10.

Michael Torbett, "More Ambiguities and Insecurities in Modula-2" *SIGPLAN Notices* 22, no. 5 (1987), pp. 11–17.

Richard Weiner, "Protecting Against Unitialized Abstract Objects," *SIGPLAN Notices* 21, no. 6 (1986), pp. 63–69.

Bjarne Stroustrup, "What Is 'Object-Oriented Programming'," *Proceedings of the 1st European Conference on Object-Oriented Programming,* Paris, France, June 1987.

and any BigInt temporaries it may have created before leaving a function, such as main(). This is to ensure that the storage used by these variables is freed.

To summarize what the C++ compiler needs to know how to do with BigInts to compile the example program, remember that it must:

- *create* new instances of BigInt variables
- *convert* character strings and integers to BigInts
- *initialize* the value of one BigInt with that of another BigInt
- *add* two BigInts together
- *print* BigInts
- *destroy* BigInts when they are no longer needed

Specifications and Implementations

Where does the C++ compiler obtain this know-how? From the file BigInt.h, which is included by the first line of the sample program. This file contains the *specification* of the BigInt abstract data type. The specification contains the information that programs that *use* an abstract data type need to have to be successfully compiled. The details of *how* the abstract data type works, known as the *implementation*, are kept in another file. In this example, this file is named BigInt.c. It is compiled separately, and the object code produced from it is linked with the program that uses the abstract data type, also called the *client* program. Figure 6–3 shows how the spec-

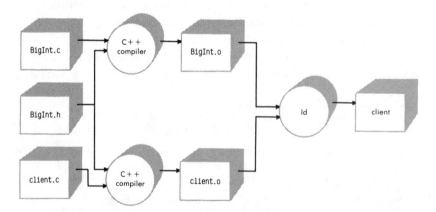

Figure 6–3 **Combining the Specification (BigInt.h) and Implementation (BigInt.c) of an Abstract Data Type (BigInt) with the Source Code of a Client Program (client.c) to Produce an Executable Program (client)**

ification and implementation of an abstract data type are combined with the source code of a client program to produce an executable program.

Programmers separate the code for an abstract data type into a specification part and an implementation part to hide the implementation details. Then the implementation can be changed with confidence that client programs will continue to work correctly after they are relinked with the modified object code. This is useful when a team of programmers work on a large software project. Once they agree on the specifications for the abstract data types they need, each team member can implement one or more of them independently of the rest of the team.

A well-designed abstract data type also hides its complexity in its implementation, making it as easy as possible to use.

The Specification

This section examines the specification for the BigInt data type, contained in the file BigInt.h. (Note that in C++, // begins a comment that extends to the end of the line.)

```
class BigInt {
    char* digits;                       // pointer to digit array in free store
    int ndigits;                        // number of digits
public:
    BigInt(const char*);                // constructor function
    BigInt(int);                        // constructor function
    BigInt(const BigInt&);              // initialization constructor function
    BigInt operator+(const BigInt&);    // addition operator function
    void print();                       // printing function
    ~BigInt();                          // destructor function
};
```

Much of this code may look odd to you, but it will be explained in the next few sections.

Classes

This is an example of one of the most important features of C++, the class declaration, which specifies an abstract data type. It is an extension of something C programmers are probably already familiar with: the struct declaration.

The struct declaration groups together a number of variables, which may be of different types, into a unit. For example, in C (or in C++) programmers can write:

```
struct BigInt {
    char* digits;
    int ndigits;
};
```

An *instance* of this structure (that is, a variable of type BigInt) can be declared by writing:

```
struct BigInt a;
```

The individual *member variables* of the struct—digits and ndigits—can be accessed using the dot (.) operator; for example, a.digits accesses the member variable digits of the struct a.

Recall that in C a pointer can be declared to an instance of a structure:

```
struct BigInt* p;
```

in which case programs can access the individual member variables by using the -> operator; for example, p->digits.

C++ classes work in a similar manner, and the . and -> operators are used in the same way to access a class's member variables. In the example here, class BigInt has two member variables named digits and ndigits. The variable digits points to an array of bytes (chars), allocated from the free storage area, that holds the digits of the big integer, one decimal digit per byte. The digits are ordered beginning with the least-significant digit in the first byte of the array. The member variable ndigits contains the number of digits in the integer. Figure 6–4 shows a diagram of this data structure for the number 654321.

However, the C++ class can do much more than the struct feature of regular C. The next section looks at these extensions in detail.

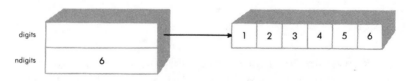

Figure 6–4   A Diagram of the BigInt Data Structure for the Number 654321

Encapsulation

In C++, an instance of class BigInt can be declared in a client program by writing:

```
BigInt a;
```

But now there's a potential problem: the client program might try, for example, to use the fact that a.ndigits contains the number of digits in the number a. This would make the client program dependent on the *implementation* of class BigInt—after all, a programmer might wish to change the representation of BigInts to use hexadecimal instead of decimal arithmetic to save storage. There should be a way to prevent unauthorized access to the member variables of the instances of a class, which C++ provides by allowing use of the keyword public: within a class declaration to indicate which members can be accessed by anyone and which have restricted access. Members declared before the public: keyword are *private*, as are digits and ndigits in this example, so C++ will issue an error message if a client program attempts to use them.

Protecting the member variables of a class in this manner is known as *encapsulation*. It is a good programming practice because it enforces the separation between the specification and the implementation of abstract data types, and it helps in debugging programs. For example, if ndigits has the wrong value in some situations, those parts of the program that do not have access to the variable are probably not at fault.

Member Functions

But how does a client program interact with the private member variables of a class? Whereas a struct allows only variables to be grouped together, the C++ class declaration allows both variables and the functions that operate on them to be grouped. Such functions are called *member functions*, and the private member variables of the instances of a class can be accessed only by the member functions of that class. Thus, a client program can read or modify the values of the private member variables of an instance of a class indirectly, by calling the public member functions of the class, as shown in Figure 6-5.

The class BigInt has two private member variables, digits and ndigits, and six public member functions. The declarations of these member functions will look unusual to C programmers for several reasons: the types of the arguments of the functions are listed within parentheses in the function declarations; three of the functions declared have the same name, BigInt;

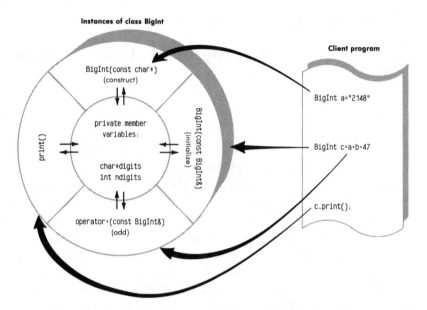

Instances of class BigInt

BigInt(const char*)
(construct)

private member
variables:

char*digits
int ndigits

print()

BigInt(const BigInt&)
(initialize)

operator+(const BigInt&)
(add)

Client program

BigInt a="2148"

BigInt c=a+b+47

c.print();

**Figure 6–5   Client Programs Can Access the Private Member Variables
of an Instance of a Class Only by Calling Public Member
Functions of the Class**

and the function names operator+ and ˜BigInt contain characters normally not allowed in function names.

Function Argument Type Checking

C++ strongly encourages a programmer to declare the types of the arguments of all functions. This makes it possible for C++ to check for inconsistent argument types when a function call is compiled and can eliminate many bugs at an early stage. For example, the C statement:

```
fprintf("The answer is %d",x);
```

will be compiled with no problem. However, when this statement is executed, the program will abort with a cryptic error message. The problem is that the standard C library function fprintf() expects the first argument to be a pointer to the stream to which the output is to be written, not a format string as it is here. On the other hand, in C++ the argument types of fprintf() can be declared:

```
extern int fprintf(FILE*, const char* ...);
```

so the compiler can give an error message when the incorrect function call is compiled, noting the discrepancy in the argument types. Conveniently, the argument types for most standard library functions are declared in system header files that can be included in programs so that programmers don't have to write all these common declarations.

Function Name Overloading

Listing the types of all of a function's arguments in its declaration has a second benefit: several functions can be defined with the same name, as long as each requires a different number and/or type of argument. For example, C++ can distinguish between two functions with the name abs:

```
overload abs;
int abs(int);
float abs(float);
```

A programmer can then write:

```
x = abs(2);
y = abs(3.14);
```

The first statement will call abs(int), and the second will call abs(float)—the C++ compiler can determine which abs to use because 2 is an integer and 3.14 is a float. When more than one function has the same name, as in this case, the name is said to be *overloaded.* One advantage of overloading is that it eliminates "funny" function names (remember ABS, IABS, DABS, and CABS from FORTRAN?). It also leads to more general programs; for example, the function call copy(x,y) will copy a y to an x without concern for their types—they might be arrays, or strings, or files, as long as the program includes a copy function to handle each case.

Calling Member Functions

Getting back to the BigInt example and the discussion of member functions, the next-to-last line in the first C++ program:

```
c.print();
```

can be explained. Member functions are called in a manner analogous to the way member variables are normally accessed in C; that is, by using the . or -> operators. Since c is an instance of class BigInt, the notation c.print() calls the member function print() of class BigInt to print the current value of c. Similarly, if the code has declared a pointer to a BigInt:

```
BigInt* p;
```

then the notation p->print() would call the same function. This notation prevents this particular print() from inadvertently being called to operate on anything other than an instance of class BigInt.

   In C++, several different classes may all have member functions with the same name, just as in regular C several different structs may all have member variables with the same name. Thus, simple function names, like print, rather than distinctive names, like print_bigint, can be used without worrying about naming conflicts. Programmers could add a new class, say BigFloat, to a program that also used BigInts, and they could also define print() as a member function of class BigFloat. The program could contain the statements:

```
BigInt a = "2934673485419";
BigFloat x = "874387430.3945798";
a.print();
x.print();
```

and the C++ compiler would use the appropriate print() in both cases.

Constructors

As you'll recall, one of the things the C++ compiler needs to know about the BigInt abstract data type is how to create new instances of BigInts. Programmers can tell C++ how to do this by defining one or more special member functions called *constructors*. A constructor function is one that has the same name as its class. When a client program contains a declaration such as:

```
BigInt a = "123";
```

the C++ compiler reserves space for the member variables of an instance of class BigInt and calls the member function a.BigInt("123"). It is the responsibility of the provider of the BigInt data type to write the function BigInt() so that it initializes the instance correctly. In this example, BigInt("123") will allocate three bytes of dynamic storage, set a.digits to point to this storage, set the three bytes to {3,2,1}, and set a.ndigits to three. This will create an instance of class BigInt named a that is initialized to 123.

If a class has a constructor function, C++ *guarantees* that it will be called to initialize every instance of the class created. A user of an abstract data type such as BigInt does not have to remember to call an initialization function separately for every BigInt declared; thus a common source of programming errors is eliminated.

Constructors and Type Conversion

The second thing C++ needs to know is how to convert a character string, such as "25123654789456", or an integer, such as 47, to a BigInt. Constructors are also used for this purpose. When the C++ compiler sees a statement like:

```
BigInt a = "25123654789456";
```

it recognizes that a type conversion must be done and so checks to see if the constructor BigInt(char*) is declared. If so, it creates a temporary instance of BigInt by calling BigInt(char*) with the argument "25123654789456". If an appropriate constructor is not declared, the statement is flagged as an error. When BigInt(char*) and BigInt(int) are defined for class BigInt, a programmer may freely use character strings or integers wherever a BigInt can be used, and the C++ compiler will automatically call the constructor to do the type conversion. This is an important feature of C++, because it lets programmers blend their own abstract data types with others and with the fundamental types built into the language.

Constructors and Initialization

C++ must also know how to initialize a BigInt with the value of another BigInt, as is required by a statement such as:

```
BigInt c = a + b + 47;
```

A programmer can control how C++ initializes instances of class BigInt by defining the special constructor function BigInt(BigInt&). In this example, this constructor allocates storage for the new instance and makes a copy of the contents of the argument instance.

Operator Overloading

The fourth thing C++ must be able to do is to add two BigInts. A programmer could just define a member function named add to do this, but then writing arithmetic expressions would be awkward. With C++ a programmer can define additional meanings for most of its operators, including +, so it can mean "add" when applied to BigInts. This is known as *operator overloading;* it is similar to the concept of function name overloading.

Actually, most programmers are already familiar with this idea because the operators of most programming languages, including C, are already overloaded. For example, programmers can write:

```
int a,b,c;
float x,y,z;
c = a+b;
z = x+y;
```

The operators = and + behave quite differently in the last two statements: the first statement does *integer* addition and assignment and the second does *floating-point* addition and assignment. Operator overloading is simply an extension of this.

C++ recognizes a function name having the form operator@ as an overloading of the C++ operator symbol @. The operator = can be overloaded, for example, by declaring the member function named operator=, as was done in the sample class BigInt. A program can call this function using either the usual notation for calling member functions or by using just the operator:

```
BigInt a,b;
a.operator=(b);
a = b;
```

The last two lines are equivalent.

Of course, overloading an operator, doesn't change its built-in meaning, but only gives it an additional meaning when used on instances of the new abstract data type. The expression 2 + 2 still gives 4.

Destructors

As described previously, C++ must be able to destroy instances of BigInts once it is finished with them. A programmer can tell the C++ compiler how to do this by defining another special kind of member function, called a *destructor.* A destructor function has the same name as its class, prefixed by the character ˜. For class BigInt, this is the member function ˜BigInt(). Since ˜ is the C++ and C complement operator, this naming convention suggests that destructors are complementary to constructors.

The function ˜BigInt() must be written so that it properly cleans up, or finalizes, instances of class BigInt for which it is called, which here means freeing the dynamic storage that was allocated by the constructor.

If a class has a destructor function, C++ *guarantees* that it will be called to finalize every instance of the class when it is no longer needed. Once again, this relieves users of an abstract data type like BigInt from having to remember to do so and eliminates another source of programming errors.

Summary of the BigInt Data Type Specification

This paper has covered a lot of territory already, so take a moment for review.

The technique of data abstraction can lead to more reliable, more readable, and more flexible programs, and many of the features of C++ support the practice of data abstraction:

- *classes,* the basic language construct for defining new abstract data types

- *member variables,* which describe the data in an abstract class, and *member functions,* which define the operations on an abstract class

- *encapsulation,* which lets programmers restrict access to certain member variables and functions

- *function argument type checking,* which helps to ensure that functions are called with proper arguments

- *constructors and destructors,* which manage the storage for an abstract data type and guarantee that instances of an abstract data type are initialized and finalized

- *user-defined implicit type conversion,* to let programmers blend abstract data types with others and with the fundamental data types of the language

- *operator overloading,* with which programmers give additional meaning to most of the existing operators when they are used with the programmers' own abstract data types, making new data types easier to use

The paper also described the idea of breaking up an abstract data type into its specification, which contains the information that the user, or client, needs to know to use the abstract data type, and its implementation, which hides the details of how the abstract data type works so that it may be programmed independently by a member of a programming team and be easily maintained.

The Implementation

Now that the specification of the BigInt abstract data type has been shown, it's time to discuss its implementation.

As mentioned earlier, the implementation of an abstract data type consists of the C++ code that embodies the details of *how* the data abstraction works. For this example, it is kept in a separate file named BigInt.c.

The implementation requires the information kept in the specification, so the first line in BigInt.c is:

```
#include "BigInt.h"
```

Because both the implementation and client programs are compiled with the same specification, the C++ compiler ensures a consistent interface between them.

The BigInt(const char*) Constructor

Class BigInt has two constructors—one to create an instance of a BigInt from a character string of digits (a char*), and one to create an instance from an integer (an int). The program must be able to create a BigInt from a string of digits, because this is the only way very large integer constants can be written in C++. The ability to create a BigInt from an int is provided as a convenience, so small integers can be written in the usual way. Here is the implementation of the first constructor:

```
BigInt::BigInt(const char* digitString)
{
    int n = strlen(digitString);
    if (n != 0) {
        digits = new char[ndigits=n];
        char* p = digits;
        const char* q = &digitString[n];
        while (n--) *p++ = *--q - '0';
    }
    else {                              // empty string
```

```
        digits = new char[ndigits=1];
        digits[0] = 0;
    }
}
```

This constructor initializes the data structure of a BigInt as described previously. The constructor determines the length of the character string argument, allocates enough memory to hold the digits of the number, then scans the character string from right to left, converting each digit character to its binary representation.

If the character string is empty, it's treated as a special case and creates a BigInt initialized to zero.

C programmers will find this code quite recognizable, with a few exceptions explained in the next few sections.

The Scope Resolution Operator

The notation BigInt::BigInt identifies BigInt as a member function of class BigInt. As was mentioned earlier, several C++ classes can have member functions with the same names. When it is necessary to specify exactly which class member is being dealt with, the programmer can precede the member name with the class name and the :: operator. The :: operator is known as the *scope resolution operator,* and it may be applied to both member functions and member variables.

Constant Types

C programmers will be familiar with use of the type char* for arguments that are character strings, but what is a const char*? In C++, the keyword const can be used before a type to indicate that the variable being declared is constant, and may therefore not appear to the left of the assignment (=) operator. When used in an argument list as it was earlier, it prevents the argument from being modified by the function. This protects against another kind of common programming error.

Member Variable References

Notice that the member variables of the instance for which the member function can be referenced without using the . or -> operators throughout the body of the member function, as for example in the statement:

```
digits = new char[ndigits=n];
```

Since member functions reference the member variables of their class frequently, this provides a convenient, short notation.

The new Operator

The C++ new operator allocates the dynamic storage needed to hold the digits of a BigInt. C programmers would call the standard C library function malloc() to do this. The new operator has two advantages, however. First, it returns a pointer of the appropriate data type. Thus, to allocate space for the member variables of a struct BigInt in C, a programmer would write:

```
(struct BigInt*)malloc(sizeof(struct BigInt));
```

whereas in C++ this is handled with:

```
new BigInt;
```

The second advantage is that if new is used to allocate an instance of a class having a constructor function (such as BigInt), the constructor is called automatically to initialize the newly allocated instance. The result is more readable, less error-prone code.

Placement of Declarations

C programmers may have noticed that the declaration of p seems to be "misplaced":

```
if (n != 0) {
    digits = new char[ndigits=n];    // a statement
    char* p = digits;                // a declaration!
```

because it appears *after* the first statement in a block. In C++, declarations may be intermixed with statements as long as each variable is declared before its first use. You can frequently improve the readability of a program by placing variable declarations near the place where they are used.

The BigInt(int) Constructor

Here's the implementation of the BigInt(int) constructor, which creates a BigInt from an integer:

```
BigInt::BigInt(int n)
{
    char d[3*sizeof(int)+1];    // buffer for decimal digits
    char* dp = d;               // pointer to next decimal digit
    ndigits = 0;
    while (n > 0) {             // convert integer to decimal digits
        *dp++ = n%10;
        n /= 10;
        ndigits++;
    }
    digits = new char[ndigits];
    register int i;
    for (i=0; i<ndigits; i++) digits[i] = d[i];
}
```

This constructor works by converting the integer argument to decimal digits in the temporary array d. How much space to allocate for the BigInt is then known, so the correct amount of dynamic storage is allocated using the new operator, and the decimal digits from the temporary array are copied into it.

The Initialization Constructor

The job of the initialization constructor is to copy the value of its BigInt argument into a new instance of BigInt:

```
void BigInt::BigInt(const BigInt& n)
{
    int i = n.ndigits;
    digits = new char[ndigits=i];
    char* p = digits;
    char* q = n.digits;
    while (i--) *p++ = *q++;
}
```

This function makes use of a reference, an important C++ feature not yet covered.

References

The argument type of the member function BigInt(const BigInt&) is an example of a C++ *reference*. References address a serious deficiency of C: the lack of a way to pass function arguments by reference.

To understand what this means, suppose a programmer wishes to write a function named inc() that adds one to its argument. In C, if this were written as:

```
void inc(x)
int x;
{
    x++;
}
```

and inc() was called by the following program:

```
int y = 1;
inc(y);
printf("%d\n",y);
```

then the program would print a 1, not a 2. This is because in C the *value* of y is *copied* into the argument x, and the statement x++ increments this copy, leaving the value of y unchanged. This treatment of function arguments is known as *call by value*.

To do this correctly in C, the program must explicitly pass a pointer as the argument to inc():

```
void inc(x)
int* x;
{
    *x++;
}
```

```
int y = 1;
inc(&y);
printf("%d\n",y);
```

Notice that the program had to be changed in three ways:

- The type of the function argument was changed from an int to an int*.
- Each occurrence of the argument in the body of the function was changed from x to *x.
- Each call of the function was changed from inc(y) to inc(&y).

The point is that passing a pointer as a function argument requires consistency in every usage of the argument within the function body and, worse yet, in every call of the function made by client programs. This, combined with C's lack of function argument type checking, results in ample opportunity for error.

Using a C++ reference, the function inc() can be written:

```
void inc(int& x)
{
    x++;
}


int y = 1;
inc(y);
printf("%d\n",y);
```

This requires changing only the argument type from int to int&.

In the function inc(), the argument x is passed using a reference because its value is modified by the function. But efficiency is another reason for passing arguments by reference. When the value of an argument requires a lot of storage, as in the case of BigInts, it is less expensive to pass a pointer to the argument, even though its value is not to be changed. That's why the argument to BigInt was declared as const BigInt&—the reference BigInt& causes just a pointer to the argument to be passed, but the const prevents that pointer from being used to change the argument's value from within the function.

The Addition Operator

Here is a first draft of the function operator+, which implements BigInt addition:

```
BigInt BigInt::operator+(const BigInt& n)
{
// Calculate maximum possible number of digits in sum
    int maxDigits = (ndigits>n.ndigits ? ndigits : n.ndigits)+1;
    char* sumPtr = new char[maxDigits];      // allocate storage for sum
    BigInt sum(sumPtr,maxDigits);            // must define this constructor
    int i = maxDigits;
    int carry = 0;
    while (i--) {
        *sumPtr = /*next digit of this*/ + /*next digit of n*/ + carry;
        if (*sumPtr > 10) {
            carry = 1;
            *sumPtr -= 10;
```

```
        }
        else carry = 0;
        sumPtr++;
    }
    return sum;
}
```

Two BigInts are added by using the paper-and-pencil method taught in grammar school: add the digits of each operand from right to left, beginning with the rightmost, and also add a possible carry in from the previous column. If the sum is greater than 10, subtract 10 from the result and produce a carry.

The BigInt(char*,int) Constructor

The first draft of the addition function has a couple of problems, which are indicated with comments in the code. The first problem is that an instance of BigInt named sum must be declared to hold the result of the addition, which will be left in the array pointed to by sumPtr. A constructor must be used to create this instance of BigInt, but neither of the two defined thus far are suitable, so a third is necessary.

This new constructor takes a pointer to an array containing the digits and the number of digits in the array as arguments and creates a BigInt from them. Client programs shouldn't use such an unsafe and implementation-dependent function, so it is declared in the private part of class BigInt where it can only be used by member functions. The declaration:

```
BigInt(char*,int);
```

is added just before the keyword public: in the declaration of class BigInt in the file BigInt.h, and the implementation of this constructor is added to the file BigInt.c:

```
BigInt::BigInt(char* d, int n)
{
    digits = d;
    ndigits = n;
}
```

Class DigitStream

The second problem is that scanning the digits of the operands in the statement:

```
*sump = /*next digit of this*/ + /*next digit of n*/ + carry;
```

becomes complicated because one of the operands may contain fewer digits than the other, in which case it must be padded to the left with zeros. This problem also occurs during implementation of BigInt subtraction, multiplication, and division, so it is worthwhile to find a clean solution: an abstract data type!

Here is the declaration for class DigitStream and the implementation of its member functions:

```
class DigitStream {
    char* dp;                        // pointer to current digit
    int nd;                          // number of digits remaining
public:
    DigitStream(const BigInt& n);    // constructor
    int operator++();                // return current digit and advance
};

DigitStream::DigitStream(BigInt& n)
{
    dp = n.digits;
    nd = n.ndigits;
}

int DigitStream::operator++()
{
    if (nd == 0) return 0;
    nd--;
    return *dp++;
}
```

An instance of a DigitStream can now be declared for each of the operands and the ++ operator can be used when it's needed to read the next digit.

With these two problems solved, the implementation of the BigInt addition operator looks like:

```
BigInt BigInt::operator+(const BigInt& n)
{
    int maxDigits = (ndigits>n.ndigits  ? ndigits : n.ndigits)+1;
    char* sumPtr = new char[maxDigits];
    BigInt sum(sumPtr,maxDigits);
    DigitStream a(*this);
    DigitStream b(n);
    int i = maxDigits;
```

```
    int carry = 0;
    while (i--) {
        *sumPtr = a++ + b++ + carry;
        if (*sumPtr > 10) {
            carry = 1;
            *sumPtr -= 10;
        }
        else carry = 0;
        sumPtr++;
    }
    return sum;
}
```

Friends

The abstract data type DigitStream looks quite elegant, but you may be wondering how the constructor DigitStream(const BigInt&) is able to access the member variables digits and ndigits of class BigInt. After all, digits and ndigits are private, and DigitStream(const BigInt&) is not a member function of class BigInt.

Well, it can't. There must be a way to grant access to these variables to just this one function. C++ provides a way to do this—making this constructor a friend of class BigInt by adding the declaration:

```
friend DigitStream::DigitStream(const BigInt&);
```

to the declaration of class BigInt.

Programmers can also make *all* of the member functions of one class friends of another by declaring the entire class as a friend. For example, all of the member functions of class DigitStream are made friends of class BigInt by placing the declaration:

```
friend DigitStream;
```

in the declaration of class BigInt.

The Keyword this

Going back to the implementation of the function operator+(), you may be wondering where the pointer variable this came from in the declaration:

```
DigitStream a(*this);
```

The paper earlier described how the members of the instance for which a member function was called could re referred to without using the . or -> operators within the body of a member function. C++ also provides the keyword this so that the entire instance can be referred to as a unit. The keyword this is essentially a pointer to this instance and for this example may be thought of as a variable of type BigInt*. Thus, the declaration DigitStream a(*this) creates an instance of DigitStream for the left operand of operator+().

The Member Function BigInt::print()

The implementation of the member function print() is straightforward:

```
void BigInt::print()
{
    int i;
    for (i = ndigits-1; i >= 0; i--) printf("%d",digits[i]);
}
```

It loops through the digits array from the most significant through the least significant digits, calling the standard C library function printf() to print each digit.

The BigInt Destructor

The only thing that the BigInt destructor function ~BigInt() must do is free the dynamic storage allocated by the constructors:

```
BigInt::~BigInt()
{
    delete digits;
}
```

This is done using the C++ delete operator, which in this case frees the dynamic storage that is pointed to by digits. The delete operator does what is usually accomplished in C by calling the standard C library function free, but in addition, if delete is used to deallocate an instance of a class having a destructor function, the destructor is called automatically to finalize the instance just before its storage is freed. The delete operator is thus the inverse of the new operator.

Inline Functions

By now you may be thinking that the overhead of calling all of these little member functions must make C++ inefficient. This would be unacceptable for a proper successor to C, which is renowned for its efficiency! So C++ allows a function to be `inline`, in which case each call of the function is replaced by a copy of the entire function, much like the substitution performed for the `#define` preprocessor command. This entirely eliminates the overhead of calling a function and makes encapsulation practical.

To make a function such as `~BigInt()` inline, its implementation is moved from the file `BigInt.c` to the file `BigInt.h` and the keyword `inline` is added to the function definition:

```
inline BigInt::~BigInt()
{
    delete digits;
}
```

The function definition must be in `BigInt.h`, because it will be needed by the compiler whenever a client program uses a `BigInt`.

Small functions make the best candidates for inline compilation. C++ has a convenient shorthand for writing `inline` functions: the function body can be included in the function declaration within the `class` declaration. Thus, `~BigInt()` can be made `inline` by writing:

```
~BigInt() { delete digits; }
```

in the declaration of class `BigInt`.

Here is a complete version of `BigInt.h` showing appropriate functions made `inline`:

```
#include <stdio.h>
class BigInt {
    char* digits;                   // pointer to digit array in free store
    int ndigits;                    // number of digits
    BigInt(char* d, int n) {        // constructor function
        digits = d;
        ndigits = n;
    }
    friend DigitStream;
public:
    BigInt(const char*);            // constructor function
    BigInt(int);                    // constructor function
    BigInt(const BigInt&);          // initialization constructor function
```

```
        BigInt operator+(const BigInt&);    // addition operator function
        void print();                       // printing function
        ~BigInt() { delete digits; }        // destructor function
};
class DigitStream {
        char* dp;                           // pointer to current digit
        int nd;                             // number of digits remaining
public:
        DigitStream(const BigInt& n) {      // constructor function
                dp = n.digits;
                nd = n.ndigits;
        }
        int operator++() {                  // return current digit and advance
                if (nd == 0) return 0;
                nd--;
                return *dp++;
        }
};
```

Summary of the BigInt Data Type

This completes the sample abstract data type BigInt. To review the C++ features presented in this section:

- With the *scope resolution operator* the class can be specified when one or more classes have member variables or functions with the same name.

- *Constant types* are used to protect variables of function arguments from unintended modification.

- *Implicit member variable references* and the keyword this are used within member functions to access the instance for which the function is called.

- The new and delete operators manage the free storage area and call class constructors/destructors if present.

- *References* are used to pass pointers conveniently to instances instead of the instances themselves as function arguments.

- Using *friends,* access to the private member variables and functions of a class is granted to other functions and classes

- *Inline functions* make data abstraction in C++ efficient and practical.

Other Uses for Abstract Data Types

BigInt is an obvious application for the technique of data abstraction because it is a numeric data type, like int, and it is natural to extend the meanings of C++'s arithmetic operators to apply to BigInts. As you become more familiar with this technique, you'll discover many opportunities for using abstract data types in your programs. Following are a few examples.

Dynamic Character Strings

A dynamic (that is, variable-length) character string abstract data type can be defined to work like the string variables in languages such as BASIC. The operators & and &= can be overloaded to concatenate character strings; the relational operators <, <=, ==, and so on can be overloaded to compare character strings; and the array subscript operator [] can be overloaded to address the individual characters of a string. The function call operator:

```
operator() (int position, int length)
```

can be overloaded to perform substring extraction and replacement.

Complex Numbers

C++, like C, doesn't have a built-in complex data type, but it's easy to define one in C++. In fact, one is distributed with the C++ compiler. Class complex has two member variables of type double that hold the real and imaginary parts of a complex number, and all of the usual arithmetic operators are overloaded to perform complex arithmetic when applied to instances of class complex. Many of the functions in the math library, such as cos() and sqrt(), are overloaded for complex arguments.

Vectors

Vectors are another useful abstract data type. Classes for vectors of the fundamental data types, such as FloatVec, DoubleVec, and IntVec can be defined, and the arithmetic operators can be overloaded to apply element-by-element to vectors. The array subscript operator [] can be overloaded to check the range of vector subscripts or to handle vectors with arbitrary subscript bounds. It's also possible to overload the function call operator () to subscript multidimensional arrays.

Stream I/O

A stream I/O package is distributed with the C++ compiler that defines the classes istream (input stream) and ostream (output stream) for doing formatted I/O. Class istream defines an instance named cin connected to the standard input file and overloads the operator >> for all the fundamental data types so the code:

```
float x;
int i;
char* s;
cin >> x >> i >> s;
```

can read a float, and int, and a character string from the standard input file, for example. The advantage of this over using the C library function scanf() is that it is not possible to make the following types of errors:

```
int i;
scanf("%f",&i);    // float format for int
scanf("%d",i);     // int instead of int*
```

Similarly, class ostream defines an instance named cout connected to the standard output file and an instance named cerr connected to the standard error file. It overloads the operator << for all the fundamental data types so:

```
cout << x << i << s;
```

will write a float, and int, and a character string to the standard output file.

Programmers can also add overloaded definitions of the operators >> and << for classes they've written so programs can read or write instances of these classes using the same notation.

Object-Oriented Programming in C++

Perhaps the most interesting features of C++ are those that support the style of programming known as *object-oriented* programming. Object-oriented programming is generally useful, but it's particularly suited for interactive graphics, simulation, and systems programming applications.

Derived Classes

Suppose a C++ class defines an abstract data type, and another abstract data type that is similar to it is needed. Perhaps it requires some additional member variables or functions, or a few of its member functions must do something differently. It's desirable to reuse the code already written and debugged as much as possible. C++ provides a simple way to accomplish this: the new class can be declared as a *derived class* of the existing class, called the *base class*. The derived class *inherits* all of the member variables and functions of its base class. The derived class can be differentiated from its base class by adding member variables, adding member functions, or redefining member functions inherited from the base class.

A base class may have more than one derived class, and a derived class may, in turn, serve as the base class for other derived classes. Thus, an entire tree-structured arrangement of related classes is possible. This provides a coherent way to organize classes and to share common code among them.

Virtual Functions

Now suppose programmers are writing a graphics package, including some classes for various geometric shapes, such as Line, Triangle, Rectangle, and Circle. All of these classes implement some of the same member functions, for example draw() and move(). The relevant class declarations for class Line and class Circle would look like this:

```
class Line {
        int x1,y1,x2,y2;                        // end point coordinates
public:
        Line(int xx1,int yy1,int xx2,int yy2)   // constructor
            { x1=xx1; y1=yy1; x2=xx2; y2=yy2; }
        void draw();                            // draw a line from (x1,y1) to (x2,y2)
        void move(int dx, int dy);              // move line by amount dx,dy
};


class Circle {
        int x,y;                                // center of circle
        int r;                                  // radius of circle
public:
        Circle(int xx,int yy,int rr)            // constructor
            { x=xx; y=yy; r=rr; }
        void draw();                            // draw circle with center (x,y) and radius r
```

```
    void move(int dx, int dy);              // move circle by amount dx,dy
};
```

These related classes should fill a couple of needs. First, it would be useful to have an abstract data type called Picture that would be a collection of Lines, Triangles, Rectangles, and Circles. Second, it should be possible to draw() and move() Pictures.

It would be most elegant if class Picture were general and contained no mention of the specific shapes. That way, a new shape, say a Pentagon, could be introduced without changing class Picture in any way.

To do this, a base class Shape is defined with derived classes Line, Triangle, and so on; Figure 6–6 shows how.

Class Shape declares functions applicable to any kind of shape (such as draw() and move()) as virtual functions and implements these functions to write out an error message if called:

```
class Shape {
public:
    virtual void draw();                // Shape::draw() prints error  message
    virtual void move(int dx, int dy);  // Shape::move() prints  error message
};
```

Declarations of classes Line, Triangle, and so forth are changed to be derived from class Shape by adding the name of the base class to the declaration of the derived class; for example:

```
class Line : public Shape { ...
class Circle : public Shape { ...
```

and the keyword virtual is added to the declarations of the functions draw() and move() in the derived classes. The implementation of these functions, however, does not have to change.

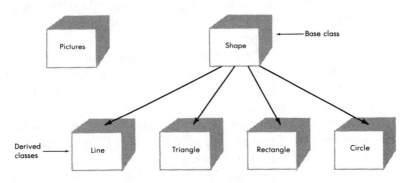

Figure 6–6   Organization of Classes for a Graphics Package

Now class Picture can be written to deal only with Shapes. A Picture can be represented by an array containing pointers to its component Shapes, and Picture::draw(), for example, can be implemented simply by calling Shape::draw() for each shape in the picture:

```
const int PICTURE_CAPACITY = 100;    // max number of shapes in picture
class Picture {
     Shape* s[PICTURE_CAPACITY];     // array of  pointers to shapes
     int n;                          // current number of shapes in picture
public:
     Picture() { n = 0; }            // constructor
     void add(const Shape&);         // add shape to picture
     void draw();                    // draw picture
     void move(int dx, int dy);      // move picture
};


void Picture::add(const Shape& t)    // add a shape to a picture
{
     if (n == PICTURE_CAPACITY) {
          cerr << "Picture capacity exceeded\n";
          exit(1);
     }
     s[n++] = &t;                    // add pointer to shape to picture
}


void Picture::draw()                 // draw a picture
{
     int i;
     for (i=0; i<n; i++)  s[i]->draw();
}
```

Because Shape::draw() is a virtual function, C++ takes care of figuring out the specific class of each component Shape when the program is executed and calling the appropriate implementation of draw() for that class. This is called *dynamic binding*.

If draw() is mistakenly not implemented for a derived class of Shape, it will inherit the implementation of draw() from class Shape. When a program tries to draw that shape, Shape::draw() will be executed, which issues an error message, as you'll recall.

Going a step further, a programmer might want to be able to build a more complicated picture out of a number of simpler pictures. This is done by thinking of a Picture as just another type of Shape and making it another derived class of class Shape, leading to the class structure shown in Figure 6–7.

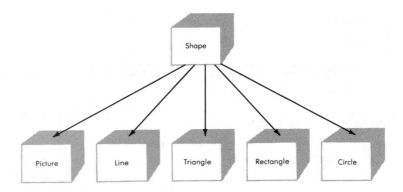

Figure 6–7   Improved Organization of Classes for a Graphics Package

Class Libraries

Taking this technique to its extreme, a class named, say, Object can be defined, and *every* class can be derived from it, either directly or indirectly. In class Object virtual functions can be declared that apply to all classes—functions for copying, printing, storing, reading, and comparing objects, for example. Then programs can define general data structures composed of Objects and functions that operate on them that will be useful for all classes, just as class Picture could work with any derived class of Shape.

I have written a library of about 40 general-purpose classes, modeled after the basic classes of the Smalltalk-80 programming language. The library, known as the Object-Oriented Program Support (OOPS) class library, contains classes such as String, Date, Time, Set (hash tables), Dictionary (associative arrays), and LinkedList.

Writing C++ programs using a class library such as this is a real delight. The classes are general-purpose, and most programs of any size will have uses for some of them. They are flexible—if a particular class doesn't quite do what is needed, it's usually a simple matter to derive a class that does. And the library is extendable. It provides a framework that makes it easy to add custom classes and make them function along with existing ones.

As an example, look at how the OOPS class library can help with the graphics package discussed here. The OOPS library has a class Point for representing x–y coordinates. It can be used in graphics classes such as Line:

```
class Line : public Shape {
    Point a,b;                              // endpoints of the line
public:
    Line(Point p1, Point p2) { a=p1; b=p2; }   // constructor
    void draw();                            // draw a line from point a to point b
```

```
        void move(Point delta);                    // move line by delta
};
```

Many of the arithmetic operators are defined by class Point, so move(), for example, can be implemented by writing:

```
void Line::move(Point delta)
{
    a += delta;  b += delta;
}
```

The crude implementation of class Picture allocated an array of fixed size to hold the pointers to its component shapes. By using the OOPS library class OrderedCltn this can easily be made a variable-length array. An OrderedCltn is an array of pointers to Objects, so it can hold pointers to instances of any class derived from Object, just as an array of pointers to Shapes was used to hold pointers to Lines, Triangles, and so on. To make class Shape a derived class of Object, its declaration is modified as follows:

```
class Shape : public Object { ...
```

Now class Picture can be written as:

```
class Picture : public Shape {
    OrderedCltn s;  // collection of pointers to shapes
public:
    Picture() {}                           // constructor
    virtual void add(const Shape&);        // add shape to picture
    virtual void draw();                   // draw picture
    virtual void move(Point delta);        // move picture
};
```

Class OrderedCltn defines member functions such as add(), remove(), size(), first(), and last() so the pointers in the array can be manipulated. It also overloads the subscript operator [] so it can subscript OrderedCltns like arrays. Using these, the functions Picture::add() and Picture::draw can be written as follows:

```
void Picture::add(const Shape& t)     // add a shape to a picture
{
    s.add(t);                         // this calls OrderedCltn::add()
}


void Picture::draw()                  // draw a picture
```

```
{
    int i;
    for (i=0; i<s.size(); i++)      // s.size() returns # of objects in s
        ((Shape*)&s[i])->draw();    // cast address of ith Object
                                    // to Shape* and call draw()
}
```

Now Pictures can have as many shapes in them as needed; class OrderedCltn manages the required storage.

Object I/O

This program uses the graphics classes just discussed to create a simple picture composed of two shapes—a line and a circle:

```
main()
{
    Picture pict;
    pict.add(*new Line(Point(0,0),Point(10,10)));
    pict.add(*new Circle(Point(10,10),2));
    pict.draw();
}
```

The first statement in the body of main() declares an instance of class Picture named pict; the second statement constructs an instance of Line with end-points at (0,0) and (10,10) and adds it to pict, and the third statement constructs an instance of Circle with the center at (10,10) and radius 2 and also adds it to pict. The result is the data structure shown in Figure 6–8.

What if a programmer wanted to save this data structure on a disk file so it could be read in later and used by another program? The OOPS class library makes this simple. The programmer would create an output stream (an instance of class ostream) named, for example, out, and write the picture to it with the statements:

```
ostream out(creat("picturefile",0664));   // create "picturefile" with protection 0664
pict.storeOn(out);
```

The function storeOn(), which is implemented in class Object, handles the details of finding all of the objects in the picture data structure and writing them to the output stream in a program-independent, machine-independent format. The storeOn() function calls the virtual function storer() to actually write out member variables. The storer() function is declared in class Object and is reimplemented by each derived class to write out its

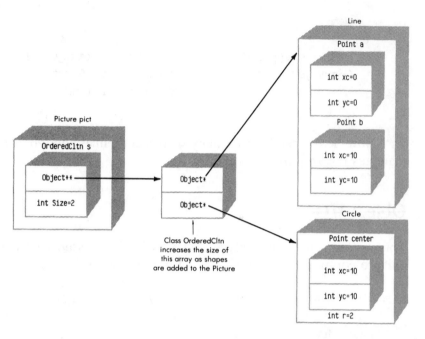

Figure 6–8   The Data Structure of a Simple Picture in Which Instances of OOPS Library Classes Are Shown as Shaded Rectangles

own member variables. This function is already implemented for all of the OOPS library classes, but one must be written for any added classes derived from class Object. That's easy to do. For example, the storer() function for class Picture looks like:

```
void Picture::storer(ostream& strm)
{
    Shape::storer(strm);    // store members of base class, if any
    s.storeOn(strm);        // store member of class Picture
}
```

To read a picture from a file, an input stream, in (an instance of class istream), is connected to the file to be read, and the picture is read from it with the statements:

```
istream in(open("picturefile",O_RDONLY));    // open "picturefile" read-only
readFrom(in,"Picture",pict);
```

The second argument tells readFrom() that it should expect an instance of class Picture to be read, and to complain if the next object on the input stream is of any other class.

The function readFrom() works somewhat like storeOn(), calling a small "reader" function that must be written for each class.

OOPS object I/O can be used to store and read an arbitrarily complex data structure containing instances of both OOPS library classes and the programmer's own classes. Since the data structure is converted into a program-independent, machine-independent format, it can be sent through a UNIX pipe to another process running on the same machine or over a network to another process running on a different kind of machine. This capability is particularly useful for spreadsheets, forms, documents, drawings, electronic mail, and so on. The OOPS class library also provides a framework to use when programmers implement object I/O for their own classes. Programmers don't have to spend time designing a storage format or worry about such issues as what to do with the pointers in a data structure, for example. They can use the general-purpose mechanism provided by the OOPS class library and concentrate on their particular application.

Further Reading on Object-Oriented Programming

For further information on object-oriented programming, the following reading is suggested:

B. Stroustrup, *The C++ Programming Language* (Reading Mass.: Addison-Wesley, 1986). This is the C++ "bible." It describes the basics of using derived classes and virtual functions for object-oriented programming.

B. Cox, *Object-oriented Programming* (Reading, Mass.: Addison-Wesley, 1986). The first three chapters of this book give an easy-to-read, entertaining introduction to object-oriented programming. The information in Table 3.1 on C++ is not correct, however. It is not impossible to add multiple inheritance to C++ (experimental implementations exist), activation/passivation is available, and C++ is now a commercial product.

Byte 6, no. 8 (August 1981). An overview and introduction to the Smalltalk-80 environment.

T. Kaehler and D. Patterson, *A Taste of Smalltalk* (New York: W. W. Norton & Co., 1986). A good introduction to programming in Smalltalk-80.

A. Goldberg and D. Robson, *Smalltalk-80: The Language and Its Implementation* (Reading, Mass.: Addison-Wesley, 1983). The authoritative work on object-oriented programming and the Smalltalk-80 language. Advanced reading!

The Current Status of C++

The C++ programming language is currently implemented as a *translator*, which accepts C++ source code as input and produces C source code as output. The C++ translator and run-time support library are written in C++, making them easily portable to most UNIX systems.

AT&T first made the C++ translator available to universities and non-profit organizations in December 1984. Release 1.0 became commercially available as an unsupported product in November 1985; the most recent update, release 1.2, was issued in April 1987.

The AT&T C++ Translator can run on your UNIX machine capable of running programs up to about 500K bytes in size, and having a robust C compilation system that can handle variable and external symbol names of arbitrary length. The C compiler must also allow structure assignments and the use of structures as function arguments and return values.

Training and third-party supported ports of the AT&T C++ Translator can be obtained for various UNIX systems, VAX VMS, MS-DOS, and others.

The Future of C++

The definition of the C++ programming language is not yet final. When the ANSI C standard is completed, C++ will undoubtedly be revised to eliminate any unnecessary incompatibilities; for example, the ANSI C rules for doing floating point arithmetic will be adopted. Historically, C++ has met the challenge of evolving while remaining compatible with C and earlier versions of C++.

Will the C++ programming language be as successful as its predecessor, or will it become just another of the countless languages that never achieve widespread use? Well, C++ has a lot going for it:

- Since C++ is, with a few minor exceptions, a superset of C, it has no fatal deficiencies. It also possesses those attributes of C that have contributed to C's success: portability, flexibility, and efficiency.

- C++ is less error-prone than C. It thoroughly type-checks programs, as is the trend in modern programming languages, but not at the expense of flexibility or convenience. A programmer may coerce (cast) types when necessary and define his or her own implicit type conversions for convenience.

- Support for data abstraction and object-oriented programming make C++ a much more powerful and expressive language than C. Yet the language remains one of manageable size, much smaller than PL/1 or Ada, for example.

- C++ programs are compatible with UNIX and with the large number of existing C libraries for graphics, database management, math, and statistics.

- There is a large existing community of C programmers who can begin to use C++ immediately, gradually learning and using its new features.

- The AT&T C++ Translator is commercially available in source form, is inexpensive, and is highly portable. It makes the language accessible on almost all popular operating systems.

- AT&T is developing a portable C++ compiler, which will compile C++ programs more quickly than the combination of the C++ Translator and C compiler now required.

- C++ was designed at the AT&T Bell Laboratories Computer Science Research Center in Murray Hill. They have an impressive track record in producing successful software, such as UNIX and C.

The main obstacle to the widespread adoption of C++ is that to realize its benefits one must master the techniques of data abstraction and/or object-oriented programming—techniques that are unfamiliar to the current generation of programmers. When this educational problem is solved, C++ should succeed C as the language of choice for a wide range of applications.

Acknowledgments

I would like to thank Bjarne Stroustrup of AT&T Bell Laboratories, Perry Plexico of the National Institutes of Health, and Sandy Orlow of Systex, Inc. for their many helpful comments that greatly improved the content and readability of this paper. My time and the computer facilities required to prepare this paper were provided by the Computer Systems Laboratory, Division of Computer Research and Technology, National Institutes of Health.

KEYWORDS

▶ Buffer cache

▶ Block mode

▶ Character mode

▶ Disabling

▶ Interrupt

▶ RAM disk

Paper Synopsis: A complete tutorial on XENIX and UNIX device drivers, this paper reveals driver theory, then shows how to write and test drivers. Both character-mode and block-mode drivers are covered. Driver functions are followed from the user level into the kernel's data structures and finally to the device.

George Pajari is a consultant with Clarendon Datex Ltd., Toronto, Canada, and has worked with UNIX and C for 10 years, writing device drivers for almost as long.

He has developed many drivers and kernel performance improvements for UNIX systems, implementing software for devices ranging from intelligent communications controllers to multiprocessor flight simulation systems.

## 7

Device Drivers Under UNIX

George E. Pajari

*D*evice drivers are the translators of the UNIX operating system kernel. They stand between the kernel and peripherals (such as disks and terminals), translating requests for work into activity by the hardware.

This paper presents a detailed overview of what a device driver is and how it works. It starts by taking an overview of a simple UNIX device driver. Once you have a general understanding of what a device driver is, you will study excerpts from working drivers in order to gain a clearer and more detailed understanding of UNIX device drivers.

The drivers discussed in this paper were developed for XENIX System V, release 2. Although other versions of UNIX may differ slightly in the details (such as the names of include files and some kernel functions and data structures), the substance will remain the same. In all cases, this paper is intended to supplement and not replace the documentation accompanying your UNIX system.

Overview

What is a device? Well, any peripheral such as a graphics display, disk drive, terminal, or printer is a device. A device is usually considered to be a piece of hardware that you can connect to your computer system and that you wish to manipulate by sending commands and data.

What is a device driver? A device driver is a collection of functions (subroutines) that

RELATED PAPERS

1 UNIX: Rights and Wrongs

8 Remote File Systems, Streams, and Transport Level Interface

9 Ethernet: A UNIX LAN

10 Real-Time UNIX

accept general requests for I/O operations and manipulate the device to perform the requested operation.

Under UNIX every device is managed by device driver functions. This group of functions is compiled as part of the UNIX kernel. The UNIX kernel contains all of the device drivers as well as the code that handles the user's requests for operating system services such as input/output, starting and controlling processes, and so on. Figure 7–1 shows high-level kernel functions and some driver functions that would be included in the kernel to enable the use of a line printer, a RAM disk, and other devices.

What a Driver Does

Now take a look at what a device driver actually does by examining a moment in the life of a line printer driver. This device was chosen because its driver is relatively simple, yet it demonstrates most of the important functions of a driver.

For this example, consider a UNIX user trying to print the date and time on the line printer by typing on the terminal:

```
date > /dev/lp
```

The first step UNIX takes is to analyze this line and to determine that:

1. a program date is to be run

2. a file named /dev/lp is to be opened

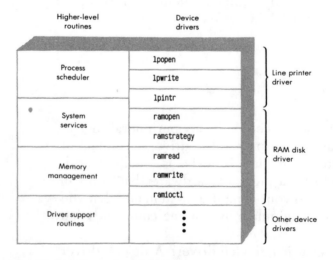

Figure 7–1 The UNIX Kernel and Device Drivers

3. any output from date written to the standard output file is to be redirected to /dev/lp

When UNIX goes to open /dev/lp, it finds that this is a special file (devices are treated by UNIX as special files rather than ordinary data files). UNIX looks it up in a table inside the kernel to see which driver is handling requests directed to this device (special file).

In this case, it would find the line printer driver. Furthermore, since UNIX is trying to open the device, the kernel calls the lpopen function within the device driver.

The lpopen function performs those functions that are required prior to the line printer being used. These functions might include:

1. checking to see that the line printer exists and is turned on
2. resetting the line printer
3. marking the line printer "in use" so that no one else can use the line printer at the same time

Recall that because the command was given to the shell with redirection (>), UNIX has redirected all output destined for the standard output to the /dev/lp file. When the program goes to write to the standard output, UNIX recognizes this as a request to write to the device and calls the lpwrite function within the line printer driver.

The lpwrite function copies the data to be printed into a buffer within the kernel. If the buffer is full or fills up before all of the data has been copied, then the driver puts the date program to sleep (suspends execution) until the buffer has emptied.

The driver then takes the first character from the buffer and delivers it to the line printer. At some later time (measured in fractions of a second) the line printer will have printed the character and will interrupt the kernel. When the CPU receives this interrupt signal, it puts aside the work it was doing to handle the interrupt. The kernel determines that the interrupt was signaled by the line printer and calls the line printer driver to handle it.

The lpintr routine is given the chore of determining why the interrupt happened and taking whatever action is appropriate. In this instance, the interrupt was caused by the line printer finishing the work it was given. The driver detects that the line printer is now ready for another character and that more characters are in the buffer. It then takes the next character from the buffer and delivers it to the line printer. This cycle repeats until all of the characters have been printed.

The example concludes with termination of the date program. This signals UNIX to close all of the files the process had opened. When UNIX goes to close the /dev/lp file, it again calls on the driver to perform the actual operation.

The lpclose routine performs those operations that ought to occur when the printer is no longer to be used by this program. In this example, operations could include marking the printer as available for use by other programs.

As you have seen, the device driver is the middleman between the UNIX kernel and the device itself. UNIX takes I/O requests from programs, determines which device they are intended for, and passes them to the appropriate driver to perform. The device driver handles the details of the interaction with the hardware and reports the results to the kernel upon completion of the operation. Figure 7–2 summarizes the flow of events from the time the process begins to the time the characters are printed.

The Two Types of Device Drivers

Now look at the two major types of drivers and the interface between the kernel and the device driver. A single device may have either or both types of driver.

Block-Mode Drivers

A block-mode driver is one that treats the device as a set of sequential blocks of data. UNIX will assume that all I/O must be performed on blocks and will issue requests to the driver to read and write blocks of data.

The block-mode driver model was designed for disk drives, but it also can work well with tape drives and other storage media. One feature of block-mode drivers is that they perform all I/O using block-sized buffers from the kernel's buffer cache. This is necessary to support a UNIX file system on the disk. Figure 7–3 shows what is involved in data transfer using a block-mode device driver.

The kernel issues requests to the device driver by calling one of the functions (entry points) in the driver.

These are the entry points used by the kernel for block-mode drivers:

open—called when any process starts to use the device

close—called when the last process is finished with the device

strategy—called to read or write a block of data to/from a buffer

---

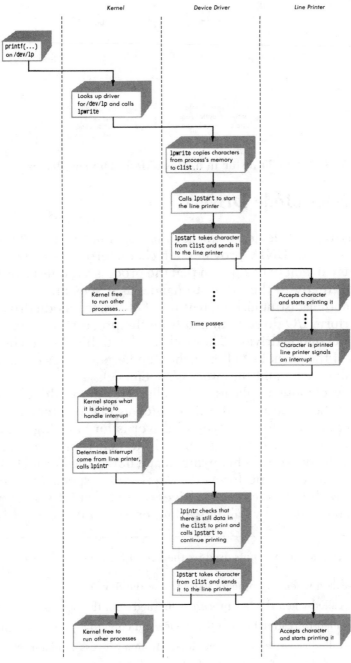

Figure 7–2   How a Message Is Printed

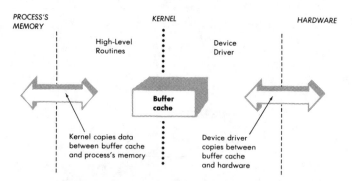

Figure 7–3   Data Transfer in a Block-Mode Device Driver

Character-Mode Drivers

For any type of device or driver that does not fit the block-mode model just described, UNIX provides for character-mode drivers. This type of driver is extremely flexible, in that the process's requests for I/O are passed almost directly to the driver to handle as it sees fit.

Another distinguishing feature of character-mode drivers is that they can perform I/O directly to and from the process's memory. Contrast this with block-mode drivers. They only deal with block-sized buffers provided as part of the kernel's buffer cache (the kernel copies the data to and from the buffer cache and the process's memory).

One obvious application for character-mode drivers is devices that handle data a character at a time, such as line printers and terminals.

Another use for this type of driver is for very high-performance devices that need to copy data directly to and from the process's memory without the overhead of copying in and out of the kernel buffers first. This can provide a high-performance interface for specialized requirements.

As with the block-mode driver, the kernel interfaces with the character-mode driver by calling certain entry points in the driver.

These are the entry points used by the kernel for character-mode drivers:

open—called when any process starts to use the device

close—called when the last process is finished with the device

read—called to read data from the device and copy to a process's memory

write—called to write data to the device from a process's memory

ioctl—called to perform special device control functions

Sometimes a block-oriented device will provide a character-mode driver along with a block-mode driver just so that an ioctl entry point is available. As you will see, the ioctl entry point is a very flexible method of performing unusual I/O requests.

Figure 7–4 shows two types of data transfers using character-mode drivers. The examples are a RAM disk driver and a printer driver. The RAM disk uses direct transfer, while the line printer uses a buffer.

Interrupt Handling

Interrupts are exactly that: signals from devices to the computer indicating that they want attention. Usually the interrupt signals that an I/O request is complete and that the device is now ready for the next operation.

When an interrupt is signaled, the CPU first checks to see if the interrupt is currently permitted. If so, the kernel is forced to stop executing whatever it is running (either a user process or part of the kernel itself)

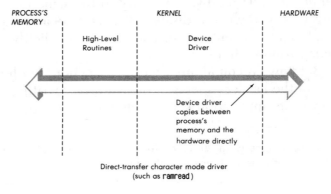

A. Direct-Transfer Character-Mode Driver (such as ramread)

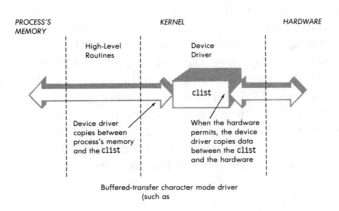

B. Buffered-Transfer Character-Mode Driver (such as pwrite)

Figure 7–4   Data Transfer in a Character-Mode Device Driver

and to start processing the interrupt. For the most part the interrupt processing will be handled by the device driver, which will check on the just-completed operation and assign the next operation (if one is waiting).

There are two very important things to remember about interrupts. They may occur at any time and, unless disabled, can interrupt the execution of the kernel or device drivers. In fact, it is possible for an interrupt to occur for a device while the device driver is working on another request. Unless properly handled, this interrupt can hopelessly confuse the device driver, leading to incorrect operation or even system crashes.

The other thing to remember is that since an interrupt can occur at any time, the user process that is currently running may or may not be the process that started the I/O operation that caused the interrupt. Therefore, the interrupt handler must not do anything that might affect the operation of the current user process.

One of the primary defenses against these problems is disabling interrupts during critical sections of code. This is achieved by raising the level of the CPU hardware priority to the same or higher level than the interrupt(s) you wish to disable. This is done automatically when the interrupt handler is entered or can be done explicitly using the splx kernel function from within the driver.

But how do you identify a critical section? With great difficulty! This is one of the harder aspects of device-driver writing. The rule is obvious; however, its application is anything but.

A *critical section* is any fragment of code that can malfunction if stopped (such as when a user runs another driver) and continued later.

Some common critical sections are: (1) code that manipulates linked lists; and (2) code that checks a condition and then sleeps until wakened by another routine when it detects that the condition has changed. Note that these rules apply only to single-CPU systems. Critical sections are much harder to recognize and to protect on multiprocessor computers.

To disable interrupts, raise the priority of the CPU to a level equal to or above the priority of the interrupt that you wish to disable. For example, if the device generates interrupts at level five, then raising the priority to level five will disable interrupts from that device.

When you are ready to enable interrupts again, you merely set the priority back to the level it was prior to your disabling interrupts.

The following list shows functions that you use and the following code excerpt illustrates their use.

spl5()—set processor priority to level five

splx(x)—set processor priority to level x

```
/* you must turn off interrupts */
oldpri = spl5();
/* perform critical operation */
splx(oldpri);
```

The Detailed Anatomy of a Device Driver

Now for the real stuff. In this section you look at the insides of two device drivers to see the general requirements for drivers and to illustrate the areas you have covered. Here a line printer driver and a RAM disk driver will serve as the examples.

For each major component in a device driver you will see an example from one of two drivers. Note that some functions are specific to character-mode drivers, while others are specific to block-mode drivers. Table 7–1 indicates the drivers and their associated functions.

Note that although this paper refers to the open, close, and other routines as though they were actual routines, they are really only generic terms describing a type of routine found in a driver. For example, the actual open routine in the line printer driver shown later in this paper is called lpopen. Similarly, the close routine for a floppy disk might be called fdclose.

Some versions of UNIX require additional specialized components such as an init or probe routine. These are frequently optional and are very specific to the version of UNIX being used. For these reasons, they are omitted from this paper.

Table 7–1   Driver Functions and the Type of Driver Required

Driver Component	Character Mode Driver	Block Mode Driver
prologue	X	X
open	X	X
close	X	X
strategy		X
write	X	
read	X	
ioctl	X	

Before proceeding with the drivers in this paper, review the role the driver plays in the path from a user program to the hardware. The driver is called by kernel routines that are responding to the program's request for system services. To help do its job, the driver calls upon appropriate support routines provided by the kernel, using function calls. Finally, the driver directly manipulates the hardware, causing the device to perform the desired function. Figure 7–5 shows how this works schematically.

The Prologue

Before you write your first line of driver code, it is necessary to provide the necessary declarations and definitions. Normally, the prologue for a device driver consists of the following parts:

- include statements for the system definitions and declarations
- definitions of the addresses and contents of the device's registers
- declarations of global variables internal to the driver

The include files that you use will depend on the system tables and services that you require, but Table 7–2 gives a short list of the include

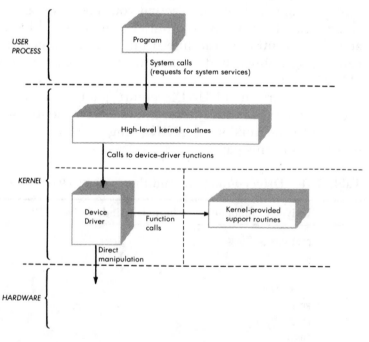

Figure 7–5   How a Process Accesses a Device

Table 7-2   Include Files Used by Device Drivers

Filename	Contents
sys/param.h	Fundamental kernel parameters (always required)
sys/dir.h	Directory structure (required if user.h is used)
sys/user.h	User area (required to access u.u_error)
sys/tty.h	Terminal and clist structures (required for most character-mode drivers)
sys/buf.h	Buffer header layout (required for all block-mode drivers)

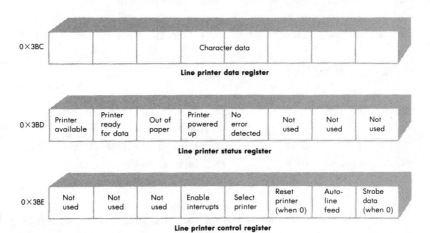

Figure 7-6   The Line Printer Registers

files frequently used by drivers. Many others exist and perusing the contents of the files in the /usr/include/sys directory can be very informative.

You will use the prologue from a character-mode line printer driver to work with this example. First, you must provide the include statements required by this driver:

```
#include <sys/param.h>
#include <sys/dir.h>
#include <sys/user.h>
#include <sys/tty.h>
```

In addition to the include files, you will need to define the location and layout of the device registers. This information is described in the manuals for the device itself. The layout of the device registers for the line printer is given in Figure 7-6.

```
/* The registers for the printer port */

#define  LPBASE     0x03bc         /* base of special I/O addrs */
```

```
#define  LPDATA     (LPBASE + 0)    /* lp data port */
#define  LPSTATUS   (LPBASE + 1)    /* lp status port */
#define  LPCONTROL  (LPBASE + 2)    /* lp control port */


/*  The bits in the printer status port  */


#define  LPERR      0x08            /* printer error detected */
#define  LPON       0x10            /* printer is enabled & online */
#define  LPPAPER    0x20            /* printer is out of paper */
#define  LPREADY    0x40            /* printer is ready for more data */
#define  LPNORMAL   0x80            /* printer is operating normally */


/*  The bits in the printer control port  */


#define  LPSTROBE   0x01            /* strobe the lp to accept data */
#define  LPLF       0x02            /* line feed is remote */
#define  LPINIT     0x04            /* initialize the line-printer */
#define  LPSELECT   0x08            /* select the printer */
#define  LPIENB     0x10            /* interrupt enable */
```

The next set of defines specifies the priority at which the driver is to wait when it is put to sleep and the low- and high-water marks for the clist. (You'll learn more about this data structure later.)

```
/*
 * Define the sleeping priority and when to sleep and wake up
 */


#define  LPPRI  PZERO+5    /* a priority that can still get signals */
#define  LOWAT  50         /* wakeup if clist drops below 50 */
#define  HIWAT  150        /* go to sleep if more than 150 on */
```

The final set of defines for the line printer driver specifies bits in the flag variable lp_flags (declared in the following code). This variable is used by this driver only and serves to indicate when certain conditions are true.

```
/*
 * lp_flags definitions (lp_flags is an internal status flag variable)
 */


#define  SLEEPING  0x01            /* sleeping */
#define  LPBUSY    0x02            /* busy */
```

Finally, you must declare the global variables that you will be using, both those defined elsewhere in the kernel and those that you are defining for your driver only. This driver uses no kernel variables, but declares two variables lp_queue and lp_flags for its own use.

```
struct clist lp_queue;      /* the clist head */
unsigned lp_flags = 0;      /* driver status flags  */
```

The open Routine

The open routine is called every time a process opens the device to perform I/O. The responsibilities of the open routine include:

1. checking to see if the process ought to be permitted to use the device
2. verifying that the device number is valid
3. initializing the device (if appropriate)
4. initializing variables local to the driver

Reasons for not permitting a process to use the device might be for security (only privileged users may access the device) or that the device is already busy and cannot be shared.

The following is an example of an open routine:

```
lpopen(dev)
int dev;
{
        outb(LPDATA, 0);
        outb(LPCONTROL, LPLF | LPINIT | LPSELECT | LPIENB);
}
```

You use the outb routine to initialize the printer by writing the NULL character to the line printer's data register and setting the appropriate bits in the line printer's control register. Figure 7–7 shows what the inb and outb functions do to the line printer registers.

The close Routine

The opposite of the open routine, the close routine is responsible for shutting down the device. One significant difference between the open and close routines is that while the open routine is called every time the device is

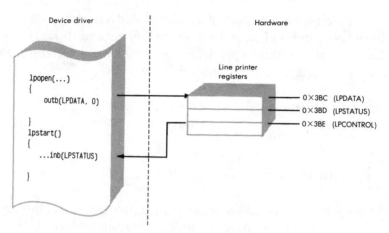

Figure 7-7 The inb and outb Functions

opened, the `close` routine is called only when the last process closes the device.

This routine needs to:

1. shut down the device (if applicable)
2. disable interrupts from the device
3. set internal flags to indicate the device is closed

When the `close` routine is called, you know that there are no other processes currently using the device and so you can shut it down. One thing to be careful of, however, is that while no one else may be using the device, the device may still be busy. It could be finishing the last I/O operation.

Often it is not necessary to perform any operation upon a close. Indeed, neither of the drivers illustrated here uses a `close` routine.

In general, a `close` routine is only required if the driver must take specific actions when the device is no longer in use. Examples of such actions might include:

- marking the device as available for use in the case of an exclusive-use device
- turning off the modem control signals on a serial port to cause the modem to hang up the telephone line

The `strategy` Routine

The `strategy` routine is only found on block-mode drivers and is the routine the kernel calls to perform input or output operations on a block device.

The kernel passes the routine a pointer to a buffer. In the header to the buffer will be information on the type and address of the I/O to be performed. The strategy routine performs the following functions:

1. It verifies that the I/O request is valid.
2. It adds the request to the queue of requests waiting to be performed.
3. It checks if the device is busy, and if not, starts it.

The following example is from a RAM disk driver. The major difference between this type of disk driver and a more traditional device is that owing to the speed of the RAM disk, I/O requests are satisfied immediately rather than being queued.

```
ramstrategy(bp)
struct buf *bp;
{
        register long ramaddr;
        unsigned iosize, disksize, blockno;
        struct ramdiskinfo *rdp;

        /* determine start and size of I/O request and size of disk */

        rdp = &Ramdisk[MINOR(bp->b_dev)];

        blockno = bp->b_blkno;
        iosize = (bp->b_bcount + BMASK) >> BSHIFT;
        disksize = rdp->size >> (BSHIFT-KSHIFT);

        /* check for valid RAM disk and that start and size are OK */

        if ((rdp->flags & ALLOC)
         && (blockno < disksize)
         && ((blockno + iosize < disksize) !! (bp->b_flags & B_READ)))
          {
                /* maybe it is a read that runs off end of disk... */

                if (blockno + iosize > disksize)
                {
                        /* if so, chop it down to size */

                        iosize = disksize - blockno;
                        bp->b_resid = bp->b_bcount - (iosize << BSHIFT);
```

```
                        bp->b_bcount = iosize << BSHIFT;
                }
        }
        else
        {
                /* no good...mark I/O as bad and mop-up */

                bp->b_flags != B_ERROR;
                bp->b_resid = bp->b_bcount;
                iodone(bp);
                return;
        }


        /* compute address in RAM for copy operation and perform copy */

        ramaddr = mltoa(Ramdisk[MINOR(bp->b_dev)].addr)
                    + (bp->b_blkno << BSHIFT);

        if (bp->b_flags & B_READ)
                ramcopy(bp->b_paddr, ramaddr, bp->b_bcount);
        else
                ramcopy(ramaddr, bp->b_paddr, bp->b_bcount);

        /* mark I/O as successful */

        bp->b_resid = 0;
        iodone(bp);
}
```

The single argument to a strategy function is a pointer to a kernel buffer header. The buffer header contains all the information needed by a strategy routine to determine where on disk the data is to be read or written, where in memory the data is to be transferred, and whether this is a read or a write operation.

The kernel buffers (more usually called "the buffer cache" or just "the buffers") are used to hold data being transferred to and from disk or tape. A buffer holds one block of data (a block may be either 512 or 1024 bytes, depending on your UNIX system). The exact size is defined as BSIZE in the include file /usr/include/sys/param.h.

The kernel converts the process's request for disk I/O into requests to the device driver to read or write a block of data. The kernel handles the problem of converting the process's request, which may be for any amount of data starting anywhere on the disk, into a request for one disk block starting at a disk block boundary. All the device driver sees is a request to fill or empty a buffer.

The complete details of the buffer are defined in the include file /usr/include/sys/buf.h. Figure 7–8 shows the most significant variables in the buffer.

Look now at the code for ramstrategy in detail. The assignment to rdp computes a pointer to the appropriate member of Ramdisk based on the device number (which tells the driver which RAM disk to use). A data structure called Ramdisk exists to store the parameters for each RAM disk, such as where in RAM it starts and how large it is. This data structure is shown in Figure 7–9.

b_flags	Write, read, done, busy, error, and so on
b_forw, b_back	Pointers used to form queue of buffers waiting for I/O
av_forw, av_back	Pointers used to form linked list of free buffers
b_dev	Number of device to use
b_bcount	Number of bytes to transfer (usually one block)
b_paddr	Address in memory of actual buffer area
b_blkno	Block on disk to read/write
b_error	Error code if I/O unsuccessful (set by driver)
b_resid	Bytes not transferred in case of error or EOF (set by driver)

Figure 7–8   The Kernel Buffer Data Structure

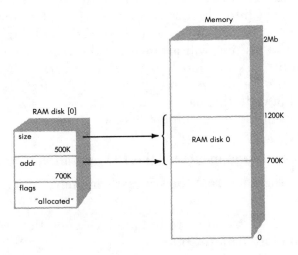

Figure 7–9   The Ramdisk Data Structure

The next three statements calculate the starting block and size of the I/O request as well as the size of the RAM disk.

The if statement checks to see that memory has been allocated for this RAM disk, that the transfer starts before the end of the RAM disk, and that either the transfer finishes before the end of the disk or the transfer is a read operation.

When all of these conditions hold, the transfer is valid. A quick check is then made (the second, nested if) to see if the read operation extends beyond the end of the RAM disk. If so, it is truncated to end at the end of the RAM disk.

When the transfer is invalid, the error flag is set in the buffer header and the I/O operation is marked as complete.

In the case of a valid transfer, you proceed to calculate the address in RAM where the transfer is to occur.

The driver then summons ramcopy (a special assembler routine not listed here) to copy the data from the buffer to the area of RAM being used to emulate the disk. Depending on whether the operation is a read or a write, the driver calls ramcopy either to copy from RAM disk to the buffer or vice versa.

The write Routine

The write routine has to get the data from the process's memory and send it to the device. The write routine is only found in character-mode drivers.

The read and write routines take one of two approaches depending on the type of device and the design of the driver. With character-at-a-time devices such as the line printer, the routine will copy data from the process's memory into a buffer within the driver. This technique is illustrated by the lpwrite routine about to be discussed. With high-speed devices such as disks, the routine will arrange for the data to be transferred directly from the process's memory to the device without using an intermediate buffer within the driver. This approach is illustrated by the ramread routine discussed later in this paper.

A write routine that buffers its data must:

1. check the arguments for the I/O operation for validity

2. copy the data from the process's memory into a buffer within the driver

3. call the start routine to initiate I/O when the buffer is full or there is no more data to copy

4. sleep until the buffer has emptied (if there is more data to write)

To read a byte from a process's memory into the device driver, you use the cpass routine. This routine takes no arguments and returns the next character from the process's memory. When the end of the memory to be written is reached, cpass returns -1. The routine is illustrated in the lpwrite function you are about to examine.

A similar routine called passc exists to write a byte into a process's memory.

To move larger amounts of data, copyio is used. This function takes as argument the source and destination addresses, a byte count, and a direction flag (read or write).

It is far more efficient for the driver to copy 50 to 150 characters from the process at once rather than copying each character as the device is ready for it. What you need, then, is a method of storing a couple of hundred characters at a time.

The UNIX kernel provides an easy method of buffering small amounts of data. This mechanism, called clists, is used by terminal and line printer type drivers to store data copied from the process. The clists are implemented as linked lists and their structure is illustrated by Figure 7–10.

A clist is created by declaring a clist header. Referring back to the prologue for your line printer driver, you declared a clist header for this driver and called it lp_queue.

The kernel routines getc and putc are then used to put characters into the clist and remove them. The clist header itself may be accessed to determine how many characters are stored in the clist.

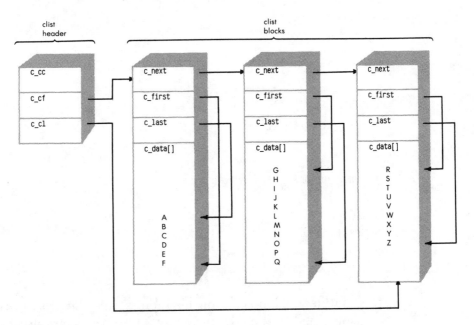

Figure 7–10   The clist Data Structure

The following is taken from the line printer driver.

```
lpwrite(dev)
int dev;
{
        register int c;
        int x;

        /* get a character from the process's memory until no more */

        while ((c = cpass()) >= 0)
        {
                /* is the clist filling up ? */

                if (lp_queue.c_cc > HIWAT)
                {
                        /* yes...start the device and go to sleep */

                        x = spl5();
                        while (lp_queue.c_cc > HIWAT)
                        {
                                lpstart();
                                lp_flags != SLEEPING;
                                sleep(&lp_queue, LPPRI);
                        }
                        splx(x);
                }

                /* put the character on the clist */

                putc(c, &lp_queue);
        }

        /* summon lpstart to start the printer */

        x = spl5();
        lpstart();
        splx(x);
}
```

In this routine you loop copying characters from the process's memory (obtained using cpass) to the clist (using putc) until there are no more characters to copy.

If the computer fills up the clist (more than HIWAT bytes), it calls lpstart to start the line printer. It then sleeps until wakened by lpstart to put more characters into the clist.

The start **Routine**

The start routine is frequently found in both character- and block-mode drivers. Although it is not a driver entry point (it is never called directly by the kernel), it is a common part of most device drivers and therefore deserves attention.

The purpose of the start routine is to take the next request or queued buffer of data and send it to the device. For a character-mode driver the characters will have been placed in clists by the write routine. In the case of block-mode drivers the buffers are queued up by the strategy routine.

The typical start routine:

1. checks to see if there is actually work to do
2. sets the busy flag
3. obtains the next item of data to process
4. sets the device register appropriately to perform the desired read or write
5. checks to see if the write routine ought to be wakened

As mentioned earlier, the RAM disk driver processes requests right away. It has no queue of requests, hence no start routine.

The following routine is from the line printer driver. As you saw earlier, the lpwrite routine copied characters from the process's memory into a clist. The lpstart routine now reads the clist to obtain the characters to be passed to the line printer.

```
lpstart()
{
        int tmp;

        lp_flags != LPBUSY;

        /* while the printer is READY and there is stuff on the clist */

        while (((inb(LPSTATUS) & (LPERR!LPON!LPPAPER!LPREADY!LPNORMAL))
                        == (LPERR!LPON!LPREADY!LPNORMAL))
                && ((tmp = getc(&lp_queue)) >= 0))
```

```
        {
                /* output the character to the printer */

                outb(LPDATA, tmp);
                outb(LPCONTROL, LPSTROBE ! LPLF ! LPINIT ! LPSELECT ! LPIENB);
                outb(LPCONTROL, LPLF ! LPINIT ! LPSELECT ! LPIENB);
        }

        /* time to wake up the lpwrite routine? */

        if ((lp_queue.c_cc < LOWAT) && (lp_flags & SLEEPING))
        {
                lp_flags &= ~SLEEPING;
                wakeup(&lp_queue);
        }

        if (lp_queue.c_cc <= 0)
                lp_flags &= ~LPBUSY;
}
```

In this example you start by marking the device driver as busy. You then loop as long as the device is ready and there is data in the clist.

By reading the printer's status register using inb you can check if the printer is ready. The bits to check and the bit pattern to look for must be determined by reading the manual for the device. If the line printer is not ready, the loop will terminate.

Inside the loop the character that was obtained from the clist using getc is written to the line printer's data register. The next two calls to outb manipulate the bits of the control register to raise and lower the strobe. This signals the line printer to accept the character that you wrote to the data register and to print it.

When you have transferred as many characters as you can, you then check to see if the clist is getting empty. If so, and the lpwrite routine is waiting to fill the clist, you wake up the lpwrite routine.

Finally, you check to see if there are any characters in the clist left to write. If not, you then mark the device as not busy.

The read Routine

The read routine is the opposite of the write routine. The read routine is only found in character-mode drivers.

As with the write routine, read routines may either buffer their data or arrange for a direct transfer. The difference between a read routine and a write routine is that a read routine transfers data from the device to the process, while a write routine transfers data from the process to the device. The ramread routine illustrated here uses direct transfer. Such read routines must:

1. verify the request as being legal
2. check to see if the device is ready to perform a read operation
3. determine the size and location of the read
4. arrange for the data to be transferred directly to the process's memory
5. set up the device registers and start the read
6. wait for the read to complete or leave information for the interrupt routine to finish the read
7. handle any errors

Because the line printer driver does not support a read function, this example is from the RAM disk driver. You will notice that the RAM disk driver is unusual in that it has both a block-mode driver and a character-mode driver for the same device. This is done to permit special high-performance access to the RAM disk and to allow the use of an ioctl routine for the RAM disk driver.

```
ramread(dev)
int dev;
{
        physio(ramstrategy, &rrambuf, dev, B_READ);
}
```

This example shows the use of the kernel-supplied physio routine to process the read request. This is standard for the read and write functions of a device driver that also has a block-mode driver.

The physio function is used to convert a character-mode read or write into a form that can be handled by a block-mode strategy function.

The intr Routine

The intr routine is the counterpoint to the start routine. The start routine kicks the device to life. The intr routine hears from the device when it has finished the work it has been given by the start routine. The purpose of the intr routine is to clean up from the last request and prepare for the next. Specifically, this routine must:

1. check if the last operation completed without error
2. mark the last operation as complete and remove it from the queue
3. see if there is more work to do
4. start the device if there is work to do

Now examine the interrupt routine for a line printer device. As with many simple character-oriented devices, there is no way of telling if there was an error with the previous operation. This routine is only concerned with giving the device more work.

```
lpintr(vec)
int vec;
{

        if ((lp_flags & LPBUSY) == 0)
                return;

        if (lp_queue.c_cc > 0)
                lpstart();
}
```

With this line printer device you first check to see if the driver is busy. If not, you can ignore the interrupt, because it either was not for you or is spurious and of no significance.

You then check to see if there are characters waiting in the clist to be written to the printer. If this is the case, you call the lpstart routine to send them to the printer.

The ioctl Routine

The ioctl routine is used to handle special requests to the driver. Examples of such requests might be baud rate changes for serial communications devices or rewind operations for a tape drive. The ioctl entry point is used only for character-mode drivers.

Examine the ioctl routine for the RAM disk driver. It handles such special requests as allocating or freeing memory for use as a RAM disk:

```
ramioctl(dev, cmd, arg, mode)
int dev, cmd;
faddr_t arg;
int mode;
{
```

```
unsigned data[4];
struct ramdiskinfo *rdp;

rdp = &Ramdisk[MINOR(dev)];

switch (cmd)
{
  case GETRAMDISK:
        if(getramdisk(rdp, arg))
                u.u_error = ENOMEM;
        return;

  case FREERAMDISK:
        mfree(&coremap, KTOC(rdp->size), rdp->addr);
        rdp->addr = 0;
        rdp->size = 0;
        rdp->flags = 0;
        return;
}
}
```

The first argument to the ramioctl routine is the device being used. The next argument is the actual ioctl command. This comes directly from the second argument to the ioctl call from within the process itself. The third argument also comes directly from the ioctl call from the process, and its meaning is established by the device-driver author.

In this case the arg parameter stores the desired size of the RAM disk and is only used when a new RAM disk is being created. The last argument indicates the mode of the device (whether opened for reading only, reading and writing, or another mode). It is rarely used.

The switch statement selects the appropriate code based on the ioctl operation to perform.

The GETRAMDISK operation is used to allocate space for a new RAM disk. The exact value of the GETRAMDISK define is not important as long as the process making the ioctl call uses the same value as the device driver.

The getramdisk function is passed a pointer to the Ramdisk data structure and the size of RAM disk to create. If insufficient memory exists, the getramdisk function will return a nonzero value, which causes the driver to place an error code in the variable u.u_error. The kernel will see this and will pass the error indication on to the process that made the ioctl request.

The other case in the switch statement is to deallocate space for an existing RAM disk. The mfree function is supplied by the kernel and is used to return allocated memory to the pool of free memory available to all processes.

Installing and Debugging Your Driver

Well, now that the driver is written, what do you do? How do you tell the kernel that your driver is now open for business and is ready to accept requests for work?

There are several things that you must do:

1. enter the name of your interrupt handler in the list of interrupt handlers
2. enter the name of your driver entry points (such as open or close) into the table of driver entry points
3. compile your driver and link it with the kernel
4. reboot with the new operating system
5. create the proper entry in the /dev directory
6. test and/or use your driver

Look at these steps one at a time.

To enter the interrupt handler into the proper table, you must locate the table for your system. On some UNIX systems there will be a table in a file called c.c in which all of the interrupt routines are listed.

```
int (*vecintsw[])() =
{
        clockintr,
        novec,
        novec,
        ttyintr,
        ttyintr,
        lpintr,
        flintr,
        dkintr,
        novec,
        novec,
        /* etc. and etc. */
};
```

You can see that the position in this list relates to the interrupt number being used by each device. If you are using an unused interrupt, then merely replace the appropriate novec ("no vector") entry with the name of your interrupt handler.

As for the actual driver routines themselves, they are listed in the cdevsw table in the case of character mode drivers and in the bdevsw table in the case of block-mode drivers. The following example shows a possible cdevsw table:

```
struct cdevsw cdevsw[] =
{
        ttyopen,  ttyclose,  ttyread,  ttywrite, ttyioctl,  /* 0 */
        sysopen,  sysclose,  sysread,  syswrite, sysioctl,  /* 1 */
        lpopen,   lpclose,   nodev,    lpwrite,  nodev      /* 2 */
};
```

Note that there is no read or ioctl routine for the line printer, so you must use a system-defined entry nodev that indicates that such operations are not permitted for this device.

On other versions of UNIX the addition of a new driver to the kernel might involve editing files called /etc/system or /etc/master. Also, a configuration program such as config may have to be run. The documentation for your system ought to cover this, and it varies greatly among different UNIX systems and vendors. The next step is to compile your driver, producing an object file. The details on how to link your device-driver object file into the kernel ought to be found in the documentation for your system.

The final step after creating your new UNIX kernel and rebooting the system is to make the appropriate entry in the /dev directory. You can do this by using the /etc/mknod command:

```
#  /etc/mknod /dev/lp c 2 0
#  ls -l /dev/lp
c-w--w--w-  1 bin      bin       2, 0 Oct 31 12:58 /dev/lp
```

The first argument to the mknod command gives a name to this device (/dev/lp). The next specifies that the entry is for a character-mode driver. The third argument specifies the major device number. The major device number specifies which line in cdevsw or bdevsw describes your driver (as given earlier).

The final argument is the minor device number, which is not used for your line printer driver so you leave it 0. More complex drivers might use the minor device number to distinguish between multiple devices of the same type (that is, if there were more than one line printer to be supported at the same time).

Debugging Your Device Driver

Testing device drivers is much more difficult than testing normal C programs. And bugs are much harder to find. This discussion looks at some of the techniques that may be employed to identify bugs in device drivers.

There are two basic techniques:

- using printf statements to print messages and the value of variables
- using the adb debugging program to access kernel variables directly

The first technique is the simplest of all. You merely place printf calls within the driver at various points to print messages indicating that the function has been called and the values of significant variables. When the printf is executed, the output will appear on the system console.

The second technique relies on the fact that the superuser can use the adb debugger to examine the kernel's memory while the system is running. Using this tool it is possible to examine and even set kernel variables while the system is running. It is also possible to crash the system very quickly by setting the wrong variables, so take care.

The following is an example of using adb to read the lp_flags variable of the line printer driver while the system is running.

```
# adb -w /xenix /dev/kmem
* $x
* /m 24 0
* lp_flags/x
_lp_flags:    0x01
* lp_flags/w 0
_lpflags:     0x01=    0x0
* $q
#
```

The command that invokes adb specifies that writes are to be permitted, that the executable file to use is /xenix (the linked kernel that you booted), and that the "core" file is /dev/kmem. In this manner you tell adb to use the actual system memory rather than a true core file.

The first command to adb is $x, which tells adb to use hexadecimal input and output. The next command, /m 24 0, is specific to the version of UNIX used here and tells adb where in memory the variables are stored. Most UNIX systems do not require such a command.

The next two commands examine and then set the lp_flags variable. You first examine the contents of the variable by typing lp_flags/x. This tells adb to print the contents of the variable as a two-byte hexadecimal integer.

The next command tells adb to write the value (here 0) into the variable.

In this way you can look at and change variables within your driver while it is running.

Some Tricks of the Trade

Sometimes the obvious approach to writing a driver will not work. Sometimes an unusual situation makes the standard approach unworkable. Sometimes you need to pull a rabbit out of your hat. This section talks about rabbits.

You are going to look at a few areas where the normal driver design techniques do not work or do not produce the best possible driver.

Lost Interrupts

As you saw early in this paper, most device drivers operate by giving some work to the device and then waiting for the device to signal the completion of that work by generating an interrupt. If the interrupt is lost or not detected by the system, then the system will wait indefinitely for an interrupt that will never arrive. The device will hang.

When this happens, it is necessary to include special code in the driver that will cause a timeout to occur if an interrupt is not received within a certain period of time. If an interrupt is expected but not received, the timeout occurs, and the device driver examines the device to see if the interrupt has occurred but was missed.

The code is in two parts. The first part (which follows) is added to the end of the code that starts the device driver off on its way. At this point the driver expects an interrupt at some later point in time. The first part is:

```
if (lp_queue.c_cc <= 0)
    lp_flags &= ~LPBUSY;
else if ((lp_flags & TOPENDING) == 0)
{
    timeout(lprestart, 0, 1);
    lp_flags |= TOPENDING;
}
```

In this code fragment from a line printer driver, you check first to see if there is any work to do. If not, you clear the busy bit from the flags variable. If there is still work to do, then you are very interested in receiving an interrupt (so you know that you may continue). You tell the timeout function to call the lprestart function in 1/60th of a second, just in case no interrupt arrives.

Note in particular that you check a special timeout pending flag (TOPENDING) to see if you need to issue a timeout. The reason for this is that a timeout cannot be canceled—you must wait for it to happen. In addition, you can only have a limited number of timeouts pending at one time. It is critical, therefore, not to issue a new timeout while one is already pending.

The second part of this code is the lprestart routine that is called when the timeout occurs.

```
lprestart()
{
    int x;

    lp_flags &= ~TOPENDING;

    x = spl5();
    lpintr(0);
    splx(x);
}
```

In this routine you merely clear the timeout pending flag and simulate the arrival of an actual interrupt. This is done by setting the appropriate priority level and then calling the interrupt handler. As far as the lpintr routine is concerned, this simulated interrupt is indistinguishable from a real interrupt and is handled in exactly the same manner.

If the real interrupt has been dropped, then this simulated interrupt will start things moving again. If everything has been working properly, this extra simulated interrupt will just be ignored.

Polling Versus Interrupts

This discussion reveals one of the lesser known secrets of device drivers: interrupts are not always best.

An interrupt-driven device driver gives the device work to do and then does nothing until the device sends an interrupt indicating that the work is done. This is the normal method of writing device drivers and is the technique used for the drivers shown in this paper. It is usually the best way because no CPU time is used while the system waits for the device to interrupt. As soon as the device is ready, the driver is signaled so that work can be given to the device as soon as possible.

A polling device driver frequently checks (polls) the device to see if it is ready.

For most devices, such as disks and line printers, interrupt-driven drivers are the most efficient. As the following example will show, however, some devices (such as serial communications ports) may be more efficiently operated by polling.

Now consider an intelligent serial I/O device. This device is connected to a communications line that is receiving data at (say) 9600 baud. This means that the device is generating about 960 interrupts per second (one per character). If you run the driver on interrupts, you have to incur the overhead of interrupting UNIX and entering the driver routine 960 times a second.

A better way exists. Assuming that the device itself has a buffer to store incoming characters, you can turn off the interrupts and poll the board every 50 milliseconds or so. When you poll the device, you can transfer 50 or so characters from the device's buffer each time. In this way you incur the overhead only 20 times a second rather than 960 times a second.

This type of driver times its polls either by using the timeout routine described previously or by adding code to the clock driver that calls the device driver as many times per second as required. For a serial device, the polling interval is the lesser of 50 milliseconds (the longest time a character can go unechoed for reasonable performance) and the time it takes to overflow the buffer at the highest supported baud rate. Figure 7–11 compares the work flow in the interrupt-driven and polled approaches.

Polling also works well with devices that are very fast and generate an interrupt very quickly after they are given work to do. An example of this type of device is a high-speed analog-to-digital converter. This device is connected to outside equipment and measures voltages, temperatures, and so on. Some devices can perform a conversion within 40 millionths of a second.

In cases such as this, it is much better for the device driver merely to sit in a tight while loop waiting for the device to complete its work. This will consume an additional 40 microseconds or so, far less than the CPU time required to exit the driver and then process the interrupt. This technique is illustrated by the following pseudocode:

```
start the A/D converter on its next conversion;

check to see if A/D conversion is finished;

while (A/D conversion is not finished)
{
        check to see if A/D conversion is finished;
}

obtain results of conversion from device;
```

257

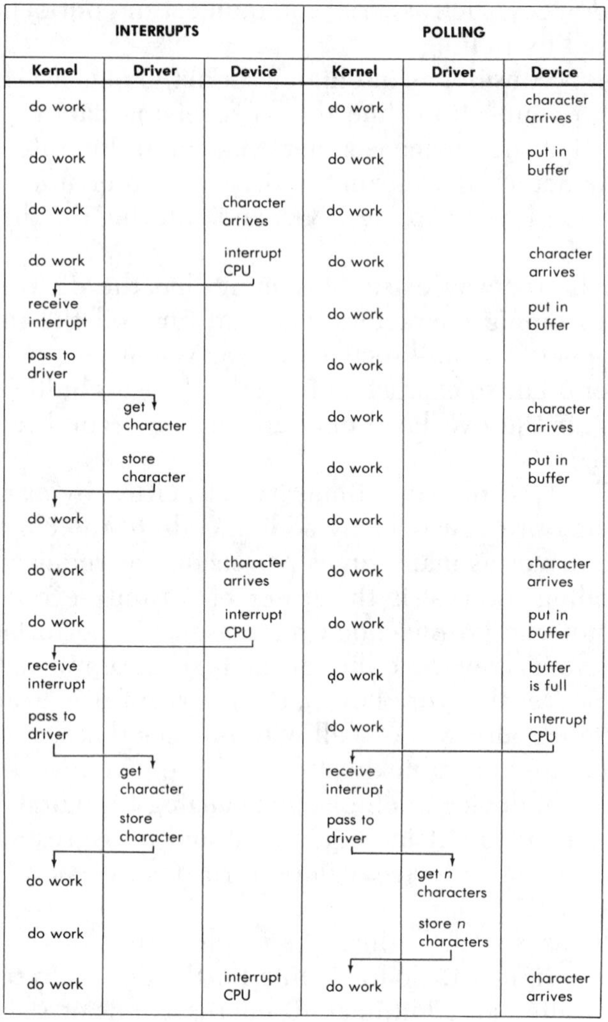

INTERRUPTS			POLLING		
Kernel	**Driver**	**Device**	**Kernel**	**Driver**	**Device**
do work			do work		character arrives
do work			do work		put in buffer
do work		character arrives	do work		
do work		interrupt CPU	do work		character arrives
receive interrupt			do work		put in buffer
pass to driver			do work		
	get character		do work		character arrives
	store character		do work		put in buffer
do work			do work		
do work		character arrives	do work		character arrives
do work		interrupt CPU	do work		put in buffer
receive interrupt			do work		buffer is full
pass to driver			do work		interrupt CPU
	get character		receive interrupt		
	store character		pass to driver		
do work				get n characters	
do work				store n characters	
do work		interrupt CPU	do work		character arrives

Figure 7-11   Interrupts versus Polling

You have seen in this section some techniques used by experienced device driver writers to implement better drivers. Remember:

1. Do not assume the hardware works as claimed.

2. Do not assume the standard way is always best.

3. Always be willing (if not eager) to learn by studying other people's drivers.

Summary

This paper explored UNIX device drivers in some detail. It showed how the UNIX kernel relies upon the device driver to translate generic requests for work into the device-specific commands actually required to perform the required operation. It examined excerpts from real drivers to see the techniques used by device driver programmers. And finally the paper discussed some of the special techniques that can be used to write efficient and polished device drivers.

Bibliography

Lions, J. *A Commentary on the UNIX Operating System Source Code Level Six.* The University of New South Wales, 1977.

Morgan, Christopher L. *Inside XENIX.* Indianapolis, Ind.: Howard W. Sams & Company, 1986.

Ritchie, Dennis M. "The UNIX I/O System," in *UNIX System Manager's Manual, 4.2 Berkeley Software Distribution, Virtual VAX-11 Version.* Berkeley: University of California, 1984.

Thompson, K. "UNIX Time-Sharing System: UNIX Implementation." *The Bell System Technical Journal* 57, no. 6 (July–August 1978), pp. 1931–1946.

"Writing Device Drivers," in *XENIX System V Development System Programmer's Guide.* Santa Cruz: Santa Cruz Operation, 1986.

KEYWORDS

► Advertise

► Domain

► Interprocess
communication

► Name server

► OSI architecture

► Queues

► RFS

► Starlan

Paper Synopsis: Remote File Sharing (RFS) is a new feature of UNIX System V, release 3. It makes any remote computer system act like it is a locally mounted file system. This means resources are allocated optimally across several machines. STREAMS and the Transport Level Interface (TLI) provide a standard way to write communications and network programs in UNIX. This paper explores how RFS, STREAMS, and the TLI work.

John Emrich is a technical consultant at the Schaumburg, Illinois branch of Analysts International Corporation, a software consulting service. He has degrees in physics and computer science, has taught courses in computer networks and programming languages, and was among the first people who experimented with implementing protocol modules in the STREAMS environment in UNIX System V, Release 3.

Mr. Emrich can be reached via electronic mail on uucp network at aicchiljee.

## 8

Remote File Systems, Streams, and Transport Level Interface

John Emrich

With UNIX System V release 3.0 (SVR3) a new feature called Remote File Sharing (RFS) was introduced. This paper addresses questions about RFS: What is this feature, and how does it affect your computing environment? What does it mean for the future? What are some of the important components in the design of RFS?

The essence of RFS is that a file system is extended over a network of computers and disk storage. To the user, the collection of computers on the network appears as one larger system. Thus, you can "grow" the RFS system one machine at a time; you are not bound by the physical limitations of one machine. This paper examines in more detail what this means to you, the user. You will see how it affects your computing environment, and how it affects the design of your programs.

UNIX SVR3 introduces two new features: STREAMS and the Transport Level Interface (TLI). STREAMS is a standardized mechanism for writing communications and networking programs within the UNIX kernel. It embodies the experiences of many programmers and desirable features they have found important in writing such programs, and does it in a standard fashion. The TLI is an interface for application programs that run outside the kernel and that communicate across computer networks. The TLI is the outcome of the Open Systems Interconnection (OSI) standardization efforts.

Both STREAMS and the TLI enhance RFS's independence from the underlying media and network by providing a general framework with which to build network applications

261

and interface to them. This helps ensure portability. Portability has always been a major factor for **UNIX** computers.

Traditional Networking Environments

You can best picture what RFS makes possible by looking at how working in a computing environment is evolving from using a network of computers to working in a homogeneous computing environment. Traditionally, a user worked on one computer, with files on one or more disks. If the user needed data in a file on a remote computer, this data was accessed via a communications link, such as a phone line. This process is illustrated in Figure 8–1. If a user on machine machA wants data from machC, the only way to get it is by copying the entire file from machC to the local machine,

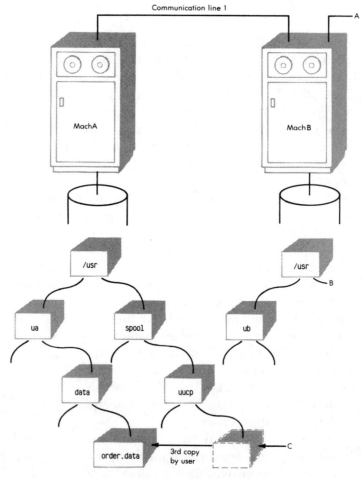

Figure 8–1   Historical Networking of Computers

machA. There are five disadvantages to this approach that don't exist when the file is local to the user's machine (machA):

1. If the user only needs a small portion of the data, the entire file still has to be copied to the user's machine. This is wasteful of communications resources, as much time is spent transferring the file. This also increases the delay in obtaining the data. If numerous users employ this same approach for their work, the problem is compounded.

2. The user must have a file copy utility that knows how to talk over the communications link to its peer (equal) on the remote machine, machC. For large files there is the additional problem of adequate disk storage space on the local machine, machA. Historically, uucp has filled the file copy role on UNIX computers.

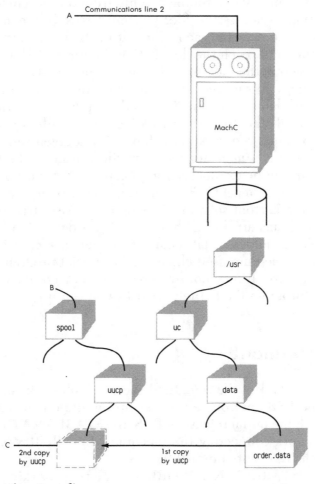

Figure 8–1 *(continued)*

3. The question of file access control, or security, has also been inadequately addressed in remote access operations. There is no password check when files are accessed, for example.

4. The name of the file must be known before you execute the file copy utility. This information usually has to be obtained via some external channel. For example, this could amount to the user logging onto machC (using cu on a UNIX computer) and searching the directory for the desired file, or someone giving the user the filename.

5. If there is no direct link to machC, then your file copy utility must be able to send the file through one or more intermediate machines or nodes.

Item 5 describes a store-and-forward method of sending a file using a gateway. It involves shipping the file from one machine to the next. This means that to access the file, you must specify a complete path to use, such as in the uucp approach. The path lists the names of the machines to ship through to reach the destination. Figure 8–1 shows the intermediate copies made in the path of a file copy from machC to machA. In order for this file copy to succeed, it is important for the intermediate node to be up and available. Intermediate nodes or links experiencing availability problems will affect the timely delivery of the file. Programs, such as uucp, will retry failed requests until they reach a given retry limit.

If there is a need for frequent file transfers, the user will probably have a custom or commercial application program for retrieving the desired data from machC. But this requires a peer application on machC. Developing custom software is expensive. Also, traditionally even when these programs are built, they have been dependent on the underlying network technology. That means if the network configuration changes or the storage medium used changes, the special program may not work the same as before. It may not even work at all. Another way of saying this is that the program limits the networks you can use.

RFS Environment

Now take a look at the remote file access problem in an RFS environment. First, the RFS environment is set up on all your machines, as in Figure 8–2. With the initial release of RFS, the STARLAN NETWORK is the local area network connecting the machines. Initially this is the only network on which RFS is operational.

The STARLAN NETWORK is a new networking product available from AT&T that consists of both hardware and software. It can be used to connect MS-DOS machines as well as some of AT&T's 3B computers. It uses standard twisted pair wiring (the same as that used for telephones) to connect the computers.

Using the **STARLAN NETWORK** product means machA doesn't need machB to reach machC. As part of the RFS setup, machine machC advertises (makes available) directories to other machines. This information is available directly through the network. These will be the directories users on other machines will see via RFS.

In Figure 8–2 the directory /user/uc/data is advertised as available by machC. To use this directory on machA, the shared directory from machC must be "mounted" on machA. This is shown as /user/remotec in Figure 8–2. Also, your directory /user/uc/data will be known on the network by the name corder. This name is used when the mount occurs. If you enter the command: ls /user/remotec on machA before you start up RFS, it will show no files. After RFS initialization, you will see:

```
ls /user/remotec
order.data
other.data
```

Now if you must obtain some data from a file on machC, you don't need a file copy utility. You only need to execute an ordinary UNIX copy command to copy the appropriate file into your target directory. If you are only interested in one item of data, you could browse the file with your favorite editor, as if it were local, copying only the desired data to a place in your target directory. An application program you run on machA would be able to use the file in machC, retrieving only the desired data. The application program would not have to know anything about the underlying network. It would be using the traditional UNIX system calls.

RFS Programming Considerations

Under RFS, a program opening a file does not know whether the file is on the local machine or a remote machine. All the standard system calls available to a program for retrieving and updating data in files on the local machine apply equally to files on a remote machine. The only difference is that the retrieval time will probably be greater when you are doing reads/writes to a remote file. Such things as file and record locking work equally well on remote files and local files. However, if programs use nonstandard locking schemes, such as in some database managers, the programs won't work. (A discussion of locking methods is beyond the scope of this paper.)

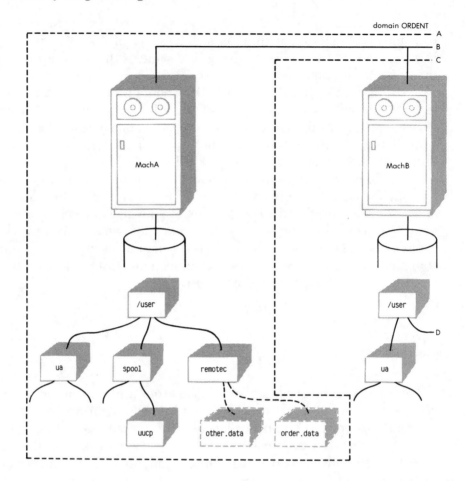

Figure 8–2   User's View, Under RFS, of Shared Files /user/uc/data **on MachC**

Locking is important when data must be read, modified, and then written back as if it were an indivisible step. Another process must not be allowed to break into this sequence. Otherwise, one of the updates could be lost and the data corrupted. Effectively, entering the read operation locks (halts) entrance to the read, modify, write sequence until the write operation completes. This is important for database managers.

Also, while you can obtain data in remote files, your process (running program) is still restricted to executing on your local machine. However, if the remote filename being used is a remote device, such as /dev/remote.dev, then you are actually using that remote device.

The same applies to writing. If the remote file is a named pipe, also known as a *fifo*, then writing to that fifo results in writing to the process on the remote machine. The same holds when sending data through the

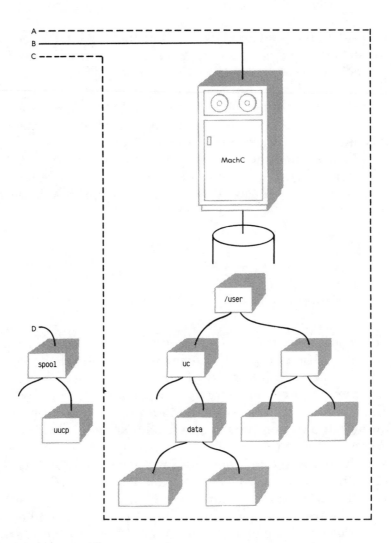

Figure 8–2 *(continued)*

named pipe in the reverse direction. Actually, you have used a named pipe to connect two processes on different machines. Remember that a pipe, designated by ¦, is used to send the output of one UNIX command to the input of another. A named pipe replaces the ¦ by a device name. Look now at a pair of commands connected by a pipe:

```
cat ord.mon ord.tue ord.wed ord.thu ord.fri ¦ sumrep >weekly.rep
```

You can place this command line in a file called ord.sh for later use. The command (program) cat is used to list and concatenate the five separate files. (In this example they are the files ord.mon through ord.fri containing order data for the respective days of the week.) The cat command pipes the data to sumrep. The program, sumrep, prints a summary report of orders placed for the week, putting the output in file weekly.rep. All the files for this command line reside in a directory of machC that machA can access. The standard output of the cat command will be sent through the pipe to standard input of the sumrep command. Typing this command line on machA means machA will execute both commands.

Now assume the existence of a named pipe, ordfifo. The significance of ordfifo is that it has an entry in the file system, whereas the pipe set up via ¦ does not. You can list the ordfifo entry in the file system with the ls command.

```
type on machA
        cat ord.sh >ordfifo
type on machC
        sh <ordfifo
```

This assumed that someone logged onto machC has started the command sh <ordfifo. The sh is just the standard shell, used here to read commands from the named pipe ordfifo instead of a terminal or file. The commands cat ord.mon ord.tue ord.wed ord.thu ord.fri and sumrep ultimately execute on machC. The command cat ord.sh executed on machA writing (sending) its output through the named pipe, ordfifo to the sh on machC, because it is interpreted by the sh there from ordfifo. In this example you have used machC to execute the set of commands instead of machA. Thus, while machC is executing this set of commands, machA would have more resources, such as CPU cycles, available for other work.

This example shows how to ship the work to another processor. This scenario can be expanded so that a set of cooperating programs on machA and machC can communicate with each other through named pipes and also split the work between them in some fashion. This has the potential for significant program concurrency and a more powerful and efficient computing environment. However, currently this is the extent to which RFS will allow distribution of executing processes. After all, RFS is a distributed file system, not a distributed operating system.

User Domains

So far you have progressed from the traditional computing environment of one machine to the entire collection of machines networked together and viewed as one machine.

In the example in Figure 8–2, machA needed data in a file on machC. If this need is frequent, it would be logical to place these two machines in the same domain. (A *domain* is just a logical grouping of machines.) Call your domain ORDENT, for "order entry." Thus, RFS would be running on machines machA and machC. Again, in the example's machine, machA is the requester and machC has the resource (data in a file). In this context, machA is a client (a requester or user of a resource), and machC is a server (owner or provider of a resource).

In reality, if there are many machines on the network, you will want to partition the network into several domains or sections. The domains will typically be set up according to application areas or normal working environments. For example, in Figure 8–2, machA frequently accesses data in machC. Because they interact frequently, they're put in the same domain. Due to the structure of the network, machines in the same domain share data more efficiently. Not only is a domain a partitioning of the network, but it can serve as a focal point for administrating and controlling the machines. This central point is where information is analyzed and actions decided. Network management functions work better with some degree of centralization. After all, the function of network management is to organize work in an orderly way as you move toward a given goal.

Locating Files on a Network

So far in the example, you have created a domain containing two computers, machA and machC. Now add a fourth machine to your network called machD, and add it to your domain, ORDENT. If machB has RFS on it, but you don't want it to be part of the domain ORDENT, you would assign it to another domain, such as MANUFAC.

In this example, the /user/uc/data directory from machC is mounted on machA at the mount point, /user/remotec. Thus, all files and directories of machC located under /user/uc/data can be seen on machA under directory /user/remotec. That is, /user/remotec/order.data and /user/uc/data/order.data are one and the same file. They are the same physical file, which happens to reside on machC's disk. Any changes made to that file by a user on either machine are immediately reflected in the file.

You can check the directories available to use through RFS on your machine, machA, using the nsquery command. This is one of the commands that comes with RFS. The output would look like this:

```
nsquery
RESOURCE      ACCESS        SERVER  DESCRIPTION
corder        read/write    ORDENT.machC    manufacturing order data
dorder        read          ORDENT.machD    yesterday's order data
```

Then you can issue the mount command to see which directories are mounted on your machA. The mount command with no parameters simply lists the mounted file systems. Any user can issue this form of the command:

```
mount
/user/remotec on          CORDER read/write on Mon Sep 1 06:00:00 1986
```

(This only displays the output from mount relevant to your scenario.) You see from the commands nsquery and mount that on machA, /user/remotec has a directory mounted from machC. To see the files and additional directories under /user/remotec, you just issue the command ls /user/remotec.

As part of starting RFS, the appropriate directories from remote machines are mounted on your local machine at some directory that you call a "mount point." You as a system user and the administrator agree beforehand on this mount point for remote directories. Only the administrator has authority to issue the mount command for this purpose. The mount point can be any directory on your local machine. It is recommended that nothing be in the mount directory on your machine, machA, before the mount request, because any previously existing files will become inaccessible while another file system is mounted on that mount point. This phenomenon is just a side effect of the standard mount command of the UNIX system.

Also as part of defining the domain ORDENT in the example, the administrator has declared machC to be the "primary name server." A *name server* is a machine that stores unique information about the other machines and domains on the network. This primary name server maintains a file of all hosts within its domain as well as their network addresses. This is similar to the way uucp keeps track of the hosts it can reach. A *network address* is the address of a machine on the network and is network dependent. Also maintained in this name server file is location information about other domains in the network. The primary name server file on machA is:

```
ORDENT    p    ORDENT.machA
ORDENT    s    ORDENT.machC
machA     a    machA.serve
machC     a    machC.serve
machD     a    machD.serve

MANUFAC   p    MANUFAC.machB
machB     a    machB.serve
```

The second entry on each line is a type field defining primary name server (p), secondary name server (s), or network address (a). For name server entries, the first entry on the line is the domain name and the third entry is the full name. The latter takes the form domain.hostname. For network address entries the first entry on the line is the host name and the third entry is the network address. (In this case it is a STARLAN NETWORK address). The machine on which the name server resides is normally the machine from which the domain is managed by the network administrator.

The name server file should be maintainable without relying on RFS. In case RFS is not running, you want an alternate way to access the file, such as cu. The name server file is a simple file that can be maintained with your favorite editor.

If the primary name server is not running, the name server file is unavailable. Thus, other machines within its domain cannot mount remote directories. In such a case, any remote directories previously mounted remain intact, and you can continue working in those directories. Any applications that read and write to files within those directories will get an I/O error on its next attempted read or write. This is because the physical file is no longer accessible. In this case, you would get one of the new error codes, ENOLINK, a STREAM-related error. ENOLINK indicates the physical link with the other machine is unavailable. Usually this is not that severe a problem, because machines and RFS itself are usually available during normal use. UNIX machines do not start and stop RFS frequently, because such machines would not be very useful.

However, for those users wanting a higher degree of availability, secondary or backup name servers can also be defined. Thus, if the primary name server is down, and secondary name servers were defined, your computing environment is not affected. It is possible for every machine in the domain to be defined as a secondary name server for an even higher degree of availability.

Making Resources Available to RFS

So far you have only seen processes about hosts and the domains to which they belong. You have not learned how the directory on machC in your example was made known to machA so it could be mounted there. After RFS is started on machC, the administrator advertises, using the adv command, the directories on machC to be shared with other RFS machines. In Figure 8–2 the adv command was used to advertise /user/uc/data and the associated resource name, corder. It is possible for another directory on another machine with the name /user/uc/data to be advertised, and you would then need to distinguish them by using different resource names. Until the administrator issues the adv command, the machine, machC here, can only serve as a client. A *client* is a computer, machC here, that can read directories on other machines, but not vice versa. When the administrator advertises the directory, machC operates as a server, a provider of a resource (the directory). A machine can be both a client and server. It is also possible for the adv command to advertise the root directory of a machine. This is not generally a good idea, because access to all files on the machine is thereby granted.

The adv command typed to advertise corder is:

```
adv -d"order data" corder /usr/uc/data
```

The adv command is the only way to advertise a resource in RFS. The parameter "order data" is just an English meaningful comment for the adv command. The parameter corder is the name by which the advertised resource is known on the network, and /usr/uc/data is the advertised directory. In fact, if you just type the command adv with no arguments, you get a list of resources advertised by your local machine. In your case you see:

```
corder    /usr/uc/data read/write      "order data"    unrestricted
```

Note how each field (corder, /usr/uc/data, "order data") correspond to the parameters on the command line adv. There are additional fields appearing on this line corresponding to options not specified on the adv command line. The additional fields appearing are all read/write, meaning write access is allowed when other RFS machines mount the resource, corder. The resource, corder, could have been advertised as read only. Then write access across the network is disallowed by your local machine, regardless of any other access permissions. Also note the field unrestricted, which just specifies those RFS hosts that you will allow to mount (access) your resource, corder. In your case, unrestricted appears, meaning any RFS host can mount this resource.

RFS Access Control

This paper has not so far addressed the issue of security. Security exists on three levels: host connection, mount directory, and user or group.

Host Connection Level

When a mount request made on machA is destined for machC as in this example, a virtual circuit is set up between machA and machC. Thus, a virtual circuit exists while a file system is mounted. You can think of a virtual circuit synonymously with a virtual route. This is analogous to telephone calls in the telephone network. When you make a telephone call, there is actual hardware dedicated to that call for the duration of that call (a circuit has been set up). On subsequent calls the dedicated hardware can change, but the telephone user is unaware of this. So when two computers set up a virtual circuit with each other, resources are dedicated for that connection (call). A partial list of resources consists of the physical link and computer memory. The appearance of a dedicated (but shared) resources is given the term *virtual circuit* (also sometimes called *logical circuit*). The users do not need to concern themselves with how it is being shared. The establishment of the virtual circuit includes security capabilities, however. If machC had requested host connection security, machC would only have accepted the call from machA if machA was in its access list. To generalize, RFS will check every host that attempts to mount your advertised directory, and a virtual circuit is only set up for those from a specified list of machines.

Mount Directory Level

In addition to the connect security, machC could have specified which hosts could mount each directory machine machC advertised. This mount directory scheme also has two sublevels of security. When the administrator of machC advertised the directory /user/uc/data, two decisions were made:

- To allow access to the specified directory only to specific client hosts—machA here
- To allow files in the specified directory to only be read

User and Group Security

The traditional UNIX read/write security at the file level is still available. However, it can become more complicated to use, because typical userids can be duplicated among multiple machines. For security purposes, what userid should be used when usera on machA is accessing data on machC? The administrator can specify a mapping, or identification conversion, to take place. Another mapping is also applicable to a groupid. This allows a given user on machA to have a unique userid and a special groupid on machC. The mapping information is maintained in a file separate from the password file containing userids. Thus, whenever the password file is modified, the mapping information may have to be updated.

RFS User Security

You may have begun to notice that substantial effort has been applied to address security concerns in RFS. There are three approaches to mapping userids across hosts. Each host can define the mapping for itself, which overrides the global mapping in the domain. The mappings for groupids are formed the same way as for userids and are established at the time a mount is performed.

No Mapping

In this case, all userids and groupids are mapped into a single default identification label on the remote machine. This default identification is one having restricted access. It can only access those files that are readable/writeable by everyone. This is the default. Figure 8–3 illustrates that all requests on machC coming from machA are mapped into the userid number 103. User 103 has no corresponding userid.

Transparent Mapping

Here each userid on machA in the example is simply carried over to machC. (This userid 158 on machA is given userid number 158 on machC). From a user's perspective, this can be less confusing, because the same identification exists across all machines. However, many UNIX machines will have been in use for some time before RFS is installed, and this makes such a mapping difficult; the userid for a user on machA may already belong to another user on machC. Many files would have to have their ownerids and groupids converted. This approach is probably only tenable when a new machine is established that has RFS on it from the beginning, as when new machines are installed. Transparent mapping works because in UNIX machines, a userid actually maps to a number internally, and it is this number that is used for security checking. Thus, as long as that number is the same, even if the userid is different, the UNIX system sees them as the same userid. This is illustrated in Figure 8–4.

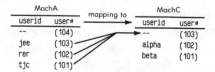

Figure 8–3 No Mapping (Default) of Userids

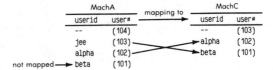

MachA		mapping to	MachC	
userid	user#	→	userid	user#
--	(106)		--	(106)
jee	(105)	→ ernie	ernie	(105)
rer	(104)	→ ron	ron	(104)
tjc	(103)	→ tom	tom	(103)
alpha	(102)	→ alpha	alpha	(102)
beta	(101)	→ beta	beta	(101)

Figure 8–4   Transparent Mapping of Userids

MachA		mapping to	MachC	
userid	user#	→	userid	user#
--	(104)		--	(103)
jee	(103)	→ alpha	alpha	(102)
alpha	(102)	→ beta	beta	(101)
not mapped → beta	(101)			

Figure 8–5   Specific Mapping of Userids

Specific Mapping

Here each user ID on the client machine is mapped onto a specific user ID on the server machine. This allows the greatest amount of regulated control. However, it can be very detailed and lengthy to set up in a large computing environment. If a userid on either client or server machine is added/deleted, this mapping must be updated. Such a mapping is illustrated in Figure 8–5. Despite these difficulties, the enhanced control makes this the more likely mapping approach to be used.

Performance and Reliability Concerns

It should be noted that together with the additional flexibility RFS provides comes additional overhead. There is a price to be paid for this additional power, as with any new feature.

User Concerns

Looking at Figure 8–6, you can picture some of the additional overhead. For usera on machA a request for data must go along path A, whereas userc's request proceeds along path C. Actually, the request along path A has much of path C in common. The usera request must reach the disk just as userc must, but in addition usera's request must traverse a network. This means accessing data on a remote disk through a network is generally slower than using a local disk. This situation is common for distributed file systems.

Requests coming in over a network represent more overhead to a UNIX machine than do local requests. This additional overhead is usually first noticeable in increased delays for your applications. If these requests

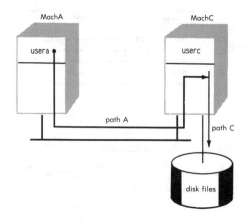

Figure 8–6   Application Data Path in a Distributed File System, RFS

are substantial, you should consider moving the user, the data files, or both to reduce this activity. However, if you have an application that is compute-bound, meaning it spends more time executing instructions than it does waiting for I/O, an application speed-up may actually occur. This can happen if you move several compute-bound tasks to separate machines on which there is more CPU time available. The increased time in doing I/O is offset by the increased availability of the machine to execute instructions. There are many examples of such programs. A partial list would be some text-formatting programs (such as mm, nroff, and troff), graphics design programs, and (typically) FORTRAN programs. The appropriate placement of programs among machines can be determined with some testing and experience.

Currently, local networks can transmit data faster than machines can access data on disks. This means that with few users, performing disk reads and writes will be the limiting factor. With many users and many machines, the network will be the limiting factor. This is because work has been distributed over many machines, each running at less than full capacity, but there is only one network, which can not distribute its work. The crossover point can be determined by experience or by testing.

Judicious use of the sticky bit can reduce the network and machine delay in loading programs. The sticky bit indicates the program can be shared in memory by several users and therefore is only loaded once. The sticky bit flag is set with the chmod command. Excessive use of this feature will reduce the main memory available for application processes and hurt performance, however.

Administrator Concerns

The standard UNIX machine utilities for performance/space monitoring— sar, fusage, and df—make available specific RFS information. The information these tools output differentiates between RFS activity and local activity. This can provide the administrator with a picture of the system utilization for load balancing and tuning.

There are limits on the number of mounts a server machine will accept; the number of directories that can be advertised has a limit, too. Additionally, there are limits on the number of file descriptors (with quite large defaults) that can be opened across RFS. These can control activity and are configurable.

RFS Summary

To this point the paper has examined RFS from a user's vantage point to see how it expands your computing environment. It has addressed security issues on several fronts. It has also noted that all standard system calls are supported for application programs. The next discussion explores the STREAMS feature of SVR3. As mentioned early in this paper, STREAMS is a separate, new feature (available with SVR3) that is used by RFS. You will see how building with STREAMS can reduce network dependence.

New Networking Features Used by RFS

So far this paper has talked about RFS, a distributed file system, without any discussion of the underlying network. It began by claiming that RFS is dependent on the transport level interface, but is independent of the network. Now it is time to look at some of the "internals" of SVR3, UNIX System V release 3, that allow this claim. First is the STREAMS feature.

Motivation for Change in UNIX Networking

STREAMS is a conceptual name for a software mechanism added to SVR3 to address situations where networking on UNIX machines did not work well. Briefly, STREAMS is a set of system calls, kernel utility routines, and kernel resources that are used to create, use, and dismantle a full-duplex path that connects a driver in the kernel and a user process. Communications for both control functions and data transmission through this path occur in terms of messages. The full-duplex feature allows messages to move in both directions simultaneously.

The traditional UNIX system, prior to SVR3, was not entirely adequate for many of the new applications put on UNIX machines today. The com-

277

munications and networking code in the kernel did not function effectively. Take a look at some examples of these problems.

TTY Architecture

Traditionally, asynchronous terminals were the way users accessed UNIX machines. Since asynchronous terminals send each character, as typed, immediately to the machine, each character can immediately be processed. This led to an architecture for terminal processing frequently referred to as a *line discipline.* However, it was difficult to have more than one line discipline active at one time. This problem of multiple line disciplines could arise when a network designer added intelligent terminals that had a very different interface.

Some of the features typically provided for terminals are:

- parsing input series of characters into lines so UNIX would process them
- processing backspace characters: this may mean blanking out a character on your terminal screen
- echoing typed characters back to the terminal
- generating signals to application process when unusual events occur, such as terminal hangup or pressing the BREAK key
- allowing a raw mode where no characters are preprocessed

In order to support this terminal architecture, clists ("character lists") evolved. These lists are program concepts that let you better manipulate lists of characters. Figure 8–7 shows these clists as used for holding characters arriving from the terminal and characters being sent to the terminal (clists are two-way, full-duplex paths for characters). Data in the clists is operated on one character at a time. This particular clist interface evolved from a time when terminals were considered dumb; the application programs on the computer provided the intelligence.

However, today many terminals have acquired sophisticated features; some actually are intelligent workstations or full-featured computers. To take effective advantage of these terminals requires an approach and an architecture different from the traditional clist-oriented line discipline.

The same need holds true for synchronous terminals and machines. These terminals are viewed as synchronous because they do not send one character at a time as it is typed. They wait for a series of characters to be typed, then send them as one transmission. These machines have a message orientation rather than a character orientation. Synchronous processing came about because it is more efficient at treating characters in a

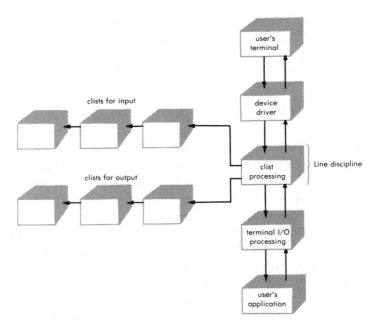

Figure 8–7   Terminal Line Discipline Character Flow

batch or "message." Within RFS, information is passed across the under-lying network a message at a time rather than character by character. This is more efficient from the perspective of optimal use of the computer and network media. There is less overhead involved in sending 100 characters at once than in sending 100 individual 1-character transmissions. When the majority of applications access files, they are more message- or record-oriented, working with such units as a line of text. The asynchronous clist mechanism usually does not contain many characters during processing, while message-oriented systems usually assimilate an entire message before processing. A "message" is usually many characters; usually hundreds to thousands of characters.

Local Area Network Demands

The recent phenomenon of UNIX local area networks put increasing demands on the buffering mechanisms for messages in the kernel. In networks many more messages can arrive within a given second because of the many attached nodes, as well as the significantly larger speeds used. The UNIX clist buffering facility has proven to be inadequate. This has led to the creation of many different buffering schemes, which are often similar, but incompatible. Many of these approaches had many good points, but they were nonstandard (non-AT&T). The lack of a standard supported architecture caused duplication of effort and duplication of functionality within the kernel. The results lacked modularity. This is most obviously seen by network maintenance people.

Open Systems Interconnection Demands

The new Open Systems Interconnection (OSI) architecture to which many vendors and users have lent support in recent years imposes some new demands on UNIX. In looking at the layers, depicted in Figure 8–8, you see that each layer adds its own header, or control information, to the message when passing it down. (You will be mainly concerned here with the layers from transport down to physical, because these are the ones typically implemented in the UNIX kernel. Note that the figure is not to scale as the user data is much longer than the layer headers.) To implement this efficiently requires headers to be linked onto the beginning of a message. That is, you want to avoid copying a message just to add a header. This may sound like a nit, but experience has shown that excessive copying of entire messages can have a significant impact on computer and network performance.

A simple example can illustrate this. Say you want to send a 1024 character (1K) message. You also use a time of .3 ms (milliseconds) as representative of the time to copy a message from one memory location to another. Examining Figure 8–8, you see that from the transport layer down to the physical layer three headers have been added. This would mean copying the message three times, using a total of .9 ms to move the message. This does not include the time to copy the message into the kernel or copy from the kernel to the physical medium. If the total pro-

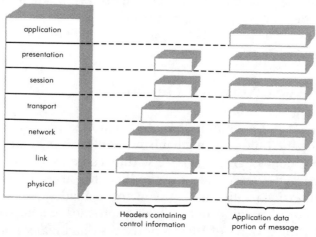

Headers containing control information   Application data portion of message

Figure 8–8   Architectural Layering

cessing time averages around 5 ms, 18 percent of the time was used in message copying. For one virtual circuit this may not be a major concern, but what if you now have 10 virtual circuits? This still means 18 percent, but it also means 18 ms. That is almost the equivalent two more virtual circuits. Another way of saying this is that the extra 18 percent represents that many fewer virtual circuits that can be supported.

Also, the layering implies a certain amount of independence of the layers. For example, the session layer is expected to work, even though the link and physical layer are changed from a phone line to a local area network. This means that each layer defines a service to the layer above. This service is available to the higher layer through an interface defined by the lower layer. How that lower layer implements that service is its concern. In this way, changing a phone line to a local network means no change in your application, providing the same interface is used. For this to be viable a standard must be followed. Another illustration is that the UNIX system calls define a service available through an interface, but the layer below (the kernel) is the implementation of the service. Another example is RFS using the OSI-defined Transport Level Interface and thus achieving increased independence from the lower layers of the network. OSI emphasizes portability, modularity, and interconnection of different vendor machines in the network. The realization is that some machines do some things better than others, so a heterogeneous computing environment is sometimes desirable.

Some of the layers, such as session and above, frequently reside in user space as library routines, while the transport level and below reside inside the kernel.[1] This means that the data portion of messages must have associated control information (header information), which is passed between layers (and into the kernel with the read/write call). The simple UNIX read/write system call does not provide a standard way of doing this. Now that you know of some of the UNIX OSI protocol-interfacing problems, see how they are tackled by STREAMS.

STREAMS Overview

STREAMS Background

To reiterate, STREAMS is a set of services and resources for communicating, with messages, over a full-duplex path between a driver in the

---

[1]A useful reference on OSI standards in local area networks is The Waite Group's *PC LAN Primer* (Indianapolis, Ind.: Howard W. Sams, 1986).

kernel and a user process. The driver in the kernel is the routine that interfaces directly with the communications hardware. STREAMS also includes a service (or function) interface definition for providing a generalized set of networking services (new system calls) for computer networking applications. The messages flow along a *stream* (a kernel component of STREAMS) between user processes and drivers similar to the way water flows in a river. Another useful analogy is that of a river delta (such as the Mississippi River emptying into the Gulf of Mexico). Just as there are numerous smaller rivers within the river delta conveying water, so there are multiple streams as components of STREAMS conveying messages. Figure 8–9 shows a stream, stream A, coexisting with a nonstream device driver for terminals.

The STREAMS feature of SVR3 evolved from version 8 of the UNIX system. Version 8 ran mostly in research areas of AT&T Bell Laboratories. You can also see the influence of 4.2BSD sockets in STREAMS.[2] SVR3 is the latest version of the UNIX system available from AT&T. AT&T is expending considerable resources into getting SVR3 accepted as the definitive version of the UNIX system. Remember, any generally accepted product will evolve and grow as user computing environments (hardware

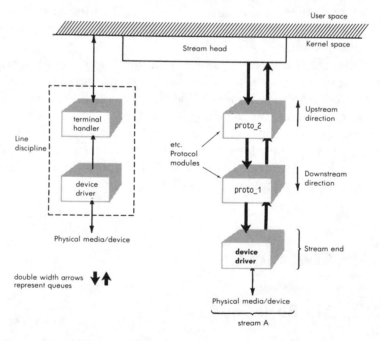

Figure 8–9   Streams Coexisting in the Kernel Alongside a Line Discipline

---

[2]4.2BSD is a version of the UNIX system available from the University of California, Berkeley campus.

and software) evolve and grow. What is needed is a stable framework upon which users can build networks. STREAMS is the UNIX system answer to this need.

User System Calls

First, look at an example of how a programmer, wishing to use the streams interface, would set up a stream in an application program. Here is a short code segment illustrating the system calls needed to set up stream A; it's also pictured in Figure 8–9.

```
        .
        .
        .

/*
 * Open the stream device
 */
if ((fd = open("/dev/strdev1","O_RDWR")) < 0)
{
        perror("open failure");
        exit(5);
}
        .
        .
        .


/*
 * Add in the lower layer protocol module
 */
if (ioctl(fd, I_PUSH, "proto_1") < 0)
{
        perror("I_PUSH #1 failure");
        exit(1);
}
        .
        .
        .

/*
 * Add in the next layer protocol module
 */
if (ioctl(fd, I_PUSH, "proto_2") < 0)
        perror("I_PUSH #2 failure");
```

```
exit(2);
    .
    .
    .
```

The open system call is written just as it always has been, with the specified device, /dev/strdev1, being a device handled by a streams driver (streams device). Just as /dev/tty01 is associated with a tty driver, /dev/strdev1 is associated with a streams driver. A *tty driver* is a kernel routine to which programs communicate using read/write and ioctl calls. A *streams driver* is a kernel routine with which programs communicate using read, write, and ioctl calls as well as the new streams system calls poll, getmsg, and putmsg. Typically a driver is associated with a real hardware device. Hardware devices (actually the associated hardware driver) have entries in the file system. For example, /dev/tty01 is the file system entry for a terminal connected to a specific place on the computer. You can see this entry by typing the command ls /dev/tty01. Therefore, you have the standard file system interface of open, close, read, write, and ioctl to that device even though there is *no disk file* containing data. The file system interface is the preferred method for communicating with a device, because it provides a simple and widely applicable way of looking at data. So, just as a terminal has an entry in the file system /dev/tty01, so does a streams driver, /dev/strdev1, have an entry in the file system. The UNIX kernel recognizes which is a streams device and acts appropriately for a streams device. Although you interface to a streams driver through the file system, the streams driver does not manipulate files, just as a terminal driver does not manipulate files.

The following ioctl calls use an I_PUSH request to add the appropriate protocols to the stream. You can think of ioctl being an abbreviation for I/O control. Its purpose is to pass control requests and information to the opened device driver and return responses to the program. The kernel may also do processing for some ioctl requests before they reach the driver. After the open for /dev/strdev1, the protocols are added, one at a time; first proto_1, then proto_2. The order is important. Note that the protocols are pushed on top of the device driver in a last-in, first-out (LIFO) stack. The protocol modules pushed could be a link layer protocol for proto_1 and a network layer protocol for proto_2. A protocol module is a kernel procedure that implements a protocol. This is all that is required to set up, or build, the stream. The protocol modules, proto_1 and proto_2, constitute a "protocol suite," which is just an implementation of a networking protocol providing a given service. In fact, you could have another protocol module, proto_x, which implemented a different link layer, but used the same STREAMS interfaces. Then proto_x could replace proto_1, without the neighboring protocol modules being aware of it. There also exists a corresponding I_POP request that can be used to remove a protocol module from a stream. The determination of which protocol module(s) to push onto the stream is left to the application program. However, this can be hidden within library routines.

This interchangeability of protocol modules gives STREAMS a major advantage: modularity. (There are also ways to have the stream be automatically set up through the open call, but that is beyond the scope of this paper.) Frequently, the term *stream end* is associated with the device driver and *stream head* with the top of the stream. Also note the stream end is device- and network-dependent, talking in terms pertinent to the networking technology and protocol. The stream head is more user-oriented, providing the standard system calls.

New System Calls

The user's application program may still use the standard UNIX System V open, close, read, write, and ioctl calls. The read/write calls are still useful for compatibility reasons as well as simple applications, but the full functionality of streams in receiving/sending messages is unavailable. Streams gives you three new system calls, shown in Table 8–1.

The getmsg system call has the same parameters as the read call, plus one more. The additional parameter is used for retrieving control information associated with the data message read. The putmsg system call has the same parameters as the write call, plus one more. The additional parameter is used for sending control information associated with the written data message.

The poll system call is used for monitoring I/O on a set of opened streams. It takes three parameters:

1. a list of file descriptors for the opened streams for which you want an indication of events that have occurred

2. the number of file descriptors in the list to be monitored

3. the event type you want to monitor. Typically, this is the presence of an input message or priority input message. Also, it occurs if a

Table 8–1 New System Calls Available with STREAMS

Call	Function
getmsg	Retrieve a message and associated control information
putmsg	Send a message and associated control information
poll	Monitor I/O on a set of opened streams

flow control situation has been relieved that would allow the
program to again send data

The standard read system call is a byte-oriented interface that has no
knowledge of message boundaries. If both control and data were put into
the same buffer returned on a read, the application program would analyze
the control information in an application-dependent manner. Another application would analyze the control information differently. In fact, different applications could have different concepts for control information
that are not necessarily compatible. There is a need to do it in a standard
way. Actually, some of the advanced network protocols, such as those
coming from the OSI effort, require sending control information with data
to carry out some functions correctly. The getmsg system call provides a
standard way of doing this independent of the application. The previous
arguments for getmsg apply equally to the putmsg system call. The getmsg and
putmsg routines are heavily used in the OSI Transport Level Interface implementation.

New Asynchronous or Concurrent I/O System Call

The poll system call is way for handling I/O events involving multiple file
descriptors. This allows an application program to retrieve incoming data
more quickly from several file descriptors. The historical way of polling
the file descriptors, although workable, is less efficient and more cumbersome to program than using the new poll system call. The old way
involved opening your file descriptors with O_NDELAY (if no data returns immediately, don't wait) and executing a loop issuing a read to each of these
file descriptors. To illustrate the historical way of polling:

```
int fd[3];      /* array for holding file descriptors */
int i;          /* work variable for looping through file descriptors */

/*
 * O_RDWR--means you plan to read and write to the file
 * O_NDELAY--means return immediately if no data
 */
fd[0] = open("/dev/ttyxx1",O_RDWR | O_NDELAY);
fd[1] = open("/dev/ttyxx2",O_RDWR | O_NDELAY);
fd[2] = open("/dev/ttyxx3",O_RDWR | O_NDELAY);
        .
        .
        .
i = 0;
```

```
while ( (nbytes = read( fd[i], buffer, 256)) == 0)
{
                if ( i == 2)
                        i = 0;
                else
                        ++i;
}
if (nbytes < 0)
{
                printf("Error on fd %d", i);
                return (2);      /* return error to caller */
}
/*
 * nbytes > 0
 * You have valid data in "buffer," up to 256 characters possible.
 * You can now process the data in "buffer."
 */
```

The while loop in this code segment is a small loop of code using the CPU until data has arrived. If data arrives infrequently, the while loop executes many times, producing no results. This is expensive in a time-sharing system. To reduce this impact, you could introduce a wait of one second, but this makes the response time worse. Whichever approach you use, the rate of arrival of data can vary, meaning the given approach is not the better one. Your program segment needs a way to be informed of data arriving over multiple opened file descriptors without incurring the side effects.

The streams poll call returns information about which file descriptors have an event, such as incoming data. The application can then decide to which descriptor a getmsg should be issued. The getmsg call will not block, because data is available. Basically, the poll system call provides a means for monitoring I/O and related events for a set of file descriptors or opened streams. A simple program segment to illustrate this follows. The three case statements after the switch correspond to the three different events that poll can detect. Notice that you are handling events for file fdpolls[0] before fdpolls[1] and fdpolls[1] before fdpolls[2], and so on. Thus, when poll returns with events for multiple file descriptors, you can decide the order in which to process them. In this example you are effectively giving preference to the files that occur earlier in the array fdpolls. This becomes important when poll returns many events on one call, because processing an event on a given file means a delay for processing on a different file. The poll system call gives you the ability to control priorities, that is, handle events (such as errors) ahead of normal processing of data.

```
        register int i;
        struct strbuf ctl, data;
        struct pollfd fdpolls[NUM_POLL_FDS];
                .
                .
                .

/*
 * There are now NUM_POLL_FDS streams opened as in the prior
 * example. Each entry in the array fdpolls represents
 * a stream.
 */
while (TRUE)
{
        /*
         * A -1 means wait forever.
         * Wait here until an event occurs on any
         * of the NUM_POLL_FDS streams.
         */
        if (poll(fdpolls, NUM_POLL_FDS, -1) < 0)
        {
                perror("poll failed");
                exit(3);
        }
        for (i = 0; i < NUM_POLL_FDS; ++i)
        {
                switch(fdpolls[i].revents)
                {
                case POLLIN:
                /* handle arrival of normal message */
                getmsg( fd[i], &ctl, &data, flags);
                        .
                        .
                        .
                        break;
                case POLLPRI:
                /* handle arrival of priority message */
                getmsg( fd[i], &ctl, &data, flags);
                        .
                        .
                        .
                        break;
                case POLLOUT:
                /* you can again send a message without blocking */
                putmsg( fd[i], &ctl, &data, flags);
```

```
                    .
                    .
                    .
        default:
        /* handle error cases */

                    .

                    .

                    .

                break;
        }
    }
}
```

The poll system call gives you the ability to control priorities, that is, handle events, such as errors, ahead of normal processing of data. A typical scenario would be to assign the first entry in the array to a management or control function. From this first entry the program could receive commands that control (such as allow and disallow) communications over the other file descriptors.

From within an application program, you can select the order in which to handle events for the related file descriptors. This can mean a significant reduction in related process switching, thus allowing your application to handle communications with more peers. Also, in some applications this facilitates a redesign for a reduction in the total number of processes, again meaning a reduction in system overhead.

The new STREAMS system calls address the present and future needs of computer networks and stress the importance networks play in the future of computing. Although there do not appear to be many new features for application programs, the key new features that have been provided allow more versatility in application design in a standard fashion. So far you have been learned the new STREAMS system calls that can be used in application programs. That is the new interface available through STREAMS. Now take a look at the kernel side of STREAMS, the implementation that supports the new STREAMS system calls, and the advantages the kernel provides.

Overview of Streams, Data Structures, and Algorithms

Queues

The design of STREAMS is based on queues of messages. When a stream is built, a set of queues is added every time an I_PUSH is performed. Figure

8–10 shows the basic building block, a pair of queues that are used to create a stream, which is a linear connected, or linked, list of queues. Figure 8–11 illustrates the results of building the stream. A queue is analogous to a line of cars stopped at a red light. When the light changes to green, the cars proceed through the intersection in the order of arrival (first-in, first-out) at the red light. On a normal drive you pass through a number of these queues. Thus, a queue is a line of messages waiting to be processed by a protocol module. Several streams can be opened that

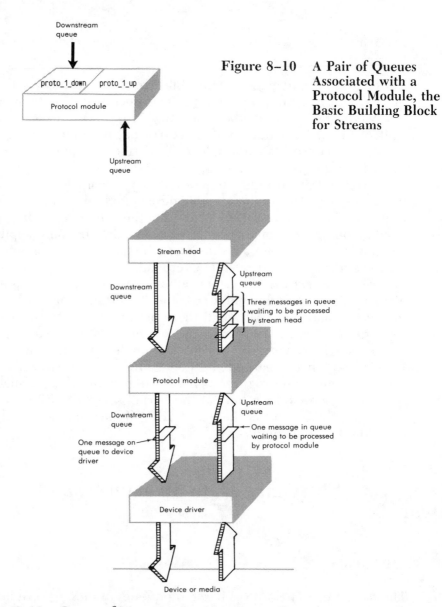

Figure 8–10   **A Pair of Queues Associated with a Protocol Module, the Basic Building Block for Streams**

Figure 8–11   **Queue of Messages Awaiting Processing**

have identical protocol modules pushed onto the stream, but each has its separate pair of queues. The push operation in the application program:

```
ioctl( fd, I_PUSH, "proto_1");
```

adds a pair of queues, as shown in Figure 8–10, and records the protocol module handling this set of queues within the queue control block. The result is in Figure 8–11. Another way of saying this is, "every queue has an associated protocol module." That means the implementation is based on a set of queues containing messages. A stream is a set of queues through which messages move. This is analogous to water flowing down a river or stream. When messages arrive in a queue, the streams scheduler will automatically call the associated protocol module to process them.

Notice the arrow in Figure 8–10, known as a *downstream queue*, that comes from above and another arrow, an *upstream queue*, coming from below. The arrows represent the queues. The act of connecting all the queues results in a stream. In fact, you can picture the linked list of queues as one large queue. The upstream queue, also referred to as the *read queue*, contains messages moving from the driver up to the user to be read using either read or getmsg system calls. The downstream queue, also referred to as the *write queue*, contains messages written by the user's write or putmsg calls and those messages moving toward the driver. This pair of queues and their associated protocol is the basic building block from which a stream is built.

These queues are created in pairs whenever a protocol module is pushed, with the upstream and downstream queues having identical interfaces. With each queue there is an associated queue control block. With the queue control block, you can locate the next queue in the stream as well as the other queue (of the pair of queues) belonging to the given protocol module.

Given the upstream queue, it is simple to locate the corresponding downstream queue, and vice versa. The pointers between queues came about because of the natural progression of messages from driver to user program and from user program to driver. This is useful when you want to echo characters to a terminal or when you return protocol acknowledgments for received data messages. When the protocol module receives character(s), in addition to sending them upward on the upstream queue (to the application process) the character(s) to be echoed are placed on the downstream queue.

Messages and Buffer Allocation

Any message not currently being processed by a protocol module is linked onto a queue. Thus, a queue is just a set of messages linked together, as in Figure 8–11, awaiting processing by a protocol module. All messages are built from one or more message blocks (or just "mb" for short) and data blocks ("db" for short). The mb's contain:

- a pointer to the db for this message block
- the length of the message text
- a pointer to the next mb for the message if any

The db's contain:

- the location of the buffer containing data
- the message type

The relationship between the message blocks and message buffer is shown in Figure 8–12. It also shows an intermediate structure, the data block, which is useful for duplicating messages without copying them. Remember earlier, under the motivation section, why you wanted to avoid copying strings of data excessively. In Figure 8–12, two messages appear on the queue for a link layer module. The link layer header is the same (for the given protocol layer), so the same data buffer is linked onto both messages. This can be determined by using two pointers to the block labeled link header. Since a message may consist of multiple message blocks, it is possible to add to the beginning of a message by simply linking an mb to the front of the message. Again, this is to avoid excessive copying of strings of data. It is just as easy to add a message block to the end of a message should the current buffer be too small. This is illustrated by the first message in Figure 8–12, to which the second message has been linked.

The messages are allocated from a buffer pool that is created at startup time. The number of different buffers and different sizes is variable and set at that time. All streams protocol modules use the same buffer pool. No one has a private buffer pool: that minimizes the amount of buffer memory allocated.

You see that the message allocation scheme is flexible, thus allowing for various ways of efficiently constructing messages. Since handling of message buffers is standard, you minimize the amount of allocated buffers and reduce the number of procedures needed to manipulate them. This is most helpful in today's network architectures, such as OSI.

Software Multiplexor

There also exists a need to funnel messages from one stream to one or more other streams. This is important in local area networks, where all

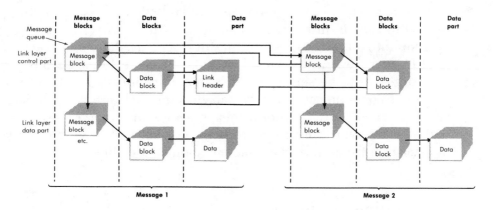

A. Message Structure for Sample Communications Link Messages

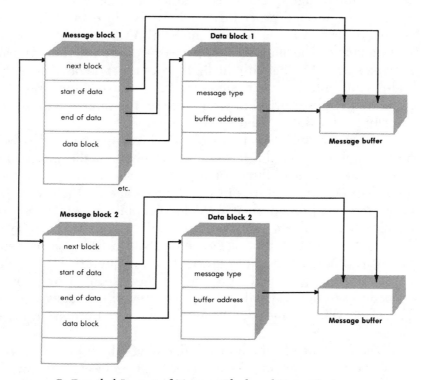

B. Detailed Layout of Message Block and Data Block

Figure 8–12   Sample Message Structure

messages must pass through one driver when going to/from the media. There are typically many virtual circuits on one machine, passing through the driver, and onto the media. Thus the streams, which correspond to these virtual circuits, must funnel down to the one stream used by the media driver. What is described here is a software multiplexor using streams.

A description of how this is implemented is beyond the scope of this paper. A multiplexor is just a way of funneling all activity from two or more streams into one stream. A multiplexor can be used in both directions. Just as I/O from several user-level processes can be funneled down to one device driver to be sent over one communications link, I/O from several different communications links can be funneled into a single stream or single opened file descriptor in an application program. An example of the latter is a network management program that is receiving error logging information from more than one communications link.

Scheduling of Queues

With each message queue is associated a *service procedure* and a *put procedure.* The service procedure is the procedure in which protocol processing occurs. It is the routine the STREAMS scheduler calls when messages appear on the queue. The service procedure will then typically remove each message, starting with the first, process it, add or remove information, and pass it on to the next queue via the put procedure. Both normal and expedited (high-priority) messages are on the same queue, with the high-priority ones always at the head of the queue.

There are only two types of priorities—normal and expedited—but within each priority the messages are added to the linked list in FIFO order. The put procedure for a given queue is called by the previous queue's procedure before putting the message on the given queue. Generally the put procedure is used for preliminary error checking of the message before placing it on the queue. Where minimum delay in message processing is crucial, that put procedure will call the put procedure of the following queue (instead of putting it on the queue). This would continue until the message reaches the end of the stream. However, use of put procedures in this way will delay processing of messages on other queues. Therefore, this one message delays processing of other messages on other queues.

The concept of scheduling is deciding which operation will execute next. The UNIX system schedules the next process to execute on the machine according to various criteria. Also, if the kernel has any work to do it will execute before any user's process will execute. However, the streams scheduler is separate from the UNIX system scheduler. When a message is placed on the queue, in either high or normal priority, it is added to the STREAMS scheduling queue in a FIFO manner. This determines the calling order for the service procedures.

Flow Control

Associated with the global buffer pool is a setting (percentage of buffers allocated), above which buffer requests will be denied for low-priority requests. At that point only high-priority requests will be satisfied until the number of available buffers increases above this setting.

Both upstream and downstream queues have associated high- and low-water marks used for flow control. The high- and low-water marks are just byte counts. Whenever a message is placed on a queue, the total byte count on that queue is incremented in the queue control block by the weighted size of the message buffer in bytes. "Weighted size" means that for small buffers, each byte counts as one byte, but for large buffers each byte counts as a smaller number. This is done to emphasize the message influence over byte influence. If the total byte count exceeds the high-water mark, that service procedure will not be scheduled again by the STREAMS scheduler until the low-water mark is reached. That means messages on that queue won't be processed until the queue in front of it processes its messages. Generally, you want the high-water mark large enough to contain several messages, such as the window size in windowing protocols, before it is reached. Also you want the difference between the high- and low-water marks to be such that several average messages can be on the queue. Experience shows this reduces the number of times the streams scheduler is called and thus reduces the overhead. The flow control rules[3] also advise against putting messages on a queue once the high-water mark is reached. However, this is purely advisory.

It is recognized that many applications share the same machine. Thus they must coexist in a fair manner, so that no one application or user hogs the resources, message processing, and buffer usage. The flow control mechanism is one mechanism to assist in the fair use of the machine for networking. This becomes most important when the system is at or near capacity, because that is the time when the flow control mechanisms are most frequently activated.

Overview of Transport Level Interface

You have viewed many of the features of STREAMS, the new system call's for application programs, and the architecture of message handling within

---

[3]The guidelines are documented in the *STREAMS Programmer's Guide*, AT&T, 1986.

the kernel. The person writing protocol modules is assisted by a large set of subroutine calls and utility routines. All is provided to ensure that programmers follow a standardized architecture, and to assist in building computer networking protocols. You have seen STREAMS providing sophisticated tools for handling messages from the user down to the communications link and back up. So far, this paper has dealt only with messages moving from a user's application program down to communications media and back up. It hasn't discussed messages in a larger sense, where two machines exchange messages. There is still a need for a protocol within which applications work and talk in a standard way with their peers on remote machines. However, STREAMS does not provide the protocols themselves; someone must build them.

By analogy, imagine that a person in the United States wants to make a telephone call to someone in Japan. There is a well-established procedure for making international telephone calls: listening for dial tone, dialing the international access code, then just dialing a sequence of numbers for the Japanese person's actual number. There also is an established procedure for answering the telephone call: picking up the receiver and acknowledging the call. Now the two telephones are connected by the telephone companies' telephone network. However, the American speaks English and the other person speaks Japanese. Just as the telephone system has provided a method for connecting to the telephone network, so STREAMS provides a method for sending messages onto a medium. Just as the telephone system in Japan has provided a way for answering the call, so STREAMS provides a way for receiving messages from the media. However, the two still cannot understand each other: a translator is needed.

To fit this need, a transport protocol is needed to reliably transport messages across a network in such a way that the two applications in the two different machines (connected by a network) can understand each other. Thus, the Transport Level Interface was developed and modeled after OSI's (Open Systems Interconnection) Transport Service Definition (ISO 8072). The TLI is also known as Transport Library Interface, because many of the user-level routines are implemented in a library (the Transport Library). The Transport Level Interface just specifies the services provided by the underlying transport provider (the protocol modules in streams). The transport provider embodies the transport protocol necessary to meet the services definition. By analogy, the UNIX user's manual contains the service definition for system calls, whereas the UNIX kernel is the provider for the implementation of those system calls.

Figure 8–13 gives a user's view of the Transport Level Interface, showing the Transport Library Interface that the user would employ in compiling programs. It provides the Transport Level Interface specific library calls. The transport provider is the implementation necessary to support the Transport Level Interface using the given technology. Writing

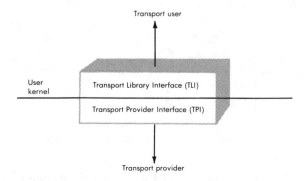

Figure 8–13   Relationship Between Transport User and Transport Provider

applications to the Transport Level Interface will in the long run enhance their independence from any specific protocol, machine, or network technology. The transport layer provides reliable end-to-end communications between transport users, regardless of the underlying network technology.

What advantages does the Transport Level Interface provide? In traditional I/O or STREAMS environments, you have a standard way of handling messages within a machine. But their definition and scope of control end where the communications link starts. They certainly do not extend into the remote machine. In a pure STREAMS environment, a write operation indicates only that a protocol module received it, not that it was sent successfully to the remote machine. Remember that STREAMS is not a protocol, but a means for protocol suites to be built. The local machine and the remote machine must still have a standard way of talking to each other for productive work to occur.

The scope of a transport protocol, as in the Transport Level Interface, on the other hand, includes the communications link and both local and remote machines. The Transport Level Interface gives you, the user, end-to-end connectivity and control. For instance, if you have an error in sending a message to the remote machine, you can distinguish between errors occurring on your local machine, the remote machine, or the path between them in a network technology independent manner. Thus, when you, the transport user, issue a t_snd (Transport Level Interface write operation), you have a high degree of confidence that the remote transport user received it. This is important because this concern increases as the size of the network (and the interactions) increases, and increases as well with the importance of the application.

Transport Level Interface Activities

From the perspective of the Transport Level Interface, there are four phases of normal activity. They are:

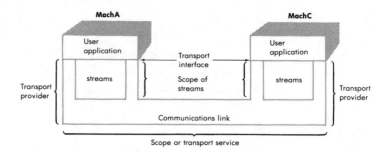

Figure 8–14   The Scope of STREAMS and the Scope of Transport Level Interface

1. local management
2. connection establishment
3. data transfer
4. connection release

Local Management

This phase is concerned with establishing the interfaces between the transport user and the transport provider. It includes setting options with the transport provider, as well as identifying yourself by name on the local machine. Following is a partial list of the more frequently used library calls. They are:

- t_open. This includes the regular open system call as well as setting up transport specific data structures.

- t_bind. This is used to identify yourself by a name to the transport provider as well as to the network. If someone wants to set up a virtual circuit[1] to you, this is the name that is called.

- t_unbind. This call is used to release the name that others have been using to set up a virtual circuit with you. Thus, you can no longer set up any virtual circuits.

- t_close. This includes the normal close system call as well as removing the transport-specific data structures that have been set up in the kernel.

- t_look. This call returns the latest action that happened on your end of a virtual circuit. This could be an indication that all is normal, or it might be some error flag.

---

[1]For a refresher on what a virtual circuit is, read the section in RFS on the host connection level.

- t_getinfo. This returns the current options the transport provider is using for the given virtual circuit.
- t_optmgmt. This is used to request certain options from the transport provider. Typically these are items such as buffer sizes, maximum number of messages to be buffered in the virtual circuit, and so on.

Connection Establishment

This phase is concerned with what is necessary to set up a virtual circuit between you and a peer application on the remote machine. The applications are the transport users. Again, the following is only a partial list of the more frequently used library calls. The relevant calls are:

- t_connect. This is used for attempting to contact another transport user on a remote machine.
- t_accept. This call accepts a transport connection from a transport user on a remote machine. You have the option of rejecting the t_connect request based on the passed information the other transport user gave to you.
- t_listen. This call is used to wait for transport requests from another transport user.

Data Transfer

This is the phase in which a transport user spends most of the time, because it handles sending and receiving messages. A partial list of its calls is:

- t_snd. This call sends data over a virtual circuit. It is analogous to the write system call.
- t_rcv. This call is used for receiving data over a virtual circuit. It is analogous to the read system call.

Connection Release

A partial list of the more frequently used library calls is:

- t_sndrel This requests the orderly termination of a virtual circuit. *Orderly* means in a way that ensures no data will be lost. All data previously sent will be received. The transport user on the remote machine will receive an indication of this request.

- t_snddis. This call is used to request the abortion of a virtual circuit. Data can be lost, as this is typically used when an orderly termination does not appear to be working for whatever reason. Again, the transport user on the remote machine receives an indication of this request.

These are the normal phases for using a virtual circuit to communicate between two transport users. There is also a connectionless-mode service (sometimes called *datagram*), which is a way of sending a message between two transport users without a virtual circuit. The message being sent contains all the information needed to get it to the remote transport user. This is analogous to the way the U.S Postal Service sends mail. There are some applications that make heavy use of this type of feature. One of these could be a sample application that monitors the temperature at different points in an office building. The temperature readings are typically taken once every minute and are not likely to change much over many minutes. If a single temperature reading is lost, the application can use the prior reading. If no temperature reading arrives in a period of time, then an error message is sent to a person who can investigate the problem. The reasons for considering using connectionless mode for this sort of application are:

- There is less overhead for sending a message once per minute from each sensor.

- An occasional lost message will not harm the application.

Transport Level Interface Summary

Designing applications to the Transport Level Interface specification may not always be straightforward. With the additional flexibility comes additional options for program design, some of which you have seen. Many of the ideas embodied in the TLI definition, and in the OSI standard, have evolved from experiences with other computer networks, and both small and mainframe computers. The paper has also tried to show in a brief space the importance of end-to-end reliability for application programs or transport users. It's impossible to stress too strongly the importance to transport users, or applications, of being able to control data movement through computer networks reliably. This concern is increasingly important as more computers are connected to more networks of differing technology. This trend will continue in the future.

Summary

This paper concludes with a brief example of a `cat order.data` command to a remote machine, machC. This example emphasizes the areas that have been discussed: RFS, STREAMS, and the Transport Level Interface. From the information you have learned so far in these discussions, you can deduce the sequence of events needed to process a simple command. This example is intended to solidify your knowledge of how all these new features fit together at a high level; no discussion of internal algorithms is attempted. This example does not imply an actual implementation. Also, because RFS is implemented completely within the kernel, and yet uses the TLI, it must interface to the kernel component of the Transport Level Interface, the transport provider (TP). However, in order to simply the example, the calls are written as if they were in an application program.

For this example, `order.data` has only one line of data. Figure 8–15 is a chart with time flowing down the page, showing requests as they traverse the key components, are modified, and passed on. When an arrow ends in a particular column, processing continues down the page. The text encountered within the column is the generated request that is sent with the arrow to the next column. The example begins with a request `open("order.data")`. This is recognized by UNIX and RFS to refer to a file system on a remote machine, machC.

Thus, RFS packages the request into a `t_snd` request with control information (`open_req,order.data`) in a data buffer. RFS sends the `t_snd` request to the Transport Level Interface. The TLI puts this into a STREAMS message format with a control part (`ctl="open\req"`) and a data part (`data="order.data"`). This is comparable to a `pútmsg` call. On the remote machine, machC, you see a `t_rcv()` has been issued waiting for any messages. It was converted into a `getmsg()` request. When the remote machine, machC, receives the `open\req` it is returned with the completion of the `t_rcv()` call. RFS on machC gives the `open\req` to UNIX to execute.

Then RFS returns to machA the result of the open, `open_ack`. The sequence of events for the `open_ack` response is similar to the `open_req`: just the message is moving from machC to machA. The `open_ack` message is a piece of data moving between machines, just as the `open_req` message is a piece of data moving between machines. When RFS on machA receives this `open\ack` request, an open successful indication is returned to the `cat` program. The `cat` program would then proceed to read the first line. Then the same sequence of events would occur as for the `open_req`, but now the request is to "read a line." This continues until an end of file (EOF) condition instead of a line of data is returned to machA. Then the `cat` program, seeing the EOF, proceeds to close the file.

This paper began by looking at an application, the RFS distributed file system, which gives you new and different ways to work. You have

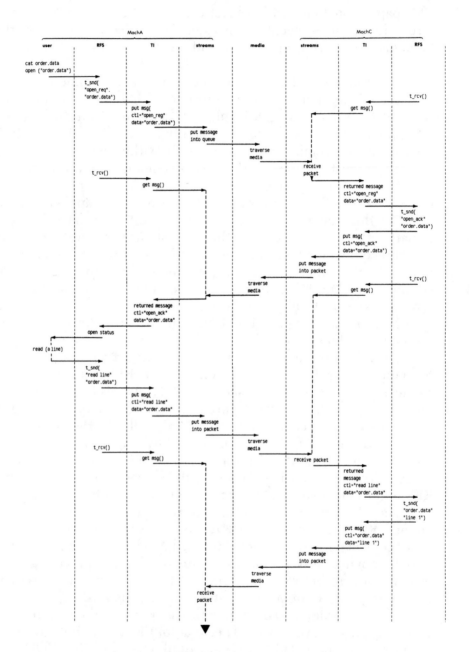

Figure 8–15   Time Diagram for a Simple Command, cat

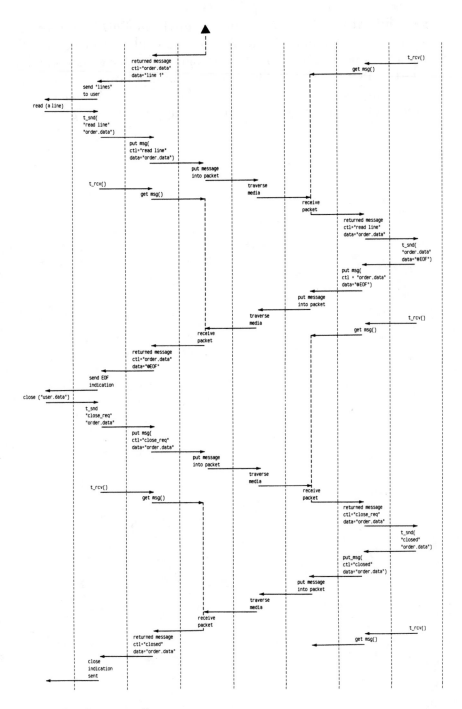

Figure 8–15 *(continued)*

seen how it affects your computing environment. You have seen how designing it on a standard, the Transport Level Interface, will allow it to be used with new networking technologies. You have also seen how the new STREAMS mechanisms allow for development of networking applications. Portability has always been a major factor for UNIX machines. STREAMS help protect the large investments in application programs.

KEYWORDS

▶ TCP/IP

▶ Ethernet

▶ IEEE 802.3
Standard

▶ OSI Reference
Model

▶ Packet

▶ Protocols

▶ Thin Ethernet

Paper Synopsis: Networking has become a necessity for many users, but it presents a bewildering array of choices and a new set of jargon. Ethernet is one of the most popular LANs in the UNIX community. In this paper, you'll learn what you need to know to design and implement hardware and software for an Ethernet LAN for UNIX systems and PCs. You will see how to take advantage of remote file servers, shared resources, diskless workstations, and multiple processors. This paper demystifies network terminology and provides sources for further information.

Charles Spurgeon is a specialist in cross-campus networks and is employed by the Academic Computing and Information Systems group at Stanford University. Mr. Spurgeon has designed Ethernet systems for computers ranging from mainframes to micros. A member of ACM and USENIX, he attended Wesleyan University in Middletown, Connecticut, where he studied cultural anthropology. (He claims that a background in anthropology is useful for understanding the obscure mating rituals observed in distributed computer systems.)

## 9

Ethernet: A UNIX LAN

Charles Spurgeon

This paper is intended to introduce Ethernet local area network (LAN) technology and to help explain how it fits into the world of UNIX systems. It also covers the basic Ethernet concepts so you'll have a general understanding of how Ethernet works. You'll also learn some Ethernet jargon to help prepare you to read and evaluate vendor literature on Ethernet LANs.

If you're familiar with UNIX systems, but have never used high-speed LANs, this paper will explain why a high-speed LAN can be a very useful addition. If you've had some experience with other LAN technologies, on microcomputers for instance, this paper shows how a high-speed LAN like Ethernet can help tie different LAN technologies together.

Why Use a LAN?

If you've never used a computer system that was connected to a LAN before, it might be hard to understand what all the fuss is about. What makes a LAN so useful? If there's a single word that sums up the advantage of using a LAN, that word is *access*. With a high-speed LAN you can have access to:

- remote file systems and file servers
- shared resources, such as a high-speed laser printer
- multiple processor types and operating systems on the same network

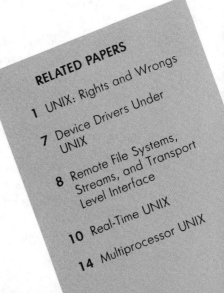

- new network-based applications, such as network file systems for diskless workstations

A LAN is a privately owned data communications system that usually covers a limited area. Different LAN technologies use different media and vary with respect to data transmission speeds, distances spanned, and other such characteristics. Ethernet was one of the first LANs to be standardized and made widely available by multiple vendors. An Ethernet LAN delivers high-speed communications and can be extended to reach several work areas in an office, floors of the same building, or even several buildings on the same compus or office park. An Ethernet LAN can handle all of these topologies and many more. Ethernet is a highly extensible network technology that is capable of growing and changing to meet your needs.

High-speed LANs support the network-based applications that are now appearing. The new UNIX-based workstation market is evolving network-based applications, such as remote file systems and server-based window systems, that require a high-speed LAN to work. The trend toward network-based applications will continue, and that makes a high-speed LAN a necessary item for sites with the new workstations.

Ethernet is particularly well-suited for linking a wide variety of UNIX and other computer systems on the same network. Ethernet can do this because it uses an open system standard, which means that it's available to all manufacturers and can be purchased to interface with virtually every computer on the market today.

Matching Technology to Your Needs

Make no mistake, installing a high-speed LAN is a big job, and it can be expensive. If all you need is the occasional file transfer and terminal session between machines, then a low-speed serial line and something like the Kermit program would probably be the best technology match. Even large file transfers, if they only happen occasionally, could be best handled with magnetic tapes or disks—a form of data transfer known in the trade as "walk-net."

You must be the judge of your own requirements, and you'll have to work at achieving the best match between the technology you need, and what the market has to offer. This paper will help by describing some of the capabilities of Ethernet and the key considerations for designing and implementing it, so that you will be better able to make an informed decision.

Ethernet Is Not New

Ethernet technology has been under steady development for over 10 years and has been available as an open system standard for over 5 years. New chips and other Ethernet technology have recently appeared, and as a result Ethernet has been steadily dropping in price. Meanwhile, the UNIX workstation market has been steadily increasing in performance, and more and more UNIX-based workstations are being sold with Ethernet built right in. Ethernet has become widely accepted in the UNIX marketplace, due to the many advantages such a high-speed, standardized, network technology can bring.

Ethernet and the Alto

Ethernet was invented in 1973 at the Xerox Palo Alto Research Center (PARC) as part of a project to build a personal computer workstation called the Alto. The Alto had a bit-mapped graphics display, mouse, hard disk, and sophisticated drawing and word processing software. It was the ancestor of the Xerox Star system, Apple Lisa, the Macintosh, and all of the latest graphics-based personal computers.

Among other advanced features, each Alto also had a high-speed connection to printers and file servers, and to every other Alto by way of Ethernet. This ability to easily and rapidly transfer information made it possible to create sophisticated electronic mail programs for the Alto, along with remote printing programs, file transfer programs, and the first interactive multiuser game for personal computers, called Mazewars. Ethernet was given its name at PARC in a memo written by one of the inventors, Dr. Robert M. Metcalfe. He proposed the name since "The essential feature of our medium—the ether—is that it carries transmissions, propagates bits to all stations."[1]

The Standards Effort

Ethernet became an industry standard in 1980 when three companies—Digital Equipment Corporation (DEC), Intel, and Xerox—announced a cooperative standardization effort. Using the first initials of each company, this effort became known as the DIX standard. After the DIX standard version 2.0 was released, Ethernet was included in the 802-series stand-

---

[1]Robyn E. Shotwell, *The Ethernet Sourcebook*, 3rd ed. (North Holland, 1985), p. xi.

ardization effort launched by the Institute of Electrical and Electronic Engineers (IEEE), which resulted in the IEEE 802.3 standard. The formal specification is now known as "IEEE 802.3 CSMA/CD," but most people continue to call it Ethernet. These standardization efforts resulted in an Ethernet specification that was available to everyone and in Ethernet equipment that could be installed in a wide range of computers instead of just machines from one manufacturer.

As everyone knows, people who speak different languages cannot easily communicate; computers built by different manufacturers share this problem, too. Standardizing the Ethernet established a common language that every machine could speak. As Metcalfe put it, "The invention of Ethernet as an open, non-proprietary, industry standard local network was perhaps even more significant than the invention of the Ethernet technology itself."[2]

Berkeley Network Software

Once Ethernet became an open system standard, many vendors began building Ethernet hardware. The VAX series of minicomputers from DEC was among the first to benefit from this new market for Ethernet hardware. At the same time, work was underway at the University of California at Berkeley on developing standard network software for the UNIX system. Berkeley had a number of VAX computers running UNIX, and it was a natural choice to develop the new network software using multiple VAX computers linked by Ethernet.

The result of the work at Berkeley has been the inclusion of Ethernet support and networking software in the Berkeley UNIX Distributions (BSD). Berkeley UNIX is used on campuses and at research centers worldwide, and has become widely accepted in the technical workstation market. Indeed, one reason for adopting Berkeley UNIX for use on technical workstations was the powerful networking capabilities that it could bring to the workstation market.

While the AT&T System V UNIX distribution does not contain the networking software developed at Berkeley, at least one workstation manufacturer has begun to merge the two distributions. Sun Microsystems is developing its own Berkeley-based UNIX system, called SunOS, into a combination of both the Berkeley and the AT&T distributions. The initial phase of this effort is complete, and it includes a System V compatibility package for SunOS. The next several phases are planned to result in as complete a merge as possible between the two UNIX distributions, including the kernel, libraries, and utilities.

---

[2]Ibid.

From the Oldest Workstations to the Newest

From its earliest beginnings with the Alto, to its use on campuses and at research centers, Ethernet has made it possible to develop entirely new capabilities for computers. Ethernet can link computers built by many different companies and allow them to transfer information reliably and at high speed.

Furthermore, Ethernet hardware has dramatically dropped in price, and the Ethernet technology has been extended to make it more suitable for offices, with the result that Ethernet has broadened its scope to include low-cost microcomputers and workstations of all types.

Next you'll see how Ethernet technology works and be introduced to some of the hardware that gets the job done.

Ethernet Basics

The Ethernet system is composed of three major elements:

1. the Ethernet hardware that moves data over a network wire that is connected to each computer
2. the Ethernet packet, which is a group of bits formed in a specified pattern and transmitted over the Ethernet hardware
3. the data carried by the Ethernet packet. The network protocols carried inside the data field of each Ethernet packet establish communications between the applications running on every computer connected to the network

The first two elements are entirely described by the Ethernet specifications. The third element is made of network protocols that have their own sets of standards. Look briefly now at how these three elements work together.

The Ethernet Packet

The Ethernet packet is an important part of the entire Ethernet system. The Ethernet hardware system, composed of network cables and controllers and so forth, is essentially a delivery service for moving Ethernet packets between computers. A diagram of the Ethernet packet is shown in Figure 9-1. Ethernet packets are more formally known as "frames," with fields of bits inside them formed as "octets." This paper uses the

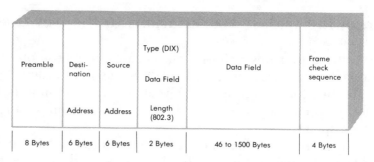

Figure 9–1   Format of an Ethernet Packet

more familiar, if less precise, terminology and calls them packets, with fields of bits formed in bytes (assumed to be eight bits long each).

The important fields to notice in the Ethernet packet are the source address, destination address, and the data field. The source and destination addresses of the Ethernet packet are also called the hardware addresses. This is because an address is assigned to the hardware of each Ethernet controller, and the controller's address is used for either the source or the destination address of the Ethernet packet, as required.

The data field of the Ethernet packet contains the bits to be transferred between computers. This data usually consists of a network protocol packet, which is just another set of bits formed in a standardized way. The applications running on each computer communicate by way of standard network protocols, which they send to one another in the data field of Ethernet packets. These "protocol packets" contain the actual applications' data being transferred.

The Ethernet Controller

Ethernet packets are assembled and transmitted by Ethernet controllers, which are located in every computer connected to the network. The controller actually does quite a lot of work on its own, both in forming packets to send and in recognizing packets on the network that are addressed to it.

The controller performs these functions automatically, without any intervention by the UNIX system. The controller is also designed to operate rapidly in order to keep up with the 10 megabit per second data rate of the Ethernet. A hardware address is assigned to each Ethernet controller when it's built, with the result that each computer that contains an Ethernet controller possesses its own Ethernet hardware address.

Ethernet packets are sent over the network one at a time. Data is sent serially on the network, one bit at a time. As the packet is transmitted, it is heard simultaneously by every Ethernet controller connected to the network. The controllers read in the bits, look at the destination address of the packet, and if it matches their own address, they store the contents of the data field of the Ethernet packet and deliver the data (in the form of the network protocol packet) to the network software running on the computer.

The controller runs constantly, watching the network and looking at every packet for an address match. When given the appropriate data and address information and the correct sequence of commands, the controller can also be commanded by the UNIX system to form Ethernet packets and send them over the network.

To the UNIX kernel, the Ethernet controller is just another device with an I/O address. The controller board also contains some memory, which allows it to read in a packet and store the data before requesting service from the UNIX kernel. There are both receive and transmit memory buffers so that the UNIX kernel can write data into the controller's memory, give it the appropriate destination address, and command it to form and send an Ethernet packet automatically.

Network Protocols Example

The Ethernet packet is used to deliver network protocols between computers on Ethernet LANs. The network protocols are also called packets, and although this may seem confusing at first glance, it's really pretty simple to distinguish between the two packets. Network protocols are easy to understand, because anyone uses some form of protocol in daily life. There's a certain protocol to writing a thank-you note, for instance, and you can compare the act of composing and delivering a thank-you note to what a network protocol does, to see how each works.

The thank-you note has a well-known form that has been standardized through custom. In the thank-you note there's the basic message, along with a greeting to the recipient and the name of the sender. After one finishes writing the note, the note is stuffed into an envelope, the sender's and recipient's street addresses are written on the envelope, and the completed note is given it to the post office or similar delivery system, which handles the details of getting the message to the right address.

A given network protocol acts much like a thank-you note. The network protocol is sent as a packet of information with a data field that corresponds to the message of the thank-you note. The sender's and recipient's names in the previous example become protocol addresses here and are added to complete the network protocol packet. After the network protocol packet has been composed by the system software, it's stuffed into the data field of an Ethernet packet, which corresponds to the envelope in the previous example. The Ethernet controller and the network system handle the details of getting the Ethernet packet to the right computer. See Figure 9–2.

Ethernet as Delivery System

The important thing to remember is that an Ethernet is basically a delivery service for networking protocols. The Ethernet packet is a standardized part of the Ethernet system. The network protocols are also standards, but independent of the Ethernet system. As far as Ethernet is concerned, each network protocol is just a set of data bits in the data field of the Ethernet packet. Ethernet with its Ethernet packets is the delivery system for those network protocols, but it's the network protocols themselves that make it possible for the application software to get things done for the user.

Ethernet controllers and Ethernet packets are both part of a larger Ethernet system composed of standard hardware components. Take a look at some of the basic hardware components in an Ethernet system.

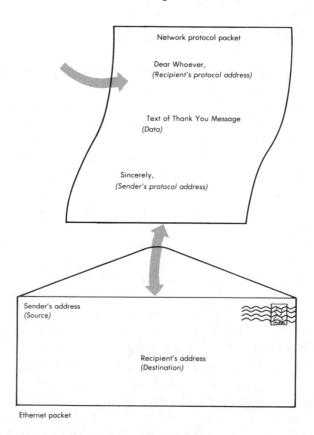

Figure 9–2   **Ethernet as a Delivery System**

Basic Ethernet Hardware

The essence of Ethernet lies in its ability to transfer data between computers quickly and reliably. To do this, Ethernet employs a set of standardized components. The names of some of these components have changed as the Ethernet standards evolved, and you'll see both old and new names here as you go along.

Ethernet Terminology

Ethernet is based on a method of data transmission called CSMA/CD. *CS* stands for carrier sense, and means that each Ethernet controller connected to the network waits until the network is idle before it sends a packet. *MA* stands for multiple access, indicating that every controller has equal access to the network and that there's no central controller or administrator in the Ethernet system.

CD stands for collision detect. It's possible for two controllers to send packets at precisely the same moment. When a collision of packets is detected, the controllers will immediately stop sending and wait for a short period of time before retrying. Each controller generates a random period of time to wait, so that they won't collide again.

Ethernet functions just like a conversation, where you wait for the other person to stop speaking (carrier sense) before speaking yourself. Assuming it's a friendly conversation, both of you have an equal chance to speak (multiple access). If you both start speaking at the same time, it's best to stop and then let one person go first (collision detect).

Ethernet is a baseband transmission system, which simply means that the Ethernet cable is dedicated to just one service—transmitting Ethernet packets. The packets are present on the network one at a time. As each packet is transmitted, it is heard by every machine connected to the network at effectively the same instant. Only the controller whose address matches the packet's destination will take any action, however. Packets come and go quite rapidly, so that on the average, an Ethernet spends a lot of its time idle, waiting for the computers to send something.

The Basic Ethernet Components

There are five basic hardware components that are used to build an Ethernet segment, as listed here and shown in Figure 9–3:

1. *Ethernet coaxial cable.* This is a special quadruply shielded, 50 ohm coaxial cable. Coaxial cable (coax) is a specially designed type of

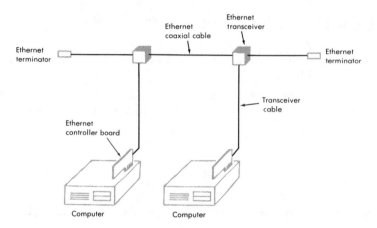

Figure 9–3   Basic Ethernet Segment

wire that can transfer electrical impulses at high speeds with low signal distortion. It's called the *network medium* in the Ethernet standards.

2. *Ethernet terminator.* This is a 50 ohm resistor that is installed at each end of the coaxial cable. The terminator prevents signals from reflecting off the end of the cable. The reason signal reflections happen on unterminated network cables is a complex subject not really worth knowing, unless you plan to get a degree in electrical engineering. The terminator prevents signal reflections by acting like a sponge for electrical signals and soaking them all up when they reach the end of the cable, instead of letting them bounce back and interfere with other signals.

3. *Ethernet transceiver.* This word is a combination of TRANSmitter and reCEIVER. The transceiver is a small box that attaches directly to the network coax and contains the electronics needed to send and receive packets on the network. The 802.3 specifications call the transceiver a *medium attachment unit (MAU).*

4. *Transceiver cable.* This cable moves the signals from the transceiver located on the network cable to the Ethernet controller located in the computer. The 802.3 specifications call this wire an *attachment unit interface (AUI).*

5. *Ethernet controller.* This component comes in two forms. One form is a board that plugs into a computer bus, such as the IBM PC bus. Now that very large scale integration (VLSI) technology has shrunk the electronics to just a few chips, Ethernet controllers are being built right into the main processor board of some workstations. In the second form, all you'll see is an Ethernet connector mounted on the back of the workstation.

Other Components

While these five components suffice to build a single Ethernet segment, many Ethernet installations are larger than one segment. Usually an installation starts with a single segment, but before long the network gets extended to connect other machines and other offices. To make this possible, there's a whole series of special Ethernet devices. The most commonly used one is the Ethernet repeater. It's used to link several Ethernet segments together according to specific rules that describe how many repeaters and segments can make up a single Ethernet network.

There are also Ethernet bridges, which are used to link large, multisegment Ethernets. A bridge is commonly installed to link the Ethernets in two different buildings, for example. There are more special devices, all of which can be combined to extend Ethernets as required. There's not enough space here to describe all the devices or to explain the rules and specifications that apply to each device. You can see where to find more information at the end of this paper.

Up until the last few years, the cost of an Ethernet connection was high enough to restrict its use to mainframe computers. With the introduction of VLSI technology for Ethernet chips, the cost of Ethernet controllers has plummeted, and new Ethernet components have also been invented that make connecting small computers much easier and less expensive. As a result, new Ethernet installations have spread rapidly, and Ethernet is now commonly used to link workstations and small computers. Next, you'll look at the new Ethernet technology that has been developed and at how it's used to connect computers of all sizes together.

New Ethernet Technology

The cost of connecting a computer to the Ethernet has dropped in the last few years, due to new technology. Using new VLSI Ethernet chips, workstations are now being shipped with Ethernet electronics built right into the equipment. While the price of controllers for the Ethernet had dropped, the cost of acquiring and installing the Ethernet coaxial cable and building the physical network remained relatively high, until recently.

This situation changed with the invention of a new form of Ethernet. The new system uses thinner network cable and a different approach to transceiver connections, with the result that installing an Ethernet cable has dropped in cost, too. Next you'll see how the new technology works and how it interacts with the original Ethernet standard.

New Ethernets for the Office

The original Ethernet coaxial cable is a large wire, with a diameter of about half an inch and a solid (and fairly stiff) center conductor. This makes for a rather heavy and inflexible cable that doesn't fit well in the average office environment. The original Ethernet cable is fine under machine room floors or in building conduits, but it just isn't well suited to smaller rooms or modular cubicles. Some way was needed to make the Ethernet cable into a reasonable office system.

The solution was to use a much thinner and more flexible coaxial cable. The new cable is called "thin Ethernet," since it is only half the thickness of the old Ethernet cable. The thin Ethernet cable also uses lower-cost connectors than the ones used in the "thick" Ethernet specification. The result is a network cable system that is a lot more flexible, lower in cost, and easier to build.

Naming Networks Through Thick and Thin

Vendor literature often uses different names for Ethernet equipment, and it helps to know how the various names came about.

The new thin Ethernet was jokingly called "cheapernet" while the specification process was underway, because a major goal of the new system was to make Ethernet lower in cost. "Cheapernet" was never meant to be an official name, but you'll sometimes see references to this bit of network slang in the literature.

The 802.3 spec officially calls the thin Ethernet system "10BASE2." That means 10 megabit data rate, baseband transmission, and, in a bit of fudging to keep things neat, 185 meters in length rounded up to 200. Don't worry about everything fitting perfectly, just realize that when a vendor says 10BASE2 in its literature, it refers to the new thin Ethernet system.

The thick Ethernet, or original Ethernet standard, is also known as "10BASE5," which means 10 megabits, baseband, 500 meters per segment.

The new thin Ethernet technology was invented at a networking company called 3COM; it became the basis of 3COM's EtherSeries product line. Other vendors have come up with different names for their thin Ethernet products. For instance, DEC has chosen to call its thin Ethernet offering ThinWire. Hewlett-Packard refers to the technology as ThinLAN. In the general marketplace, however, the use of the name thin Ethernet seems to have caught on. The original 3COM thin Ethernet specifications have changed and have become more conservative now that thin Ethernet is part of the 802.3 standard. That's the usual process that occurs when a new technology is standardized for use industry-wide.

The Three New Components of Thin Ethernet

The thin Ethernet system consists of three new components:

- lower cost, thin coaxial cable
- lower cost connectors
- single-chip Ethernet transceivers

The thin Ethernet system is based on the development of new single-chip transceiver electronics. Once the transceiver electronics had shrunk to the size of a single chip, it became possible to incorporate the transceiver and Ethernet controller onto the same board. This eliminates the need for an external transceiver and transceiver cable. In practice, the thin Ethernet coax is connected directly to the controller board with a T connector. The result of this innovation is to make attaching a workstation to the Ethernet much less expensive. Another result of the new technology is to make Ethernet cable easily fit into normal office environments. See Figure 9–4.

Mixing Thick and Thin

Thin Ethernet is compatible with standard thick Ethernet systems. The thin Ethernet uses the same Ethernet packet, runs at the same speed, and

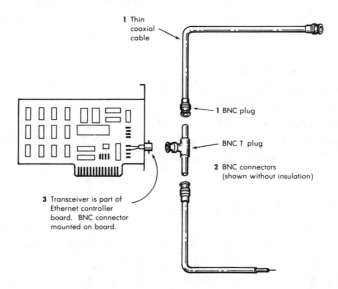

Figure 9–4   Three New Components of Thin Ethernet

can even connect to old style Ethernet transceivers that have been equipped with the new thin Ethernet connectors. Both old and new style equipment can be mixed on a thin Ethernet installation with no compatibility problems. Using the new specifications, each thin Ethernet segment can be 185 meters (about 600 feet) long, which is shorter than a standard Ethernet segment, but still suffices in the average office area.

Ethernet repeaters can be used to link several thin Ethernet segments together to cover a larger area, just as in the old style Ethernet standard. One design for a building-wide Ethernet is to use thick Ethernet as a main network "backbone" with branches of thin Ethernet dedicated to the task of bringing the network to individual offices. Of course, if you only have a single office, or a floor of offices to network, then thin Ethernet alone can do the job.

Network Protocols

Once the network is installed and everyone's computer is connected to it, then what? Application software capable of using network services is required; and not just any application software, either. One theme in this description of the Ethernet has been the advantage of using open system standards. An open system standard is available to all and makes it possible to link many different computers together. The advantages of open system standards extend to the world of network protocols, too. For applications on many different computers to cooperate, the application software must be based on open system protocol standards as well.

Take a quick look now at one network protocol family in wide use on UNIX systems today—the TCP/IP protocol suite. There are many other network protocols, including a new international standard protocol suite being developed right now. Some of these new protocols may become widely accepted in the future, but for now, the TCP/IP protocol family is the one in common use on UNIX systems that support high-speed LANs. (You'll see what the initials mean in a moment.)

Berkeley Leads the Way

Researchers at the University of California at Berkeley have made extensions to the UNIX kernel to support standard network protocols for the UNIX systems they have been developing. These new system calls are designed to be general enough to support many different protocol standards, but one of the first major protocol implementations was the TCP/IP suite. The work on TCP/IP was funded by the Defense Advanced Research Projects Agency (DARPA, commonly referred to by its old acronym, ARPA) which is a part of the U.S. Department of Defense. For many years, ARPA has been involved in the development of computer network technology, and it has sponsored work in this field at research centers across the country.

As a result of this work, the first major computer network spanning the entire country, called the ARPAnet, was developed. A whole series of network protocols were created for the ARPAnet, culminating in the TCP/IP protocol suite. *IP* stands for Internet Protocol, and refers to the fact that the ARPAnet is made up of many individual networks. The IP portion of the protocol suite deals with managing these individual networks so that they all look like one big network to every computer.

TCP stands for the Transmission Control Protocol. This portion of the protocol suite provides a set of mechanisms for establishing reliable communications among software applications that run on the computers linked by the network. These protocols and the applications based upon them were developed under federal funding, and as a result they are in the public domain.

With Berkeley researchers incorporating the TCP/IP protocols into their distributions, it wasn't long before TCP/IP became a de facto network protocol standard for the UNIX workstation market. Sun Microsystems' SunOS UNIX contains the Berkeley support for TCP/IP, as does DEC's version of UNIX called ULTRIX. There's even software that allows IBM PCs equipped with an Ethernet controller to run TCP/IP-based applications.

The ISO OSI Reference Model for Networks

While TCP/IP is now a viable standard, no true industry-wide network protocol standard has emerged yet. The development of industry-wide standards is generally the last thing that happens in the computer business. The usual cycle is for years of confusion to occur before some given hardware or software technology finally gets accepted as the standard way to do things. The network market seems to have learned from this sorry past, and network vendors are actively supporting the effort to arrive at new standards. The network market is still fairly chaotic at the moment, but a set of solutions is in sight. The solutions are coming from work now underway at the International Organization for Standardization (ISO) based in Geneva, Switzerland.

The ISO is developing a new set of network protocol standards based on the Open Systems Interconnection (OSI) Reference Model. The OSI Reference Model defines all of the network functions as a set of seven layers.

Figure 9–5 shows these network layers. The bottommost layer of the model is the physical layer, which defines such things as the transceiver that connects to the network cable. Layer number 2 is called the data link layer, and it covers matters such as synchronization and error control of data transmissions on the physical channel. The Ethernet specifications deal with the network functions covered by these first two layers.

Layer 3 is the network layer, and its task is to standardize the way networks provide routing information to devices located on a single network or to devices connected via multiple networks. Layer 4, the transport layer, is concerned with the reliability of the actual data transfer between the applications running on different computers. Layer 5, the session layer, establishes reliable communication sessions between the applications.

Layer 6, called the presentation layer, concerns itself with data formats, such as whether the data is encoded in ASCII or EBCDIC, and is intended to help provide standards that ensure that the data transmitted between hosts can be understood at each system. Layer 7 is the application layer, which manages resources for standardized network applications such as electronic mail, file transfer, and so on.

Seven Layers for Descriptions

The seven-layer model is a way of separating the network functions, and is intended to provide a coherent method of describing and comparing network standards. The model makes it possible to discuss network functions piece by piece, and by dividing things up this way it becomes possible to standardize things in independent sections. Instead of the hopelessly large task of trying to generate a single standard for the entire range of network functions, you have a set of layers that helps divide the task into manageable pieces.

The lowest layers are already well-defined by existing standards such as Ethernet, token ring, or even slow-speed serial line communication standards like RS-232-C. A major benefit of the layered structure of the OSI model is that various standards at different layers can be mixed and

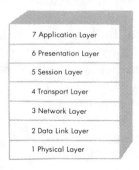

Figure 9–5   The Seven-Layer Reference Model

matched. Although the TCP/IP suite is almost always run over Ethernet in the UNIX market, there is no reason you can't run TCP/IP-based applications over serial lines. Ethernet gives high performance at a reasonable cost and has become very widespread, but the original TCP/IP development for the ARPAnet was done over a network that included many phone line connections.

Layers Make It Possible to Predict What Works

From a UNIX programmer's point of view, an important function of the seven-layer architecture is that it gives you the ability to predict what network applications will work together with applications running on other machines. Eventually, the new OSI protocol specifications being developed with the help of the seven-layer Reference Model will fully specify all seven layers. At that point, applications that employ the entire OSI protocol suite will be guaranteed to interoperate. This will slowly come about over the next several years, so that you will be able to pick out applications in your area of interest (technical offices, manufacturing floor, and so on) that will be guaranteed to work together. Meanwhile, the seven-layer model can help you understand which protocol families and their applications will work together today.

One major reason that TCP/IP has become so widely used on many machines is that TCP/IP-based applications such as electronic mail and file transfer have been standardized. While the development of the TCP/IP suite was not based on the OSI model, the network functions in TCP/IP have been standardized up to the application layer. This means that TCP/IP applications running on different machines and different operating systems can communicate with one another and will work together to get the job done for the user.

In contrast, other network protocol families use standards based on the lower layers of the Reference Model, but the applications developed using these network protocols have never been standardized across the upper layers. That means that while applications based on these protocols can coexist on the same network, due to their use of lower-level standards, they cannot interoperate and cannot communicate on the application level between different machines.

Organization by Layers Doesn't Guarantee Interoperability

One thing to watch out for is the statement made that "the XYZ protocol suite adheres to the OSI seven-layer Reference Model." All this means is that the XYZ protocol suite is organized according to the latest thinking in network protocols. It does not mean that the protocols or the applications based upon them use the new OSI protocol specifications, or that they will interoperate with any other network-based applications. The OSI Reference Model is just an architectural description and not an actual protocol specification. You cannot assume that simply adhering to the model will mean anything when it comes to compatibility between applications running on different machines. On the other hand, applications based on the forthcoming OSI protocol specifications will be designed to work together.

The whole issue of interoperability can be a tricky one. You have to investigate vendor's claims carefully and be sure to ask for a demonstration before buying any software. The seven-layer model helps explain why the TCP/IP applications work together, and it also shows that different protocol families can use the same lower-level standards, such as Ethernet, and can coexist on the same network. This means that you may have a single Ethernet connecting computers using many different network protocols. As long as they all use standard Ethernet, they can each send packets to the appropriate Ethernet controllers and will not interfere with one another.

Network-Based Applications and High-Speed LANs

Applications like electronic mail and file transfer are nothing new, and they don't depend upon the existence of high-speed LANs in order to work. These older applications can also run on slower communication channels such as serial RS-232-C ports. Using Ethernet makes them run faster, however, and makes it possible to link these applications across many different kinds of computers.

New applications are being developed that depend on the existence of high-speed LANs to work well. One such is the Network File System (NFS) developed at Sun Microsystems and whose specifications have been placed in the public domain. The NFS specifications describe a set of mechanisms for translating among different file systems on different computer systems. Obviously, you want this to happen as fast as possible, so that files accessed on the remote machine linked with NFS can appear almost as rapidly as files on a local disk. This makes the Ethernet an important part of the NFS application. AT&T has developed a similar network-based file system called remote file sharing (RFS). The two network-based file systems had different goals to satisfy and use different approaches to the same general problem. Depending on your needs and the equipment you have, you may want to use one or the other, or even both.

Another recent development that exploits the power of high-speed LANs is the network-based laser printer. This is a printer that connects to an Ethernet and communicates via TCP/IP protocols. Any number of UNIX systems on the same network can spool files to this printer. Laser printers are high-performance machines, and tend to be fairly expensive. The presence of the network allows many different users to share the cost of this resource.

Protocols Hold It All Together

The network protocols that travel in Ethernet packets make it possible for application programs to deliver useful results. There have been many different network protocol families developed by various companies, but applications based on these protocols are often based on proprietary standards and are often tied to an individual company's machines and operating system.

In contrast, both the TCP/IP protocol suite and its application specifications are in the public domain. This has helped make the TCP/IP protocols a de facto standard for UNIX systems. The new international standard protocols are under development, and the first implementations based on this effort are just starting to show up in the network market. Until implementations based on the new OSI standards become much more widespread, however, the TCP/IP suite will remain a widely used protocol family for UNIX and high-speed LANs.

A Guided Tour of a Thin Ethernet Installation

Now that you've seen how network protocols help applications communicate, take a look at how a thin Ethernet installation works. Thin Ethernet can be used to link workstations in a single office or in many offices located in the same building. Like the basic Ethernet it evolved from, thin Ethernet is an extremely flexible network technology that can be extended to meet many different needs.

Many different kinds of computers can be connected to the same thin Ethernet, just as in the original Ethernet system. Figure 9–6 shows a thin Ethernet installation with several different kinds of computers connected to it. Take a look at how these computers can work together over the network.

The workstations shown here are a good example of today's new high-powered UNIX-based workstations. The example here features a couple of diskless Suns located in an office area and a file server running UNIX

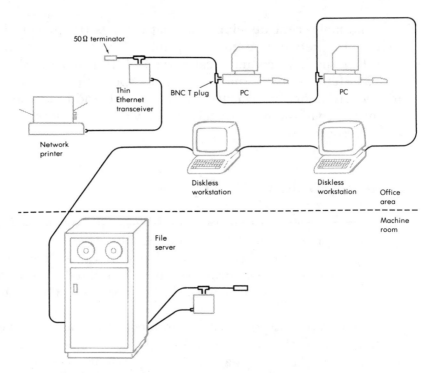

Figure 9–6   Thin Ethernet Installation

and equipped with high-speed disks located in a machine room area. Disk-less workstations rely entirely upon the network and the remote file server for disk access. Each workstation has its own private file space on the server. All workstations can use the same set of public files also located on the server, and in order to save the files for many different workstation users, you only need to back up the files on the server system. The shared printer is part of this system, since each workstation can send print requests to the printer by way of the print spooler on the server.

There are software packages available for the IBM PCs shown on the sample network that allow them to use TCP/IP-based programs such as Telnet and File Transfer Protocol (FTP). The Telnet application establishes what is known as a virtual terminal connection between the PC and a host computer on the network, such as the file server. The PC then acts as a terminal connected to the remote host system, able to log in like any other terminal. The PC user can then do the usual sorts of things such as editing files, reading mail, and so on. FTP allows the PC user to transfer specific files one at a time between the PC and the remote host.

By running given TCP/IP-based applications such as FTP or Telnet, PC users are able to take advantage of the resources available on many other UNIX systems linked by the network. At least one software package for IBM PCs also implements the Berkeley UNIX variations of the TCP/IP applications such as `rlogin`, `rcp`, and so on. These programs allow remote log-in, remote file copy, and other such interactions between a PC and a UNIX host. This same package implements the TCP/IP standard for electronic mail and will allow a PC to receive mail from a UNIX system over the network.

The diskless workstations mentioned earlier use the Network File System to link their local file systems with files on the remote server. Sun also licenses its UNIX implementation of NFS to various vendors, with the result that many UNIX systems can now automatically mount and use file systems located on other UNIX hosts. Software has been developed that allows IBM PCs to run NFS, so that that PC users can store files on a UNIX system.

Prepackaged Network Systems for IBM PCs

Another approach to linking IBM PCs over an Ethernet is to purchase a given vendor's file server or other such prepackaged system. Prepackaged systems can be a useful approach, because they often involve special protocol implementations that are optimized for speed and low overhead, compared to full-blown implementations of an open system protocol standard. Prepackaged systems are also tightly integrated with the PC's file system, so that users don't need to learn a new set of programs for saving files, for instance. The major disadvantage is that the prepackaged systems are not based on TCP/IP application standards, so they won't work with TCP/IP applications running on UNIX systems. Vendors of prepackaged systems often have special software available for UNIX systems that allows the PCs to communicate, but this requires that you buy their product and run it on every UNIX system you want to communicate with.

There are other ways various systems can interact using Ethernet and TCP/IP-based applications. As you've seen, as long as common standards are used, and as long as the applications are standardized over the whole range of network layers, it doesn't matter if the applications are running under UNIX, ULTRIX, SunOS, MS-DOS, or whatever. You've just seen a few of the most common types of applications available. There are many different packages available, and the big problem is sorting out exactly what mix of applications you need and which packages meet your requirements.

No matter which applications you choose to run, you've got to get a network built first. This means that you need to know how to go about designing and building an Ethernet LAN. This subject alone could occupy an entire book, but you'll be introduced to a few of the main ideas behind network design next.

Designing Ethernet LANs

So far you've seen some of the components used to build Ethernet LANs, with both thick and thin cable. You've looked at how Ethernet communicates using packets, and at how the application software communicates via network protocols carried inside Ethernet packets. And you've seen how applications based on open system network standards can work between different machines and different operating systems. You've also seen a little of how Ethernet technology fits together and how Ethernet can be extended to fit many different environments, from areas as small as a single office to very large installations linking hundreds of computers.

You'll now see some of the items involved in designing and building an Ethernet for your own use. There's much more information than can be covered in a short space, and this will only be an overview of network design issues, with further sources of information at the end of this paper.

The Range of Ethernet Technology

There are Ethernet devices that make it possible to link several segments together to cover several floors in a building with one network. There are other special devices that can be used to link networks in several buildings on a campus or office complex. As you can see, Ethernet technology covers a large range of installations, involving all sorts of special Ethernet devices. The range of topologies, and the number of special devices available, can make designing an Ethernet a daunting task.

How Many Computers, and How Far?

In order to cut the task down to size, you first need to draw up a list of your requirements. You need to know how many stations will be attached and how large an area you have to cover. This information is used to determine just what mix of Ethernet technology is required to get the job done.

If you have a small number of stations to connect, and you only need to network a single office space, then the thin Ethernet technology will probably be the best solution. This also makes the task of design and construction much more manageable, because you need only follow the simple rules for a single Ethernet segment. On the other hand, small networks rarely stay small. This is a phenomenon you might call the First Law of Network Design, which can be stated, "Networks always grow larger than you had originally planned."

A small installation usually ends up being so useful that it becomes necessary to add more stations, more file servers, more print servers and oh, yes, the folks down the hall want a connection to the net so that they can send files back and forth. You get the idea. Network design must try to reach a balance between the installation that you can afford today and all the possible extensions that you might want to make in the future.

Basic Rules for Ethernet Segments

The basic 10BASE2 thin Ethernet specifications are:

- Maximum cable segment length is 185 meters (approximately 606 feet).
- Maximum number of nodes per segment is 30.
- Minimum node connection spacing on segment is .5 meters (approximately 1.7 feet).
- Nodes may be attached directly via BNC T or with standard transceiver cable and BNC-equipped transceiver.

The basic 10BASE5 thick Ethernet specifications are:

- Maximum cable segment length is 500 meters (approximately 1640 feet).
- Maximum number of nodes per segment is 100.
- Minimum node connection spacing on segment is 2.5 meters (approximately 8.2 feet).
- Nodes are attached via transceivers and transceiver cables. Maximum transceiver cable length is 50 meters (approximately 164 feet).

The maximum number of nodes per Ethernet is 1024. Multiple segments may be connected together with repeaters, so long as there are no more than two repeaters in the path between any pair of nodes on the network. Multiple Ethernets of up to 1024 nodes each may be connected together with Ethernet bridges.

Large Scale Nets

If your network design includes cabling an entire building, there are many more things to know. You need to become familiar with the many Ethernet devices available to help make Ethernets cover large areas. Wiring an entire building also requires that you know about wire access systems such as cable trays and conduits, not to mention fire safety codes, wiring codes, and on and on. It's a big job, and you should consider giving the task to a contractor who specializes in Ethernets to make sure it's all done according to the rules. Figure 9–7 shows a few basic Ethernet topologies, with repeaters and bridges used to link multiple segments and multiple networks.

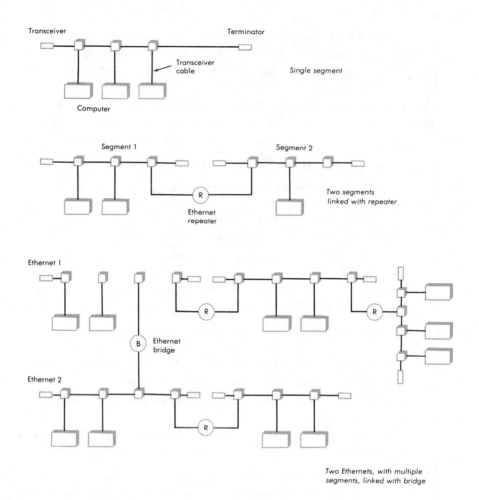

Figure 9-7   A Few Basic Ethernet Topologies

Ethernet Rules of Behavior

Speaking of rules, there are good reasons to be sure that you don't violate the Ethernet specifications. Ethernet is a high-speed, high-performance network technology, and it pays to be careful when designing an Ethernet LAN. Ethernet is standardized, and it's very reliable, but that doesn't mean that it will work no matter what you do to it.

Ethernet will stay reliable as long as you understand the rules and do nothing that violates them. Stretching the rules may actually work today, but it can fail tomorrow when one more station is added to an already over-long network, for instance, and everything grinds to a halt.

Buying an Ethernet LAN

There so many ways to design an Ethernet LAN that it's not easy for manufacturers to offer a prepackaged network in a box, all set up and ready to go. On the other hand, a small thin Ethernet installation of a few IBM PCs would be a reasonable candidate for a prepackaged approach. Several vendors do offer thin Ethernet supplies, but they're usually bundled together with a specific product such as a PC file server.

These prepackaged systems often involve small computers linked over an Ethernet with proprietary network application software. If you purchase one of these systems, you are limited to using one vendor's software on the computers and also one vendor's hardware for the file server. This can be a very useful approach for people who want a centralized file server and don't want to set it all up themselves, but you need to be aware of what you're locking yourself into.

Finding Ethernet Design Information

If you want to build your own Ethernet LAN, you have to understand the rules on how things are put together. There are several sources of information that describe these rules, and you'll find a list of a few of them here. More names and addresses can be found at the end of this paper.

Several vendors supply design information that describes both thick and thin Ethernets. Naturally, these design manuals feature the vendor's product line and usually exclude other vendors' network products available on the market. You need to read these manuals carefully, and remember that no single vendor has all the answers. One approach to take is to obtain design manuals from several vendors. That way you can compare the different ideas presented and get a better notion of the range of equipment and designs that is available.

Two vendors that have published useful design information for Ethernet are DEC and Hewlett-Packard. There are many other Ethernet vendors, and you should try to collect literature from as many vendors as possible to widen your knowledge of what's available in the networking marketplace.

DECconnect System General Description Manual

Order Number EK-DECSY-GD-001, January 1986.
For ordering information, see Access to Further Information at the end of this paper. This manual describes DEC's integrated building wiring

system, called DECconnect. There are also descriptions of several different network topologies, including an appendix that describes both thin and thick Ethernet configurations. DECconnect includes ThinWire, which is DEC's name for thin Ethernet. DEC's ThinWire system is based on the use of the multiport repeater. The multiport repeater is a special device for establishing up to eight thin Ethernet segments. The multiport repeater also connects to a thick Ethernet backbone cable. There are several advantages to this approach, not the least of which is the isolation of any network problems to a small number of users.

For instance, if someone disconnects the network cable on the back of his or her workstation without understanding how to do it, it's possible for that user to partition the network and disrupt service to the other users on that segment. A multiport repeater makes it easy to design multiple thin Ethernet segments so that the users can be spread across a number of segments instead of everyone connecting to a single wire. That way, any accidental disruptions of the network only affect a small number of users.

LAN Cable and Accessories Installation Manual

Hewlett-Packard Company, January 1986. Manual Part Number 5955-7680.

For ordering information, see Access to Further Information at the end of this paper. This manual describes both standard and thin Ethernet, which Hewlett-Packard calls ThinLAN. This is a very useful compendium of network specifications and designs. It also contains specific information about the tools required and the steps to take to build your own network cables, both thick and thin. Good information on network planning, installation, testing, and documentation can be found here. Note that the transceivers shown in the January 1986 version of this manual feature an installation method that has been superseded by a newer, easier to install mechanism found on most thick Ethernet transceivers being sold today.

Building a Thin Ethernet

Now that you've learned a few of the design rules, look at the steps you need to follow in order to build a small thin Ethernet. You'll build a sample network that has been chosen to make the task as easy as possible, because there's not a lot of space to explain a more complex design. In this example, you've also made the decision to use cable segments that are cut to length and supplied by vendors with the connectors attached.

This is more expensive than buying the raw materials and doing it yourself, but it's also the most reliable and quickest way of getting a network up and running. Buying the parts and assembling things yourself is lower cost, but also means that you must have the crimping and cutting tools, plus some basic test equipment and the hardware skills to manage it all. It's not a terribly difficult task, but it requires much more information than can be presented here.

List of Materials

Figure 9–8 shows the sample network you intend to build. As you can see, there's not a lot to it. The computers are located in open modular offices, since that's the easiest space to network. The list of materials needed, with approximate prices added, follows:

1. Two thin Ethernet (BNC) 50 ohm terminators, with plastic insulation: $12 each, $24 total.

2. Six 6 foot long thin Ethernet cable segments: $20 each, $120 total.

3. Seven BNC T connectors with plastic insulation: $15 each, $105 total.

The total for purchasing just the network wire is $249, not including labor. Of course, the network is of little use if you don't have any equipment attached. Now the list continues with the parts needed to add Ethernet capability to the IBM PCs and to attach the file server and printer, which are assumed to contain 10BASE5 thick Ethernet type controllers:

1. Three Ethernet controller cards with on-board transceiver chips and thin Ethernet connectors: $500 each, $1500 total.

2. Two thin Ethernet transceivers: $200 each, $400 total.

3. Two 6 foot long transceiver cables: $55 each, $110 total.

The total for controllers is $2010, and the grand total for parts and network equipment is $2259.

BNC Connectors

The diskless workstations are assumed to have thin Ethernet built in and only to need a connection to the network via a BNC T in order to work. The BNC parts just listed are slightly more expensive than stock BNC parts, but come with plastic insulation, unlike the cheaper BNC connectors. This helps eliminate any problems with stray electrical ground cur-

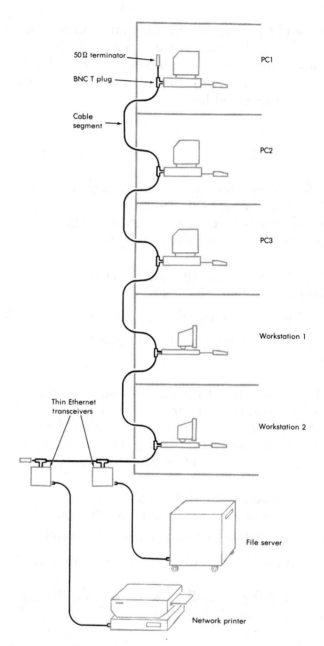

Figure 9–8 Building a Thin Ethernet

rents that can occur when metal parts on the connectors accidentally touch equipment or conduits that have voltage on them. The 802.3 thin Ethernet specs recommend insulated BNC connectors for this reason.

The prices listed were the lowest found in a selection of two vendors' catalogs at the time of writing (May 1987). No doubt you could find lower prices by looking in more catalogs and shopping around a bit.

This paper's sample network is much like the installation described in the guided tour of a thin Ethernet. There is a mix of powerful UNIX workstations and small computers sharing the same network and able to interoperate by running application and network software based on TCP/IP protocols. Because many UNIX workstations come with this software and networking capability, you're able to take advantage of some very powerful networking capabilities for a low total cost. To complete the network, you'll have to purchase networking software for the IBM PCs. There are several reasonably priced packages available to choose from, depending on what you wish to accomplish.

Routing Cables and Other Considerations

Because of space limitations, this paper leaves out lots of other issues that deserve to be mentioned. For instance, one of the trickiest parts of routing any network is access to office spaces surrounded by walls. What's the best technology available for doing this, and how do you do it? One system for networking offices, the ThinWire system from DEC, has been described; DEC's manuals offer installation ideas.

Another consideration is the amount of network traffic your stations will generate on the network you build. For the great majority of network implementations, network load is not a problem. On the other hand, a single segment with lots of high-speed, diskless workstations can really stress a network, because they're using the network cable for their disk I/O.

Vendors of diskless workstations can help with recommendations for the maximum number of stations per segment. The packet traffic on individual Ethernet segments can also be isolated, while the communications are still possible, by linking the segments together with an Ethernet bridge. This device looks at all the packets on both segments it's connected to and builds a list of every node address seen on each segment. The list allows the bridge to determine whether or not a packet on one segment has to be transferred to the other segment to reach its destination. The bridge transfers only those packets that have to get from one segment to the other and restricts the local packet traffic to its own segment.

Ethernet Load

Network load can be hard to determine, since the packet traffic rises and falls, reaching a peak for a few moments, and then subsiding to a background level. Network load is also affected by the varying size of Ethernet packets. The data field of the Ethernet packet carries protocol packets.

The protocol packets carry the application data in their own data field, and this field can vary in length as each packet is filled with different amounts of application data.

The average Ethernet packet size measured on a busy campus network with several mainframe computers, a dozen or so workstations, and scores of terminal sessions, is on the small side; 95 percent of the packets are between 64 and 128 bytes long. Assuming an average size of about 120 bytes per packet, an Ethernet segment can handle a constant rate of about 4500 packets per second and still be at roughly 50 percent capacity. If you exceed 50 percent capacity by much, the Ethernet controllers will start having problems finding an idle moment in which to transmit.

A constant rate of 4500 packets/second is quite a lot, actually. The campus network mentioned earlier runs at an average rate of about 100 packets per second, with momentary peaks of up to 650 packets per second at its busiest. As you can see, there's plenty of room for growth, on what many people would consider a large and busy network. The "back of the envelope" load calculations given here are not very scientific, but they show that network load considerations are not a limiting factor in most Ethernet designs.

The newcomer to network design may feel overwhelmed by all the options and all the designs that are possible. But as you've seen, given a set of equipment like this small installation, it can be quite easy to build a network for it. More complex environments will take more work to design and implement, but the results in terms of high speed and reliable network access are well worth it.

UNIX and Ethernet Are Alike

A major advantage of using the UNIX system is the wide range of machines it makes available to you. UNIX is almost entirely written in a high-level language and has been made available to many other companies, so that UNIX now runs on a large number of computers—from micros to the most powerful machines built today.

The same kind of advantage comes from using Ethernet technology. Ethernet has been made an open system standard, and the technology is available to any manufacturer. Installing an Ethernet makes it possible for you to network a wide range of computers. Ethernet is organized around Ethernet packets, so it's not dependent on any specific data rate or wiring system. Basic Ethernet and the newer thin Ethernet operate at 10 megabits, but the standard allows for other data rates to be developed, when they are needed.

Linking Other Networks

There are many other LAN technologies available today, and Ethernet can help link them together, too. Different network technologies can be linked together with devices called *gateways.* For example, a gateway can have an Ethernet interface on one side, an AppleTalk interface on the other side, and special software that allows for translating data between the two, as shown in Figure 9–9.

There are several products available that will link AppleTalk networks to other AppleTalk networks, using the Ethernet as a bridge between them. One such, the FastPath AppleTalk bridge sold by Kinetics, is also capable of serving as an Ethernet gateway when the appropriate software is used. This makes it possible to write TCP/IP-based applications for the Macin-

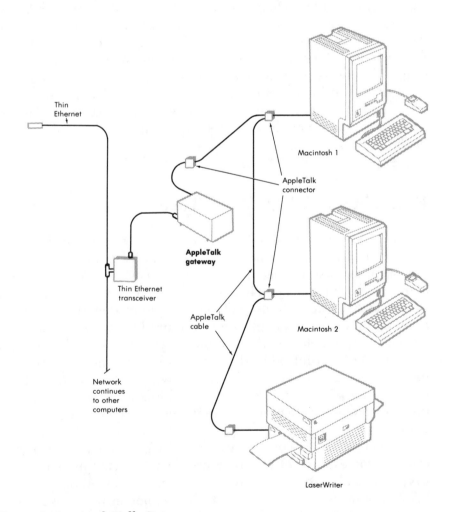

Figure 9–9   AppleTalk Gateway

tosh that will be able to interact with similar applications on other machines, located on an Ethernet.

New Network Protocols Are Evolving

The world of network protocols and network-based applications is complex and undergoing rapid change. The UNIX marketplace has adopted TCP/IP as a de facto standard for the time being, and applications based on TCP/IP can work between such radically different machines as high-powered UNIX workstations and the "lowly" microcomputer.

While the TCP/IP family of network protocols is in wide use on UNIX systems today, the new OSI protocols now under development will eventually replace them. One advantage of the new effort is that it will help vendors standardize such things as data representation between machines. As it stands now, you can use the FTP program to transfer files between different machines, but if the files contain special formatting codes or graphics software, you're out of luck. The new network standards are being used as a base for developing applications standards that can deal with translating special document codes between any machines. This will make connecting machines through networks much easier and more powerful in the future.

Ethernet and UNIX Work Together

There's a lot to know about Ethernet and how it operates, and too much to cover in one paper. You've seen that the Ethernet LAN is a hardware and software system that provides a low-cost, reliable way to establish high-speed communication between many different computers. You've also seen that Ethernet is only half the story and that the other half is the network protocols and applications required to make information move in a standard way between the computers you attach to the network.

You've been introduced to quite a bit of Ethernet jargon, so you'll be able to read the vendor literature without wondering what half the words mean. And you've seen that building an Ethernet can range from the very simple installation in a single office to complex campus-wide networks.

Ethernet has become a widely used LAN technology precisely because it solves a lot of different problems for computer users. Just like UNIX, it can be used on many different machines. And just like UNIX, it helps turn many different computer technologies into a useful computing environment. With the new thin Ethernet becoming the office network of choice, Ethernet and UNIX will be working together for many years to come.

Access to Further Information

The following is a list of sources for further information. The list begins with addresses for acquiring the Ethernet standards. The standards documents are formal specifications and do not contain the kind of real-world information you need to design and build a network. For that reason, this discussion also includes access to the DEC and Hewlett-Packard network manuals. The list continues with information about where to get network protocol specifications. It concentrates on the TCP/IP family, because that is one in very common use on UNIX systems, but also includes some access information for the newer OSI protocol standards.

Ethernet Specifications

Carrier Sense Multiple Access with Collision Detection (CSMA/CD), ANSI/IEEE Std 802.3, 1985

This is available from, IEEE Service Center, 445 Hoes Lane, Piscataway, New Jersey 08854, or by telephoning 1–201–981–0060. A list of IEEE standards with prices is available from the Institute of Electrical and Electronics Engineers (IEEE), 345 East 47th Street, New York, New York 10017. The IEEE 802.3 standard may also be found in technical bookstores or from a document broker (listed later).

Ethernet Local Area Network Specification Version 2.0, Part Number: AA–K759B–TK

This is available from: Digital Equipment Corporation, P.O. Box CS2008, Nashua, New Hampshire 03061, or by calling 1–800–258–1710 for the latest access information.

The IEEE specification is the one all new Ethernet equipment is based on. There are a few differences between the two specifications, but network vendors have been careful to offer new products that maintain compatibility with older equipment.

The IEEE specification can be difficult to read, due to the kind of language used in formal specification documents. For this reason you'd be wise to get a copy of the version 2.0 DIX Ethernet specification. When it comes down to designing and building Ethernet products, the IEEE 802.3

specification is the last word. But if all you want to do is read about the basic thick Ethernet rules and get an idea of what Ethernet topologies are allowed, the old DIX standard can be more approachable. Neither standard contains any information about network design and implementation. For that, you need to look into the design and construction manuals listed next.

The thin Ethernet specifications should be in the 802.3 specification, but you won't find them in the 1985 revision. Instead, you will find section 10 of that document reserved for them in a future revision. Even though vendors have been building thin Ethernet products for several years now, they've been doing so by using a draft standard. Things happen at a deliberate pace in the standards world, and it takes time for new standards to show up in the formal specification documents.

Ethernet Design and Construction Manuals

The two manuals cited previously are available from the individual vendors.

LAN Cable and Accessories Installation Manual, Hewlett-Packard Company, January 1986, Part Number 5955–7680

This manual is available from Hewlett-Packard's direct sales catalog by writing to: Hewlett-Packard, HP-Direct, P.O. Box 3640, Sunnyvale, California 94088–3640 or by calling 1–800–538–8787 for latest price and ordering information.

DECconnect System General Description Manual, Digital Equipment Corporation, January 1986, Part Number EK–DECSY–GD–001

This manual is available from: Digital Equipment Corporation, P.O. Box CS2008, Nashua, New Hampshire 03061 or by calling 1–800–258–1710 for the latest access information.

DEC also has a direct sales catalog, called DECdirect. This catalog has a section on the network products DEC offers with pictures of the items, size information, and pricing. To receive a copy of this catalog, call the toll-free number just listed.

LAN Vendors

There are hundreds of LAN vendors, and there's simply no way to list them all. A technical librarian can help you if you want to compile a list of vendors in the business. LAN vendors may also be found by looking in the ads of specialized magazines and tabloids. You can often find such publications in engineering libraries.

Network Protocols

A large amount of information about the TCP/IP protocol suite is available from the Network Information Center (NIC) at SRI International. TCP/IP protocol documentation, and much other material available from the NIC, are published as a series of numbered reports called "Requests for Comments" (RFCs). A good place to start is RFC 980, "Protocol Document Order Information" available for $5 from: SRI International, DDN Network Information Center, Room EJ291, 333 Ravenswood Avenue, Menlo Park, California 94025, or by calling 1–415–859–3695 or 1–800–235–3155.

The NIC is also the place to call for information on how to obtain a registered IP network number, whether or not your network is connected to the ARPAnet.

Finally, you may want to order RFC999, which contains an annotated list of the RFCs from RFC900 through RFC999.

OSI Standards

The ISO series of OSI standards is a large subject in and of itself. The OSI standards are made available in this country by the: American National Standards Institute, 1430 Broadway, New York, New York 10018 or by calling 1–212–642–4900.

Document Brokers

There are several technical document brokers who sell protocol specification documents. One such who deals with OSI standards and also IEEE standards is: Omnicom, Inc., 501 Church Street, NE, Suite 304, Vienna, Virginia 22180, or by calling: 1–703–281–1135.

Omnicom can send you an information package including a list of the OSI protocol specifications they have available.

KEYWORDS

▶ Buffer

▶ Latency

▶ Predictability

▶ Process scheduling

▶ Shared memory

▶ Signal mechanisms

Paper Synopsis: UNIX provides an excellent way to control physical devices and processes, such as the machines on a factory floor or test equipment in a laboratory. Most often these devices require that the computer controlling it respond almost instantly, in what is called "real time." UNIX is capable of making a practical real-time system, but there are important considerations to know. The paper discusses alternatives for achieving real-time performance with standard UNIX, "enhanced" UNIX, and UNIX clones.

Geoff Kuenning is vice president of Interrupt Technology Corporation, a consulting firm specializing in UNIX and real-time systems. Prior to joining Interrupt Technology, he worked as an operating systems and real-time consultant, participating in projects as diverse as UNIX ports and real-time simulators. Mr. Kuenning holds bachelor's and master's degrees in computer science from Michigan State University, and is a member of both IEEE and ACM.

## 10

Real-Time UNIX

Geoff Kuenning

UNIX has been advocated and used as a real-time operating system since fairly early in its history. It is used by AT&T as the basis for switching systems, and it has also provided a basis for transaction-processing systems (discussed later) for a number of years. In addition, there are several vendors who offer UNIX-like operating systems for more general real-time use.

When real-time project managers investigate UNIX as an operating system for their project, they are likely to discover that the system has its detractors as well as advocates. Under the label "UNIX" there is a bewildering variety of choices, and the confusion is aggravated by the prevalence of myths and misinformation. This paper is intended both to reduce the confusion and to provide the project manager with a decision-making framework with which he or she can cut through the myths and hype. In addition, a number of suggestions are made that may help the reader more effectively use his or her current system.

This paper:

- defines real time and considers the major types of real-time systems

- discusses UNIX as a real-time system in the context of the definition

- reviews user options for situations when UNIX is not suitable

- examines the future for UNIX as a real-time system

RELATED PAPERS

1 UNIX: Rights and Wrongs

7 Device Drivers Under UNIX

8 Remote File Systems, Streams, and Transport Level Interface

9 Ethernet: A UNIX LAN

14 Multiprocessor UNIX

What Is Real Time?

Before discussing UNIX as a real-time operating system, the paper briefly defines and discusses *real time*. The focus is on identifying the critical requirements for each type of real-time system.

The origin of the term *real time* lies in a literal interpretation of the words. One part of the definition involves getting things done within time constraints imposed from outside the computer. An example is computer-produced video effects. Scene-generation systems produce a frame of movie film every few minutes, so effects specialists must suffer through a tedious wait before seeing the fruits of their labor. Ideally, a movie maker would like to be able to view a scene at full speed, as it was being generated.

Instead of seeing it come out in the stretched time of ultra-slow motion, it would be much more desirable to be able to see it at full speed, the way the audience will see it. If the computer is fast enough to generate 24 frames per second (the speed of sound movie film), the scene will come out in a nonstretched time frame that matches the sweep second hand on a wall clock: "real" time.

This suggests a simple definition of the term "real-time computer system." A real-time computer system is one that

1. deals directly with the world external to the computer
2. is fast enough to keep up with it

Note that this is a pretty fuzzy definition. The field of real time is a very broad one; in the broadest sense it includes all computer systems. (In particular, any interactive computer system can be viewed as a real-time system.) Even the telephone company's billing system is real-time in some sense. After all, you'd be pretty annoyed if your payment went unrecorded because the phone company's computers couldn't keep up with the load! However, systems that are called "real-time" usually involve times on the order of seconds or less.

Take a look at some examples of real-time systems.

Data-Generation and -Collection Systems

The simplest type of real-time system is the movie scene generator already discussed. This system operates under an extremely simple "output-rate" constraint: the frames must be generated at a rate of 24 per second. As long as the frames come out fast enough, the movie maker will be happy.

The computer cannot take longer than one twenty-fourth of a second to generate a frame, however. Even a slight hesitation will cause the movie maker to see the scene differently from what the eventual audience will see. A longer hesitation will be clearly visible as a stop in the action. If this goes on for more than one frame, the movie maker will be back to watching things in slow motion.

If most frames can be generated within one twenty-fourth of a second, but a few take longer than that, a designer may be able to get real-time performance by using a "buffer" to hold frames as they are generated, as shown in Figure 10–1.

The idea is that the computer "primes" the buffer with a few early frames before beginning the display. As fast as additional frames are generated, they are put in the buffer; a separate part of the system pulls frames from the buffer at exactly 24 per second and displays them. If the computer slows down for one frame, there will be no problem as long as there are already enough frames in the buffer to keep the display going. Later, the computer will be able to "catch up" on frames that it can generate faster than 24 frames per second, and thus build a new backlog in the buffer.

The opposite of such a data-generation system is a data-collection system. These are often used in scientific and medical applications, where a large number of instruments must be monitored simultaneously. In a data-collection system, there is an outside factor that determines how fast the computer must be. If 10,000 samples of data are generated every second, the computer must be able to swallow them at the same rate. If it cannot keep up, some information will be lost. This constraint, which is called a "sampling-rate" constraint, is a major difference between a data-collection and a data-generation system. In the field of data collection, a delay is more than an inconvenience. As with data-generation systems, short-term delays can be smoothed out using a buffer.

Transaction-Processing Systems

So far, the only systems discussed have been "unidirectional": information flows either from the computer to the world or from the world to the computer, but not both. This greatly simplifies the demands on the computer. To see why, the paper next examines a system that connects both ways.

In many applications, the computer provides a service to the outside world. Frequently, this "outside world" is either a human or a computer

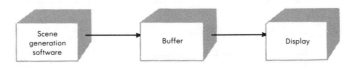

Figure 10–1   Buffered Data Generation

that can afford to wait a short time for a response. An example of such a system is an airline reservations computer, shown in Figure 10–2. The travel agent requests flight information from the computer and, with customer approval, confirms the reservation.

In this system, for the first time, there is a "response-time" constraint. The travel agent presumably has a customer waiting and will insist on getting an answer reasonably promptly. However, as in a data-generation system, an occasional extra delay is not the end of the world. This is the primary characteristic of "transaction-processing" systems: there is no "hard" time constraint. As in this example, it is not possible to pin down the time constraint precisely. Although a user works interactively, a delay of a few seconds for each response can cause frustration. The exact time parameters are application-specific and must be determined through a combination of experimentation and technical judgment. It is, however, safe to say that less delay is almost always better.

Despite this flexibility in processing individual transactions, a transaction-processing system makes heavy demands on its computer. Typical applications involve hundreds or even thousands of terminals, all demanding fast responses. Occasionally, of course, the computer gets overloaded. To remedy this, imagine taking a design idea from the data-generation and data-collection systems, and introducing a buffer to smooth out the load (Figure 10–3).

What happens? As long as the buffer stays empty, everything works just as before. But suppose a large number of requests come in all at once, increasing the system load, so that the buffer develops 10 seconds' worth of backlog. Now a travel agent's request must spend 10 seconds percolating through the buffer before it even gets to the computer. If the computer

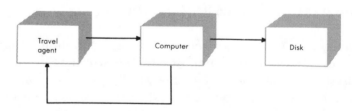

Figure 10–2   Transaction-Processing System

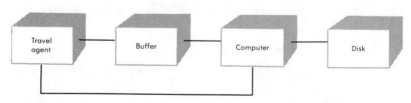

Figure 10–3   Transaction-Processing System with Buffer

then spends 1 second on the request, the agent will see a 11-second delay. The buffer hasn't helped response time at all!

The nature of "bidirectional" systems (where the computer both receives information from the outside world and sends it back) is such that the computer cannot work ahead, because nothing can be done until there is input (in this example, from a travel agent). The best that can be done is to try to empty the buffer as quickly as possible. Until the input load lightens, a backlog will stay in the buffer, adding to the response time. As the load lightens, the system will eventually empty the buffer and thus reduce the response time back to one second.

This illustrates a basic property of bidirectional real-time systems: If the computer isn't fast enough, there's nothing you can do.

Real-Time Control Systems

The final, and most demanding, category of real-time systems arise when a computer actually is used to make decisions about how to control some external device or process. A dramatic example of real-time control is the flight-control system for a rocket. A climbing rocket is balanced on its exhaust, just like a broomstick on a fingertip (Figures 10–4a and 10–4b). Like that broomstick, if it gets too far out of balance, you won't be able to recover control.

To keep the rocket in control, the computer periodically reads the current position, compares it with the desired course, and applies a correction to the control fins (Figure 10–4c). When the fins move, the rocket changes course, which affects the readings of the inertial guidance system. This is indicated by the dotted line in the figure.

As with the transaction-processing system, there is a response-time constraint. If the computer finds that the rocket is about to topple, a correction must be applied before it reaches the point of no return. This is a constraint on the speed of the computer itself, because the calculation of the correction cannot begin until the data is available. Once the data is in, the remaining delay is caused by CPU speed. If the calculation takes even a millisecond too long, the rocket will pass the point of no return and the flight will be a failure. Real-time control systems are characterized by hard time constraints; or in the words of James Ready, of Ready Systems (manufacturer of the VRTX real-time operating system), "late results are wrong results."

Summary of Real-Time Systems

You have learned the definition of *real time* and have seen that there are three basic system types: data-generation and data-collection systems,

A. *Broomstick Balanced on a Finger*

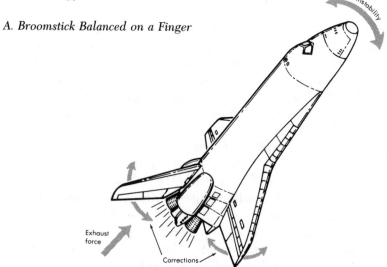

B. *Rocket Balanced on Its Exhaust*

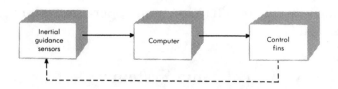

C. *Rocket Balanced Under Computer Control*

Figure 10–4   Balancing Broomsticks and Rockets

transaction-processing systems, and real-time control systems. Each of these system types puts different demands on the underlying computer and operating system. Although the exact demands vary with the application, real-time control usually puts the most stringent requirements on the computer.

Real Time with UNIX

You now have a framework within which UNIX can be evaluated as a real-time operating system. You have seen that different types of real-time applications put different constraints on the system design. Real-time control frequently has hard time constraints, in which being even a little late with results can spell disaster. On the other hand, most other real-time systems have much less demanding constraints. Traditionally, UNIX has been considered to be a poor choice for demanding real-time applications.

One might ask, "why use UNIX if it's not really suited for real time?" Despite its many deficiencies for real-time applications, many project managers still select UNIX as the preferred system for their application. This is because UNIX, as the only available standard and portable operating system, offers so many advantages in flexibility that it is worthwhile to suffer its real-time deficiencies. For many less-demanding applications, these deficiencies are very minor.

Another reason why UNIX is used as the real-time operating system in many applications is because development costs and risks are reduced by using UNIX for both the development system and real-time system. This is because in general, it's easier to develop and test software that will run on the system it is being developed on. In addition to technical considerations, marketing or strategic reasons may influence the choice towards UNIX.

This section examines UNIX in the light of real-time demands. It considers the problems that UNIX presents and discusses solutions. You will see that for hard constraints such as those presented by real-time control systems, UNIX is generally unsuitable. For other, less-demanding systems UNIX is more appropriate, and in many cases either clever use of a standard UNIX or using a UNIX look-alike will provide a quite satisfactory solution.

In consideration of alternatives here, it's assumed that you do not have the option of modifying UNIX. If you have UNIX source code and your project will allow a custom operating system, you have many advantages—at least until it comes time to upgrade to the next UNIX version.

If, for whatever reason, you cannot modify UNIX but are faced with a UNIX deficiency, there are three basic solutions: a clever use of UNIX, switching to a UNIX look-alike, or using some other non-UNIX operating system for the real-time application. These options will be discussed more extensively later.

Raw Performance

The most basic thing a real-time application needs from a computer is simply performance. If the computer doesn't have the power to keep up with the constraints, no amount of ingenuity will make the system work. Some applications demand excellent CPU performance; others require high-performance peripherals, most often disks.

Raw performance alone is only the beginning, however. The operating system used on the computer will have a major impact on system performance. The performance of an operating system is a complex issue that depends on the exact application, so it is difficult to make a general statement about the performance of UNIX (or any other operating system). Usually, it is best to run benchmarks on several different systems to determine which has the best performance for a particular project. For many applications, UNIX systems have more than enough power.

If the performance of the computer or the operating system is inadequate, there is usually little that can be done to improve the situation in software. In a few instances, the application can be significantly redesigned to place lower demands on critical parts of the computer. In most cases, however, the only recourse is to change the operating system or the computer.

Predictability

You have seen that raw performance is critical, but performance is not the only key issue. To be certain that response time meets some limits, the response time must be predictable. Part of the response time is the running time of the real-time application. The rest depends on the predictability of the operating system itself.

Process Scheduling

A few real-time applications are small enough to write as a single program, which can run under a simple single-tasking operating system such as MS-DOS (or the application may even be "standalone," with no operating system at all). However, most complex systems must be written as a collection of programs, or "processes," each of which handles part of the whole problem. If these processes are to share a single computer, a "scheduler" is required to coordinate the use of the computer among them.

When you are writing a real-time application, the scheduler introduces several kinds of delays and uncertainties. The two most important of these are scheduling priority and scheduling latency. With the former, the scheduler's main job is to decide which process gets to use the computer next. This is usually done by assigning a numerical "priority" to each process, then giving the CPU to the one with the highest priority.

In the rocket, for example, you would assign a higher priority to flight control than to watching the fuel supply, because the rocket can go out of control much faster than the fuel can run out. To make absolutely sure that the flight-control process can use the CPU when it needs to, a "preemptive" scheduler is commonly used. It has the capability of interrupting a lower-priority process (fuel supply) so that a more important one can run.

With scheduling latency, once a process becomes ready to run, or to use the CPU, there is an unavoidable time delay before it actually begins running. This delay, known as *latency*, is caused by operating system overhead that is incurred while the system suspends one process, decides which new process has the highest priority, and sets it up to use the CPU. If some other process is the highest-priority process, additional latency may be incurred because higher-priority processes run first. From the point of view of the real-time programmer, latency is wasted time that directly adds to the delays in the system.

Although the UNIX scheduler is adequate for time-sharing systems, it is very weak for real-time applications. The user has some limited control of process priority through the nice system call, but this control is not absolute. UNIX has a very complex idea of process priority, and the nice value is only a small factor in the final priority. None of the other factors are under user control, so that even a process with a very high nice priority (indicated, unfortunately, by a low numerical value) may not be first in line to use the CPU.

In addition, UNIX has a high and variable scheduler latency. Where most real-time operating systems have latencies on the order of a few tens of milliseconds, UNIX has been measured with a latency of over one second (though the average latency is quite short).[1] This is a time frame that is disastrous in many real-time applications.

As with the performance issue, there is little that can be done about this deficiency of UNIX. Naturally, the nice system call should be used to control process priorities to the extent possible. Extra system load should

---

[1]D. Lennert, "Decreasing Realtime Process Dispatch Latency Through Kernel Preemption," in *Proceedings of the Summer USENIX Conference,* 1986.

be minimized by reducing the number of unnecessary processes in the system. The real-time application developers can also try to avoid using expensive kernel operations. According to Lennert, these include:

- forks of large processes
- execs of large processes
- certain I/O operations, notably "canonical" terminal I/O
- process exit
- shared memory setup
- the link and unlink system calls

Swapping and Paging

When the processes that want to run on a computer do not all fit in memory simultaneously, the operating system must resolve the conflict by temporarily storing some of them on disk. This is referred to as "swapping." In a virtual-memory system, an operation called "paging" is also used; from the point of view of a real-time programmer, paging and swapping are very similar.

When a process has been "swapped out" (stored on disk), it cannot be run until it is read back into main memory. This can introduce long and unpredictable delays that are unacceptable in real-time applications. A paging system introduces similar, though shorter, delays. Real-time operating systems that have swappers or pagers usually provide a "lock-in-memory" primitive to allow a process to prevent swapping. Such a primitive (plock) is available in the System V variant of UNIX.

Locking a process in memory is very good for that process, but it tends to decrease overall system performance. If this is unacceptable, the performance of the swapper or pager becomes important. In older UNIX versions that lack virtual memory, swapping should be avoided if possible, because the swapper is not very effective. For similar reasons, the swapper and pager in 4.2BSD should be avoided. System V.2 UNIXes and some enhanced UNIXes, on the other hand, have pagers and swappers that perform better under heavy loads, and they may be more suitable for real-time projects.

A final note: some systems also have special system calls that allow a knowledgeable programmer to exert more precise control over the pager's behavior (such as the vmadvise system call in BSD UNIX). In a demanding application, such features can be a great help in solving deficiencies in a virtual-memory system.

Interrupt Latency

As you have seen, real-time systems often demand a fast response to external events. Frequently, the computer learns of these external events through a hardware interrupt. To produce a fast response to the event, then, the computer must be able to respond quickly to an interrupt.

The fastest way to get a response to a device is to put the relevant code directly into a device driver. This is a common technique in real-time systems. For this reason, "interrupt latency" is usually defined as the time that elapses between the moment a hardware device actually requests an interrupt, and the moment that the first instruction of the device driver's interrupt routine is executed. (The author of the interrupt routine is presumed to be responsible for any further delays). The interrupt latency can be thought of as the time that elapses between when the work (of responding to the external event) should begin, and when it actually begins.

Interrupt latency has several components:

- the unavoidable overhead introduced by the hardware

- the unavoidable overhead introduced by the operating system. On many operating systems, especially those designed for real-time use, this can be zero. In standard implementations of UNIX, there is a small assembly language "wrapper" that sets up a proper environment for interrupt routines that are written in C, which adds a small amount of overhead.

- the latency introduced by having interrupts periodically disabled by the kernel and by other interrupt routines. Unfortunately, UNIX is one of the worst offenders in this respect. Unless your vendor has improved the code (which is not particularly difficult), you should expect a high (and variable) interrupt-disable latency

It is difficult to arrive at an accurate figure for the interrupt latency of a computer system. Some vendors quote zero interrupt latencies; however, only operating system latency can ever be zero. Most of the time, it is not practical to calculate the total latency. When possible, the maximum interrupt latency should be measured using an oscilloscope or in-circuit emulator (ICE). Otherwise, the designer will be forced to settle for an educated guess.

If the interrupt latency of a computer system is too high, a way must be found to reduce it. Unfortunately, there are very few viable options. Sometimes, the incoming interrupt rate can be reduced by changing to intelligent interface hardware or by eliminating noncritical activity. But in many cases, a new hardware or software vendor must be found who offers better performance.

File System and Disk Driver

Many real-time applications require some sort of disk file to store data. This can be either data that they are collecting or information that they use to help perform their tasks. In such systems, the performance of the disk subsystem becomes critical to the success of the application. This performance is significantly affected by the resident operating system.

The disk file system used in UNIX is a compromise among efficiency, flexibility, and reliability. While it is nearly ideal in the time-sharing environment it was designed for, UNIX disk I/O is less perfect for real-time applications. The major problems are described here.

Reliability   One of the most famous features of the UNIX implementation is the "buffer cache," which is a method for saving the most frequently used sections of the disk in the computer's memory to enhance disk performance. Although the buffer cache significantly improves performance, it can also reduce reliability. Since information may be temporarily saved in main memory, even when the programmer thinks it has been written to the disk, a system crash can cause that data to be lost.

Performance   The UNIX file system is designed to maximize flexibility and to make it efficient to store small files. This causes a small (but significant) degradation compared to the capabilities of the underlying hardware. This degradation is most noticeable when you create or access large files, especially if the access patterns are random.

Priority   UNIX assigns equal importance to all disk operations, regardless of the priority of the process making the request. If a real-time process needs to access the disk, it frequently cannot afford to wait while several lower-priority processes get their turns.

Some real-time UNIX look-alike systems offer features to address some of these problems.

Synchronized Writes   In UNIX System V.2 and later versions, a file can be opened with the O_SYNC option. This causes all writes on that file to bypass the buffer cache. This ensures that the data on the disk matches what the programmer expects, even if there is a system crash, at the expense of performance. Other UNIX variants may make a similar facility available on a per-write, per-file, or per-disk basis.

Contiguous Files   Your choice of optimization techniques is significantly influenced by the presence or absence of other applications competing for the same resources. If the real-time application has exclusive use of a disk and the application needs to access large files, then contiguous files can provide major performance gains. In hardware terms, these gains come primarily because the disk head(s) don't have to be repositioned between accesses. Thus, large transfers can be done at hardware speed, random access is quicker because the data are all in one small area of disk, and the operating system can easily calculate the location of any block in the file.

The major disadvantages are that space for most files must be allocated ahead of time ("preallocated"), that it may be difficult to find sufficient contiguous space on a crowded disk, and in general that disk management is made more difficult.

File Preallocation   Regardless of whether the vendor supports contiguous files, space for a file can be preallocated, so that the operating system does not have to engage in a time-consuming file-extension operation in real time. Even if a particular implementation of UNIX does not offer a system call to do this, it is quite easy to write a program to handle the function.

BSD Fast File System   One of the innovations in the 4.2BSD release of UNIX was a complete redesign of the file system, with a specific goal of improving performance. Many vendors, including some System V vendors, have adopted these modifications.

Disk Priorities   It is quite easy for a vendor to modify the operating system so that each disk request inherits the priority of its parent process. I/O from high-priority processes will then get the first shot at the disk. In systems that do disk head sorting (true of most UNIXes), the process priority should be more important than the disk head position—this is an important point to check when you evaluate vendors. (*Disk head sorting* refers to the use of algorithms to sort the list of queued disk accesses into an order that minimizes head seek time and other overhead.)

In addition, on any UNIX or UNIX look-alike system, some of the following may help.

Sync the Disks Frequently   If the application must ensure that its data is actually written on the disk, it can issue the sync system call to make sure that the disk matches what is in the buffer cache. The disadvantage of this is that a sync takes a long time, so that overall system performance will suffer. Under BSD UNIX, the fsync call can be used instead, so that only the buffers relevant to a particular file will be written. (Be warned, however, that in many implementations fsync simply calls sync.) If there is only one file with critical data, it may be better to use raw disk I/O (discussed later), which bypasses the buffer cache entirely, than to continually issue sync calls.

Eliminate Unnecessary I/O   If the real-time application is having difficulty accessing the disk because of the total disk load, reduce unneeded disk I/O.

Organize the Free List   New space for UNIX files is allocated from a disk structure called the "free list." If blocks on the free list are organized optimally, files will be created with that same optimal structure. Conversely, if the free list is random, files will be created randomly, and performance will suffer. The free list can be reorganized with the fsck utility.

Organize Existing Files   If existing files on the disk were not created from an optimal free list, it may be profitable to reorganize them as well. The dcopy utility, if available, can do this.

Use Raw Disk I/O   Many real-time applications need top performance only on a few large files and do not need the more advanced file system facilities, such as directories and automatic file extension. In such cases, "raw" disk I/O can be used to achieve performance limited only by the hardware. An entire disk partition is dedicated to each large file, and the real-time program opens the appropriate special file in the /dev directory to access it.

I/O transfers on such files bypass the buffer cache and usually are executed directly by the hardware at maximum speed. The disadvantage is that an entire disk partition, which is usually quite large, must be dedicated to a single file.

Interprocess Communications Facilities

As was discussed earlier, real-time applications are often composed of a family of processes working together. To work together, the processes must be able to communicate with each other. A good real-time system supplies a rich set of "interprocess communications" facilities to the programmer.

Synchronization Facilities

All interprocess communications facilities have performance limits. The performance characteristics most important to the real-time programmer are latency and bandwidth. The "latency" of an interprocess-communications method is the amount of time it takes for a message to arrive. Usually, the latency is determined by how long it takes the scheduler to run the receiving process, so it is similar for all communications facilities in a given operating system.

The "bandwidth" of a communications facility is the amount of information that can be passed in a given amount of time. For example, a 300 baud modem has a low bandwidth, because it can only pass 30 characters per second. An Ethernet, by contrast, has a very high bandwidth of 1.2 million characters per second. If a lot of data must be transferred, a high bandwidth is necessary for adequate performance. The bandwidth of the various facilities will be discussed later.

The simplest form of interprocess communications is synchronization: one process must inform another that it's time to do something. There are two facilities found in UNIX systems for this purpose: *signals* and *semaphores.*

The signal mechanism is available in all implementations of UNIX, although it behaves slightly differently on BSD and System V. The problem with signals is that they are difficult to handle correctly. From the point of view of the application process, a signal is just like a hardware interrupt and is just as hard to deal with. It is very easy to introduce race conditions accidentally that will produce intermittent bugs. (In this context, a *race condition* is an intertask communications problem usually caused by (near) simultaneous messages from both tasks. For example, either task may send the other a request for data and suspend execution until the data is ready. With both tasks asleep, neither can send data to the other; thus, the system is hung.)

Worse, in System V (though not in BSD), the signal mechanism is inherently unreliable. When a signal is sent to a System V process, there is an unavoidable time window during which a second signal of the same name will terminate the target process. The window extends from the time the first signal is delivered until the process manages to issue a system call to reset the signal handler. This window can be reduced by careful coding, but it cannot be eliminated. In fact, if the target process is swapped out between signal delivery and the system call, the "danger window" can become arbitrarily large.

System V also provides a synchronization mechanism, the semaphore. Semaphores, which were invented by Edsger W. Dijkstra, can be thought of as an extension of the signal concept. When events are signaled using semaphores, a count of events is kept. Because of the counter, semaphores are reliable even if multiple signals are sent. The implementation of semaphores in System V is a particularly powerful and flexible one that is sufficient for a wide variety of applications.

Communications Facilities

Both signals and semaphores have very low overhead and high bandwidth, with semaphores winning slightly on most systems. Often, however, it is not enough simply to notify a process that some event has occurred. In addition to or instead of this information, it may be necessary to communicate something more complex. For example, in the rocket example, the position of the fins may be controlled by a separate process. If the flight-control process wants to change the fin position, it is not sufficient to simply say "move the fins." You must also tell the fin process what fin position you want. There are two communications mechanisms available in UNIX: messages (which also includes UNIX pipes and similar facilities), and shared memory. (Files can also be used for interprocess communications, but this is not common in real-time applications for performance reasons.)

Messages, Pipes, Sockets, and Streams   A message facility allows a process to say "send the following n bytes of data to such-and-such a process" (Figure 10–5).The sending process does not have to wait for this to happen; instead, the operating system will collect the message in an internal buffer and deliver it to the receiving process later. If the receiving process asks for a message when none is available, it may get an "empty" indication, or it may just wait for the next message to arrive, depending on the particular implementation. Each message-send operation is matched by exactly one message-receive operation, and each message arrives as a separate unit. Usually, more than one message can be in transit at a particular time. If the backlog becomes too large, the sending process either waits until some messages have been removed or receives an error indication (again depending on the implementation).

All UNIX implementations have an interprocess communications facility, the pipe; some implementations also provide pipe-like facilities called *sockets* and *streams*. For practical purposes, a *pipe* is simply a type of message facility that does not preserve the boundaries between messages. Thus, the sending process could write 10-byte chunks and the receiving

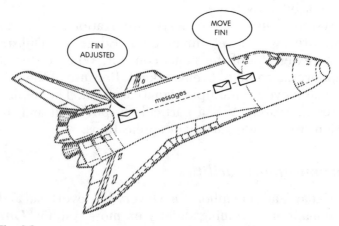

Figure 10–5   Messages

process could read 15-byte chunks; after every 30 bytes the message boundaries would line up again. As long as the programmer is careful about message boundaries, a pipe can be just as useful as a message facility. In some older variants of UNIX, pipes can only be created between certain processes. However, this does not apply to sockets or streams, and all modern UNIX variants support either these or arbitrary piping.

Sockets are like pipes with more power. They are bidirectional and may cross network or other machine boundaries. In addition, sockets allow limited control information as well as data.

Streams are more general still, with extensive control information-passing capabilities.

On most UNIX systems, messages (if available) have the lowest overhead and highest bandwidth, with pipes following close behind. Because they support complex networking facilities, sockets are probably less efficient than streams, but because they rarely appear on the same machine as streams, the question is somewhat academic. They certainly have much lower bandwidth than pipes or messages.

Shared Memory   Sometimes, it is not appropriate to organize interprocess communications as separate messages. In some cases, large amounts of data must be passed, so the bandwidth of a message facility (which must physically copy every message) is too low. Or perhaps the communication does not fall neatly into the one-in-one-out model of messages.

For example, consider again the rocket's flight-control and fin-control processes. The fin-control process has a simple job: put and keep the fins in the position currently requested by the flight-control process. The key word here is *currently*. You don't really care what the flight-control process wanted six seconds ago, or even a tenth of a second ago. If the flight-control process uses a message facility to request position changes, and the fin-control process is delayed, a backlog of out-of-date requests will develop. On the other hand, if the fin-control process tries to receive a position message and none is available, it will wait for one. This may prevent the process from accomplishing required tasks, such as making minor corrections in the fin position to compensate for turbulence-induced fin motion.

The solution to this problem is shared memory, which allows the same physical memory to be available to two different processes. You can create a shared memory area to contain the fin-position variable. Now the flight-control process can simply store the desired fin position, and the fin-control process can read it when convenient (without waiting), and it will always get the latest value. (In cases where values prior to the latest are required, this technique may be generalized by using an array instead of a variable in shared memory. This becomes in effect a buffer, usually a ring buffer. If the reading task tags the last-read entry, the writing task can detect the condition of overwriting unread values. If this occurs, the buffer needs to be made larger or a different algorithm selected.)

There are many situations with shared memory in which some sort of synchronization code must be used in addition to storing the data. Suppose the rocket has separately controllable left and right tail fins. Now consider the following sequence:

1. The flight-control process calculates and stores a new left fin position. It then goes to work calculating the corresponding right fin position.

2. The fin-control process reads the desired left and right fin positions, getting the new left fin position and the old right fin position.

3. The flight-control process now gets around to storing the right fin position that matches the new left fin position.

The fin-control process is now operating with incorrect data. Unless correctly dealt with, these "stale-data" problems are a prescription for disaster. In this example, the problem can be avoided by a sequence number associated with each data item. Then the fin-control process will not use the data for the left fin until the right fin sequence number matches the left fin's sequence number. The flight-control process writes the left fin sequence number, then the left fin position number, then the right fin position number, and finally the right fin sequence number. If the fin-control process then reads the data and sequence numbers, *reading the left-fin (first written) sequence number last,* and it still matches the right sequence number, it is guaranteed that the data is correct. Because of the problem with making sure data in a shared memory is all self-consistent, real-time programmers tend to avoid shared memory when possible. Used carefully, however, it is the most powerful interprocess communications tool. Shared memory has the highest bandwidth of any communications method.

Asynchronous I/O

Most modern computers have the ability to carry on input/output operations in parallel with computation. This is called *asynchronous I/O*. It allows early read data to be processed while additional reads are going on or allows processing to continue in parallel with a large write. Real-time programmers often want to take advantage of this capability to squeeze a little more performance out of the computer. Doing this requires special support in the operating system.

The most basic facility needed is a way to tell the system not to wait for an I/O request to complete after it is issued. In UNIX this can be accomplished by selecting the O_NDELAY option with either the open or the fcntl system call.

However, this is rarely sufficient. The programmer is almost always interested in being notified when the I/O operation finally completes (often so yet another operation can be issued). For example, the rocket's flight-control process must periodically read navigation instruments to be sure the rocket is still on course. If the programmer uses asynchronous I/O, the process could start reading the navigation instruments well before they were actually needed, then continue with other work. At some point, it will be time to work with the navigation data; the flight-control process will then need some way to be sure the data has actually been read in.

Unfortunately, System V provides no way to learn about I/O completion. This makes the O_NDELAY option much less useful than it should be. BSD UNIX does a better, though still imperfect, job. There is a signal, named SIGIO, that will notify a process that an I/O request has completed. (Remember that in BSD, unlike System V, signals are reliable.) However, SIGIO only tells you that some request is finished; it gives no indication of which request it was. To solve this, BSD provides the select system call, which accepts a list of requests that might have completed and returns an indication of which ones have actually done so.

The BSD select mechanism, together with SIGIO and O_NDELAY, provides all of the facilities needed to do asynchronous I/O. However, these facilities need additional support in the individual device drivers. Some vendors may not provide this support in all drivers, so that select may be available on one device and unavailable on another. When evaluating possible hardware systems, you should be sure to check that asynchronous I/O is actually available on the devices you will be using.

Suppose you have a version of System V UNIX that does not have select—what do you do? You can still achieve asynchronous I/O, but you will have to do a bit more work. You will need a separate process for each I/O operation that can go on simultaneously. For example, suppose you need to write two disk files asynchronously and simultaneously carry out computations. You will need three processes: one for each disk file, and one for the actual computation, as shown in Figure 10–6. The System V shared-memory facility can be used to pass disk-bound data to a disk process, and semaphores can be used to tell them that there is more data available. The overhead will be higher than an equivalent implementation using select, but you will still be able to satisfy your requirements.

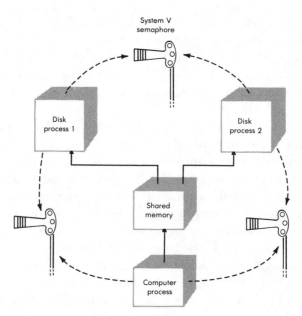

Figure 10–6   Asynchronous I/O on System V

Timing Facilities

Real-time applications, by their very nature, are intimately involved with time. Two basic facilities are needed: the ability to measure the passage of time, and the ability to suspend a process for a certain amount of time. Standard UNIX provides both of these facilities. However, because of its time-sharing history, UNIX timers have a resolution of only one second. Many real-time applications need to accurately measure times shorter than a second.

Version 4.2 BSD UNIX offers augmented system calls that can be used for high-speed timing. Most vendors of enhanced real-time UNIXes and UNIX look-alikes also offer this feature.

Projects working under System V can make use of the return value of the times system call to obtain a timer with subsecond resolution. In some circumstances, this can solve timing problems that would otherwise require going to an enhanced UNIX. The poll system call can also be used in some cases to suspend a process for less than a second.

Support for Specialized I/O Devices

Real-time programs must deal with special input and output devices that are not part of "normal" computer systems. These include analog-to-digital (A/D) converters, digital-to-analog converters, digital inputs and outputs, graphics displays, and other special devices.

All of these devices require software support, at least in the form of drivers. Many also require library support for the applications programmer, because the form of requests to the driver is inconvenient. Graphics devices are usually the most complex, and thus they require the most support, but even A/D converters require library support to convert the binary code from the hardware device into an actual voltage. The quality of the support library for real-time devices can be a big factor in the success or failure of a real-time project.

Usually, it is the vendor's responsibility to provide drivers and a support library. This is something that should be checked when you are evaluating hardware choices for a real-time project. If you purchase an interface board from a vendor who does not provide a UNIX driver and library (or, even worse, not even a C-callable non-UNIX one), you will have to write one yourself. It may be more cost-effective to go to a different vendor, even if the hardware cost is slightly higher.

Robustness and Crash Recovery

Robustness refers to how the computer system responds to minor errors and difficulties. If a disk drive fails, does the entire computer come to a halt, or does it merely work around the problem? Similarly, if the operating system detects a software problem, does it repair it or does the whole system crash? How many operating system bugs are there, and how often do they cause either system crashes or application program failures? If the protections fail and the computer does crash, how much information is lost during a reboot? And how long does the reboot take? These *crash recovery* issues can be critical in some real-time applications.

When you consider robustness, UNIX is something of a compromise. The system has been around long enough, and is in use in enough installations, that most of the software bugs that cause system crashes have been removed. Many UNIX sites run for months at a time without software crashes.

However, UNIX was written for time-sharing applications, and the authors did not attempt to write a system that would continue running in the face of serious failures. As one example, an I/O error on the main disk can make the entire system fail, even if all the other disks are still running perfectly. UNIX also has a tendency to crash when it runs out of space in certain fixed-size internal tables. (However, it is frequently possible for the developers to increase critical table sizes to avoid this problem.)

Because UNIX was originally written for a time-sharing environment, there is no extensive crash recovery facility. All modern UNIX implementations come with fsck, which is sufficient to allow completely automated recovery from nearly all crash-induced file system problems. However, fsck cannot recover the state of processes that were running at the time of the crash. If the real-time application has long-running processes that must be recovered after a crash, the programmer must provide special recovery code to handle the situation. Usually, this consists of taking frequent checkpoints of the state of the application, and then providing crash-recovery code that can read in the latest checkpoint and restart things from there.

A final, and serious, problem with UNIX crash recovery is the time that it takes. UNIX crash recoveries can be very long-running, mostly because the fsck program is very slow. For projects that require rapid crash recovery or process state saving, standard UNIX is probably not suitable.

One fact should be clear from this discussion: you must know the requirements your application will place on the system. For example, if portability is a requirement, then using standard UNIX is probably important. If, however, there are hard response-time constraints or other severe demands, this almost certainly excludes standard UNIX.

UNIX is suitable for projects that are not too demanding, but that do require multitasking, a file system, and other features. If the task is demanding, or conversely if the task is very simple, UNIX is not likely to be suitable. In most cases if UNIX is suitable or nearly so, then there are UNIX look-alikes that are also acceptable. Use of a look-alike may significantly impact portability, however. In the selection of UNIX systems and look-alikes, the quality of the vendor is very important. The UNIX world is one where the buyer must beware. With requirements in hand, you can evaluate existing products and select one that meets the demands, without the expense of overkill.

Summary of Real-Time Operations

Real-time applications demand performance, predictability, and robustness from the underlying operating system. They also need special facilities to support high-accuracy timing, interprocess communication, and special devices. Most standard UNIX implementations satisfy some, but not all, of these requirements.

When Standard UNIX Isn't Suitable

When you decide that standard UNIX is unsuitable for the application in question, you have several other options:

- If it is clear that the real-time application requires either no operating system or a true real-time control system, then UNIX and its look-alikes are out. In this case UNIX can still be used as the development system by using cross-development techniques.

- If standard UNIX is more nearly suitable, then you may choose a UNIX look-alike that has the needed improvements.

- A final approach is to buy a UNIX source license and make the needed improvements in-house.

This section briefly addresses each of these approaches.

Using UNIX as a Cross-Development System

When a real-time application is extremely demanding or when the power of UNIX is unneeded (such as in the rocket-control example) it may be best to avoid UNIX completely as an application base. Instead, an operating system designed for real-time use can be specified, using UNIX only as a development system. This approach was pioneered by AT&T itself with the Programmer's Workbench (PWB) product. The advantages and disadvantages of this approach are the normal trade-offs of cross-development. The target machine can be specialized to the real-time environment, but special software support is needed for compiling and debugging on a different machine, so development will generally be somewhat slower.

UNIX Look-Alikes with Real-Time Enhancements

A UNIX look-alike designed for real time may be suitable if standard UNIX is not appropriate. Such systems are available from several vendors, including Alcyon Corp. (Regulus), Charles River Data Systems (UNOS), Databoard, Inc. (D-NIX), Hewlett-Packard (HP-UX), Masscomp Corp. (RTU), and Whitesmiths, Ltd. (IDRIS), among others.

Advantages of this approach include:

- The system may be supported by an experienced, stable vendor and may have been debugged in the field. The quality of the UNIX look-alike *vendor* is a very important issue.

- Because the system is a close analog of UNIX, programmers will find it familiar, and it will be easy to staff the project with experienced people.

- Because the system is not derived directly from AT&T UNIX, it does not have UNIX's historical deficiencies in its real-time performance.

- License fees for the system may be lower.

- Because the system used for development is the same as that used for the actual application, there are no cross-compilation or cross-debugging problems. This can save a significant amount of project time.

- The system will have specialized support for real-time software that cannot be found in AT&T UNIX. This support will include special real-time system calls, support libraries, and superior CPU and disk performance.

- Because the vendor is targeting real-time as a major market area, the vendor will often be more knowledgeable in the field and will be able to provide better support than a vendor who is simply repackaging AT&T UNIX.

Disadvantages of this approach include:

- A UNIX look-alike is not UNIX. Small differences will exist, and these differences frequently surprise programmers who are expecting "real" UNIX. Portability, both in bringing software to the system and moving resulting applications to other systems, may be difficult.

- Despite the best efforts of vendors to match the System V Interface Definition (AT&T's official specification of how UNIX is supposed to behave), errors and ambiguities in that specification will cause discrepancies.

- AT&T UNIX is not a static operating system. Whenever AT&T improves UNIX, look-alike vendors have to play catch-up. Thus, features that the project may require could be unavailable in a look-alike.

- UNIX look-alike systems are generally provided by hardware vendors and are available only on hardware supplied by that vendor. Thus, one of the biggest advantages of UNIX (hardware independence) is lost.

Enhancing UNIX with Real-Time Features

Still another approach to doing real-time operations under UNIX is to start with the AT&T UNIX kernel and add the real-time support necessary for the particular application. This is an approach that has succeeded for a number of companies.

The enhancement approach works best when standard UNIX is almost good enough for the application in question, so that the changes that need to be made are small. A common change is a modification to the UNIX scheduler that makes the nice (priority) level more meaningful; this is often combined with other scheduler improvements such as reducing the time-slicing interval (the rate at which the scheduler changes to a new process).

Advantages of this approach include:

- Because the system is based on standard UNIX, there are few or no compatibility problems or surprises, and programmers find themselves in a familiar environment.

- Since the changes that need to be made to support the application are small, the kernel-modification project can be low-cost.

- If the changes are done in-house (as opposed to being purchased from a vendor), the real-time changes can usually be made machine-independent, so hardware portability is not lost.

- As UNIX evolves, the real-time enhancements can often be merged into later releases with only a little work. This allows the project to take advantage of new UNIX features such as STREAMS.

Disadvantages of this approach are:

- If the enhanced kernel is purchased from an outside vendor, you are locked into that supplier, just as with a UNIX look-alike.

- If the enhancements are developed in-house, it will require a staff that understands both the UNIX kernel and the design of real-time systems. The success of the project will depend critically on the quality of these people.

- An in-house kernel project can be a dangerous thing, ballooning in time and money until it eats the entire project budget.

- As AT&T (or other UNIX supplier) releases updated versions of the kernel, existing changes will have to be repeatedly merged into these new versions. In the best case, UNIX tools like sdiff can make this a fairly simple task, but "fairly simple" can still mean a lot of days and dollars. In the worst case, the vendor may have rewritten or discarded all of the code you so carefully improved, and you will have to repeat the entire enhancement project.

- The real-time application will be dependent on home-grown, nonstandard features. This will add programmer training costs and may make it much harder to move to a different hardware base.

Summary of Nonstandard UNIX Approaches

If standard UNIX is not suitable for the project, you have three basic choices: cross-develop (useful when a powerful real-time operating system is a must), use a UNIX look-alike with real-time features, and (least desirable) enhance UNIX with the required capabilities.

Future Directions

As UNIX continues its rise in popularity, there is continually more demand for ways to use UNIX in real-time projects. As you have seen, many companies have already begun to address this demand in various ways. In the future, you can expect more of this, as well as attempts to standardize a real-time variant of UNIX.

The IEEE P1003.1 Standard (POSIX)

The leading UNIX standardization effort is being undertaken by the Institute of Electrical and Electronic Engineers (IEEE). The committee, known as P1003.1, is responsible for producing a portable operating system standard, to be known as POSIX. A draft of the POSIX standard has been published for comment, but it does not specifically address real-time features.

The /usr/group Users' Organization

The UNIX users' organization known as "/usr/group" also has a committee that is working on a real-time UNIX standard. This group is further along than the IEEE committee and will probably produce a recommendation for the IEEE effort. As of early 1987, the /usr/group committee has generated several preliminary proposals which are being reviewed and worked on.

AT&T: MERT, UNIX/RT, and DMERT

Within AT&T, UNIX has been used for a number of successful real-time projects. In the mid-1970s, Bell Labs undertook a research project to build a real-time kernel that could support UNIX functionality. The result of this effort was called MERT (for multienvironment real-time) and was described in the first special UNIX issue of the *Bell System Technical Journal* in July 1978. MERT was used as the basis for a real-time UNIX called UNIX/RT. UNIX/RT has not been well-described outside of AT&T, but it appears that several internal projects used it successfully. In addition, the 3B20D computer system runs DMERT (for duplex MERT), which is described in another *Bell System Technical Journal* special issue dated January 1983.

AT&T is, of course, well aware of the demand for a real-time UNIX. As of this writing in early 1987, AT&T's plans in terms of a real-time variant of UNIX have not been announced. Whatever AT&T does, real-time UNIX is here to stay. But an official version or certification standard would provide a big boost.

Summary

Real-time applications make many demands on the computer and operating system. The most demanding are real-time control systems, which may require extremely short response times for proper operation. If properly understood, these demands can be often limited to what UNIX can deal with. For applications that are beyond UNIX's capabilities, there are several other options for making at least some use of UNIX in the project, ranging from cross-development to enhancement of UNIX. In the future, AT&T and other vendors can be expected to address UNIX's deficiencies with a standard real-time UNIX, but this will be some time in coming.

## Part Three

ESOTERICA OF IMPLEMENTATION

One thing was clear when the contributors set out to write *UNIX Papers:* market conditions were ripe for licensed AT&T UNIX clones to appear on new 32 bit microprocessors, such as the Intel 80386 and the Motorola MC68030. As UNIX proliferated on these chips, programmers would find themselves faced with opportunities to write code for these machines. We thus felt that knowing how these UNIX ports were accomplished and what trade-offs had to be made would be of interest to application programmers, because any quirk of the microprocessor would also be present for the application program. Also, at the time of this book's publication, there was increased interest in parallel processing, using multiple computers to work on a single program, and the uses of UNIX in real-time environments.

This part first explores the implementation of UNIX on three important microprocessors: the Intel 80286 and 80386, and the Motorola MC68030. The difficulties of the segmentation scheme of the Intel 80286 port is mainly overcome in the port to the 80386 with its true MMU, full 32 bit "paged" (overlapping segmented) addressing, and ability to run MS-DOS in the "virtual" mode. A paper on the Motorola MC68030 shows that it provides a rich platform for running UNIX and has features that make it perhaps the best choice from a strict performance view. For the person interested in state-of-the-art performance, we present a paper on loosely and tightly couple multiprocessing under UNIX, where several hardware processors run programs as parallel tasks. The last paper explores where UNIX is heading—the trends that are shaping its success, such as "open system standards" and the adoption of UNIX by mainstream PC vendors, and the types of features and changes we can expect to see in future versions of UNIX.

KEYWORDS

▶ Segmented
  Memory

▶ Descriptor

▶ Memory
  management

▶ Memory models

▶ Protected mode

▶ Real mode

▶ Segmentation
  Selector

Paper Synopsis: UNIX can run effectively on computers that contain the Intel 80286 microprocessor, but you must understand how the 80286 architecture affects the way UNIX processes can be compiled and run. This paper explains the major decisions that have to be made in porting UNIX to the 80286.

Anthony D. Andrews is a systems programmer with Wildridge Consulting, which specializes in UNIX porting and networking. A specialist in UNIX system ports, Mr. Andrews earned a bachelor's in electrical engineering at Purdue University in 1981. He may be reached on uucp at ihnp4!onecom!wldrdg!tony.

## 11

A UNIX Port to the 80286

Anthony D. Andrews

This paper examines UNIX on the Intel 80286 (iAPX286) microprocessor. You'll first review the architecture and memory management of the 80286 and see how they affect the C language. Then the paper considers how UNIX actually uses the memory management features of the 80286 and also looks at some of the problems involved in running UNIX on this microprocessor. This paper should be of interest to anyone considering running UNIX and writing programs on an 80286 system.

One of the most popular microprocessors on the market today is the Intel iAPX286. This processor, more commonly known as the 80286, is used in the IBM PC/AT and many other PC-compatible systems. While remaining compatible with the older 8086 and 8088 chips, the 80286 provides a substantial increase in performance.

The future market for the 80286 seems quite solid, at least for the next few years. IBM's new Personal System/2 line of computers includes the Model 50 and Model 60, which both use the 80286. This trend will most likely continue, making the 80286 the processor of choice for most new PC-compatible machines, with the new 80386 reserved for the highest-performance machines.

The 80286 also provides many new features rarely used in these PC-compatible machines. These features, which include memory management and protection, make the 80286 eminently more suitable than its 8088/86 predecessors for use in multiuser, multitasking operating systems such as UNIX. Given these features and the popularity of the 80286, it's worthwhile to consider the value of the 80286 as a UNIX machine. (By the way, in this paper,

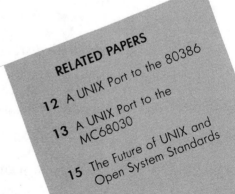

"UNIX" refers to System V release 2 as ported to the 80286 and supplied by AT&T, unless stated otherwise.)

C on the 80286

This section explores the C language as implemented on the 80286. It starts with a general discussion of the 80286's segmented memory organization. Next it will show how the C language is implemented in such an environment. Finally, it takes a closer look at the memory management features of the 80286 in both the real and protected modes of operation. This will prepare you to look at the problems of running UNIX on the 80286.

Segmentation

In segmented memory architectures such as the 80286, physical memory is broken up into contiguous regions called *segments.* A program consists of a number of segments. A given segment contains code or data (but usually not both).

In a segmented system, a logical address consists of two portions: a segment name and an offset. The segment name tells which segment is being referenced. It is a 16 bit number. There are 65,536 possible segments. The offset specifies the location of interest within the segment. Offsets on the 80286 are also 16 bits, giving a maximum segment size of 64K bytes. Figure 11–1 shows the segment and offset portions of a logical address being mapped to a physical address in memory.

For now, you don't need to be concerned with how a segment name specifies where the segment is. Later, you'll look at this translation process in detail.

Segment Registers and Memory References

Because there are 64K different segments, segment names are represented by 16 bit numbers. Four special registers are used to hold the segment names of those segments that are currently being used. These registers are:

- CS—code segment
- SS—stack segment

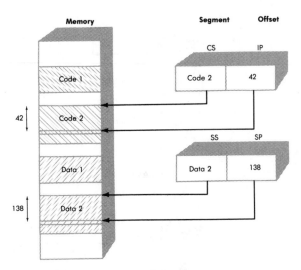

Figure 11–1   Addresses in a Segmented System

- DS—data segment
- ES—extra segment

When a program is running, the code segment register (CS) and the instruction pointer (IP) give the segment and offset of the next instruction to be executed. The stack segment register (SS) specifies the location of the program stack segment. The stack pointer (SP) on the other hand, gives the current offset of the top of the stack. The data segment (DS) and extra segment (ES) registers are used to access general program data. The DS register is used most often and is the default segment register used in most memory references.

The CS register is referenced implicitly by the processor, along with the IP register (which also gets incremented) each time it fetches an instruction for execution. To set the CS register, special forms of the 80286 jmp and call instructions are used. The jmp and call instructions transfer program control to a given destination (the call instruction makes a subroutine call). Both instructions set the IP to the offset of the destination. If the destination is in a different segment, the CS register is set as well. In this case, the instruction is said to be an "intersegment" jump or call.

Figure 11–2 shows each kind of jump graphically. The top half of the figure shows an intrasegment (within the segment) jump from offset A to B. The CS register remains unchanged, and the contents of the IP register is replaced with B. In the bottom of the figure, an intersegment jump is made from offset A in segment code1 to offset D in segment code2. In this case, both the CS and IP are modified.

Like the CS register, the stack segment register (SS) is often used implicitly. All stack operations (such as the push and pop instructions) use

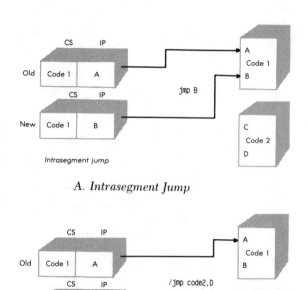

A. Intrasegment Jump

B. Intersegment Jump

Figure 11-2   Intrasegment and Intersegment Jumps in the 80286

the SS register. The SS register is set using the 80286 mov instruction. Since most programs have only one stack, this is normally done just once during program startup.

The data segment (DS) and extra segment (ES) registers are used for general data access. Most instructions that reference memory use the DS register by default, although the ES register can almost always be used instead. Like the SS register, DS and ES are set using the 80286 mov instruction.

Figure 11-3 shows a program with four segments: one for code, another for the stack, and two more for data. Each segment is shown addressed by the appropriate segment register.

One advantage of segmentation is that it makes it easy to relocate programs in memory. In some systems, programs must be compiled to run at a specific physical address, which makes relocation difficult. In a segmented system, relocation of a segment can be done by simply copying it to the desired location and then changing the corresponding segment register value to point to the new location.

In UNIX systems, processes may be "swapped" (copied) out to the disk if there isn't enough memory to hold all processes at once. When a process that was swapped out is to be run again, it must first be copied

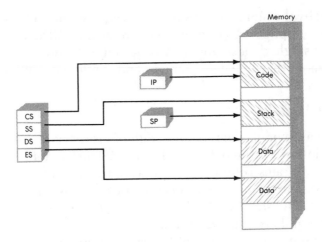

Figure 11–3   Segment Registers in the 80286

back into memory. In a segmented machine, the operating system can copy the process back into any area of memory that is free. If that doesn't happen to be the same location as before, the system can just set the segment registers for the new location and let the process resume execution.

Another benefit of segmentation is that it promotes program modularity. It does this by allowing related data to be placed in a single segment separate from the data of other program modules. On the 80286, each segment can have different attributes and privilege level, allowing a fine level of control over the memory used by each program module.

Memory Models in C

The term *memory model* refers to the number of code and data segments that are used by a program. Programs that contain multiple data segments, for example, are compiled differently from programs that need only one. In this section you'll look at the two most common memory models in detail and see the advantages and disadvantages each has for UNIX.

The System V C compiler is given a short piece of C code here so you can look at the 80286 assembly code it generates for each model. An examination of the code will reveal the effects of the different models on assembly code and speed. Finally, you'll learn about the merits of some of the less common memory models.

Most C compilers for the 80286 support at least two memory models, and some support up to 11. A command line option tells the compiler what model has been selected and determines the style of assembly code that will be generated. The choice of a memory model is usually determined by the memory consumption requirements of the particular program being compiled. A program with only a small amount of data will only need a single data segment. A program with more than 64K of data would need more than one data segment and would use a different memory model.

Small Model

In a small-model program, one segment is reserved for the executable code, and another for the data and the stack. This model is suitable for relatively small programs requiring less than 64K each of code and data or a total of 128K maximum bytes. This includes the vast majority of standard UNIX utilities. The standard UNIX cat command, for example, requires only 10K of code and around 5K of data.

The main advantage of the small model is that because there is only one segment each of code and data, the segment registers can be set up just once when the program starts and forgotten from there on. Figure 11–4 shows the code and data segments of a small-model program with the segment registers initialized appropriately.

Now you can try compiling a small C code fragment using this small model and look at the code it generates. The C code is:

```
1       /* small-model C demo */
2       int     x, y;
3       sub1()
4       {
5               x = y;
```

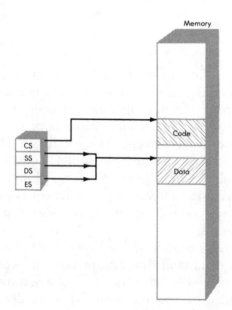

Figure 11–4   Segment Registers in a Small-Model Program

```
6                 sub2();
7        }
```

This code declares two ints, x and y. It then defines a function, sub1(), which sets x equal to y, and then calls another function, sub2(). Here sub2() is a C function already defined elsewhere. This is a simple example, but it lets you see how both code and data are referenced without getting bogged down with too many other details.

The assembly code you'll be looking at is for the System V UNIX assembler, which uses a different syntax than most standard Intel assemblers. The major difference is that the source and destination operands on the 80286 mov instruction are reversed; the leftmost operand is the source. Also, register names are preceded by a percent sign to avoid conflicts with variable names.

If you run this example through the UNIX C compiler (cc) on an IBM PC/AT, the assembly code it generates looks like this:

```
1        sub1:    enter    $0, $0
2                 mov      y, %ax
3                 mov      %ax, x
4                 call     sub2
5                 leave
6                 ret
```

The 80286 enter instruction on line 1 sets up the stack for this routine and allocates space for any local variables (none, in this case). Line 2 moves the contents of variable y into the AX register. Line 3 moves the contents of the AX register to variable x, completing the assignment statement x = y;.

The call to subroutine sub2 is accomplished by the 80286 call instruction on line 4. Finally, the 80286 leave instruction reverses the effects of the enter (restoring the stack pointer, and so on). The ret line returns to the function that called sub1.

In this example no segment registers were directly referenced at all. To access a variable, you only had to use its offset within the data segment. Because there is only one data segment in this model, no segment changes were needed. The 80286 mov instruction, by default, uses the DS register unless told otherwise. Likewise, to make a subroutine call, the compiler used the short, intrasegment form of the call instruction. In each case, the compiler could assume that the segment registers were already initialized by the operating system and pointing to some segment in the system's memory space. The exact location of the program's segments in memory might change each time the program is run.

To summarize, the small model works well for programs that don't require large amounts of code or data. Since the segment registers don't have to be manipulated, the resulting assembly code is small and efficient.

Large Model

Suppose you have a program that has more than 64K of code and that uses very large arrays or structures. The large model is designed for such programs. In a large-model program, there may be multiple segments of code and data (not just one of each) and the program can thus exceed the 64K limits. A program needing 100K of data would use two data segments in the large model.

Figure 11–5 shows how a large-model program might look in memory. In this figure, the DS register currently points to segment D1. To reference data in segment D3, either the DS or ES register would first have to be loaded with the appropriate segment value. Similarly, to call a routine in segment C2, the long, intersegment form of the call instruction would be used.

In a large-model program, the stack is given an entire segment of its own. In fact, the stack is limited to a single segment and so must not exceed 64K bytes in size. (This is seldom a problem.) A similar restriction applies to the data segments; no single data structure or array may be larger than 64K.

Now take the same C fragment you used in the last section and see what code the compiler would produce for the large model. Again, the C code you're using is:

```
1       /* large-model C demo */
2       int     x, y;
3       sub1()
4       {
5               x = y;
```

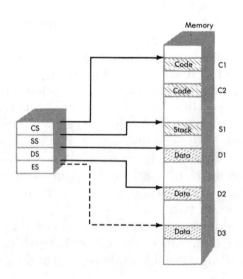

Figure 11–5   Segment Registers in a Large-Model Program

```
6              sub2();
7        }
```

This time, an option on the command line was used to tell cc to use the large model. The compiler produced the following assembly code:

```
1        sub1:   enter   $0, $0
2                mov     $<s>y, %ax
3                mov     %ax, %ds
4                mov     y, %ax
5                mov     $<s>x, %dx
6                mov     %dx, %ds
7                mov     %ax, x
8                lcall   sub2
9                leave
10               lret
```

The first line sets up the stack for this routine. Lines 2 and 3 work together to load the number of the segment for variable y into the DS register. (You can't load an immediate value directly into a segment register, so a two-instruction process is needed.) Line 2 loads the segment number into the ax register (the <s> notation is used by the System V assembler to reference the number of the segment that contains a symbol). Next, line 3 moves the segment number from AX to DS. Now that the segment register has been initialized, in line 4 the value of variable y can be loaded into AX with the same instruction that was used for the small model. Note that when a variable is referenced without the <s> prefix, only its 16 bit offset is used.

Lines 5 and 6 perform the same segment register initialization for the variable x, this time going through the DX register to get to DS. These two lines may seem, at first glance, to be redundant, since the DS register was set up by lines 2 and 3. But when the compiler is generating this code it can't assume that the loader will place the variables x and y in the same segment. Finally, line 7 stores the value of y from AX to location x.

It is possible to eliminate the redundant segment register load if x and y do wind up in the same segment. To do this, the program is compiled and linked once to find in what segment each variable is placed. This information is then used during a second compilation to eliminate redundant segment register loads when they occur. Unfortunately, this is a manual procedure and is also extremely slow. It has been used to optimize the UNIX kernel, but it isn't a standard function of the UNIX C compiler.

The call to sub2 is again performed in a single instruction, but this time the long, intersegment form of the instruction is used (lcall sub2). This instruction implicitly loads the CS register with the segment value for sub2.

On line 9 the effects of the enter instruction are reversed by leave. The function uses lret on line 10 to return, because sub1 would also have been called with an lcall instruction. You know this because all parts of a program must be compiled for the same memory model.

Through this example you've seen how the large model can be used to compile programs that don't fit the small model. You've also seen how the resulting assembly code becomes larger and slower in comparison to the small model. The code is slower because more instructions were required (for segment register setup) and because some of the instructions used (lcall and lret) were slower than their small-model counterparts (call and ret). Later on, you'll learn about the performance differences in more detail. The next section takes a quick look at some other memory models that try to address situations that can't be handled optimally with either the small or large model.

Other Memory Models

The small and large models are sufficient for nearly all applications and, in fact, are the only models supported by UNIX System V on the 80286. But there are still some cases that can't be easily handled by either model.

Huge Model

With the large model, you still have the restriction that no single data or code item can exceed the maximum segment size of 64K bytes. The "huge" model removes this limitation, allowing arbitrarily large structures and arrays to be created. To support this, the compiler has to generate more code than it did for the large model. This makes huge-model programs even larger and slower than large-model programs.

Medium Model

In some cases a program may require more than one segment of code, but only need a small amount of data. This can happen in some scientific applications when complex processing must be performed, but only a small amount of data is involved. The large model would certainly work in this case, but would needlessly reload the DS segment register on every data reference, slowing program execution considerably. The "medium" model addresses this specific situation, by combining the long calls and returns of the large model (allowing multiple code segments) with the short data references (only one data segment) of the small model. The resulting performance is close to that of the small model, because data references are generally much more common than subroutine calls.

The huge and medium models each serve a useful purpose and are supported by the XENIX compiler.

This section covered 4 of the 11 existing models. The others are all minor variations on 1 of the 4 more common models. Remember, though, that memory models only exist to adapt the C language to the segmentation of the 80286. On machines with a uniform address space like the Motorola 68000 that don't have segmentation, the concept of memory models doesn't even exist.

Real Mode

Until now, this paper has described the segment address as something that points to the start of a segment. This section and the next considers segment addresses in more detail to show just how a segment address leads to a physical address.

When the 80286 first starts execution, it is running in what is called the "real mode." In this mode, the 80286 is fully compatible with the 8086 and 8088 processors. In 80286-based computers that run MS-DOS, the processor always stays in real mode. This is why a PC/AT running MS-DOS can be completely compatible with other MS-DOS machines with 8086 or 8088 processors.

In real mode, the conversion from a "logical" to a "physical" address is quite simple. *Logical* refers to the style of addresses visible to the programmer, while *physical* refers to the addresses actually used by the processor to access memory. The segment address is multiplied by 16 (that is, shifted left four bits) and then added to the offset. Figure 11–6 shows this process graphically. The result of this addition is a 20 bit physical address, which means the 80286 can directly address one megabyte of memory in real mode ($2^{20} = 1MB$).

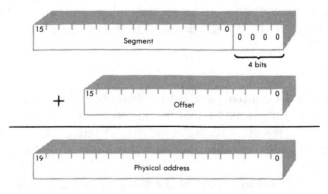

Figure 11–6   Mapping a Logical Address in Real Mode

In real mode, there is no way to limit the range of offsets that can be used within a segment. All 64K of a segment is always accessible to a program even though only part of it may actually be needed. Likewise there are no restrictions on the values that may be loaded into a segment register. The practical implication of all this is that in real mode, any application can access any part of memory.

This lack of memory protection in real mode makes it generally unsuitable for multitasking operating systems. The danger is greater for large-model programs that routinely modify segment registers. An invalid pointer could easily overwrite parts of the operating system or another task. If only small-model programs are allowed, the range of an errant pointer is limited to 64K and the danger can be minimized.

UNIX has been implemented in real mode for the older 8086 and 8088 processors that don't support the memory management features of the 80286. The two major versions of real-mode UNIX are XENIX/86 by The Santa Cruz Operation, and PC/IX by Interactive Systems Corporation. Although the lack of memory protection is always a danger, in practice it really isn't a problem for the single-user machines for which these systems are targeted. Typically these machines run a small number of tasks that are unlikely to contains major bugs. The risk is greater when the systems are used for software development where unstable programs are frequently executed.

Protected Mode

To take full advantage of the features of the 80286, it is necessary to enter a "protected mode" operation (by altering a bit in a special register while you are using the real mode). This enables several new system-level instructions and the memory management unit (MMU). The MMU is the portion of the processor that translates logical addresses to physical ones in protected mode. This section ignores most of what happens in protected mode, however, and sticks to the subject of how address translation is performed by the MMU, because that's of the most importance to UNIX.

Selectors

To be able to control access to segments and manage memory, a number of pieces of data must be maintained for each segment. In protected mode, segment names are called "selectors." Figure 11–7 shows a selector containing an index, a table indicator bit, and two RPL (requested privilege level) bits.

The 13 bit index part of the selector contains a number that identifies the segment of interest. There are two kinds of segments in protected

Figure 11-7   Contents of a
Protected Mode
Selector

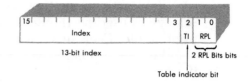

Figure 11-8   Global and Local Segments in the 80286

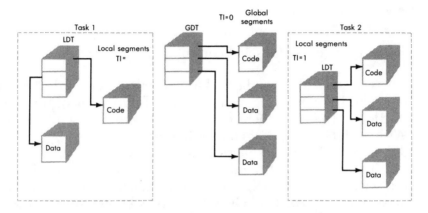

mode: global and local. Global segments are accessible to all processes in the 80286. Local segments are reserved for code and data that is private to a single process. Each process has its own set of "local" segments. The table indicator bit tells which of these two kinds of segments is being accessed; the bit is zero for global segments and one for local segments. In Figure 11-8 two processes are shown, each with its own set of local segments.

In addition to their local segments, each process also has access to the three global segments shown. The table indicator bit (TI) determines which group of segments (global or local) will be accessed, and the index selects a particular segment in the group. The RPL bits are used for memory protection. You can ignore them for now.

With 13 bits reserved for the index portion of a selector, 8192 different segments of each type (global and local) can be accessed by each process on the 80286. Each of these segments can contain between 0 and 64K of data, giving a maximum of one billion addressable bytes.

Descriptors

The 80286 uses two tables in memory to hold detailed information about the segments in the system. One, the global descriptor table (GDT) is for all the global segments. The other table, the local descriptor table (LDT) holds information about the local segments for a process. Each process has its own LDT describing its local segments.

385

Rather than pointing directly at a segment, the index portion of a selector is used by the 80286 as a pointer to a single entry in the appropriate table. Each such entry is called a *descriptor* and holds information about its corresponding segment. The three fields in each descriptor specify the:

- base address of the segment
- size of the segment (limit field)
- access permissions and control information of the segment

The base address is the 24 bit physical address of the beginning of the segment. In referencing memory, the offset portion of the logical address (the lower 16 bits) is then added to this base to yield a full physical address. With 24 bits of physical address information, the 80286 can directly address 16 megabytes of physical memory.

The limit field of the descriptor gives the maximum usable offset for the segment (up to 64K). Since most segments are less than the full 64K maximum, the limit field allows the UNIX kernel to only reserve as much memory for the segment as is really needed. If a program attempts to use an offset larger than the limit given in the descriptor, the 80286 generates an interrupt and the kernel can take the appropriate actions.

The access field provides other information about the segment. The segment may contain code or data. If it contains code, the code may or may not be readable. Some operating systems make code executable but not readable for security reasons. If it contains data, the data may be marked read-only.

Code and data segments use offsets starting at zero and increasing in size. Segments containing a stack start at high offsets and expand down as the stack is used. The contents of the access field determine which of these options have been selected.

Figure 11–9 shows how a logical address is converted to a physical address in protected mode. A 32 bit pointer consists of a 16 bit selector and a 16 bit offset. From the selector, the 13 bit index points to an entry in a descriptor table. The base field of that descriptor then points to the start of the segment in memory. Finally, the offset is used to reference a particular location within the segment.

In practice, programmers rarely need to be concerned with the actual contents of a pointer. When you take the address of a variable in C, as in p = &x, the compiler and linker take care of setting up the selectors and offsets properly.

Protection

In protected mode, a process on the 80286 only has access to segments listed in the GDT or its own LDT. Since the GDT and LDTs are managed

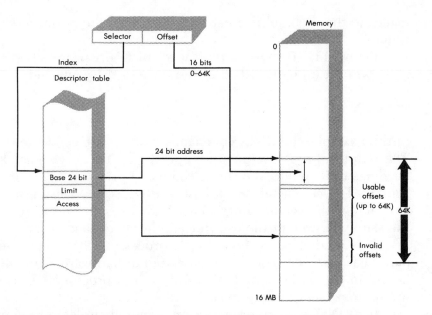

Figure 11–9   Mapping a Logical Address in Protected Mode

by the operating system, processes can't access arbitrary memory locations or the memory of other processes. In protected mode, each process only has access to those segments explicitly given to it by the UNIX kernel. This removes the danger with real mode UNIX and explains why the 80286 is a better processor for UNIX than the 8086 and 8088. In protected mode, a pointer error simply causes the offending program to be terminated. There is no danger to the operating system or to other tasks that may be running.

UNIX on the 80286

The remainder of this paper looks at how small- and large-model programs run as processes under UNIX on the 80286. First it reviews the concept of a process in UNIX and considers the basic assumptions UNIX makes about processes in general. The next section covers processes on the 80286, for both the small and large models. Finally, it discusses a number of problems that arise from the segmented architecture of the 80286.

Processes in UNIX

Processes are the basic unit of computation in UNIX. Each user on a UNIX machine communicates with the system through a shell. Through commands to the shell, users create more processes to perform the work they request.

Figure 11–10 shows a typical set of UNIX processes. This arrangement was set up by the shell in response to the command:

```
pr f.c ¦ lp
```

In this example, the UNIX commands pr and lp are connected with a pipe. The output of pr is used as the input to lp. The pr command adds page headings to its input, and the lp command prints its input on the default printer. The command line just shown generates a listing of the file f.c complete with page headings. When pr and lp are done, they will exit, and the shell will prompt the user for another command.

This section talks about UNIX processes without reference to any particular machine. You'll see what kind of hardware assumptions are inherent in the UNIX kernel and what kind of process structures flow naturally from these assumptions.

In a UNIX system, processes are generally isolated from one another by the memory management hardware of the machine. As far as any process can tell, it is the only thing in memory. Processes communicate with their environment through system calls, which are just "traps" to the operating system. (A trap transfers control from the user's process to the kernel.) Everything a process does, other than accessing and modifying its own memory, is done by making a system call. A programmer uses system calls to communicate with I/O devices, read and write to files on the disk, allocate more memory, and so on.

The address space of a UNIX process contains three basic regions; text (or code), data, and the stack. Figure 11–11 shows the typical arrangement of these regions in memory. When one process "forks" or starts another process to do some work, the exec system call is used to replace the calling process with the new program, whose name is passed as an argument to exec. When an exec system call is used to start execution of a program, these three regions are initialized. The text region is loaded with the executable code for the process. The data region is loaded with the

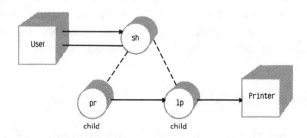

Figure 11–10   Processes in UNIX

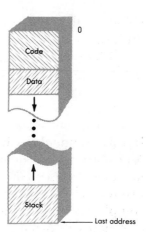

Figure 11–11   Memory Layout of a
Typical UNIX Process

initialized data for the process, and any space for uninitialized data is cleared. Space is allocated for a stack, and process execution begins at the first instruction in the text region.

The text region is essentially static and may or may not be readable. On UNIX systems code is generally readable, but this isn't a strict requirement. The data region must, of course, be readable and writable.

Frequently, programs may need to allocate space for data during execution. If the amount of space needed tends to vary, then it makes sense to allocate it dynamically when the program runs, rather than allocating it statically (by declaring an array, for example). UNIX allows programs to do this with the brk and sbrk system calls. These calls are used to expand the data region, allowing access to more memory.

To do this, the UNIX kernel allocates more physical memory for the process and sets up the memory management hardware to extend the data region for the process, allowing the program to access more logical addresses. The new logical memory seen by the process corresponds to the physical memory that the kernel allocated.

Dynamic memory allocation in this fashion is very common. Some applications put executable code into memory that is dynamically allocated. This is sometimes done in very large programs that don't usually need to call very many of their subroutines. When the program determines that a subroutine will be needed, it can allocate memory for it, load it into memory, and then execute it. This use of dynamic memory trades execution time for memory. To support programs like these, memory obtained via brk or sbrk should be executable.

UNIX makes few assumptions concerning the stack area. It generally starts after the end of process memory and grows toward the data. Processes do not request stack growth; it is either preallocated or expanded automatically by the kernel as needed. There is no fixed minimum stack size required by UNIX and most applications require little. But in certain applications (recursive algorithms, for example) the stack can grow large quickly.

Processes on the 80286

Now that you've seen some general assumptions behind UNIX processes, you'll examine the two kinds of processes that UNIX supports on the 80286. Note how the layout of large- and (especially) small-model processes is influenced by the memory management unit of the 80286.

Small Processes

You'll recall from the earlier discussion of memory models that a small-model program consists of one segment for code, and another for data. Figure 11–12 shows a small-model program as it is implemented in UNIX on the 80286. The size of the code segment is fixed when the process starts and does not change.

The data segment contains both the data and stack. The stack pointer (SP) starts at the offset labeled S in the figure and moves toward zero. The stack region doesn't grow in the small model. The area from the start of the segment to S is always allocated even though only a small part of it might be needed.

Static data starts at S and extends to the current end of the segment. The brk and sbrk system calls dynamically allocate data by changing the limit field of the segment's descriptor, increasing the size of the segment and allowing access to more memory. The UNIX kernel allocates more

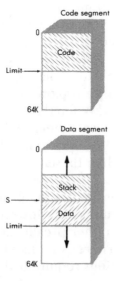

Figure 11–12   Memory Layout of a Small-Model Process

physical memory for the segment to match the increase in logical memory, as was discussed earlier.

The dividing point, S, between the stack and data can be moved by a command line option to the compiler. By default, 8K is reserved for the stack. Programs that require more stack or data may increase one at the expense of the other, but only at compilation time.

Another way of arranging the data segment would have been to place the stack at the end of the segment and the static data at the beginning. The stack and dynamic data could then grow toward each other in the normal fashion.

There are several problems with this approach. First, it requires the kernel to allocate a full 64k of physical memory for each such segment. Segments on the 80286 may grow up or down, but not both. There can't be a hole in the middle of a segment. Also there is nothing to prevent the stack from expanding on top of the data area.

Large Processes

A large-model process consists of multiple code and data segments. Figure 11–13 shows the layout of a typical large-model process. Segments C1

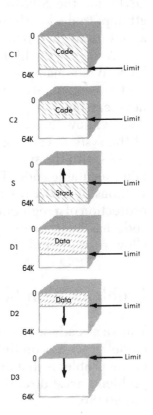

Figure 11–13   Memory Layout of a Large-Model Process

and C2 contain the executable code for the process. Note that C1 is not quite full. In general it isn't possible to use all 64K of a segment, since C functions can't be split between segments. This isn't a problem, because the 80286 provides a large virtual address space, and the limit field of the segment descriptor keeps physical space from being wasted on unused virtual space. Notice how the limit is maintained for each segment shown in Figure 11–13.

In a large-model process, the stack is given an entire segment of its own. The segment is set up by the kernel to start at high addresses and expand toward zero. As the stack grows, this expansion is performed automatically. Expansion beyond 64K is, of course, not possible.

Static data segments are set up much the same as the code segments were. The brk and sbrk system calls can be used to extend the limit of the last segment (D2) or to allocate new segments (D3). It's not necessary to use all 64K of a segment before moving on to a new one. In Figure 11–10, segment D3 could be allocated without using the rest of the available space in D2. But if this were done, it would not be possible to allocate the space at the end of D2 later, because of the way brk and sbrk work.

The existing UNIX system calls really weren't designed to deal with dynamic memory allocation in a segmented environment. In System V UNIX for the 80286, brk and sbrk have been modified somewhat in an attempt to deal with the problem. Unfortunately, this causes problems for applications that assume the normal UNIX return values and behavior.

And even the higher-level allocation routine, malloc, isn't without problems. When many requests are made for small amounts of space, the current version of malloc wastes segments, allocating only the first 4K of each new segment it requests from the kernel. Although this is rarely a problem, it shows how the effects of segmentation can propagate up to higher levels of the system, causing unexpected problems.

As with the small model, dynamically allocated memory may not contain executable code. To support dynamic linking of executable code, some versions of UNIX for the 80286 have added a system call to change the protection of a segment to allow it to be executed. After dynamically linked code has been loaded into a segment, its protection can be changed to allow execution of the code.

Problems with Segmentation

You've already seen some of the problems that arise with small- and large-model processes on the 80286. This section considers in more detail some of the problems that arise when you run UNIX on the 80286. All of these problems arise directly or indirectly from the segmented architecture of the 80286.

Kernel Support

A secondary effect of segmentation is the need for multiple process types (small and large). For each process in the system, the kernel needs to know whether it is small or large model. This information is needed in several parts of the kernel to determine how various operations will be performed. The areas most affected by this are:

- the exec system call
- the brk and sbrk system calls

The exec system call replaces the current process image with the executable code specified in the parameter list. The processing of this system call is especially complicated because there are four possible combinations to deal with. Both the current process and the new process can be either small- or large-model programs.

The memory allocation calls brk and sbrk are similarly affected. Processing for the small model is relatively simple, but the large-model case requires dealing with allocation of new segments and of data within segments.

Memory Model Limitations

An earlier section showed the various memory size restrictions of both the small- and large-memory models. In addition to these, some additional limitations apply when you use UNIX on the 80286.

The only major limitation of this kind in System V release 2 applies to shared memory. System V supports a feature allowing programs to create regions of memory that will be shared by multiple cooperating processes. Each such process makes a system call that maps such a shared region into its own address space. Because the smallest manageable unit of memory in the 80286 is the segment, each shared memory region is one segment.

Figure 11–14 shows two processes that are sharing a segment of memory in this fashion. Both processes have several private segments accessed through their local descriptor tables. In addition, they each have an LDT entry that points to the same segment of physical memory. This segment can be accessed and modified equally by both processes, allowing them to exchange data quickly. Because small-model processes don't know how to address multiple segments, shared memory can only be used by large-model processes.

Multiple Libraries

UNIX systems have several different libraries of routines available for use by C programmers. Since different assembly code is required for the small

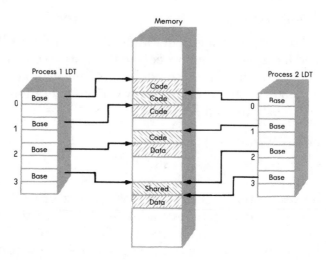

Figure 11–14   Shared Memory on the 80286

and large models, two copies of each of these libraries are needed on the 80286. From a user's point of view, the only problem with this is that twice as much disk space is required for the libraries. This is a bigger problem for system administrators and UNIX developers, since it greatly increases the amount of code to be debugged and maintained.

C Portability

If properly written, C code is very portable, meaning it will run with little or no change on a large number of machines. Unfortunately, most C programmers have picked up some bad programming habits and write code that is less portable than it ought to be. Much of this has arisen because of differences between the "typical" larger UNIX machine and the 80286. While portability problems can't be blamed on a particular processor, it's worth pointing out some of the common errors that can cause problems on the 80286.

The most common error arises because most UNIX machines have a word size of 32 bits. Many programmers declare variables of the C type "int" and then write code that requires the variables to be 32 bits wide. On the 80286, the "int" type is 16 bits wide (in both small and large models) causing such code to fail. If a variable requires a 32 bit word size, the C type long int should be used.

Another common error is to assume that pointers and ints are the same size. This also tends to happen a lot because it's true on most UNIX machines. On the 80286 this is true in small model, but not in large model, where an int is 16 bits, but a pointer is 32 bits.

As an example of this kind of error, suppose a C function named putname is used to output a log-in name passed as a character pointer. As a special case, a pointer value of zero indicates that the log-in name of the current user should be used. The wrong way to pass a zero pointer to putname is:

```
putname(0);
```

In C, constants such as this zero are of type int by default. On the 80286 in the large model, the above function call would pass a 16 bit integer of value 0 to putname and would likely result in a memory fault error. The correct way to make this call is:

```
putname((char *) 0);
```

In this case, the constant zero has been typecast to a character pointer that is the true type of the parameter. This code works properly regardless of the memory model that is used. This kind of error is also fairly common when a program that had been developed in the small model is changed to the large model.

Performance

The performance of UNIX as a whole on the 80286 is reasonable. An IBM PC/AT running System V will support two or three users fairly well. But even an 80286 system with plenty of memory and disk space would be hard pressed to support more than five users.

As was discussed earlier, small-model processes don't need to modify the segment registers, and this contributes to pretty efficient code. Most of the processes running in an 80286 UNIX system will be small-model. This contributes to the good overall performance of the system in general.

Large-model processes, on the other hand, load segment registers quite often; either implicitly by using long, intersegment call instructions, or explicitly by loading the DS or ES registers. This has an impact beyond the simple addition of some extra instructions to the program.

This paper noted earlier that UNIX works best on the 80286 in protected mode. Whenever a segment load occurs in protected mode, however, the 80286 has a lot more work to do than it did in real mode. For each segment register, the 80286 keeps a copy of the current segment's descriptor. Whenever a segment register is loaded, the 80286 fetches the new segment's descriptor into this cache. In the process of doing this it verifies that the segment does exist and that the process is permitted access to it.

Once this work is done, subsequent memory references are just as fast as those of a small-model process. It's only during segment register loads that being in protected mode has a large impact. The following shows the two most common instructions that perform segment loads and the number of clock cycles they require in real and protected mode:

	Real	Protected
Intersegment call	13	26
Move register to ES or DS	2	17

The net effect of this is that the performance difference between small- and large-model programs is much more profound in protected mode than in real mode. This is because most of the additional instructions that the C compiler generates for the large model involve segment register loads.

In general, a small-model program slows down by around 20 to 50 percent when compiled for the large model and executed on a protected mode UNIX system. The exact amount depends on several factors. References to local variables are fast because the stack segment register never has to be reloaded (because there is only one stack segment). References to global data, however, always involve a segment register load, because any given data can be in one of several segments. The relative frequency of these two kinds of references determines to a large extent the performance degradation of the large model.

The following table shows an example of this effect using the standard UNIX od (octal dump) command. This command is a small-model program used to print the contents of a file in octal or hex format. The table compares the program size (code and data) and execution time (in seconds) for od and a copy of od that was compiled using the large model. The execution times were measured on an 80286 system running UNIX System V, release 2. Each version of od was given a large (250K) input file and the execution time was measured using the UNIX time command.

	Program Size	Execution Time
Small model od	14130	50.8
Large model od	17028	68.6

In going from the small-model to the large-model version, program size increased by 20 percent and execution time increased by 35 percent. Execution time was affected more than program size because, as noted earlier, the instructions that get added for large model tend to involve segment register loads and are especially slow in protected mode.

Summary

This paper looked at many reasons why the 80286 is not a good processor for UNIX. In spite of all that, it's important to remember two things. First, UNIX does work on the 80286. System V release 2 and XENIX are two versions of UNIX currently available for the 80286. Both are supported products running on the IBM PC/AT. Second, the 80286 provides memory management features such as protection that at least make it a safe and reliable processor for UNIX. Unlike the older 8088 and 8086 processors, the 80286 can safely support a multiuser UNIX system.

Given these two points, it's reasonable for owners of PC/ATs or other 80286 machines to consider UNIX as an alternative to MS-DOS. UNIX has several advantages over MS-DOS that may make it attractive in certain circumstances. The biggest advantage is the ability to support multiple users on a single 80286 system. This may make it easier to justify the cost of a system.

And while the 80286 isn't ideal for C and UNIX, it isn't an inherently bad processor. It would certainly be possible to design a language and operating system that would work quite well within the architecture of the 80286. Such a language would be able to make assumptions about whether variables are in the same segment. This could be done by having the programmer explicitly group data items into "modules." All variables that are in the same module would be forced to be in the same segment. Unlike C, the compiler for this language would then have some information about the placement of variables in segments and would be able to eliminate redundant segment register loads. This hypothetical language wouldn't have the concept of memory models. The assembly code it generates would look like it was for the large model but without the redundant segment register loads.

An operating system designed for the 80286 would have memory allocation primitives more tailored for segment-based operations. Because it would be based on the language just described, it would only support one kind of process. In any case, a language and operating system designed for the 80286 would not end up looking much like UNIX. It would sacrifice portability for efficiency.

In summary, UNIX can and has been implemented on the 80286, and in many cases it's an attractive alternative to MS-DOS. But there are several processors on the market that provide a much better foundation for UNIX. The Motorola 68010 and 68020, the National Semiconductor 32032, and the new Intel 80386 are all better hosts for UNIX.

The Future

Intel's latest entry in the microprocessor market is the 80386, its successor to the 80286. The 80386 is largely compatible with the 8086 and 80286, but eliminates most of the problems you've seen with the segmentation of the 80286. As with the 80286, pointers on the 80386 consist of a selector and an offset. On the 80286, the selector and offset portions are each 16 bits. Selectors on the 80386 are still 16 bits, but offsets have been expanded to 32 bits. This means that the maximum size of a segment is 4 gigabytes on the 80386.

On the 80286, segments are indivisible units of memory. To access any part of a segment, the whole segment must be in physical memory. This would not be practical on the 80386, because segments can be so large. To solve this problem, the 80386 supports paging within segments. This means that you don't have to treat a segment as one large chunk of memory. Individual pages (each page is 4K in size) can be moved in and out of memory and those that are in memory can be accessed normally. If a program references part of a segment that isn't in memory, the 80386 notifies the kernel. The kernel can then make room for the page, load it, and resume execution of the program.

These two features (larger segments and paging) can be used quite effectively by UNIX. Consider how a small-model process would look on the 80386. It would have a large, 32 bit address space. Paging could be used to allow dynamic data and stack growth. In fact, a small-model process on the 80386 satisfies all the basic requirements of a UNIX process discussed earlier.

The problem on the 80286 was that no one memory model would work well for all situations. On the 80386, a small-model process will be fine for all but the most bizarre cases. The 80386 is a good processor for UNIX, not because of its segmented architecture, but rather because it finally provides segments large enough that one memory model can be used by all programs. In David Robboy's paper, you'll see how UNIX was ported to the 80386. By effectively ignoring segmentation, virtually all of the problems with it on the 80286 were avoided.

KEYWORDS

▶ Address translation

▶ Context switching

▶ Descriptors

▶ Memory management

▶ Paging

▶ Processes

▶ Protection

▶ Regions

▶ Segmentation

Paper Synopsis: The 80386, with its 32 bit addressing and paged architecture, is well-adapted to the UNIX operating system. This paper introduces the 80386 processor architecture and describes how the UNIX kernel was adapted to this processor. Because the SVR3 UNIX kernel implementation was influenced by the WE 32100 processor, it had performance problems when ported to the 80386, and solutions to these problems are described. The paper discusses how 16 bit applications can run on a virtual machine monitor as UNIX processes.

David Robboy earned a bachelor's degree in mathematics from Reed College. He has worked as a jazz musician and carpenter, and he is currently a project manager of UNIX development at Intel Corp. in Hillsboro, Oregon. He was part of the team that ported UNIX SVR3 to 80386 systems.

## 12

A UNIX Port to the 80386

David Robboy

T he most interesting and demanding problem in porting the UNIX kernel to a new processor is to adapt the kernel and the processor to each other's model of memory management. To adapt the processor to a UNIX implementation means deciding which features of the processor to use and how to use them together in order to achieve an easy port, keep it maintainable, and have good system performance. A team of engineers at Intel Corp., including myself, ported the UNIX System V release 3 kernel to the Intel 80386 microprocessor in early 1986, and this paper discusses some of the problems we faced and how we dealt with them.

The Intel 80386 (386 for short) is a 32 bit microprocessor with an on-chip memory management unit, including support for demand-paged virtual memory. The 386 can directly execute binaries from the 16 bit members of the Intel 86 family of processors, the 8088, 8086, and 80286. The 386 can do this by running a standard 16 bit operating system, but the more interesting case is that it can run 16 bit applications under a multiuser, 32 bit UNIX system.

First, this paper explores some of the basic features of the 80386 architecture as it pertains to memory management, protection, and task switching. Next, it looks at what the UNIX system expects and requires from a processor architecture. Along the way, some examples show how the 80386 architecture can be adapted to serve this purpose. Because the 80386 is both versatile and well-adapted to the UNIX architecture, it did not take many changes to the kernel to get it running on this processor. However, once it was running, we found that the design of UNIX System V release

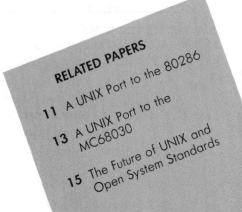

401

3 was not well-suited to the relatively large page size of the 80386, and some optimizations were called for in order to exploit the advantages of the processor. Finally, the paper describes how it is possible to run 8086 personal computer applications as processes under the UNIX system on the 80386.

Intel 80386 Processor Architecture

What follows is not a complete discussion of the 386 architecture, but it will cover the concepts you need to learn about the memory management, protection, and UNIX context switching. The important parts of the processor architecture for this paper are concerned with paging and segmentation. It avoids, as much as possible, discussing the instruction set, the register set, and features such as the instruction prefetch queue and page translation cache, which mostly affect overall chip performance.

The 386 supports both paging and segmentation. This may seem terribly complex, but the best way to understand it is not to think of segmentation and paging at the same time. They occupy separate universes, and each one is easier to understand in isolation from the other. This section takes a quick overall look at address translation on the 386 in general, and then a more detailed look at paging and segmentation separately. After that, it looks still more deeply into memory protection.

Overview of Address Translation

Figure 12–1 shows how segmentation and paging work together. A *virtual address* is an address as seen by executing code. It consists of a *selector*, which defines a segment, and an *offset* into the segment. The segmentation logic converts this 48 bit virtual address into a *linear address*, which is a 32 bit address in a flat address space. Then the paging logic maps the linear address to a *physical address*, which is the address seen by the hardware bus. The paging logic can be turned off, in which case the linear address is the physical address.

To summarize this, segmentation works on top of paging. That is, first the segmentation logic maps an address, and then the paging logic takes the result of that mapping and maps it to the physical address.

It may seem that the double mapping of segmentation and paging would be time-consuming, but the 386 typically does the entire computation of virtual to linear to physical address in 1.5 clock cycles, including all the protection checks. Furthermore, since the memory management

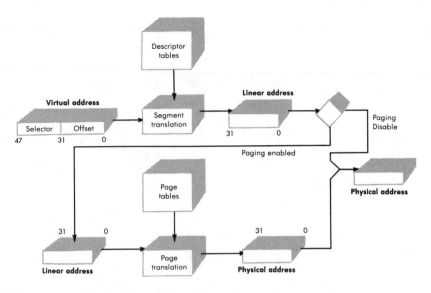

Figure 12-1   Address Translation Overview

unit is integrated into the 386 chip, the 386 is usually able to pipeline instructions and do the address translation in parallel with other activities.

Paging

A page is the basic unit of memory allocation, and occupies 4K bytes of memory. As the terms are usually used, a "page" is a logical page referred to by a linear address; and the paging logic maps each page to a "page frame," which is a physical page of memory.

Figure 12-2 shows how the pages are mapped by means of a two-level mapping involving "page tables" and "page directories." Each page directory entry contains the address of a page table, and each page table entry contains the address of a page. The linear address itself has three fields, giving the offset into the page directory, the offset into the page table to which the directory entry points, and the offset into the page to which the table entry points.

A page table occupies 1 page (4K bytes) and contains 1024 entries, each containing the address of a page frame. Thus each page table covers 4 megabytes of linear memory. A page directory also occupies 1 page and has 1024 entries, each representing a page table, so a page directory covers 4 gigabytes of linear memory, or the entire linear memory space. A CPU register called *Page Directory Base Register (PDBR)* points to the currently active page directory, which defines the current mapping of memory.

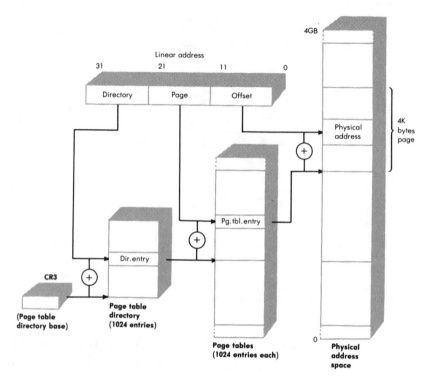

Figure 12–2   Linear to Physical Address Translation

An Example of How Paging Is Used

As an example, here is how the UNIX system organizes linear memory. The kernel associates each user process with a page directory, so that each process, while it is running, has access to the entire linear memory space, as shown in Figure 12–3. The kernel itself resides at the high end of linear memory. Each page directory has entries pointing to the kernel's page tables, so all processes share the page tables for the kernel, and the kernel occupies identical linear memory for each process. One of the things that happens during a context switch is that the PDBR register is changed to point to a new page directory, which remaps memory for the incoming process.

Each page of code or data, at the time it is being used by an instruction, must be mapped to a page frame. When the page is not being used, it can happen that it is stored on an auxiliary device *(paged out)* and not mapped to a page frame, in which case the page is said to be *not present*. When a process tries to access a page that is not present, the hardware generates a fault and the operating system can respond by getting the required page and restarting the instruction. Figure 12–4 shows what a page table entry

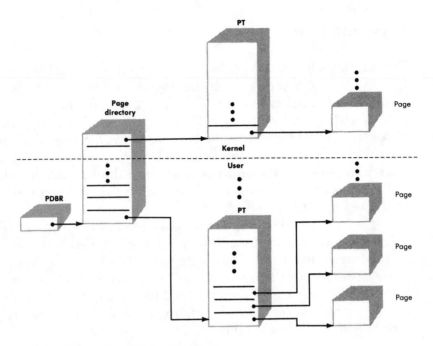

Figure 12–3   Example of Page Table Usage

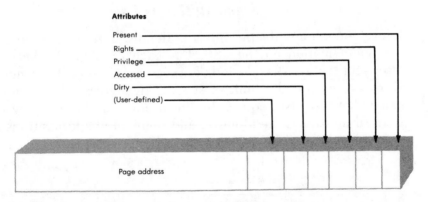

Figure 12–4   Principal Page Table Entry Fields

looks like. The *present* bit tells the hardware whether the page is present
in memory. The rights field controls read, write, and execute access; the
accessed and *dirty* bits help the operating system to implement its virtual
memory algorithms; the privilege field controls who can access the page.
The privilege field is actually a bit whose two values can be thought of as
user and *supervisor*. Later, the paper shows how these privilege levels are
established, but the point of interest here is that the kernel can protect
its code and data from user access on a page-by-page basis.

Segmentation

Considering segmentation, the 386 architecture looks like the 286 except that the size of a segment can be anywhere from 1 byte to 4 gigabytes rather than being limited to 64K bytes. A virtual address on the 386 consists of a 16 bit *selector* and a 32 bit *offset*. The selector is stored in one of several special registers called *segment registers*, and the 386 hardware uses this value to locate the *base address* of a segment; that is, where it starts. The offset is the address relative to the base of the segment. The 386 maps a virtual address to a linear address by adding the base address of the segment to the offset.

The way the 386 finds the base address of a segment is to use the selector as an index into a *descriptor table*. A *descriptor* is a hardware-defined structure that defines a segment; it contains the base address and other attributes of the segment. So the selector identifies the descriptor, which tells where the segment is, and the offset gives the address relative to the segment's base address. Figure 12–5 illustrates the mapping from virtual address to linear address.

An Example of How Segmentation Is Used

Before you get any deeper into the details, here is how the UNIX kernel uses segmentation on the 386. For each process, the kernel sets up a descriptor table with code and data segments, but each segment has a base address of zero and a limit of several gigabytes. A base address of zero means that the offset equals the linear address, the mapping from virtual to linear address is the identity, and segmented address translation effec-

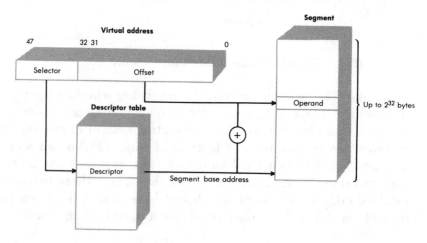

Figure 12–5 Logical Address Translation

tively disappears. You get a 32 bit flat address space, where every address is completely defined by its offset.

However, the UNIX system does make use of other segmentation-based features. For example, segmentation is used for protection and the operations of context switching and kernel entry. Also, the 386 is capable of running 16 bit applications, which are segmented. Therefore, you need to learn some more details. This paper does not attempt a complete and general description of the 386 architecture, but it will discuss how it is used in UNIX implementations. Even so, if it gets too tedious, skip ahead to the section that deals with the 386 processor architecture and refer back here when it becomes necessary.

Protection

The term *protection* has many different uses and meanings. This paper discusses protecting the operating system and applications programs against the effects of programming errors or intentional corruption by users. For example:

- The kernel's code and data are protected against modification by user code, which would likely result in the system crashing. A programming error can cause unpredictable and erratic behavior in the offending program, but it should not be capable of bringing down the whole system.
- The kernel's data is protected against reading by users, and its code against execution by users, for security reasons.
- The kernel operates at a higher privilege level to which users do not have access. This keeps system facilities such as I/O devices, interrupts, and memory under the control of the kernel, which can allocate them to users in an orderly and equitable manner.
- Users have no access at all to each other's memory space, so that no programming error by one user can affect the program of another.

The fundamental purpose of segmentation is for the protection of the kernel from users, and protection of users from each other. A segment is defined by a descriptor, which is a hardware-defined structure. There are several different kinds of descriptors, but for this discussion the important fields of a descriptor are:

- base

- limit

- type

- descriptor privilege level (DPL)

You have already been introduced to the base and limit fields. The type field tells the type of a segment and its access attributes (read only, writable, executable, and so on). The DPL field defines the privilege level of the segment. The 386 supports four privilege levels, of which the UNIX kernel and processes use two. The kernel runs at level zero, which is the most privileged, and user code runs at level three, which is the least privileged. Level zero gives the kernel several special privileges:

- ability to execute privileged instructions that control the hardware, such as modifying registers that point to the descriptor tables

- access to all segments, regardless of privilege level

- access to both user pages and supervisor pages

To review this a little more concretely, think of kernel code and user code running with different values in the code segment (CS) register. These two selectors refer to two different descriptors, which both describe the same extent of memory (base = zero, limit = big value).[1] So the kernel code segment and the user code segment are the same segment in the sense that a given object has the same offset in both segments. However, these two segments have separate identities because they have different protection attributes. User code cannot get access to segments at a more privileged level, including code segments; that is to say, a user cannot execute kernel code except under specially controlled conditions, by making a system call. The kernel's code segment is what gives it the attributes normally associated with a supervisor, including access to supervisor pages. Notice that segmentation ties in to paging in one respect: the code segment privilege level is tied to the user/supervisor bit in the page table entry, so they are not quite orthogonal.

Descriptor Tables and Other Friends

The 386 has two kinds of descriptor tables, known as a *global descriptor table (GDT)* and a *local descriptor table (LDT)*. In UNIX memory management there is a single, global GDT; there is one LDT per process. The

---

[1]Actually, the kernel code segment is a superset of the user code segment. The kernel is located in high memory, and the user code segment has a segment limit below the kernel's code.

GDT contains descriptors for the kernel's code, data, and stack segments and also for several special objects including LDTs, since an LDT itself is a segment of a special kind. Each LDT contains descriptors for the user's segments.

The 386 features a variety of special kinds of segments and descriptors that this paper lacks room to describe fully, but a few are important to a discussion of UNIX implementations on this processor.

A *call gate* is a special kind of descriptor that permits calls to code at a higher privilege level, and it is the mechanism for making system calls. A call gate, instead of containing the base and limit of a segment, contains the selector and offset of the destination of an intersegment call (also known as a *far call*). Ordinarily, if a user attempted to make a far call to a code segment at a more privileged level, it would cause a protection trap. However, a user can make a far call to a call gate, and it will transfer control to destination specified in the call gate, which is under the control of the kernel. The LDT of each UNIX process contains a call gate for making system calls. A UNIX process on the 386 ordinarily would not make far calls, because all its code is in one segment. A special library function written in assembly language makes the call to a predefined call gate in the LDT, and the kernel initializes this gate with the correct destination address for making system calls.

A *task state segment (TSS)* is a special kind of segment used for context switching. A *process* is a single thread of execution in UNIX terminology; the architects of the 386 call this a *task*, which is the same thing. You should distinguish between a *context switch*, which is how UNIX processes are switched, and a *task switch*, which is a 386 hardware operation. A TSS is a structure containing the contents of all the CPU registers, which collectively define the state of a process. A CPU register called the task register contains the selector of the TSS of the currently active task (that is, a selector into the GDT, which must contain a descriptor for the TSS).

When the operating system wants to do a task switch, it executes an intersegment jump to the TSS of the new task. The 386 recognizes that the destination of the jump is a TSS rather than a code segment, and accordingly it executes a task switch rather than an ordinary jump. A task switch saves all the registers in the current TSS (identified by the task register), restores all the registers from the new TSS (the destination of the jump), and reloads the task register with the selector of the new TSS so it can be restored later. Among the registers restored are CS and EIP (*extended instruction pointer*), which cause execution to resume at the address stored in the TSS; PDBR, which points to the page directory and hence maps paged memory for the process; and LDTR, which points to the LDT for the process and defines the segmentation mapping.

Another structure, the *interrupt descriptor table (IDT)* is what you would intuitively expect: a vector of descriptors that control the destinations of interrupts. A register called IDTR tells the CPU where in memory the IDT is. The entries in the IDT are *interrupt gates,* which are very similar to call gates.

If all of this sounds complex, it can be ignored except when you are actually dealing with the issues of protection, kernel entry, and context switching. The kernel initializes most of these structures and registers when it boots; then the kernel does no more with them. All of this machinery is invisible to application programs, and most of the kernel is not concerned with it either.

Example of How the UNIX Kernel Uses Paging and Segmentation for Protection

To review some of these concepts, here is a continuation of the example of UNIX paging and segmentation. You have seen that UNIX memory management uses a page directory per process in order to map each process into the entire four gigabyte memory space, and that it superimposes kernel and user segments. Here is how the kernel protects itself from users, and users from themselves and each other. Users are protected from each other because they operate in different memory maps, so they have no access to each other's memory space. The kernel uses the paging mechanism to protect its own code and data: these pages are accessible by the supervisor only. They are also doubly protected by segmentation, since the user's segment limits are below the start of kernel code and data. Segmentation does not protect a user program against accidentally writing on its own code, because the data segment covers both data and code, but the code is protected by paging because text pages are read-only.

A side effect of this use of segmentation is that a process can read code into its own data space and then execute it. That is, the process reads the code into its data segment and then executes it at the same offset in its code segment, because the two segments are superimposed.

UNIX Implementation and Processor Architecture

AT&T implemented UNIX System V release 3 on the WE 32100 Microprocessor. System V release 3 (SVR3) in this paper denotes the AT&T release on the AT&T processor. Engineers at Intel ported this release of the UNIX kernel to the 386 processor in early 1986. System V.3/386 denotes the 386 port of this release. SVR3 has several new features, including STREAMS, remote file sharing, a file system switch, and shared libraries. These are portable features; porting them to the 386 consisted mainly of recompiling the code, and this paper does not describe such features. SVR3 was the first UNIX release from AT&T to support paged virtual memory, which gives rise to the topics covered in this paper. This section is a very brief summary of some aspects of the SVR3 kernel; it does not come anywhere near being a general explanation of how the kernel works.

To get an idea of the parts of the kernel involved in this paper and how they fit into the whole kernel, imagine that you could list all the C language functions in the UNIX kernel, in descending order of abstraction. At the least machine-dependent level are functions to do things like networking, file system I/O, system call handling, interprocess communication, and the like. Getting less abstract but still very machine-independent are functions to do things like schedule processes and create regions of memory. These two categories constitute the great bulk of the kernel source code. Getting down to a more concrete level, there are functions for which you would have to be on the lookout for machine dependencies, such as loading programs, handling signals, and the algorithms for demand-paging. At a still more concrete level are the functions that are definitely machine-dependent and that are the meat of this paper: mapping memory, managing pages of memory, and context switching.

At a still lower and more concrete level, a small amount of the kernel code was highly machine dependent but not very interesting, such as the code to program the timer and interrupt controller, to program drive devices in general, to catch hardware interrupts, and to translate the interrupts into error conditions.

In terms of memory management, the kernel represents a process as a set of *regions*, which are contiguous extents of linear memory. Typically there are three regions per process: text, data, and stack. A process may have additional regions, namely, shared data and shared libraries. The motivation for the concept of regions was to create general mechanisms for the operations of allocating, freeing, expanding, shrinking, sharing, and duplicating pieces of memory. The kernel maintains regions globally rather than on a per-process basis, which permits it to share regions between processes. Sharable regions are text (in case two processes are running the same program), shared libraries, and shared data (a mechanism for processes to share memory).

The kernel maintains each region internally as a list of page tables, so the granularity of a region is the extent covered by a page table (four megabytes on the 386). When processes share a region, they also share the page tables for that region. This does not mean the entire extent covered by the page table is allocated to the region. Some of the page table entries may represent nonexistent pages, and the region can expand dynamically in the cases of data and the stack. The stack can expand a page at a time as needed when data gets pushed on it. The data region can expand when the process executes the sbrk system call to allocate memory.

In this case the kernel increases the size of the region to indicate which pages may legitimately be used, and then when the process touches a page it generates a page fault and the kernel allocates a page frame.

To make this a little more concrete look at some of the data structures involved in managing regions. The kernel keeps data for each region in a structure called a *region* (see Figure 12–6). The region structures reside in a table called the region table, which is global in the sense that it contains the region structures for all regions associated with all processes. Each region structure contains a field called r_list, which is a pointer to an rlist, an array of pointers to page tables. The rlist defines the contents of the region. To clarify this a little, an rlist is an array of pointers, while the name r_list is a C language variable.

On a per-process basis, the data structure that binds a region to the process is called a *pregion*, as shown in Figure 12–7. For each process, data about that process is contained in a proc structure, stored in the proc table. A field of the proc structure is p_region, which is a pointer to a list of pregions; one for each region attached to the process. Among the data in the pregion structure is a pointer to the corresponding region structure in the region table.

When a process creates a new process ("forks," in UNIX terminology), typically the parent and the child processes share the text region, so they also share the page tables for text. They do not share the data and stack

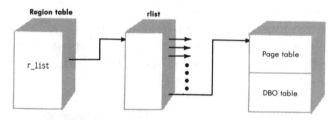

Figure 12–6   Region Table and R_list

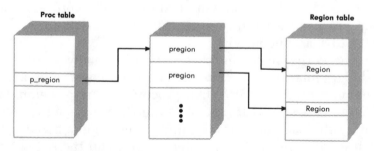

Figure 12–7   The P_Region Structure

regions, so these page tables are duplicated for the child. However, the pages of data themselves are not duplicated until one process or the other modifies some data in the page; then the page containing the data is duplicated. The status of these pages is said to be *copy-on-write*, and the kernel uses the "rights" bit of the page table entry to make the page nonwritable, so the 386 will generate a page fault the first time a process tries to modify the page.

Parallel to each page table, the kernel maintains an array of structures called *disk block descriptors (DBDs)*, each of which contains the device number and disk block address of a page when it is not present. Since there is a DBD for each page table entry, the array of DBDs associated with each page table is the same size as the page table itself; on the 386 that is one page. By convention, this page-sized array is called a DBD, though it would be more proper to call it a "DBD-list." Each DBD element contains the disk address of the page plus other information about the state of the page that will not fit in the page table entry. For example, there are several possible reasons for a page to be not present: it can be paged out to the swap device; it can be text that has not yet been loaded from the program file; it can be logically allocated, uninitialized data that has not yet been touched; or the stack can expand to a page that has not yet been allocated.

The pages of memory in active use are called the *working set;* other pages are paged out until needed. In order to maintain a supply of available page frames, the kernel runs a process in the background to monitor which pages have been recently accessed. This process is called vhand, so named because it circulates among the pages like the hand of a clock. When vhand finds a page that was not recently used, it makes the page frame available, paging out the contents of the page if necessary. For each active page, the kernel keeps a record of whether it was recently accessed and, for efficiency, whether it was modified since it was last paged out. The 386 hardware supports this recordkeeping, in the form of "accessed" and "dirty" bits in the page table entries.

The kernel keeps a working set of active pages in memory for each process, and it also monitors which processes are active. A process may be idle while waiting for a system resource such as I/O or waiting for another process to do something. In this case, the kernel may *swap out* the entire process, which is to say it pages out all its pages. When this happens, the process is flagged as being swapped out, and the scheduler passes over it until it becomes runable.

This section has briefly discussed a few concepts about the kernel that are necessary for an understanding of the port to the 386. The next section will discuss some design decisions we made in doing the port.

UNIX Ports to the 80386: Design Decisions

Beyond rewriting the lowest-level, machine-dependent code, porting the UNIX kernel to the 386 did not require extensive changes. The low-level code involved fundamentally uninteresting things like initializing the processor, the interrupt controller, and other devices; handling hardware interrupts; setting up structures such as descriptor tables; and driving devices such as the disk and console. Low-level coding also involved substituting the 386 hardware dependent definitions of structures such as page table entries and TSSs, and then making adjustments in all the places where the code depended on these definitions. Beyond that, the "interesting" modifications required to get a UNIX implementation running on the 386 boil down conceptually to two changes in actual algorithms, plus some optimizations.

At this point it is worthwhile to look at how the concept of regions maps onto the 386 architecture. Figure 12–8 shows the layout of a process in linear memory and the page tables involved. A page directory defines the memory map for the process and has an entry pointing to a page table for each region, plus one for the kernel. A typical region, being under

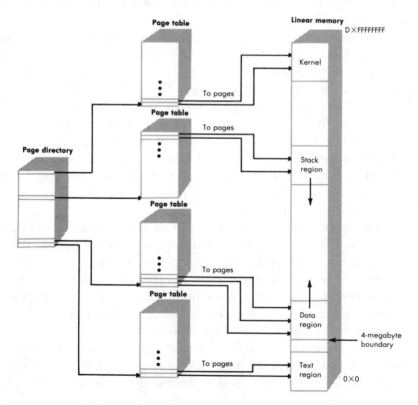

Figure 12–8   Page Tables and Regions

four megabytes, needs only one page table. The text region is in low memory, and the data region is nearby. Each of these regions is aligned at a four-megabyte boundary, so as to use pages at the beginning of a page table. The data region, growing dynamically, can use additional page tables if necessary. The stack is at a high address so that it can grow toward the data across a wide expanse of linear memory, and starts just below a four-megabyte boundary, so that as it grows downward additional pages can be allocated in the same page table.

Growing a Region

The most significant modification was due to the fact that on the 386, the stack grows downward. That is, the push instruction causes the stack pointer to be decremented, while on the WE 32100 it is incremented. Two kinds of regions can expand—stack and data—so on the 386 the function to expand a region has to allow for expansion in either direction to handle these two cases. Also, the function to create a region must make a special case of the stack, and allocate pages at the top end of the extent covered by a page table, so that the stack can expand downward into pages covered by the same page table.

It only took one short paragraph to describe this modification, but the reason it's considered significant is that it involved algorithmic changes in some of the region-handling functions. Most of the other modifications involved more superficial changes in the coding.

Context Switching

The WE 32100 processor has a structure called a *PCB* for context switching, analogous to the TSS on the 386. The SVR3 code uses the PCB, and as a result this code was portable to the 386 with minor changes beyond substituting a TSS for the PCB. However, these "minor" changes are subtle and require considerable explanation. The 32100 processor has an instruction to save the context of the current process in its PCB without switching tasks. Also, just as on the 386, a task switch is accomplished on the 32100 by jumping to a new PCB, but the 32100 has the option of saving the current context or not when switching to a new context. The following pseudocode shows how the AT&T code handles task switching when the kernel gets down to actually doing the hardware task switch:

```
Save the context of current process in its PCB
Still running in the current context:
    Decide what process to run next
```

> Set flag to switch tasks without saving context
> Jump to PCB of new process

Here is what this accomplishes. When the kernel is ready to run its scheduler and decide what process to run, it saves the context of the current process. The kernel then continues in the same context to decide what process to run and switches to it. The jump to the new PCB does the actual task switch.

Here is how to accomplish the same thing on the 386:

> Find what process to run next
> If new process is different from current one:
>   Fix up a GDT descriptor to point to new TSS
>   Jump to TSS of new process, using that selector
>   Reload task register with old TSS selector

The slight complication here has to do with the fact that the TSS is a segment. At any given time, the TSS of the current process is mapped to a fixed location in linear memory, represented by a static C language structure. As a segment, the TSS is mapped by a fixed selector, via a descriptor in the GDT. The TSSs of other processes also exist somewhere in the kernel's memory space, but they are not distinct segments. In order to execute a far jump to a new TSS, the kernel must fix up a descriptor to map that TSS into a segment. During the task switch, the old context is saved in the TSS whose selector is in the task register, so the GDT must contain descriptors for both the old TSS and the new one. After the task switch, the kernel fixes up the task register in order to set up the hardware to save the context in the correct place on the next task switch.

To give an idea of how big a job it was to port the kernel to the 386, it took three people about three months to get the kernel and a few key utilities to a reasonably stable state. The changes outlined in this section and the associated side effects and debugging took about two staff months. The other seven or so staff months were spent on low-level, machine-dependent code: device drivers; the boot loader; and finding problems with the development tools, including the C compiler and a firmware debugger. The only utility program with significant machine dependencies is ps, which tells what processes are running and what files they were loaded from. This program is machine-dependent because it must read the process table in kernel data.

This discussion is as short as it is due to the versatility of the 386 and its suitability to the UNIX architecture. Our guiding philosophy was always to make the smallest possible changes to the code, for several reasons:

- to make it easier to track future UNIX releases
- to reduce the total effort and time for the job

- to avoid creating new bugs
- AT&T certification requires minimum changes to the source, within reason

The first of these was particularly important, because the UNIX system is definitely still evolving.

Optimizations and Other Topics

Memory Overhead

Once a kernel is running on a new processor, the next step is to optimize it to get it to run more efficiently on that processor architecture. On the 386 it was quickly apparent that this would involve reducing the kernel's overhead in memory per process. The reason for that is that each process in SVR3 has at least three regions: text, data, and stack. Each region is represented as a list of page tables and has at least one page table. Associated with each page table is a list of disk block descriptors. A page table and page directory on the 386 each occupy one full page, as does a DBD list. Each region also has an rlist structure, which occupies a page of its own. If you do the multiplication, you'll see that this already involves considerable per-process memory overhead.

Before you go on, some more information about the 386 architecture is necessary. To ensure high performance in page translation, the 386 has an on-chip cache for paging information, called a *translation lookaside buffer (TLB)*, which contains the mapping information for the 32 most recently used pages. The TLB does not contain page table entries; each TLB entry contains the information from a page directory and a page table necessary to map linear addresses to a page frame. Whenever an instruction touches a page that is not cached in the TLB, the processor has to go out and look at a page directory and a page table in memory. On the other hand, the TLB provides on-chip mapping for 128 kilobytes of memory, giving an expected hit rate of 98 to 99 percent.

A computer architect has trade-offs to consider when choosing a page size for a processor architecture. The bigger each page is, the more memory will be wasted, because each contiguous extent of memory (such as a UNIX region) will waste half a page on the average. On the other hand, the smaller each page is, the more pages there are to manage, and also the more page tables, because it takes more page table entries to manage more pages. The page table size also involves trade-offs, because a page table does not necessarily have to occupy a full page. If a page table were half the size of a page or a fourth the size, the software would have to allocate multiple page tables per page, which would complicate the job of managing page tables. On the other hand, in the case of the UNIX system, which creates many small regions, page table space is wasted, because only a few of the 1024 entries in most page tables are used.

If the page size or the page table size were smaller, then managing more pages and more page tables would involve software overhead to do tasks such as maintain and search lists. More important, it would involve additional hardware overhead because it reduces the hit rate of the TLB. Intuitively speaking, the more information there is per page, the more information there is in the TLB, which is a major rationale for a large page size. There are other considerations, such as the expected rate of page faults due to pages that are not present, which this paper cannot address.

To sum all of this up, the 386 has a good strategy for optimizing virtual memory performance, at the expense of memory. SVR3 was designed on a processor in which pages are cheap and page tables are cheaper, but when this design is moved intact to the 386, the expense in memory rises to a point where optimizations are necessary.

Optimizations

At the time this is written, some optimizations have been implemented and others are being discussed and considered. This section will necessarily be somewhat theoretical, if not vague, and it only gives the flavor of what kinds of optimizations are possible or desirable. There is a key point to be made here, and it is that programmers do not necessarily have to redesign the operating system in order to optimize it. We found that SVR3 was not optimally designed for a processor with a large page size, but that does not inevitably lead to the conclusion that the design of the operating system must be changed in order to port it. It may be possible to look more closely at the 386 itself, reinterpret its architecture, and adjust the UNIX implementation so it is a better fit.

Various optimizations are possible, such as swapping out page tables for a process when it is swapped out, swapping out other data structures, and allocating less than a whole page for some data structures such as the rlist. Most of these would require a lot of detailed explanation and are not architecturally interesting in themselves, because they involve changing the way some particular piece of data is stored. This discussion focuses on one optimization, which is to cut down the overhead of a page table and a DBD per region. To show how versatile the 386 is, three optimization strategies are outlined, none of which involve a major redesign of the region handling code. This will also give you some insight into ways of using the 386 architecture in general.

Collapse the Stack and Data into One Region

The stack and data regions have in common the properties of being private (nonshared) and expandable. It is convenient to keep them in separate regions because they each need room to grow, so it is natural to locate them far apart in linear memory, especially on a machine where both stack and data grow upward. However, it is possible to rearrange the layout of memory and keep both stack and data in one region, cutting the total number of regions by about a third—or more, in case of processes that are sharing text.

It is customary in Intel processors for the stack and data to grow toward each other across an expanse of memory. Using this arrangement, we could not save a page table unless the combined stack/data region was limited to four megabytes (the extent covered by a page table). This is an undesirable limit. However, the layout can be rearranged so the stack is below the data (see Figure 12–9). In this arrangement, the stack grows downward across a gigabyte or so toward the text, and the data grows upward across a gigabyte or so toward the kernel. The region itself grows

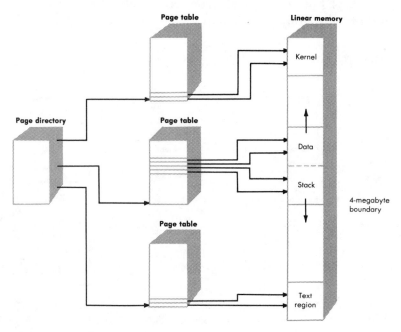

Figure 12–9   An Alternative Memory Layout

at both ends. If either the stack or data grows to be over two megabytes, it grows out of the extent covered by a single page table, in which case the kernel must allocate another page table for it.

Alias the Page Tables

Collapsing the stack and data into a single region is a way to get rid of a page table and a DBD, but there is a simpler, if less intuitive, way to do the same thing, and it does not require moving the stack and data around. Looking at Figure 12–8, one entry in the page directory points to a page table for the data region, of which processes typically use only a few entries near the low end of the page table. Another page directory entry points to a page table for the stack region, of which processes typically use only a few entries near the top end. Suppose both of these page directory entries pointed to the same physical page table, as shown in Figure 12–10. The physical page table would have two separate page directory references, or aliases, so it would serve for two separate regions. The data would still reside in low linear memory and the stack in high linear memory; nothing would have been moved around. The only complication would be that the kernel would have to do limit checking when regions grow and avoid contention for page table entries by allocating a new page table when necessary. For the typical process, which does not have multimegabyte regions, this would never happen.

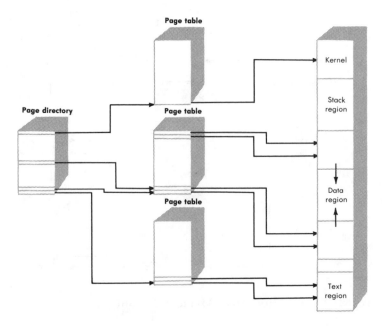

Figure 12–10   Aliasing a Page Table

What was just described is harder to understand than merging the stack and data into one region, but it is simpler because the UNIX region-handling code does not have to change at all, except for the limit checking. The stack and data are still separate regions, separated by a wide expanse of memory, but one physical page table has two incarnations as two logical page tables. If a page table is aliased, then a DBD can be aliased also, because there is a one-to-one mapping of page table entries to DBD entries. So two pages per process are saved in this way.

The next step to consider is triply aliasing a page table and including the text region, too. If you tried this, you would immediately run into contention, because text and data both occupy pages near the bottom end of the page table. However, it is a simple matter to change the linker defaults to align the data in the middle of a four-megabyte extent instead of at the beginning. Then the text could use entries near the start of the page table, the data in the middle, and the stack at the top end. This is illustrated in Figure 12–11. You still would have to do the same checking for contention between the expanding stack and expanding data, and allocate a new page table if necessary. This scheme would save two page tables and two DBDs per process, or about 16K.

The cost of this optimization is that the kernel has to do limit checks when regions grow.

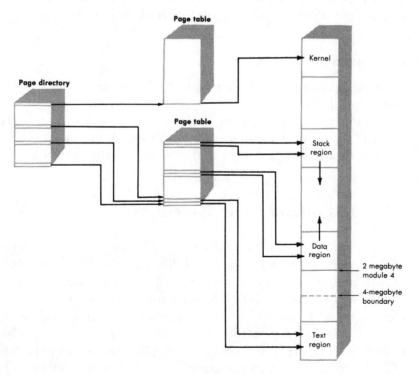

Figure 12–11   Triply Aliasing a Page Table

Multiplex the Page Tables

A typical process such as a system utility, compiler, or shell usually has relatively small text, data, and stack regions; that is, they do not consume megabytes of memory. That means many regions use only a few entries of each page table. A simple, if not pretty, optimization is possible. The kernel can maintain the page table data for most regions in small data structures, and it can only copy the entries into the page tables when the relevant processes are active, which is to say on each context switch. This would optimize for small regions, assuming they are the usual case.

To keep such a scheme simple, you would want to distinguish between "small" and "large" regions, where a large region is larger than some fixed size. Large regions would have their own page tables, so you would not have to deal with allocating and copying variable amounts of data.

Multiplexing buys you approximately three page tables and three DBD's per process, less a small amount of data to store the entries you need. Since many processes are using the same page tables, they can also share a page directory, so you also save a page directory per process. The saving is approximately 7 pages per process, or 28K. This is a greater saving of memory than aliasing gives, but the cost is that data has to be copied on every context switch, and there is also some complexity involved in distinguishing between small and large regions and in allocating new page tables when a region grows enough to become large.

Conclusions

Three optimization strategies were outlined very briefly—just enough for you to get the idea of what the strategy is. Each of these strategies reduces the memory overhead per region without significantly modifying the design of the region handling code, and they show that the 386 is versatile enough to adapt to a design that was not ideally suited to its page size.

8086 and 80286 Code Execution

A paper on the 386 is not complete without mentioning virtual 8086 and 80286 code execution. This capability can occur in protected mode with paging enabled, so the operating system can maintain control of a multiuser system while running individual 16 bit processes as well as 32 bit ones. Clearly, most users will be interested in executing code from the 8086/88, and PC-DOS applications in particular. However, it is also instructive to look at protected mode 80286 execution, especially since the available PC-DOS monitors are proprietary to other vendors, and I don't have access to their inner workings.

In principle, it is possible to enhance the UNIX kernel with all the features necessary to emulate another operating system, but this would make the kernel large and unwieldy. It would also be severely limiting, because a single release of a single target operating system would be entombed in the kernel, and it would have to be maintained there. A more flexible solution is to create a *virtual machine monitor*, which is a program that runs as a UNIX application and emulates the target operating system. With the appropriate kernel hooks, one can potentially emulate several different operating systems with different monitors. The virtual machine monitor might be the actual target operating system, ported to run on top of the UNIX environment instead of on bare hardware, or it might be an emulator written from scratch.

The 386 has a bit in its flags register called the *VM86 flag*. When this flag is set, the processor is in "virtual 86 mode," which is a subset of full protected mode. In virtual 86 mode, the processor behaves very much like an 8086 (or an 80286 in real mode), but paging is still enabled. Whenever an interrupt occurs, the flags are changed so that the UNIX kernel runs in ordinary 32 bit protected mode. The kernel can handle the interrupt or pass control back to an interrupt handler in the monitor. Whenever the kernel returns from the interrupt, the flags are restored and the processor passes back into VM86 mode. It is important for paging to be enabled, because each virtual 86 process occupies the first megabyte of linear memory, so the processes must all be mapped to the same place.

Executing 80286 code in protected mode is a little different. The processor does not enter a special mode; the 80286 instructions are a subset of its instruction set. A bit in the descriptor of each code segment tells the processor whether to execute that code as 16 bit or 32 bit code. This implies that a UNIX process could contain both 16 bit and 32 bit code, in separate segments. For example, a virtual machine monitor can be compiled as ordinary 32 bit code, and it, running as a UNIX process, can allocate segments, load 16 bit code into them, and execute 80286 applications.

To get an idea of what kinds of kernel hooks are needed to support virtual 86 execution, consider the interfaces between an application and the UNIX kernel. They can be summarized in four categories:

- the executable file—the program loader has to be able to recognize the executable file, load parts of it into memory, initialize hardware registers, and begin execution at the correct location.
- system calls—when the program makes system calls for operating system facilities, the operating system has to interpret the arguments, perform the service, and return control to the program.
- error conditions—when a program generates a hardware fault due to a programming error or a page fault, the kernel must handle it

in the appropriate way and either terminate the program or return control to it.

- signals—the kernel must be able to send the process a signal, which is to say, a simulated asynchronous interrupt. This can involve tricky manipulations of the stack in order to simulate an interrupt, because a stack for 16 bit code looks different from a stack for 32 bit code.

When a user executes a program, the kernel must have hooks to recognize what type of executable file is being invoked. With 16 bit programs, the kernel does not have to understand the inner structure of the program file, because the virtual machine monitor can actually load the file, but the kernel must be smart enough to invoke the monitor. In case the monitor itself runs in virtual 86 mode, the kernel must be able to load the monitor unless it is always resident. Once the monitor is running and reading the program file, another kernel hook is needed in order to allocate 16 bit segments for the program to run in.

An application program makes system calls by means of either an interrupt or a call gate; in either case, the interrupt or gate is a specifically predefined one. The UNIX kernel needs the appropriate gate in its interrupt descriptor table or its global descriptor table to catch these system calls and feed them back to the monitor. The monitor will handle the system calls, and in the process it may make UNIX system calls.

A *fault* is a software-generated interrupt. Programs can generate faults in several ways; for example, they can divide by zero, or in protected mode they can violate the limits of a segment. A fault always transfers control to the UNIX kernel via the IDT, in order to preserve system security. However, a virtual machine monitor may simulate the interrupt vector of an 8086 in its own memory space, and it may have system call interfaces for allowing the application to determine how to handle interrupts.

In certain cases, an application program can respond to external interrupts; for example, pressing CTRL-C will interrupt the program and abort its execution. Application programs can also have functions to handle interrupts themselves. The UNIX kernel does not let an interrupt pass directly to the application; the kernel itself catches the interrupt and simulates its effects with software by sending the process a signal, but this is more or less equivalent to the process getting the actual interrupt. The main differences are that the process may not get interrupted immediately (especially if some other process is running at the time), and that the signal handler returns with an ordinary return instruction instead of an interrupt return. This discussion skips the gory details, but the point is that the kernel must cooperate with the monitor to simulate interrupts properly, and the kernel must maintain the stack consistently for all cases, whether it is sending a signal to a 16 bit application or a 32 bit application, or in case a hardware interrupt comes in while one or the other type of code is running, while an interrupt handler is running, and so on.

These examples, while brief and superficial, show how it is possible to execute 16 bit programs directly on the 386, and they also indicate what kinds of "hooks" are needed to support virtual machine monitors. At the time of this writing, two virtual machine monitor products are available for executing PC-DOS applications on System V/386.

KEYWORDS

▶ Caches

▶ Flat addressing

▶ Memory management

▶ Processes

▶ Translation tables

▶ Transparent segments

▶ Supervisor and user mode

Paper Synopsis: The MC68030 is another leading alternative for UNIX on microprocessors. This paper provides an introduction to its architecture and how UNIX can take advantage of it. It also discusses some closely related MC68030 support chips, including the 68881/82 hardware floating-point coprocessors.

Michael Cruess is a section leader at the Microprocessor Products Group of Motorola. He received his bachelor's degree from Rice University and his master's from the University of Texas. Although both of his degrees are in electrical engineering, his career has shifted to software over the last several years. He currently is involved with providing system software for the M68000 microprocessor family.

## 13

A UNIX Port to the MC68030

Michael Cruess

The Motorola MC68030 is the newest addition to the M68000 family of microprocessors. For many years, the M68000 family has been a popular choice for computers running UNIX. This paper talks about why the MC68030 is a good choice for a UNIX system. It also discusses some things that you should be aware of when using or porting UNIX on the MC68030.

In addition to the MC68030, the discussion includes some closely related integrated circuits. Hardware floating point is added to an MC68030 system by using either the MC68881 or MC68882 coprocessors. The UNIX kernel needs to take into account some characteristics of these circuits, so they are briefly covered. The predecessors of the MC68030 are the MC68020 microprocessor and the MC68851 memory management unit. Most of the material in this paper can be applied directly to them. Exceptions will be explicitly noted.

Since there are many releases of UNIX and many "UNIX-like" operating systems available, this paper does not attempt to describe one version specifically. If a comment applies to a version of UNIX that used demand-paged memory allocation (like UNIX System V release 3) instead of swapping (like release 2), then that fact will be mentioned.

The rest of this paper will outline the MC68030 hardware and how the hardware affects UNIX. Special attention will be paid to the memory management unit. Following that, the specific issues of exception handling and the UNIX "signal" mechanism will be discussed.

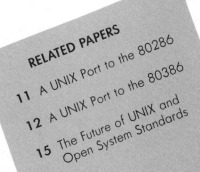

RELATED PAPERS

11 A UNIX Port to the 80286

12 A UNIX Port to the 80386

15 The Future of UNIX and Open System Standards

Hardware Architecture

The MC68030 is manufactured by Motorola, Inc. It is one of a series of processors that began with the MC68000. A block diagram of the MC68030 is shown in Figure 13–1. The *central processing unit (CPU)* executes instructions and controls the operation of the circuit. The CPU uses the *address translation cache (ATC)* to translate the logical addresses used by a program into the physical addresses used by memory. The memory used by the MC68030 can be slow compared with the speed of the CPU, so the MC68030 has an instruction cache and a data cache to help speed things up. These caches remember information that was read from memory (up to 256 bytes in each cache). If the CPU tries to use any of the remembered information again, the caches can provide it faster than the memory. Information can be accessed by the MC68030 from both caches and from the external memory simultaneously. The bus control unit controls the interface between the MC68030 and the outside world.

Basic CPU Structure

The MC68030, like its predecessors in the M68000 family, has a structure that is well-designed for implementing the UNIX operating system. It has features similar to the processors on which UNIX was originally designed and implemented. This section gives an overview of the MC68030 CPU architecture and its implications for UNIX.

Registers and Data Types

The programmer's model for the MC68030 is shown in Figure 13–2. There are eight 32 bit wide data registers (D0 to D7) for integer arithmetic and

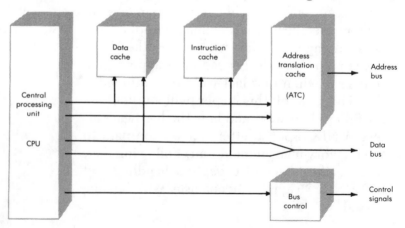

Figure 13–1   MC68030 Block Diagram

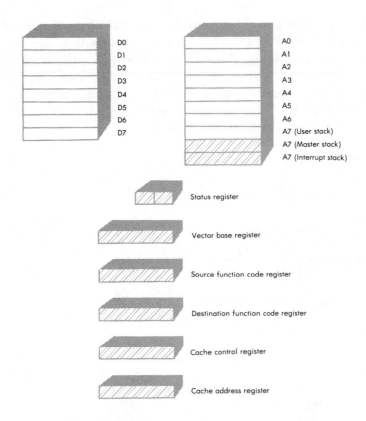

Shaded registers are only available in supervisor mode

Figure 13-2   MC68030 CPU Programmer's Model

logical operations. There are eight address registers (A0 to A7) available to a program at any one time. Register A7 serves as the hardware stack pointer. The stack pointer is used for things like saving the return address for a subroutine and for holding local variables in a C program. One of the three A7 registers is selected by the CPU hardware whenever a program uses register A7. The paper discusses later how and when these different stack pointers are used.

For the user of an MC68030 UNIX system, the most important thing to notice about the register set is that both the address and data registers are 32 bits wide. This allows pointers and integers to be the same size. Many existing C programs assume that integers and pointers can be assigned to each other without any special precautions. Most C compilers for the M68000 family use an integer size of 32 bits for this reason. There are some, however, that may use a 16 bit integer. If you are not sure about your system, compare the results of the C functions sizeof(int), sizeof(long), and sizeof(char*) on your compiler.

Your C compiler should hide most of the details of using the address and data registers, but there is a situation in which a programmer should be aware of them. Many C compilers place the return value of a function in register D0. Some compilers are smarter and place return values in D0 if they are integers and in A0 if they are addresses. If your compiler does this, then the following program may give trouble. The program consists of two files. The first one contains:

```
main()
{
        int *p;

        p = function();
        printf( "%d", p);
}
```

The second file contains:

```
extern  int two;

int *function()
{
        two = 2;
        return( &two);
}
```

This program is supposed to print the number 2. Notice that in the first file, function is declared (implicitly) to return a type of int. The compiler will generate code to look for the result of function in register D0. In the second file, function is declared to return a pointer to int. A compiler may generate code that places the return value into register A0. If this happens, the main routine will not use the correct return value. In this example it will cause the wrong value to be printed, but in real programs it may cause subtle bugs. Some C compilers will deliver function results in both D0I and A0 to avoid this problem at the expense of a small loss in performance. Careful programming, and using the UNIX utility lint, should uncover these mistakes before they cause major problems, no matter how your compiler returns values.

Another characteristic of the MC68030 that makes it good for UNIX is that the memory addressing is "flat." In other words, a pointer is a single quantity that can be manipulated with integer arithmetic instructions. As mentioned before, both the address and data registers are 32 bits wide. This is a good size for an address, because a 32 bit address can span 4 billion bytes. Four billion bytes is more than the number of bytes of disk storage on most UNIX systems today. Since programs in UNIX cannot be larger than the amount of disk available to hold them, a 32 bit address is more than adequate for UNIX. There is no need for different "models" with the C compiler. Some other processors have a segmented address in which the address is composed of two parts. This type of address is more difficult to deal with because regular integer arithmetic may not work with addresses.

The MC68030 directly supports all the data types needed by UNIX and C. In addition to the 32 bit integers and pointers, 16 bit and 8 bit integers are also available. Typically, MC68030 C compilers make the types int and long int 32 bits wide. The type short int will be 16 bits wide, and 8 bit wide integers can be obtained with the type char. Character strings are represented as strings of 8 bit integers. No character string instructions are provided, but character manipulations can be done by short loops that take advantage of the MC68030 caches. Using the string library routines from the C library on your machine should provide efficient code for string operations. Bits and bit fields are manipulated with special instructions. Single, double, and extended precision floating point is implemented by an MC68881 or MC68882 floating-point coprocessor attached to the MC68030.

MC68030 Processing Modes

M68000 family processors have two processing modes: user and supervisor. User mode allows a program to execute most instructions, but only allows access to areas of memory that belong to the program. Supervisor mode is the way that M68000 family processors keep the operating system safe from user programs. In supervisor mode, all of the resources of the MC68030 processor are available. The shaded registers of Figure 13–2 and the instructions that control memory management can only be accessed by the supervisor. These modes map directly onto the UNIX model of user mode and kernel mode.

Most of the time, a UNIX system should be executing a user process. When it is required, supervisor mode is entered in one of several ways. Software errors, such as attempting to divide by zero or trying to access protected memory, will cause the system to enter supervisor mode. Executing the trap instruction is an important way to enter supervisor mode because it is the way user processes make system calls to the UNIX kernel. Certain hardware conditions and interrupts from peripheral devices also cause a change to supervisor mode. On entry to supervisor mode, the MC68030 hardware places information on the supervisor stack about the event that caused the change to supervisor mode. One of the pieces of information is a number indicating why supervisor mode is being entered. Since the format of the information placed on the top of the stack is always the same, the UNIX kernel can use a common piece of code to set up an environment and jump to the appropriate C language handler routine.

The registers that are restricted to use in supervisor mode are used by the UNIX kernel to control critical functions of the MC68030. The cache control register and cache address register are used to turn the instruction and data caches on and off, and to empty them of old information. The source and destination function code registers are used by the moves instruction to move data between user and kernel memory spaces. The vector base register tells the CPU where to find the routines that are to be executed when supervisor mode is entered. Control for the processor interrupt level, instruction tracing function, and processor mode is provided by the status register. These registers are discussed later, when you need them.

Memory Management Unit Structure

The structure of the memory mapping and protection hardware on a computer has a great influence on many parts of the UNIX kernel. This is because the kernel has to know how to access the user process, how to protect certain areas of memory from being written to, how to share memory between processes, how to protect user processes from one another, and how to protect itself from user processes. For a given computer, the memory management hardware determines the best, or only, way to perform some of these functions. The MC68030 provides a *memory management unit (MMU)* integrated with the CPU. This MMU treats the addresses generated by programs running on the CPU as specifying a location in a logical (or virtual) address map. This map can be up to four billion bytes in size. The MMU treats addresses that leave the chip as specifying locations in the computer's memory. These are called physical (or real) addresses and they are part of the physical address map. The physical memory map can be up to four billion bytes in size, but it typically has only a few million bytes of real memory. The main task of the MMU is to translate addresses from the logical address map to the physical address map. Both the logical and physical address maps are composed of fixed size units called *pages*. The translation process replaces the page number of the logical address with a physical page number, as shown in Figure 13–3. The MMU uses tables in physical memory to determine the physical page number that corresponds to a logical page. The remainder of this section gives an overview of the MMU and how it is used.

MMU Registers and Instructions

The MMU on the MC68030 is controlled using special instructions. These are shown in Table 13–1.

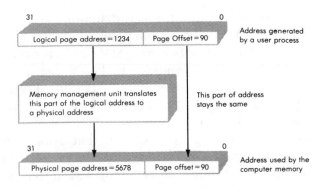

Figure 13-3   Address Translation in the MC68030

Table 13-1   MMU Control Instructions

Instruction	Meaning
pload	Force an entry to be loaded into the ATC the ATC
ptest	Interrogate the MMU for information about a logical address
pmove	Load and store MMU registers
pflush	Invalidate selected ATC entries
pflusha	Invalidate all ATC entries

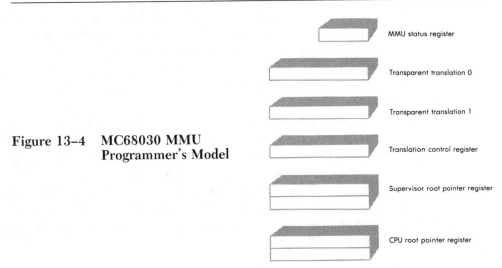

Figure 13-4   MC68030 MMU Programmer's Model

The registers of the MMU are shown in Figure 13-4. The CPU root pointer (CRP) and supervisor root pointer (SRP) point to the address translation tables used by the MMU. The number and sizes of the tables are set by the translation control (TC). The MMU status register receives the results of the ptest instruction. Finally, the transparent translation registers (TT0 and TT1) set the windows in which the MMU will be bypassed. These are discussed more later.

433

Now examine how these instructions and registers are used in the UNIX kernel. When the system boots, the kernel loads the TC register using a pmove instruction to set up the MMU. Each process has its own address translation tree. The kernel loads the CRP register with a pmove instruction as part of setting up a process to run. This loading automatically invalidates the entries in the ATC that belonged to the previous process.

Occasionally, a user process causes a memory fault. A memory fault occurs when the MMU determines that a memory access is illegal. For example, the process might have tried to write to the kernel. The kernel uses the ptest instruction to get information that helps determine what to do about the fault. The ptest instruction puts the information into the MMU status register. If the kernel decides to fix the memory fault and let the process continue, it can use the pflush instruction to empty the ATC so that the corrected address translation can be loaded.

MMU Options

Some memory management hardware allows only one way to set up an address map or to perform certain other functions. This may or may not be the best way for a UNIX kernel to do tasks. The MC68030 is not that rigid. Within the basic address translation model provided by the MC68030 hardware, the UNIX kernel can configure many aspects. Items that the operating system programmer can adjust are shown in Table 13–2.

Logical addresses in the MC68030 MMU are treated as if they contain several distinct bit fields. The number and width of these fields are set by system software. The maximum number of fields is six, as shown in Figure 13–5a. The initial shift (IS) field defines bits of the logical address that are not used in translating addresses. Any logical addresses that are different in these bits, but the same in all other bits, will be treated by the hardware as the same logical address. The table index fields (TIA, TIB, TIC, and TID) are used as indexes into the address translation tables. As each level of translation table is searched, the next table index field is used to select an entry. Finally, the page size (PS) field is the byte offset of the data in the page. It is not changed by the MMU.

Table 13–2   MC68030 MMU Options Configurable by Software

Item	Configurations Possible
Page size	256, 512, 1K, 2K, 4K, 8K, 16K, 32K bytes
Number of table levels	1–5
Size of table entries	4 or 8 bytes
Restrictions for pages	Supervisor only, read only, don't cache
Special features	Transparent translation windows

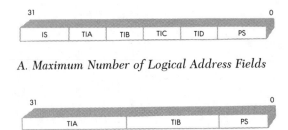

A. *Maximum Number of Logical Address Fields*

B. *Logical Address Fields Typical for UNIX*

Figure 13–5 **Sample Logical Address Breakdowns**

You do not need to use all of these fields, and a UNIX system does not require all six. A more typical configuration is shown in Figure 13–5b. Since there is no IS field (the IS field width is zero), all 32 bits of the logical address are used in the translation. There are two TI fields, so there are two levels of translation tables.

The Address Translation Tables

Translation tables for the MC68030 MMU are organized into a tree structure. As described earlier, the MMU contains two registers, CPU root pointer (CRP) and supervisor root pointer (SRP), which point to the roots of two translation tables trees. If a memory access by the CPU requires a search of the address translation tables, the CPU selects one of the two trees. The SRP register is used if the access is supervisor mode and a control bit in the MMU's TC register is set. The CRP is used otherwise. For each level in the table structure, a TI field is extracted from the logical address and used to index into a table. The selected table entry provides the pointer to the next level of table, or, for the last level, the physical page number. This process is shown for the two-level table in Figure 13–6.

In this example, the logical address is divided into three pieces. The TIA and TIB fields are both 8 bits wide, and the PS field is 16 bits. Assume that a user mode program generated this address, so the first thing that the MMU does is to use the pointer in the CRP register to find the first table. Now that the MMU has found the first table, it has to pick an entry in the table. The TIA field has a value of 2, so the MMU selects the third entry (entries are numbered beginning with 0). The pointer in the third entry points to another table. The MMU uses the value of the TIB field (3) to select the fourth entry from this table. There are no more tables, so the pointer is does not point to a table. Instead, it contains a physical address. To complete the translation, the MMU constructs the complete physical address by replacing the TIA and TIB fields of the logical address with the corresponding bits from the last pointer. The PS bits are not changed.

435

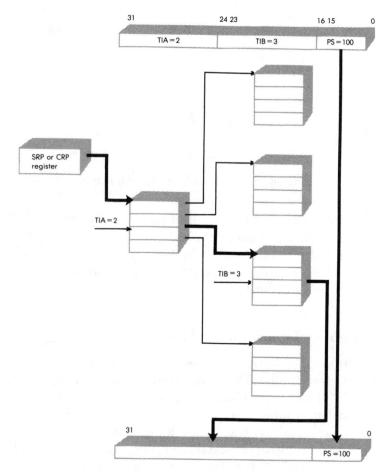

Figure 13-6   Sample Address Translation Table Search

In addition to pointers, entries in the address translation tables contain protection information. Of interest to the UNIX system are the abilities to prohibit writing to an area of memory and to restrict access to an area of memory to supervisor mode only. The restrictions are turned on in the MC68030 by setting bits in the translation tables. They can be used at any level in the translation table tree. This allows protection of a large area of memory by setting only 1 bit.

The Address Translation Cache

The MC68030 contains an *address translation cache (ATC)* that allows it to save the results of recent searches of the address translation table. It is automatically loaded whenever the MMU makes a search of the address translation tables. This means that the MMU does not have to search the address translation tables every time the CPU needs something from memory. The ATC contains 22 recently used logical-to-physical-address translations. Entries in the cache stay there until they are removed to make space for another entry or until they are explicitly flushed.

Differences Between the MC68030 MMU and the MC68851

As mentioned in the Introduction to this paper, the MC68030 is very similar to its predecessors, the MC68020 and MC68851. For UNIX systems that must run on both, there are some features to be aware of. Both support the same range of translation table structures and page sizes. The MC68851 is able to keep entries for more than one process in its ATC. This requires an explict flush of the ATC when a process dies to make sure that there are no stray entries in the ATC. The MC68851 also provides some instructions for using the MMU that are not on the MC68030. These should not be used by software that will need to run on both MMUs.

Finally, the MC68851 hardware leaves loading the ATC during cas, cas2, and tas instructions to the software. These instructions run multiple bus cycles that cannot be interrupted. They provide a hardware-guaranteed synchronization between multiple processes or processors. In a UNIX system, they can be used to provide synchronization between processes sharing a memory segment without using the kernel semaphore facilities. If a table search to fill the ATC must take place for one of these instructions, the MC68851 cannot get the bus from the MC68020 CPU to do it. The memory fault handler routine is run by the CPU, and it must recognize this situation and be prepared to deal with it. Since on the MC68030 the CPU and MMU are integrated, the hardware handles this situation automatically.

The Instruction and Data Caches

The MC68030 contains two cache memories for storing recently used pieces of information from main memory. The purpose of these cache memories is to speed up programs. Main memories in small computers are often slower than the MC68030 requires. This means that the microprocessor has to wait for the memory when it needs data from main memory. The cache memories are small, fast memories that are inside the MC68030 itself. The idea is that if some piece of program code or data has been used recently, there is a good chance that it will be used again in the near future. The cache memories remember the information and can provide information faster than the main memory. On the whole, this operation makes the MC68030 execute programs faster.

One of the cache memories is for storing information that is part of the instruction stream. It is called the *instruction cache*. The other cache is for storing data that is fetched as an operand for an instruction. It is called the *data cache*. Each of these caches can store 256 bytes. They are direct mapped caches, meaning that every time that information from a particular address in main memory is loaded into the cache it goes at the same location. It also means that addresses in main memory that are separated by multiples of 256 bytes will go into the same cache location. If a cache location is full when a new piece of information must use that location, the old information is thrown away and replaced by the new information.

As far as the UNIX kernel is concerned, the most important characteristic of the caches is that they are attached to the logical address bus. This allows both caches to be accessed simultaneously, improving performance. It also means that the memory management unit does not translate the addresses used by the caches. The UNIX kernel must be aware of this; it is discussed more in a later section.

Setting Up the MC68030 for UNIX

For the most part, the casual user of a UNIX system can ignore the way in which memory is organized. The kernel and the C compiler will get a program linked together and put in memory at appropriate addresses. Similarly, the casual user can ignore the caches and the details of how shared memory works. The following material is provided for people who may need to implement UNIX on the MC68030 or for users who want to know how their computers work.

Setting Up the MMU

The MC68030 allows the creation of literally thousands of different address translation table structures. The widths of the index fields can be varied, address spaces can be overlaid, and bits of the logical address can be ignored. Each of these structures gives a different memory map for UNIX. Most of these memory maps are not particularly useful in a UNIX system. While requirements will vary among implementations, a few basic guidelines can be given.

In a UNIX system, the page size selected will affect performance. Setting it too small causes many searches of the address translation tables. In a demand-paged UNIX system, a small page size will also cause more disk activity.

The number of levels of translation tables should be kept small. This reduces the time for each search of the tables. Depending on the memory map that you use in your UNIX system, however, a table structure with more levels may reduce the time it takes the system to manipulate the tables. The net effect will vary depending on many factors. There is no fixed answer.

The MMU should be set up so that the when the kernel addresses either program or data, the logical addresses refer to the same physical addresses. This is called overlaying the program and data address spaces. Similarly, the user program and data address spaces should be overlaid. There is little to be gained from separating address spaces unless you plan to be running programs that will require more than a billion bytes of code or data. A possible example of a need for this much space is artificial intelligence systems that allocate small amounts of widely scattered memory.

With all of this in mind, look at two plausible address map layouts for a UNIX system. Each of the layouts has advantages and disadvantages to examine.

Memory Map 1

The first alternative is shown in Figure 13–7a. This map arranges logical addresses so that the supervisor program and data spaces are merged, and start at logical address 0. The user program and data spaces are also merged and start at logical address 0. Note, however, that logical address 0 for the kernel and logical address 0 for the user process are not the same. The MMU can tell when a memory reference is for the user and when it is for the supervisor, so it keeps the kernel and user maps separated. As you can see from Figures 13–7b and 13–7c, there are two levels of translation tables used to translate addresses.

The primary advantages of memory map 1 are that it provides four billion bytes of address space per user process, and that it provides a good separation between user and supervisor. Once the MMU is turned on, user mode and supervisor mode memory references are translated by different translation tables. This makes it less likely that a kernel error will allow a user process access to supervisor areas of memory.

The disadvantage of this structure is that it requires a special instruction, moves, to transfer data between the kernel and a user process. The moves instruction allows the supervisor to make a memory reference to the user address map. Without this capability, the kernel would not be able to get to the user address map at all. Unfortunately, using the moves instruction, data can be transferred no more than four bytes at a time. Also, the transfer must be to or from a data register. These restrictions, coupled with the fact that a C compiler cannot generate a moves instruction, make the transfer of data between the user address map and the kernel unwieldy.

439

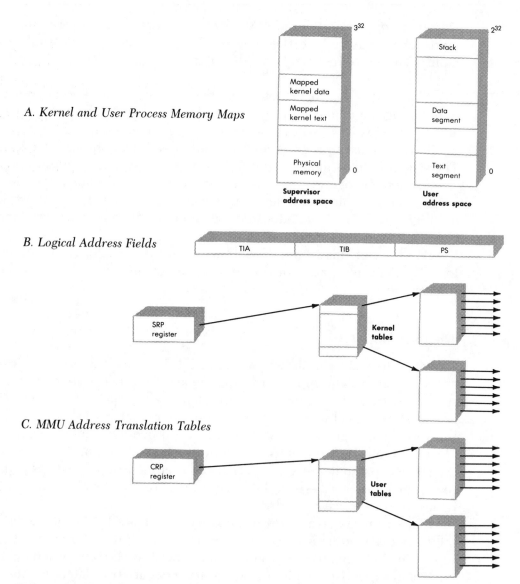

A. Kernel and User Process Memory Maps

B. Logical Address Fields

C. MMU Address Translation Tables

Figure 13–7   First Sample Memory Maps and Translation Tables

In spite of the drawbacks, the moves instruction does have a benefit that may make it attractive. In some UNIX kernels, the memory fault handler does not expect to see memory faults generated by the kernel. Using the moves instruction to access a user process causes the reference to appear as a user reference. The complexity of the fault handler can be reduced if it can assume that any fault on a supervisor reference is an error. In a demand-paged system, the user space reference by the kernel can automatically initiate page fault processing.

Memory Map 2

The second example memory map is shown in Figure 13–8a. It shows the kernel occupying the lower half of a single address map and the current user process in the top half. All of the address spaces, user program/data, and supervisor program/data are overlaid.

    Using this configuration, all memory references are translated using the translation table pointed to by the CRP register. Since the CRP register is still reloaded when switching from one process to another, each process must have tables to translate the kernel. The most convenient way to do

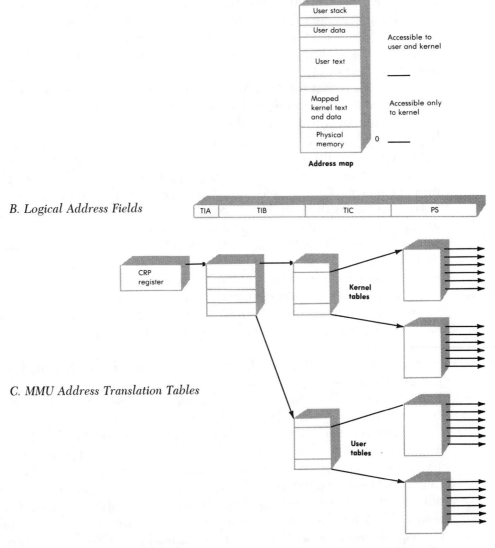

B. *Logical Address Fields*

C. *MMU Address Translation Tables*

Figure 13–8   Second Sample Memory Map and Translation Tables

this is to have one set of tables for the kernel. Each process then shares this one set. To accomplish this sharing without requiring very large tables, the logical address is broken down, as shown in Figure 13–8b.

Creating a table that is indexed by two bits as the uppermost table in the tree breaks the address map into four pieces. The first (lowest-addressed) two pieces belong to the kernel, and the other two belong to the user process. When the translation table for a new process is created, all the kernel has to do is copy the two pointers for the kernel translation tables into the first two entries of the table for the new process. It now has all of the mapping for the kernel without having another set of kernel tables created. Protecting the kernel from access by user processes is done by setting a control bit in the two kernel table entries.

The advantage of this address map layout is that it allows the kernel to access the current user process with instructions that can be generated by C compilers. When you do accesses this way, there are three things to notify the kernel of.

The first is that the MC68030 data cache should be used in its "write allocate" mode. This mode is discussed later. Using this mode ensures that data written by the kernel into the user process does not accidentally bypass old data (marked as user references) for the same address in the data cache. An alternative action is to invalidate the data cache on returning to user mode from the kernel if any data was written to the user process image. This second alternative appears to require fewer cache entries to be invalidated, but it requires more overhead in the kernel to decide when the data cache must be cleared.

The second thing that the kernel must be prepared for is the possibility that an access to a user memory segment may cause a memory fault. The fault handler routine must be ready to handle this case. This is especially likely to occur in a demand-paged system, because not all of a process is required to be in memory at once. It is possible, for example, that the user has requested a disk transfer to a page that has been moved out to disk itself.

The last thing that the kernel must watch out for is a bad address passed to it as part of a system call. Since the user can generate an address that may point into the kernel itself, all addresses received as part of a system call must be checked by software for validity.

Using the moves instruction will get around all of these problems. As mentioned earlier, it might be used with the memory map shown in Figure 13–7. In the case of memory map 1, you have to use it to allow the kernel to access the user process at all. In this case, using the moves instruction is not required. The kernel can directly address the user process. The moves instruction allows the kernel to access the user process and have memory protection enforced as if the access was made by the user process. This allows hardware, instead of software, to check the validity of addresses passed to system calls by user processes. The drawbacks of using the moves instruction were discussed earlier, and they remain. The use of one method or the other is a matter of personal preference, or of already having code that either can or cannot handle these situations.

A final advantage of the second memory map (Figure 13–8) is that logical address 0 is not accessible to a user process. Since the value of the NULL pointer in UNIX is typically 0, all attempts to use a NULL pointer will result in a memory fault. This makes debugging programs that contain this type of problem much easier. It also guarantees that a NULL pointer bug sleeping in a program will cause a hard fault instead of strange behavior when it is finally tripped.

The primary disadvantage of memory map 2 is that it does not allow the entire four billion byte address space of the processor for use by a user process. Because there are still two billion bytes left for the user, this should not be a severe restriction.

These examples should not be taken as the only ways to use the MC68030 MMU for UNIX. There are many others that are just as good. Other considerations, such as special system requirements, availability of existing code, and personal preference, may lead you to different solutions.

Transparent Segments

The MC68030 provides two "windows" in which logical addresses bypass the MMU's translation and are used directly as physical addresses. These windows are called *transparent segments*. They are controlled by the TT0 and TT1 registers. The registers provide a base and bound for each transparent segment, as well as fields that can control access to the segments based on user or supervisor mode.

There are two advantages to using these windows. The first is that they do not require address translation tables. This means that references to addresses in these windows never require a table search. The second advantage is that references using these windows do not cause entries to be made in the ATC. Using large amounts of data through a window will not cause entries in the ATC to be replaced and then refetched later. This means that fewer searches of the address translation tables are required.

UNIX systems can benefit from using these windows in two ways. One is to map physical memory into the kernel address space. A UNIX kernel typically needs to address physical memory directly from time to time. Using a transparent window allows this mapping to be done easily, and at minimum cost. User processes are prohibited from getting to physical memory because the windows can be restricted to access by supervisor mode code only.

Providing controlled access to a physical device by a user process is another way that the transparent windows can be used. An example of a device that might require fast access and have a large data throughput is a video display buffer. To request access to the buffer, a user process could request that a special shared-memory segment be attached. This segment would be a special one created by the kernel that contains the buffer. To allow a user process to access the buffer, the kernel would load a TTx register with the appropriate values when the process is set up to run. The user process can then access the buffer without further intervention of the operating system.

Figure 13–9 illustrates the logical and physical address maps for a process using a transparent segment for a video buffer. The display buffer responds like memory at some high address in the physical map. The text, data, and stack segments of the program are mapped by the MMU into the regular RAM memory of the system at whatever physical addresses the kernel decides on. The display buffer is mapped using a TTx register, and appears in the logical map at an address equal to its physical address.

Note that the MC68851 MMU does not implement transparent windows. Any kernel code must run on both MMUs should have an option to provide translation tables for the MC68851. Often these can be truncated tables, using a single page descriptor instead of a set of tables. The MC68851 requires ATC entries for each page accessed, but because it contains more entries in its ATC this should not degrade system performance.

Shared-Memory Segments

Shared-memory segments are a way in which UNIX allows two processes to communicate. Using UNIX system calls, one process creates an area of

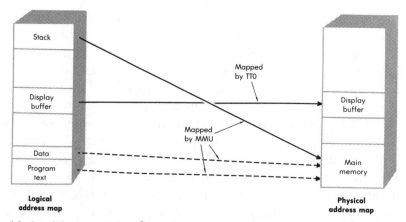

Figure 13–9   Memory Map for a Process Using Transparent Segments

memory and allows it to be shared by other processes. Another process can then request that this shared memory segment be "attached" to its logical address map. Data that is written into the shared segment by one process can be read from the segment by another process.

Shared-memory segments can be easily implemented using the MC68030 MMU. A segment size is chosen to be the same as the amount of memory that can be translated by one self-contained set of translation tables. This self-contained set of tables is then simply attached to the translation table of each process that is sharing the segment. Figure 13–10 shows a diagram of this arrangement. Each process can have either read/write or read only access to the segment.

The action of the MC68030 data cache must be taken into account with shared-memory segments. One of several precautions must be taken by the kernel to make sure that the cache handles data from the shared segments properly. These precautions are needed because the data cache monitors logical addresses, but not physical addresses. It may be confused by data that has more than one logical address but only one physical address. The easiest precaution is to operate the cache in its "write allocate" mode. This will allocate space in the data cache whenever a piece of data is written. The write allocate mode is discussed in the next section. Another solution is to make all shared segments not cacheable. A third solution is to identify segments that are attached more than once to the same process and to make only those segments uncacheable.

The relative performance of each of these alternatives can vary wildly, depending on how processes use the shared segments. Operating the cache

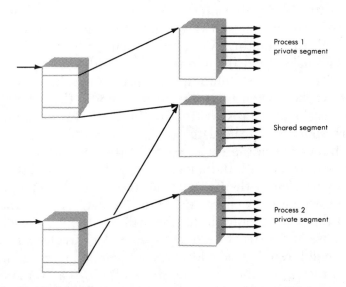

Process 1
private segment

Shared segment

Process 2
private segment

Figure 13–10   Translation Tables for Shared-Segments UNIX on the MC68030

in "write allocate" mode is the easiest for the operating system to deal with.

Using the Instruction and Data Caches

Normally, no special care needs to be taken by the UNIX kernel with the instruction cache other than flushing it when switching from one process to another. A program that has self-modifying code may not run, however, because the instruction cache does not pick up the writes that modify the code. This is because the instruction cache works by monitoring an internal bus on the MC68030 that only handles memory reads, never memory writes. If a program with self-modifying code may be run, the simplest solution for the UNIX kernel is to disable the instruction cache.

The data cache presents more interesting problems because it must also deal with data that is written as well as read. More than one logical address sharing the same physical address is the cause of these problems. Since the data cache is on the logical side of the MMU, it has no way of knowing which logical addresses refer to the same physical memory. This situation can occur when the same memory segment is attached to more than one address in the same process. It can also occur when the user and supervisor address spaces are overlaid. While none of these problems is difficult to deal with, again, it is something that the UNIX kernel must take into account.

The MC68030 hardware offers the system software two ways of dealing with the problems just mentioned. They boil down to "fix it in hardware" and "fix it in software." The "fix it in hardware" approach probably appeals to operating system writers initially, but there are drawbacks to it that make it worthwhile to look at both solutions.

The hardware solution is to turn on the "write allocate" mode of the data cache. When in write allocate mode, the MC68030 looks into the data cache as data is written by the CPU. The location in the data cache corresponding to the data being written is selected. In addition to data, each location in the cache contains the address of the stored data. If the address stored with the selected cache location and the address of the data being written by the CPU are not the same, the data in the cache location is thrown away. A characteristic of the data cache is that logical addresses that differ by a multiple of 256 will use the same cache location. This is because of the structure of the cache. A characteristic of the MMU is that if two different logical addresses are mapped to the same physical address, then they must differ by a multiple of 256. The reason for this is that the page sizes used by the MMU are multiples of 256. The combination of these facts is what allows the write allocate mode to solve the problem.

An example may help to explain this. Assume that the data 1000 is being written to logical address 0. Data at address 0 will be placed in entry 0 of the data cache. Also assume that the data that is in entry 0 in the data cache came from address 1024, and is 2000. The cache remembers the address 1024 for location 0. In write allocate mode, the cache will invalidate entry 0 and allocate it to address 0. The data cache cannot be sure that address 0 and address 1024 are not being mapped to the same physical page by the MMU. The drawback to the hardware solution is that, nearly always, the address of data being written and the address of data in the data cache are not mapped to the same main memory address. This results in perfectly good data being thrown away.

The software solution is to operate the cache in its no write allocate mode. This mode does not invalidate entries in the cache. If the write is for a complete 4 byte cache entry, to an address already in the cache, then the cached data is replaced. Otherwise the cache is not touched on a write. The advantage of this strategy is that good data is kept in the cache. The disadvantage is that the software has to determine when dangerous situations arise.

Interrupts

An interrupt is a request to the CPU by another piece of hardware for some service. This request can cause the CPU to stop executing its current program and automatically begin executing the service program for the hardware that caused the interrupt. UNIX systems typically handle hardware interrupts by running a very short interrupt service routine that schedules work to be done later.

The amount of time that it takes for a computer system to respond to an interrupt is called the *interrupt latency*. In the past, UNIX systems in general could tolerate a fairly long interrupt latency because they were primarily software development systems. Today, some UNIX systems are being made with real-time extensions. These systems may require the ability to respond to hardware interrupts in a very short time. Another consideration as you determine the maximum interrupt latency that a system can tolerate is the requirements of peripheral devices. Some peripheral devices need a quick response to operate properly. This section discusses the interrupt response of the MC68030 and how it is determined for a particular system. It also discusses special considerations involving interrupt handlers and the floating-point hardware. Finally, it looks at how to use the MC68030's interrupt stack pointer in a UNIX system.

447

Calculating Interrupt Latency

It is very difficult to calculate the exact amount of time that an operation will take in a complex computer system. The effects of cache memories, address translation hardware, main memory speed, instruction pipelines, and other features can interact in ways that are not obvious. This example attempts to find the worst case by making some assumptions. You can assume that the cache memories are empty. The following discussion is meant to point out what to look for in determining the interrupt latency for your system. It is not a specific answer for all MC68030 systems.

Most processors will only begin servicing an interrupt at the end of an instruction. This is true of the MC68030 when it is operated without a floating-point coprocessor. You know then that the interrupt latency cannot be less than the length of the longest instruction. Added to that is some overhead involved in saving the state of the program that is executing and transferring control to the interrupt handler. In the MC68030, searching the address translation tables is considered to be part of the instruction. Interrupts are not taken until the instruction, including the table searching, is finished. This paper looks at each of these factors in turn.

Start with the overhead, since it is the easiest to deal with. On an interrupt, the MC68030 must save the status register and program counter for the current program on the stack. It then has to figure out which entry in the interrupt vector table to use. This value is also placed on the stack. The processor reads the vector table to get the new program counter value for the interrupt handler. Finally it reads instructions from the interrupt handler code to fill its internal instruction pipe. This process takes about 35 clocks. If an interrupt occurs under the best possible conditions, it will take 35 clocks to begin executing the first instruction of the handler.

The time taken to execute the longest instruction is the next thing to consider. There are several candidates for longest instruction. The longest instruction that a user can execute on the MC68030 is the signed divide instruction divs, with a memory indirect addressing mode. This can take, worst case, 119 clocks. The longest instruction that the supervisor can execute is the return from exception (rte) instruction that restores a long format fault, followed by the longest user instruction. This is because the MC68030 CPU will not service on interrupt until the first instruction after an rte has executed. Returning from a page fault in a demand-paged version of UNIX is a common use of the rte instruction. rte itself can take 94 clocks with fast memory, but because it does 24 memory reads, it could take longer than the divide instruction if memory is slow.

Finally, you have to account for the time it takes to search the address translation tables. In a UNIX system this time will easily swamp the time taken by other components of the interrupt latency calculation. UNIX systems will typically have two- or three-level address tables. Searching tables of this size will take 30–40 clocks, plus the number of wait states required because of slow memory. This time is very dependent on the exact configuration of the tables and the speed of memory. You should consult the *MC68030 User's Manual* for details.

Since table searches are expensive in terms of time, you need to look for instructions that can cause a lot of table searches. The worst case is to rte to a memory-to-memory move when both addressing modes are memory indirect. Complicating matters is the fact that the operands and the instruction stream can all cross page boundaries. A *page boundary* is an address that is a multiple of the page size used by the MMU. Assume that the instruction and data caches are empty, so that crossing a page boundary causes the MMU to search the address translation tables. The move instruction in the following code segment can cause up to nine searches of the address translation tables.

```
#       assume that page size is 1000 hex
#       set up some symbols to use


        org     $1ffe           # right at page boundary
op1addr dc.l    op1             # insert addr of op1
        org     $3ffe           # another page boundary
op2addr dc.l    op2


        org     $5ffe           # data at a page boundary
op1     dc.l    $1234
        org     $7ffe           # another page boundary
op2     dc.l    $0


#       now for the program


        org     $90ee           #gets the move ins at a page bound
start:  lea     op1addr,a0
        lea     op2addr,a1      # rte to this instruction causes
        move.l  ([a0]),([a1])   # up to nine table searches
```

Here is a sample calculation for the time taken for an interrupt. Note that it includes the assumptions used, followed by the time (in clocks) for the various operations, and finally a translation of clocks into microseconds for representative clock frequencies.

Assumptions Used

- A memory fault occurs on the last write of the instruction sequence shown.
- The ATC is completely empty when the sequence starts.
- The supervisor (master) stack crosses a page boundary because of the fault.
- An interrupt occurs during the stacking for the memory fault, the interrupt stack is being used, and it crosses a page boundary because of the interrupt.
- Table searching takes 35 clocks.

Clocks Used by Operations

Instruction	Calculation	Clocks Used
rte instruction		94 clocks
move instruction		49 clocks
Tables searches for move	9*35	315
Memory fault (short)		50
Table searches for fault	5*35	175
Interrupt		36
Table searches for interrupt	5*35	175
Total		844 clocks

Time–Frequency Relationship

Clock Frequency	Time for 894 Clocks
16.67 MHz	50.6 μsec
20 MHz	42.2 μsec
25 MHz	33.8 μsec
33.33 MHz	25.3 μsec

In contrast to the worst case, look at the typical case now. Since UNIX programs are most often written in C, what do C compilers generate? Instructions used heavily by C compilers will be branches, moves, and arithmetic instructions. Common addressing modes will be indexing off of the stack pointer (for parameters and local variables) and absolute (for global variables). For these instructions, even the worst-case timing is less than 10 clocks. The "typical" instruction does not require a search of the address translation tables. This is because the memory page containing the instruction is probably the same one used by the last instruction, and the data the instruction used was probably used recently too. On the other hand a "typical" UNIX process might use enough entries in the ATC that the entries for the supervisor stack, vector table, and interrupt handler are replaced. Using the numbers for interrupt and table searches for interrupt from the table, note that a "typical" interrupt takes only a little over 200 clocks.

In summary, the average interrupt latency in an MC68030-based computer will be short. If your system requires the CPU always to respond to interrupts within a certain amount of time, you should evaluate the effect on the interrupt latency and structure your software so that your time constraints are met.

Interrupts and Floating Point

Some instructions on the MC68881 or MC68882 can take over 1000 clock cycles to execute. You should look at the effect that this has on interrupts. The long instructions allow interrupts at certain points. According to the *MC68881 User's Manual*, the longest that the floating-point hardware can cause interrupts to be delayed is 312 clocks. This is less than the interrupt latency caused by the MC68030, so the floating-point hardware will not be a factor in interrupt latency.

There is another consideration involving UNIX and the floating-point hardware, however. A UNIX kernel typically has no need for floating-point arithmetic. Integer arithmetic is sufficient for its work. It will save and restore the state of the floating point hardware during context switches, but that should be all. For most of the kernel, there are no special restrictions on using floating point anyway. In interrupt handlers, however, a decision must be made to allow floating point or to prohibit its use.

The problem is that the MC68030 and the floating-point hardware can run concurrently. That is, they can both be executing parts of different instructions at the same time. This is good for the UNIX user, because it means that a program will run faster. It is a problem for the kernel, however. During some of these long instructions, the MC68030 can fetch the next instruction for the floating-point unit and deliver it to the MC68881/2. The MC68030 then waits either for the first floating-point instruction to finish or for an interrupt. If an interrupt occurs, the MC68030 services it without telling the floating-point hardware. This leaves the floating-point unit with a half-finished instruction, plus another opcode loaded and ready to go. It cannot accept another opcode without finishing the work it has started. The interrupt handler must be aware of this or it may cause errors in the floating-point calculation.

An interrupt handler has two choices. The first is to leave the floating-point hardware alone. When the user process resumes, the floating-point instructions will pick up where they left off. The floating-point hardware will never know the difference. The second choice, if the interrupt handler wants to use floating point, is to save the state of the MC68881/2 with the fsave instruction. If the handler tries to use floating point without doing this save, an error will be signaled by the hardware and the user's calculation will be lost.

The reason that this decision must be made by the kernel programmer is that UNIX systems have a piece of assembly language code that runs before the C language interrupt handler. This assembly code sets up the environment that a C routine expects to see. It is this assembly language code that would do the save operation for the floating-point hardware. If this save is not done and a later programmer writes an interrupt handler that uses floating point, the result will be system crashes that may be difficult to trace.

A dangerous aspect of this problem is that it may be inadvertently caused by a C compiler. A compiler that generates floating-point instructions will also generate an instruction to save floating-point registers at the beginning of a C function. An unsophisticated compiler may generate a move instruction with no registers to move. This unneeded move will cause the problem described earlier.

To illustrate how subtle this can be, consider the following incident. A compiler is being used to develop a UNIX kernel. The kernel doesn't use floating point anywhere, so the compiler does not generate any floating-point instructions. In trying to track down a bug, the compiler is told to generate debug information. Generating the debug information automatically turns off the compiler's optimizer. One of the functions of the optimizer is to remove the extraneous floating-point register move instructions at the beginning of every function. The result is a kernel that is fine until you run a program that tries to use floating point, at which time the system crashes mysteriously.

The Interrupt Stack Pointer

One last area of interrupt handling will probably be of interest only to UNIX kernel programmers. The MC68030 can use three stack pointers. As shown in Figure 13–2, they are the user stack (for user mode operations), the master stack (for use in supervisor mode when entered by a trap instruction), and the interrupt stack (for use in supervisor mode when entered by an interrupt). These stacks can be used to solve a small, but potentially annoying, problem with UNIX kernels.

Most UNIX systems keep a kernel stack for each process. This is used to keep information that is specific to each process, such as system call or memory fault information. In most computers, a pointer to the kernel stack is maintained in a register that is used only when the computer is executing kernel code. In the MC68030, this happens when the CPU selects one of the A7 registers. Unfortunately, some computers have only two stack pointers, and the kernel stack must also be used for storing information about interrupts. This means that each kernel stack has to be large enough to hold information for all of the interrupts that can occur at one time, including the local variables of the interrupt-handling routines. The usual solution is to provide a good size area for each stack and hope that nobody installs an interrupt handler for a new device driver that needs a lot of stack space.

Using the separate interrupt stack pointer on the MC68030 allows one interrupt stack to be kept for the entire system. The per-process kernel stacks only have to be large enough to hold system call and memory fault information. This is usually a well-known amount of information and will not be changed over the life of the system. Certainly it will not be changed by simply adding a new device driver. The single interrupt stack can be made very large, because it will not have to replicated for each process.

Signals

Signals are the way that UNIX lets a user process handle special conditions. These conditions range from trying to divide by zero, to memory protection violations, to the user typing the interrupt character at the keyboard. A list of the signals provided by System V/68 release 2 is shown in Table 13–3. To use signals, a program calls the signal(2) library routine to specify a signal name and the name of a user routine to execute when the signal occurs. Executing this routine is called "catching" a signal, and the routine

Table 13–3   System V/68 Release 2 Signals

Signal	Meaning
SIGHUP	Loss of carrier from a modem
SIGINT	Typing the interrupt character
SIGQUIT	Typing the quit character
SIGILL	Illegal instruction
SIGTRAP	Trace mode trap
SIGIOT	iot instruction
SIGEMT	emt instruction
SIGFPE	Floating-point exception
SIGKILL	Sent by another process
SIGBUS	Hardware bus error
SIGSEGV	Addressing outside allocated segments
SIGSYS	Bad argument to a system call
SIGPIPE	Write to pipe with no reader
SIGALRM	Alarm clock timed out
SIGTERM	Software termination signal
SIGUSR1	User defined
SIGUSR2	User defined
SIGCLD	Child process terminated
SIGPWR	Power failure

itself is called a "signal-catching" routine. When the signal-catching routine returns, the user routine continues executing where it left off.

Signals have various uses in a system. A common one is to catch the interrupt signal sigint so that the program can do some cleanup work when the user types an interrupt character. The shell on many UNIX systems catches sigsegv and allocates more data space for temporary storage. A program may be able to catch sigfpe, try to fix the result of a bad floating-point calculation, and continue processing.

There are two major characteristics of signals that you must be aware of as a programmer in order to use signals effectively. The first is that they are asynchronous with respect to the process. In other words, you cannot predict exactly when they will occur. This is not true for things like the illegal instruction signal sigill, but it is safer to think of all signals in this way as much as possible. The second thing to keep in mind is that the behavior of signals tends to be very system-dependent. For example, dividing by zero may produce sigfpe on some systems and a special not a number result on others.

How Most UNIX Systems Handle Signals

Most UNIX kernels handle signals in a fairly straightforward manner. A signal for a process may occur when the process is executing (like sigfpe) or when another process is executing (like sigint). Whenever it happens, the kernel figures out what process the signal is meant for and makes a note of it. When the process is ready to run, the kernel checks to see if there are any signals waiting for it. If there are, the kernel arranges the kernel stack and user stack to make it appear that the process called the signal-catching routine and that the signal-catching routine was interrupted just before it executed its first instruction. The kernel then resumes the process in the signal-catching routine, which runs and returns to the point at which the user process had originally stopped.

In an MC68030-based system, this approach cannot be used. The reason is that the method described earlier assumes that the process stopped between instructions and can be restarted at any other instruction. The MC68030 can stop inside an instruction and can be safely restarted only at the place at which it stopped. This restriction affects both the kernel and, to some extent, the user.

Why Signals Are Different on the MC68030

Now look at the two situations that can cause problems. The first is a memory reference that causes a hardware exception to occur. This can happen when the stack needs to be extended, when the process tries to access unallocated memory, or (in a demand-paged UNIX) as a result of a page fault. An example is shown in the following code:

```
long    int test_var = 0;  /* Assume this 32 bit integer falls across a page
                               bound */
        int  (*catch)();
main()
{
        int a = 0;
        signal(SIGINT, catch);

        while(1) {   /* forever*/
                a += 0x00010001;  /* Increment upper and lower halves */
                test_var = a;   /*
                                Fault could occur after first half of test_var
                                is updated.  User presses interrupt key while the
                                fault is being processed
                                */
        }
}


catch()
{
        /*
        User expects test_var to be 00010001 or 00020002, and so on
        but never 00020001.  UNIX kernel should ensure this
        */
        printf( "test_var equals %x\n", test_var);
}
```

This example shows a very typical piece of code that happened to cause a page fault. While the page fault was being processed, the user typed the interrupt character from the terminal and a SIGINT waited for the process. What the kernel wants to do is to run the signal-catching routine for SIGINT and let the routine return to the assignment. Because the processor stopped inside an instruction, the kernel cannot do what it wants to directly.

The second situation in which a process can stop in mid-instruction happens when you use the MC68881 or MC68882 floating-point coprocessor. This is the same problem discussed in the previous section. A sample code sequence is shown in this code sequence:

```
float   b;
```

```
int  (*catch)();

main()
{
        register float a;
        signal(SIGINT, catch);

        while(1) {    /* forever*/
                b = a / 10.0;
                /*
                This C statement  will compile to something like
                        FMOVE   FP2,FP0
                        FDIV    #10.0,FP0  *interrupt happens late in FDIV
                        FMOVE   FP0,b
                */
        }
}

catch()
{
        /*
        User expects to be able to look at the variable b.  The UNIX kernel
        should ensure this, also.
        */
        printf( "b equals %f0", b);
}
```

The floating-point hardware will work on the divide. Meanwhile, the MC68030 will get the opcode for the fmove and send it to the floating-point hardware. If an interrupt occurs before the divide finishes and the fmove starts, the MC68030 will honor the interrupt and the floating-point hardware will finish the divide and stop in the middle of the fmove. In the example you again have a sigint pending. If the kernel tries to run the signal-catching routine for SIGINT and let it return to the fmove instruction, the MC68030 and MC68881 will be out of the signal-catching routine for sigint and let it return to the fmove instruction, the MC68030 and MC68881 will be out of synchronization. The MC68030 will be at the beginning of the fmove and the MC68881 will be in the middle.

There are two possible solutions to this situation for the kernel. Each one has different implications for the user. Take a look at each one.

How Signals Are Handled on the MC68030

The most desirable solution is to force the process that is receiving the signal to an instruction boundary before you run the signal handler. As mentioned before, most signals are asynchronous, so it will not matter if the process runs another instruction or two before getting the signal. The kernel can tell from the saved state of the process whether or not it stopped on an instruction boundary. If the process did stop between instructions, the kernel can start the signal-catching routine in the way described at the beginning of this section. Otherwise, the kernel turns on the trace mode of the MC68030 CPU and returns to the process where it had stopped. The trace mode causes the process to execute one more instruction and return to the kernel. This is guaranteed by the CPU to be on an instruction boundary. The kernel can now restart the process in the signal-catching routine.

The benefit to the user of this method is that it lets the signal-catching routine see the process in a consistent state. All global variables are accessible, as is the floating-point hardware. The signal-catching routine can do anything that a normal subroutine can do. This is the model of signal catching that programmers expect from other UNIX systems. It does introduce some complications for the kernel.

The second way for a UNIX kernel on the MC68030 to take care of signals is to arrange things so that signal-catching routines exit back to the kernel, instead of directly to the previous user routine. The kernel restores the original process state and returns. This is usually handled by using some special code as a front and back end to the signal-catching routine. This special code is linked into a program from a library along with the signal(2) routine and is invisible to the programmer.

The benefits of this method, compared with the first one, is that the kernel does not have to deal with the trace mode of the processor. The return to the kernel from the signal-catching routine can be done with an extra system call. There are disadvantages for the user with this method. The signal-catching routine sees the process in an unknown state. In general, the state of a global variable is unknown. The process could have been in the middle of modifying one when a fault occurred. The floating-point unit can be in the middle of an instruction. In addition, the signal-catching routine cannot use the longjmp(2) routine to return to another place in the program. This may cause portability problems with existing programs.

Even though it is not desirable, the second method of handling signals is required in one case. This is when a memory fault is the reason for the signal being sent. The memory fault will prevent the instruction from completing, so turning on the trace mode will not get the process to an instruction boundary. The signal associated with this situation is sigsegv. For the user, the only reasonable things for the signal-catching routine for sigsegv to do is to try either to allocate memory for the faulted address with sbrk(2), or to terminate the process. The kernel must keep the state of the process at the time of the fault and restore it after the signal-handler exits.

For most UNIX systems, the kernel will only find it feasible to store information for one memory fault at a time. This means that a signal-catching routine for sigsegv that causes another sigsegv will kill the process.

Summary

This paper covered some of the aspects of UNIX on the MC68030 microprocessor, including the basic structure of the CPU. You saw that there are not any characteristics of this processor that make it difficult to use UNIX. The paper also talked about the MMU and other parts of the MC68030 and showed how they can be used by UNIX. Finally, because there were no serious problems to discuss, the paper looked in some detail at more minor aspects of implementing UNIX on the MC68030.

References

Kelly-Bootle, Stan and Bob Fowler, The Waite Group. *68000, 68010, 68020 Primer*. Indianapolis, Ind.: Howard W. Sams & Company, 1985.

MC68020 User's Manual, 2nd ed. Englewood Cliffs, N.J.: Prentice-Hall, 1985.

MC68851 User's Manual. Englewood Cliffs, N.J.: Prentice-Hall, 1986.

MC68881 User's Manual. Motorola, 1985.

MC68030 User's Manual (in preparation).

System V Interface Definition, Issue 1. AT&T, 1985.

System V/68 User's Manual. Motorola, 1985.

KEYWORDS

▶ Context switching

▶ Interprocess communication

▶ Loosely coupled processors

▶ Multitasking

▶ Scheduling

▶ Semaphores

▶ Synchronization

▶ Tightly coupled processors

▶ Vector processor

Paper Synopsis: A new growth area for UNIX is multiprocessing systems—computers that allow UNIX processes to run in parallel at full speed. This paper explores the current UNIX multiprocessor market and defines the different types of multiprocessor architecture that exist.

Tom Jermoluk is director of high-performance systems for Silicon Graphics Inc. where he is responsible for the next generation of high-perform-ance graphics workstations. He was the coarchitect (with Dr. Forest Baskett) of the new hardware design to support multis and attached special-purpose processors. Previously Mr. Jermoluk was a member of the Bell Labs UNIX Development Laboratory and was responsible for porting System V UNIX to Hewlett-Packard's RISC architecture.

## 14

Multiprocessor UNIX

Tom Jermoluk

The availability of relatively high-performance, low-cost microprocessors such as the Motorola 68010 and National Semiconductor 32016 created the boom in technical workstations. For the first time it was cost effective to give individual engineers their own machine. Companies such as Sun Microsystems and Apollo made fortunes by selling into markets previously dominated by the DEC VAX and IBM 4341 class of machines.

Now a new breed of company is intent on leveraging this price performance into markets previously held by the largest VAX, IBM mainframe, and even CRAY computers. Companies such as Sequent, Alliant, Convex, Encore, and others are introducing multiprocessor UNIX systems; complete UNIX systems that use more than one CPU working in concert to enhance performance. Meanwhile, CRAY and IBM seek to maintain their technical markets by putting UNIX on their large scale multiprocessors.

This paper starts by looking briefly at multiprocessors in general. Then it explores what happens when UNIX is run on a collection of microprocessors rather than just one. You'll see why this is such a hot market area, and should be able to determine whether it's right for you. In starting this discussion, it is necessary to understand where this movement began and how far it can go. Questions that must be addressed are:

- What are general features of multi-processors?
- What are the different multiprocessor architectures?
- How well does UNIX fit on multiprocessors?

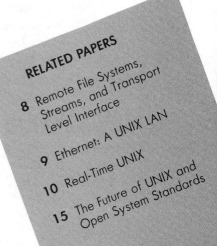

- What is the history of multiprocessor UNIX?

- What are the advantages/disadvantages to the user?

- Where is the technology going from here?

General Features of Multiprocessors

Multiprocessors provide several general features that are not specific to UNIX, but which mesh well with the UNIX marketplace. The features include:

- reliability—running code on more than one processor provides inherent system redundancy. The processors can be run in "lockstep," where each is running the exact same code at the same moment. If one processor is lost, the other(s) will continue to process. Alternatively, the systems can be run as general purpose, where if one goes down the load migrates across the rest of the complex. Although the performance may slow, because there are fewer processors per job, the system stays up.

- cost—microprocessors are inexpensive today. It costs relatively little to put 20 or more in a box. The company saves money on the expense of designing faster processors and new architectures. Small companies that cannot afford the development costs of a new processor to achieve higher performance can instead tie many microprocessors together. These chips are in such wide use that the costs are relatively insignificant compared to system price.

- performance—if parallelism can be achieved in user applications, system throughput can be speeded enormously. Any one program will use the same number of CPU cycles, but many will run at once. The actual time (or "clock" time) the program takes can be much less.

Multiprocessor Architectures

A process is the execution of a set of instructions on a collection of data. Computers today can be divided into four classes, depending on the way they handle the instructions and data:

- single instruction, single data (SISD)
- single instruction, multiple data (SIMD)
- multiple instruction, single data (MISD)
- multiple instruction, multiple data (MIMD)

Most computers today can be called SISD. This implies one CPU that operates on a single stream of data. It is the simplest configuration to build, has the lowest cost, and is a necessary first step in the life cycle of digital computers. Most single workstations such as the Sun 3, Apollo 580, and SGI 3030 would be classed as SISD. Figure 14–1 demonstrates the basic nature of the single instruction single data computer.

An SIMD computer is more commonly called an *array processor* or *vector processor*. In this case, there is one stream of instructions that operates on multiple streams of data as shown in Figure 14–2. In this manner, many units of data may be added or multiplied in a single cycle. Applications such as fluid dynamics that involve repetitive matrix multiplications are well-suited for this class of machines.

There are no generally accepted machines operating today that are referred to as MISD. There are machines that are multiple SISD, such as the CRAY 1 or CDC Cyber 205. The distinction is that they have multiple functional units but single control units.

The most interesting class to this paper is the MIMD. In this class are included Alliant Fx8, CRAY XMP, and most other systems being used for multiprocessor UNIX today. As shown in Figure 14–3, in this scenario there are multiple processing units, each of which is capable of operating on an independent stream of data. Each of the processing units has access to memory, and can function on independent programs.

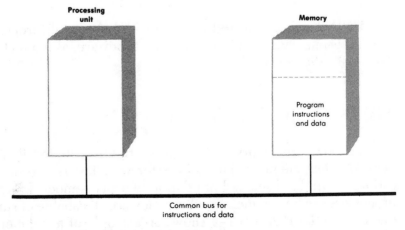

Figure 14–1   Single Instruction, Single Data

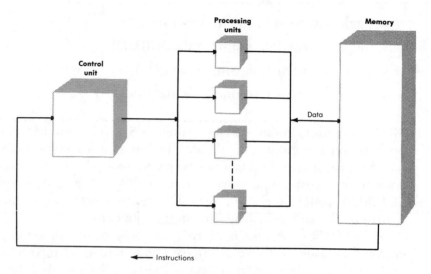

Figure 14–2   Single Instruction, Multiple Data

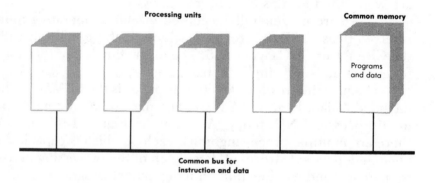

Figure 14–3   Multiple Instructions, Multiple Data

UNIX has been ported to several styles of multiprocessor architectures. It is important to understand what they are, as it affects significantly what tasks they do well.

Tightly Coupled Architecture

Two or more processors are said to be tightly coupled if they share the same physical memory. This allows for very fast interprocess communication, as will be discussed in relation to process models. Tightly coupled processors can be symmetric, where they are all capable of running exactly the same code. Figure 14–4 shows an example of a symmetric dual processor. If they are not symmetric, certain tasks are dedicated to one or

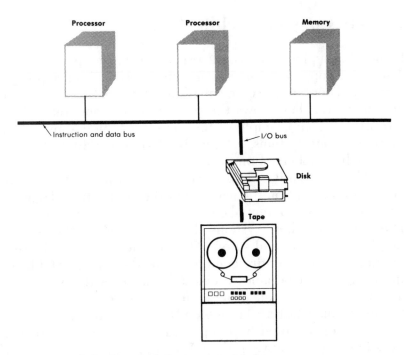

Figure 14–4   Tightly Coupled Symmetric Multiprocessor

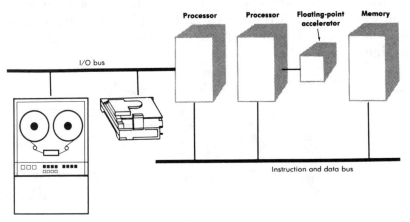

Figure 14–5   Asymmetric Multiprocessor

more of the CPUs, a condition referred to as *asymmetric*. Figure 14–5 shows an asymmetric system with dedicated I/O and floating-point units.

One example of asymmetric processing is where only one processor handles the I/O. Many companies call this an "attached processor" (AP) or "master/slave." Other common tightly coupled AP configurations are special-purpose units, such as math or graphics function units. Common symmetric tightly coupled systems would be the VAX 8650, IBM 3081K, and CRAY XMP.

465

Loosely Coupled Architecture

In loosely coupled systems, the processors have separate physical memory. A separate copy of the operating system resides in each processor's private memory. There exists some communications path, either as a common bus or a network, that allows the processors to cooperate. The Convergent Megaframe is an example of the loosely coupled approach. Figure 14–6 shows separate systems, each with a Motorola 68020, that are connected via a high-speed common bus.

Whether tightly or loosely coupled microprocessors are better is completely dependent on the makeup of the application. Tightly coupled systems have a lower potential cost, given the same throughput requirements. This is because these systems share the frame of the system, the power supply, backplane, and so on. They use less memory because one OS is running across the entire complex instead of one per CPU. However, the application must be able to take advantage of this style of architecture. And any one monolithic program (one which consists of only one task) will still only run as fast as the one CPU it is able to use.

A loosely coupled system provides better fault tolerance. With fewer parts in common between the CPUs, there are fewer parts whose failure would make the whole system fail. As each CPU runs a copy of the operating system, the complex can run with one or more nodes down. As you will see later, it is often easier to implement the operating system for loosely coupled systems, but the cost in overhead for general applications is high.

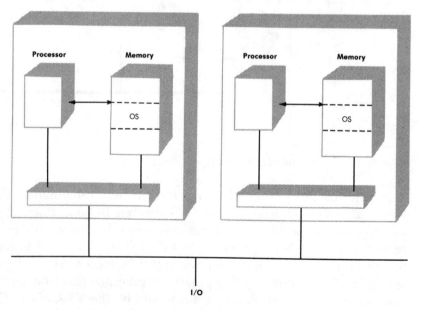

Figure 14–6   Loosely Coupled Multiprocessor

Vector Processors

Since many of the multiprocessors that run UNIX are vector processors of the SIMD type, it is worth looking into their potential uses. A vector unit can be thought of as a very fast, somewhat specialized processor that can operate on a very wide piece of data. Where a normal microprocessor might be "16 bit" or "32 bit," a vector unit could be "512 bit." What this refers to is the quantity of data that will actually be added (or divided, multiplied, and so on) in a single execution phase. If you consider an example, this can be demonstrated fairly easily. Examine the following programming loop:

```
for i in 1 2 3 4;
do;
a(i) = b(i) * 2;
done;
```

There are four elements in the arrays a, b, and c. On a scalar microprocessor, such as the 68020, only one 32 bit multiply can be done at once. This code would be executed like this:

```
load b(1) into a register
multiply by the constant 2
store the result in a(1)
load b(2) into a register
multiply by the constant 2
store the result in a(2)


--repeat for a(3), a(4)--
```

On a vector processor, this code would look as follows:

```
load b(1) b(2) b(3) b(4) into a vector register
multiply the register by 2
store the register into a(1) a(2) a(3) a(4)
```

This code is then about four times faster than the equivalent scalar code. For applications that need lots of raw compute power, vector processors are a clear win. These type of applications are usually modeling, fluid dynamics, mechanical design, or others that deal with large numbers of variables.

In order to run code on a vector processor, you need a vectorizing compiler. This is a compiler that knows about the interface to the vector unit and how to structure code for it. There are two types of vectorization

467

that are performed. The first is implicit. In this case the compiler tries to figure out from the user's source code what pieces can be vectorized. In the earlier example, the compiler figured out that it should put all four elements of the a and b arrays in the vector unit at once. The second method is explicit vectorization. In this case, the user tells the compiler using "directives" to vectorize a certain section of code. If it is too hard for the compiler to figure out how to vectorize, it has to be explicitly directed to do so. This requires extra awareness and work on the part of the programmer.

The important point is that the better the vectorizing compiler, the more it can implicitly vectorize. This leads to faster execution with less work for the user. Companies such as CRAY and Convex have invested hundreds of engineer years in developing compiler technology for vectorization.

UNIX Multitasking Model

It is important to understand the difference between a program and a process (also called a task). A process is the instance of a program that is actually executed on a processor at any point in time. A UNIX process is an individually schedulable, accountable unit of work. It has access to all system resources such as the memory, I/O, and CPU. The process is divided into instructions (or text), data, and BSS (block started by symbol or un-initialized data). Figure 14–7 shows this division. All of the areas together are known as the *process address space*. It is a mapping of the areas against a private view of memory for the process. This is called the *virtual mapping*. One program can have several processes running at the same time. This is where the terms *multitasking* and *multiprogramming* come from. Take a look now at how UNIX implements multitasking.

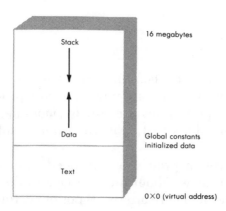

Figure 14–7   Process Address Space

The basic UNIX primitive for creating new processes is fork(). The process calling fork is known as the "parent," while the resulting new process is referred to as the "child." A single parent can have multiple children through successive calls to fork. Children may become parents themselves by calling fork. The fork primitive copies the address space of the parent and gives the child a new stack (used for system calls, I/O, and so on).

Multitasking is the ability of the user to start multiple processes that will then compete for system resources. Conceptually, to the user the processes are all running at the same time. This allows the user to code in a manner that allows logical separation of simultaneous tasks into multiple processes. Because this concept is at the heart of the UNIX on multiprocessor question, the next discussion examines two examples in detail.

The first example is an obvious application that is immediately useful. A user wants to transfer a file, such as mail or a document, to another user. Using common UNIX facilities for data communication, such as uucp, a program is called to transmit the file. If this user were to try the transmission on a PC running DOS, for example, he or she would usually be prevented from running any other program while the transfer were taking place. (Some DOS applications can appear to be doing two things at once, but they really aren't.) So if the user wanted to continue editing a memo, or use the printer, he or she is out of luck. A PC is a single-user single task system.

On the UNIX machine however, the user would simply call the communications program, and run it in the "background." This is the UNIX term for programs that are running without user interaction with them. The program that the user interacts with is called the "foreground" program. A user could have more than one background task. In the example in Figure 14–8, the user is sending mail to a friend, printing a memo, and editing a spreadsheet.

Look at how the CPU was used in the first example. A user who is editing is using very little of the available resources of the machine. The load from processing incoming characters at typing speed is very small, and there are long periods of idle time while the user is thinking about what to type next. Perhaps 90 percent or more of the CPU time would have been available to another program, such as the mail program example, if the system were multitasking. Now if the user wanted to run two programs, each of which could fully use all of the resources of the processor, multitasking isn't going to speed the programs up. This is where multiprocessors are able to contribute. By spreading the second program onto another processor, the total time required to run both can be cut in half. Thus, the user has parallelized the previously serial execution of these programs. Programs such as these that are already coded to run multitasking will spread across multiprocessors transparently. The user need never know that the programs were running on a multiprocessor.

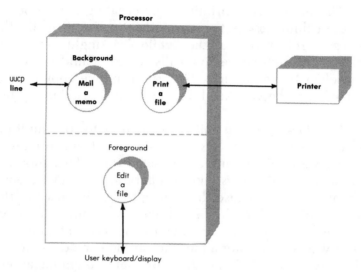

Figure 14–8   **Multitasking on UNIX**

Now look at a second, more complicated example. A common use of UNIX systems is as a file server. In this case there are multiple computers spread around a department. The computers may be running DOS or UNIX, but the file server must run UNIX, as you will see. The user's computers have small hard disks, or maybe just floppies. They want to share large databases, however, for applications such as accounts receivable. Many people often want to retrieve and deposit data on the file server at the same time. This situation is shown in Figure 14–9. If the server were a single-tasking DOS system, it would be like going to a bank that had one teller and a long line. You have to wait until everyone who got there before you was served. Now if the server ran UNIX you could have a separate task on the file server talk to each user. In this manner, it appears as if there is a system there whenever the user needs it. However, what is really happening is that there are now several windows open at the bank, and one teller is running between them as customers show up. If two customers show up at the same time, and each needs the full attention of the teller, service will slow down. If there were two or more tellers, this would be avoided. So the file server example comes full circle. Depending on how many users in the department are asking for files from the file server, the department can add more processors (or tellers) and speed up the service.

This concept works well for other applications, such as compute servers in a technical environment. Instead of providing files on demand, the system provides CPU resources from one big system to many smaller systems.

Now in the first example, the mail program and the editor that were running at the same time were fairly independent processes. However, in

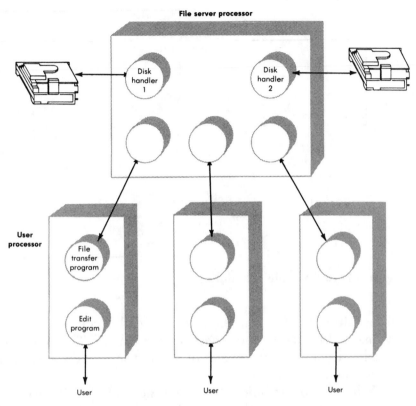

Figure 14–9   File Server Under UNIX

the second example the file server processes had to cooperate. They needed to be able to move data between users and to share the file system and the network. In order to cooperate they need to communicate. This communication in UNIX is called *interprocess communication (IPC)*. There are several different IPC mechanisms in current UNIX. The first was pipes. These are simply a data path between two processes. Here's a simple example of an IPC using pipes:

```
ls -l /usr/bin ¦ lp
```

One program ls lists the names of the files in a directory and "pipes" them into the line printer program lp to be printed. Later came more sophisticated methods, such as Berkeley sockets and system V's shared memory, semaphores, and messages. Later, in the discussion of possible changes to be made to UNIX, the paper takes a look at why the IPC method is important for multiprocessors.

It is also useful to understand how UNIX currently schedules processes. The nominal case is shown in Figure 14–10. There is a single queue of "runnable" processes maintained. Whenever a process that was blocked

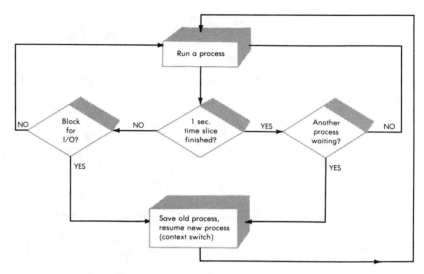

Figure 14–10   Simple Scheduling

while waiting for I/O, an alarm, or a signal receives the required event, it is marked runnable and placed on the queue. The scheduler runs periodically (usually every second or so) and selects the next process on the basis of highest priority.

When a process blocks because it needs I/O or it wishes to sleep, the kernel saves the currently running state of the machine. This is known as the *context* of a process. When one process blocks and another is scheduled, the kernel restores the state of the waiting process to the processor. This is called a *context switch.*

So this is how the appearance of multiple programs executing at the same time is implemented. All the programs that want to run get put into the run queue. Then the scheduler divides up time and gives each process a one-second shot at the processor. If the process blocks before its second is up, the scheduler will put the next waiting process on. This is naturally a simplification of a complex concept, but an important one to understand at this level before the next section's discussion.

Changes to UNIX for Multiprocessors

There are three levels of concern in a discussion of changes to UNIX for multiprocessors, and each has to do with synchronization. These levels are the hardware, operating system, and user code. Each of these areas have several solutions for how to synchronize, and as with any system, the best solution depends on the application.

Hardware Synchronization

The hardware presents several problems to an operating system that needs to control more than one CPU. Each processor in a tightly coupled system needs to have a map of what memory looks like to it. This is sometimes called a *memory management unit (MMU)* or a *translation lookaside buffer (TLB)*. This needs to be kept properly updated for consistency across processors. Each processor may have a cache for instructions and data. As a process moves from CPU to CPU, these may get out of sync. Imagine the simple case of one processor deciding to page out (to disk) a real memory page that another processor is using! It is beyond the scope of this paper to discuss the cause of all of these problems, but the solutions are important. Hardware synchronization can be done by hardware or by software. The more that is done by hardware, the less overhead is required from software. At the same time, this adds cost to the hardware. Thus, it is an important trade-off. It is very significant that the companies that can build the easiest and least expensive hardware to solve these problems will also provide the best performing systems.

The most fundamental hardware element for multiprocessing is a method of reading and modifying a variable in an atomic fashion. What this means is that software can be absolutely guaranteed that it can read and modify a variable in a single cycle. No interrupt or exception—no matter how high a priority—can occur during an atomic operation.

These instructions are called variously "test and set," "read modify write," or "load and clear." The reason why this is so important is that it is the basis for synchronization. It can take software hundreds of cycles to guarantee an atomic read and write, while the hardware can do it in one. This synchronization is used for mutual exclusion. This means the synchronization ensures that in a particular section of code, known as a *critical section*, only one process is executing the code at a time. Mutual exclusion is also used to ensure that only one process can write data into a particular memory location at once. For instance, consider a case where two processes are generating data and placing it on a linked list. In Figure 14–11 the critical section is not protected, and the result is the loss of data. Then, in Figure 14–12, the same code is run, but now the critical section is protected via synchronization, and the data is filled in the list properly.

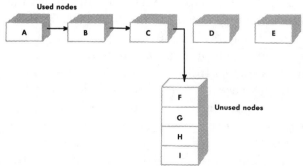

Time processor 1	Process 1	Process 2	Time processor 2
Clock 1	Generate data	Generate data	Clock 1
Clock 2	Select next free element (selects F)	Selects F also (not off unused list yet!)	Clock 2
Clock 3	Take F off of unused list	Also takes F off of list	Clock 3
Clock 4	Write data into F	Writes data over data processor 1 Just wrote!	Clock 4

Figure 14–11   Critical Section Unprotected

Why does the UNIX kernel need to be modified to use these synchronization primitives? Recall there were three areas of problems: hardware, operating systems, and user code. Let's look at the second of these: operating systems.

Operating System Synchronization

Although the UNIX user interface presents a view to the user that is appropriate for an MP system, the UNIX kernel was not originally designed to run on more than one processor. The UNIX kernel uses a "run to completion" style. This means that once entered via a system call, the kernel must complete the call before there can be a context switch. This is one way in which the kernel protects its data structures. Because it knows that no other process can be in the kernel, it always assumes that modifying data is atomic, and need not occur in a particular order. The only exception to this rule is interrupts. Because an interrupt can happen at any time, the kernel must prevent interrupts from occurring while it is modifying a data structure. However, it only needs to do this if the data structure could be modified by the interrupt handler code. Otherwise it is safe, because any process that is scheduled as a result of the interrupt will not run until the previous process has completed the system call. The method of preventing interrupts is called spl(). This blocks interrupts of a

Time processor 1	Process 1	Process 2	Time processor 2
Clock 1	Generate data	Generate data	Clock 1
Clock 2	Lock critical section	Try to lock section, Find Process 1 already there. Begin wait	Clock 2
Clock 3	Select next element	Wait	Clock 3
Clock 4	Take F off of unused list	Wait	Clock 4
Clock 5	Write data	Wait	Clock 5
Clock 6	Unlock section	Wait	Clock 6
		Lock section begin modification	Clock 7

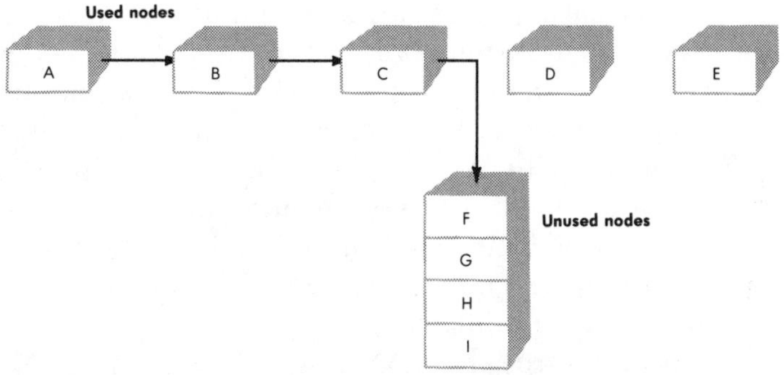

Used nodes

A → B → C → F

Unused nodes

F
G
H
I

Figure 14–12   Protected Critical Section

specified level from occurring until the next spl() specifies a lower level. Interrupts can be grouped together by level. The grouping normally associates interrupt handlers that touch the same data structures.

Because the kernel expected that only one process was asking to do something at one time, it was called "single-threaded." Now look at an example of something you can do in a single-threaded kernel. The user does a read() system call and the kernel is going to oblige by giving the user a piece of memory (known as a *buffer*). In this memory will be data for the user's read. So the kernel looks at its list of buffers and selects one for the user, then it assigns it to the user and is done. Now imagine that the kernel is multithreaded so more than one process can do system calls at once. If another user had done a read(), and the kernel was looking for a buffer to give that user, a problem develops. These two processes are now executing that same code to acquire a buffer. Suppose process 1 selects buffer number 4, but before it can give it to the user it is interrupted. Now process 2 wants a buffer, and process 1 has selected buffer 4, but has not yet given it to the user or marked it as used. Therefore process 2 thinks it is free and selects it. You now have selected that same buffer for two different processes. Woe is you, for you have corrupted your system. This is known as a *race condition*. It is a race to see who gets there first.

Wouldn't it be nice if the kernel could say exactly in what order things should execute?

Well, that's not an easy problem to solve. And that is why the first multiprocessors were master/slave where the kernel was single-threaded. Rest assured that the problem has been solved using methods of synchronization. However, this synchronization does not come free. It requires overhead on the part of the system. Such things as how many points of synchronization are in the kernel, and how often processes have to wait for another process to get out of a critical section, are very important. Once again, this is an area in which companies can take different approaches that will cause their system to perform well or very poorly for your application.

Another important area of modification of system software is the I/O subsystem. On systems with lots of users and I/O devices, such as disk and network, the amount of time spent in the kernel handling interrupts and I/O gets very large. It can consume more than half the resources of a VAX 780 running with 32 users and associated peripherals. On multiprocessors in which a system may now handle hundreds of users, the design of the I/O system becomes critical. The interrupts must be distributed intelligently across the entire complex. The methods of dealing with the disk need to change fundamentally.

Another area that does not scale well in UNIX as you add processors is memory management. As a complex adds more processors and more users, it needs to add memory to remain a "balanced" system, where no one part becomes the bottleneck. There are systems now such as the Convex C1 that run with up to 1 gigabyte of real memory. Most UNIX systems today run with 1 to 8 megabytes. This means from 100 to 1000 times more memory on the new systems than on current machines! The memory management algorithms in UNIX have no user input or intelligence about the program. This makes it very difficult to tailor memory management to the needs of larger more complex systems. This is an obvious area for new work in the kernel.

On general-purpose UNIX multiprocessors, where you are not trying to make one program run faster but just to run more programs, things don't have to change from the user code perspective. Recall the previous discussion of compilers that know how to parallelize and vectorize. Also remember the examination of the UNIX user interface, where it was found that the interface already supports a multitasking view that is perfect for multiprocessors. Those two things take you a long way toward the solution. But to achieve maximum throughput gains with a single program, there must be some recoding, and the operating system should make this as easy as possible.

The current UNIX interprocess communications primitives discussed earlier, such as pipes and messages, all require a system call. This involves the kernel. On a uniprocessor, the kernel is involved any time you change between two processes, because it is doing the context switch. So anything else it needs to do while starting the other process is done while in the kernel for the switch.

On a multiprocessor there is an important difference. The two processes do not just look like they are running at the same time, they *are* running at the same time! You can call the kernel to send another running process a message, but it would be a shame to have to do that if they are both already on the processors, because it creates unnecessary overhead. This model is shown in Figure 14–13. One way around this that many multiprocessor people use is shared-address space processes. If you remember the description of a process address space, imagine now that two processors are now executing that process at the same time. They don't have to be in lockstep, just both in the same code. This might sound complicated, and it is somewhat tricky to implement, but the benefit is great. The two processes can now both view the same memory. If one updates it, the other sees it without the kernel having to copy it from one process address space to the other. It is like having a UNIX shared-memory area for your entire address space. In Figure 14–14, process A can send a message to B by simply writing in its own address space, thus eliminating the kernel overhead.

Now in order to coordinate who is writing what, you need a synchronization primitive. Otherwise the user has the same "race" condition described earlier for the kernel. In System V this is the semaphore() system call. Once again the user has to call the kernel, though, again introducing overhead. If you remember the earlier test and set variables discussed, and imagine those being in the shared-address space of these processes, then the user does not need to call the kernel. The two processes can write data and signal each other when it is okay to read by using the

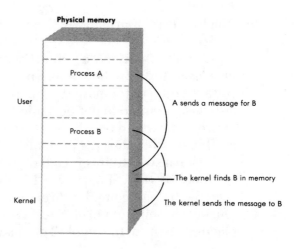

Figure 14–13 Messaging

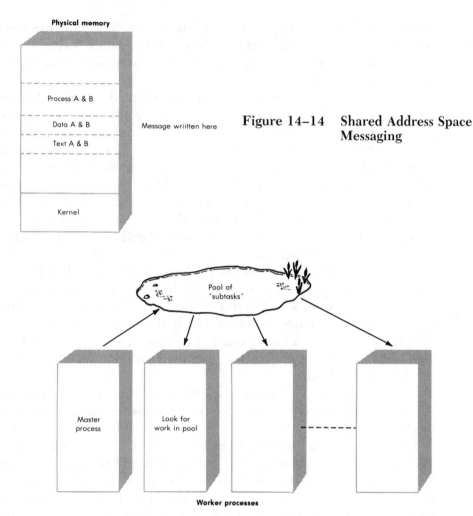

Physical memory

Process A & B

Data A & B

Text A & B

Kernel

Message wriitten here

Figure 14–14   Shared Address Space Messaging

Pool of "subtasks"

Master process

Look for work in pool

Worker processes

Figure 14–15   Self-Scheduling

synchronization primitives. These are then referred to as *cooperating processes.*

There is one more subject you may be wondering about. Does the user have to know how many processors there are? It would be hard to code if you had to know that there were 4, or 20, or even 2. This would also make your code not portable to other systems with different numbers of processors. And one of the reasons UNIX shows up on so many different machines is because it's portable.

The answer to this is called "self-scheduling." Imagine that you have one pool of work. Figure 14–15 shows such a pool. One master process with the help of compiler directives for parallelization, and operating system synchronization primitives, is creating independent units of work and placing them in the pool. This may be loops in programs that are not dependent on each other, or subroutine calls that can be done in parallel. Each processor sees the same memory space and the collection of processes that have been discussed. The operating system creates as many processes as there are processors. So the user doesn't have to know.

Now the processes all look in the pool and see if there is any work for them. If there is, they take it and execute the code. This is why this concept is called self-scheduling. The master process figures out what can be done when, thus scheduling the order of the execution. The master doesn't have to know how many workers are taking things out of the pool. And the workers don't have to know how many other workers there are. When they are done with their unit of work, they put it in the "done" pool and either the master or other workers can see it and perhaps use it in a later calculation.

It sounds somewhat complex, and it is. Thus, it is the challenge of the operating system to make these primitives as easy and understandable to use as possible. For without them the programmer can't optimize the application for multiprocessing, and the user is not realizing the full potential of the hardware and may not think your company's system is fast enough.

The Development of MP UNIX

As early as 1975, people were considering the possibilities of running UNIX on a multiprocessor. At the Naval Postgraduate School in Monterey, California, the MUNIX operating system was specified. Although it never saw the light of day outside of research, MUNIX marked a first in the history of UNIX.

One of the earlier known multiprocessor UNIX systems was developed at Purdue University in 1979. This system was done on a VAX in the master/slave style. In this case, all UNIX kernel code ran on the master, while user code ran on the master or the slave. This clearly makes the master the system bottleneck, but system throughput would be increased to the amount of user code the system had available to run. For specialized applications, this could provide throughput enhancement. Take the example of the program used to format this document. It needs to use the kernel to read in the document from disk. But once the document is in memory, the program has no need for further kernel services until it is ready to print the result. So this program can indeed benefit from a slave. However, if you then place multiple users on the system, each of which is preparing a document, they bottleneck on the master. Regardless of the application, at that point in time the Purdue system was an important first step in the technology.

Meanwhile, at Bell Laboratories a project then known as "UNIX/370" got underway. This system was designed to run UNIX on an MP version of the IBM 370 mainframe. UNIX/370 is especially important, because it was the first system to face the task of protecting kernel data structures via semaphores. This allowed the kernel to run on more than one processor, thus reducing one system bottleneck. The first version of UNIX/370 was done as a port of UNIX layered on the kernel of an IBM operating system called TSS. Its kernel, called SSS, was used to interface UNIX with the hardware. This UNIX system went into production at Bell Labs in 1982 and is still being used today. The layout is shown in Figure 14–16. It was the basis for the system now being shipped by IBM known as IX/370. It proved to be an excellent solution for a rather large project that was developing software for a digital phone switch. This project had over 1000 engineers who had a need to share a common database and environment. They had previously been developing on PDP and VAX computers. The IBM 370 was the fastest general-purpose computer available to try to solve the problem. In 1983 more than 10 machines in the 370 class existed, representing over 100 MIPS of available processor.

This project proved highly successful. It allowed many more users to share large amounts of data, up to 10 gigabytes per system. It also made possible running large software builds in hours that previously took days to complete on the VAX.

Some of the original team from UNIX/370 went on to do a "native" port of UNIX onto a Bell-designed computer known as the 3B20A. The *A* implied an attached processor. But although the system was asymmetric for I/O, the kernel ported onto it was multithreaded. This system achieved at the time greater than 70 percent performance improvement over the single-processor version. Much attention was paid to the contention on the semaphores, and the length of critical sections. Indeed, over 95 percent of the time a process found itself able to get into a critical section without waiting for any other process. As the port was now native, it was trans-

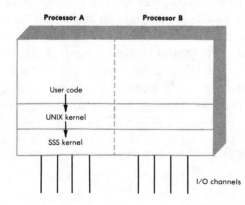

Figure 14–16   UNIX on a IBM 370

parent to all users that there were two processors doing their work. Even for most administration, the systems appeared to be normal UNIX systems.

One of the better implementations of a multiprocessor UNIX system is the Sequent Balance 8000 system. The Sequent represents a machine for which considerable effort was undertaken to reduce the overhead associated with multiprocessing. First, there is a bus-watching system for cache consistency. This alleviates much of the need for the software to manage the cache. The system implemented a set of atomic synchronization variables. Some of these are separate from the bus and very high speed; others are bus mapped and slightly slower, but there are many of them. This allows great flexibility and performance of the synchronization variables mentioned earlier. There is also a separate high-speed chip used for processor synchronization and interrupt distribution. The system is thus capable of running up to 30 National 32032s at a time with near linear throughput speedups. It is a traditional, tightly coupled symmetric system, yet through paying attention to the right areas it is a major step forward in multiprocessor performance. Figure 14–17 shows a block diagram of the Sequent architecture.

As a general-purpose UNIX system, this provides an excellent enhancement for the user. By running multiple users that each have multiple tasks, the system is assured of having enough work to keep its processors busy. The inherent parallelism of the UNIX multitasking interface, as discussed earlier, lends itself well to generating multiple units of work.

That is fine for multiple UNIX users, but what about a different class of problem? Take a look at processors that maybe don't have large numbers of users.

The Alliant Fx8 is designed to solve a more specific task. It is an example of a multiple SIMD machine. There is a complex of general-purpose processors, each of which is capable of controlling one or more vector processors. The software combination of the operating system and

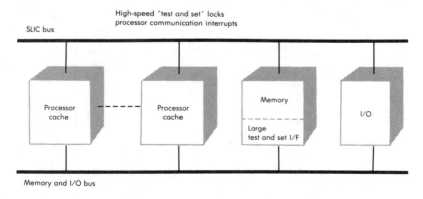

Figure 14–17   Sequent Balance 8000

compiler combine to try to parallelize the user's application. This application is then distributed across the processor complex. The scheduling and control had to be modified to accommodate the more complex structure of this architecture. The success at either automatic or manual parallelization of the program is crucial to this style of machine. However, if the programmer does recode to take advantage of the hardware features, dramatic throughput increases of greater than 100 percent can result. A diagram of this more specific, and more complex, structure is shown in Figure 14–18.

What's in It for the User?

With the migration of UNIX onto these various architectures, the user is now presented with a pleasant variety of choices. The common thread is the familiarity with UNIX. A company can have workstations, department computers, and number crunchers all running a common operating system and presenting a common programming interface.

The bottom line is that UNIX does go well with multiprocessor computers. There is inherent parallelism in the interface that is presented to the user. General-purpose UNIX systems built on multiprocessors can give immediate transparent throughput increases. The ability to push high-throughput tasks such as networking and document formatting onto separate processors frees resources to provide quick response time to interactive users.

As UNIX moves from the technical to commercial markets, the fault tolerance aspects of multiprocessors become big factors. For a bank to lose a computer that is perhaps controlling automatic teller machines is a dis-

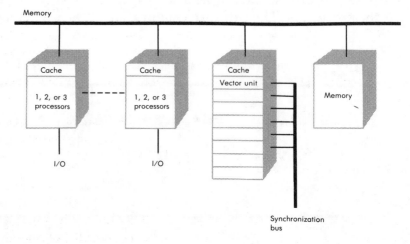

Figure 14–18   Alliant Fx8

aster. Imagine the chaos if the computers running airline reservations systems failed. These customers demand uptime from their systems that can only be achieved through use of multiple processors.

The areas covered here that need to change when you move UNIX to a multiprocessor are not generally visible to a user. Multithreading the kernel, new memory management, and hardware synchronization are all worries for the architects and kernel programmers. How good or poor a job they do will only show up in the end as how well the system performs, and how much it costs.

Some Performance Considerations

How well it performs will be completely dependent on the use. All systems will have bottlenecks at some point in their performance. The key question is: for the applications that a particular user wants to run, does the system perform adequately? What are the bottlenecks that we have looked at so far?

1. I/O. If the disk devices for a system are only accessible by a single processor, this creates a potential bottleneck. Is such a system is to be used as a file server, it may not perform as well as one whose I/O is distributed across multiple processors. On the other hand, it probably would perform better than a single processor trying to do both I/O and computation at the same time.

2. Operating System. Programs that do many system calls will not run as well on processor completes that have a single version of the operating system. They will tend to queue up in waiting for service, and as a result take longer in terms of clock time to execute. However, for a user running code with few demands from the operating system, a system with a single copy of the system may be cheaper, and sometime faster.

3. Memory Bandwidth. A tightly coupled system is potentially bottlenecked by its access to memory. All programs execute from the same physical memory. If these programs all require large and frequent references to memory, the multiple processors may be wasted because the system is trying to satisfy all the demands for memory references. There are many different designs for memory interfaces, ranging from large caches to no cache, a single memory controller to many memory controllers. How far a system needs to go to provide memory bandwidth for the processors is a function of the application that the complex is trying to run.

Be sure to look at benchmarks on a system that indicate the workload you plan to run. Ensure that the target market of the company's product matches your business and application. Finally, and most important of all, try running some of your code on the system before you make a purchase.

In general, UNIX has shown itself to be easily tailorable to many different architectures. It is proving to be a generalist of operating systems. Although perhaps not as good as any specialist given a specific task, it fits in well enough that programmers embrace the familiarity when they move from one machine to the next.

What's Next?

Multiprocessor UNIX is still relatively immature at this point. In order to truly take advantage of parallelism, compilers need to get smarter at detecting inherently parallel sections of code. Tools need to be developed that can generate better code for users in a fashion more conducive to multiprocessors.

In hardware, new technology is being developed that will lead to hundreds of processors instead of tens. This will lead to complete redesign of I/O subsystems, memory management, and the user interface. Busses will get faster and continue to take over synchronization overhead from the software.

The program development environment needs to get better. A system capable of creating and debugging multiprocessor applications requires much more intelligence in tracing and profiling code.

A large body of UNIX libraries and utilities can be rewritten for multiprocessing. Imagine being able to use the fsck(1) (file system consistency) program on your disks all at once, each with a different processor! Some systems can do this today. This can also be done with make(1), so that large program builds can be spread across machines. There are dozens of these utilities that can take advantage of multiprocessing.

Advances will also be made in the administration of the system, for example, the capability to take processors on- and offline for repair. The ability to reassign a processor dynamically across a complex as the load requirements change would also improve efficiency.

Summary

This paper has demonstrated the usefulness of UNIX on multiprocessor computers. It discussed some of the advantages that one architecture may have over another for a specific application. The changes that were required from the system and user standpoint were covered, with an eye toward how the implementation may affect the system. The paper traced the origins of multiprocessor UNIX and described where it may go in the future.

Overall, UNIX can be a powerful tool when placed in the hands of the right system, to solve the right problem.

Acknowledgments

Thanks to all who started it: Bach, Buroff, Goldman, Wilde, Johnstone, Felton, Dvor, Ernst, et al. Thanks to Jim Barton for good ideas.

Bibliography

Bach, M. J. *The Design of the UNIX Operating System.* Englewood Cliffs, N.J.: Prentice-Hall, 1986.

Bach, M. J., and Buroff, S. J. "Multiprocessor UNIX Operating Systems," *AT&T Bell Laboratories Technical Journal* 63, no. 8, October 1984.

Barton, J. M., and Jermoluk, T. A. "Multiprocessor Software Specification." *Silicon Graphics Technical Memorandum.* September 1986.

Beck, Bob, and Kasten, Bob. "VLSI Assist in Building a Multiprocessor UNIX System." *USENIX Summer Conference Proceedings*, 1985, pp. 255–75.

Dijkstra, E. W. "Solution of a Problem in Concurrent Programming Control," *CACM* 8, no. 9, September 1965.

Dongarra, Jack J. "Advanced Architecture Computers." *Argonne National Laboratory Technical Memorandum*, no. 57, October 1985.

Goble, G. H., and Marsh, M. H. "A Dual Processor VAX 11/780." *Purdue University Technical Report*, TR–EE 81–31, September 1981.

Hawley, J. A., and Meyer, W. B. "MUNIX, a Multiprocessing Version of UNIX," Master's Thesis, Naval Postgraduate School, Monterey, California, 1975.

Hwang, Kai, and Briggs, F. A. "Computer Architecture and Parallel Processing." New York: McGraw-Hill, 1984.

Johnstone, Ian. "Strength in Numbers." *UNIX Review* 4, no. 2, February 1986.

Test, Jack. "Concentrix—A UNIX for the Alliant Multiprocessor." *USENIX Winter Conference Proceedings*, 1986.

KEYWORDS

▶ POSIX

▶ USENET domains

▶ X Environment

▶ X3J11 C
Standard

▶ PostScript

▶ MINIX and GNU

▶ IBM PS/2 and
OS/2

▶ Mac II

Paper Synopsis: This final paper analyses the technical and market impact of recent evolutionary developments in UNIX, C, and various application-area standards. Aspects of the general industry trend toward open system standards are examined, with a focus on recent microcomputer developments including the IBM PS/2 and Apple Macintosh II announcements. Implications for the future are discussed.

Eric Raymond is a software designer, independent consultant, and writer in language design, system tools, and portability/standards issues for UNIX and MS-DOS environments. He has been published in *PC Magazine* and the *PC Tech Journal.* Mr. Raymond was also the principal author and researcher of *Portable C and UNIX System Programming* (Prentice-Hall 1987, under the *nom de plume* J. E. Lapin). His current projects include a complete rewrite and enhancement of the USENET software (for the public domain).

## 15

The Future of UNIX and Open System Standards

Eric Raymond

Over the last 15 years the UNIX operating system has grown out of roots in computer science research, and academia to become an important force in mainstream computing. UNIX has come to dominate a number of technical application and development areas, especially in the workstation and minicomputer markets. Its example has created transforming pressures, even in many areas of the industry in which the operating system itself is not generally accepted (many features of MS-DOS releases after 2.0, for example, are modeled on UNIX). And it is now assuming a wider role in business computing.

To understand the probable pattern of UNIX's future growth, it needs to be examined in the context of other ongoing changes in the computer industry. A powerful synergy between UNIX software technology and other trends in software standardization and hardware design is developing. This paper looks at UNIX's present and future in that context and touches on some important structural changes the combination may bring to computing.

Much of UNIX's appeal has been in the promise of application portability across different families of machines, from desktop to supercomputer. End users want to avoid having to throw costly software investments away at each change in vendor and new generation of hardware; software developers want a uniform environment in order to lower their development and maintenance costs and to reach more potential customers. These economic realities are what is behind the increasing trend toward development and use of UNIX software.

In the real world of work environments that use heterogeneous mixes of machine types, *portability* is the ability to transform an application from a collection of source code written in a common high-level language into a set of executables for each of the target machines without having to do a significant amount of modification for each. For this to work, relevant parts of the software environment of each machine have to be guaranteed to look alike.

UNIX is one of the most successful examples of a functioning *open system standard,* a set of conventions and capabilities that hides differences in the underlying system and enables software environments to look alike to applications.

For an open system standard to be valuable, it must have:

- a consistent, well-documented interface that can cleanly express all the usual kinds of actions used in the class of applications it addresses

- implementability across a wide range of hardware (multiple processor families and sizes of system)

- sponsorship by an established standards body that will be responsible for keeping conformance requirements publicized and relatively stable.

The UNIX operating system itself has all of these properties. In addition, UNIX's technical strengths well equip it to serve as a base for open system standards in high-level languages, software development tools, and (most importantly) application areas such as graphics and communications. The effect of these combinations can be much more than the sum of their parts.

The development of powerful desktop computer hardware is the most important single cofactor accelerating the open system trend. The computer industry's hardware technologies, driven in the 1950s and '60s by mainframe engineering and during the '70s by minicomputer designs, is now driven by the technology of microcomputers. Customer expectations are likewise increasingly conditioned by what they see on desktops rather than in computer rooms. This has created a sort of democratization of computing and a huge demand for powerful portable software to control the bewildering array of hardware alternatives available to the developer and user.

It seems most likely, then, that the future of UNIX and other open system standards will be hammered out in the microcomputer market. Accordingly, the remainder of this paper will examine developments in that arena as well as developments in the UNIX operating system proper and in general open system standards.

Recent Developments in UNIX Environment Standardization

UNIX has been the leading contender for the role of general-purpose operating system standard since it was reimplemented in C in the mid-1970s. No other system has ever combined UNIX's level of capability with its breadth of hardware base. UNIX implementations run on literally hundreds of different machine types; no other commercially significant operating system has ever migrated successfully off the processor family it was born on.

But UNIX itself suffered from some standardization problems (see Daniel Franklin's paper). And by itself, UNIX was incomplete; it didn't include adequate standards for (to name just three areas) the C programming language, networking, or desktop-style windowing interfaces. The paper will examine important developments in UNIX standardization and these application areas.

AT&T Takes the Lead: The Impact of the System V Interface Definition

The key recent development in the standardization of UNIX has been the widespread acceptance of AT&T's System V Interface Definition (called SVID, or "the Purple Book," after its cover and by analogy with Kernighan and Ritchie's famous "White Book," *The C Programming Language*).

In the technical and standards world, despite internal troubles AT&T has successfully cooperated with other UNIX standards groups to avoid conflicts and duplication. As a result, the various UNIX-like programming environment descriptions now being prepared by standards-making bodies are compatible to a remarkable and unprecedented degree.

More specifically, the X/OPEN environment standard (informally called the "Green Book") now being developed by AT&T and a consortium of European computer manufacturers, is committed to SVID compatibility. The IEEE's P1003 Portable Operating System Standard (informally and generally known as POSIX) will also be SVID-compatible—though in that latter case it might almost be more appropriate to say that SVID is POSIX-compatible; the SVID Edition 2 indicated that the rules for some system operations would be changed to match some superior technical proposals made in early drafts of the POSIX document.

The SVID standard also now has commercial teeth, as large customers including General Motors and several agencies of the U.S. government are now formally requiring conformance from their suppliers.

Vendors have responded to this trend. One can now take pretty much for granted that new hardware in the general-purpose computing market will be offered with a UNIX option. Even IBM now offers, however reluctantly, SVID-compatible UNIX across almost its entire strategic product line, from the PC/AT on up. These are developments that would have been next to unthinkable even five years ago.

One important piece of recent news in this area is the early 1987 announcement by AT&T and Microsoft that XENIX and System V UNIX are to be (effectively) merged on the 80386 microprocessor. Future XENIX versions on the 80386 will be SVID-compatible and will be able to run old XENIX applications from the 80286, eliminating a possible source of division in the 80386 applications world.

Berkeley Redux: The Long, Slow Fall of BSD UNIX

Another important development in UNIX standards has been more difficult to see, because it hinges on the absence of something rather than its presence. During the four years between the University of California at Berkeley's release of 4.1BSD in 1981 to AT&T's massive commitment to System V UNIX at the beginning of 1985, one of the great debates in the UNIX world was whether AT&T's or Berkeley's UNIX would define the future of UNIX and UNIX-like operating systems.

The debate involved more than pure technical points; it represented a contrast between two cultures. The BSD system, which had generally accepted technical superiority over the AT&T Version 7, System III, and early System V implementations it competed with, came out of the University of California at Berkeley. It was beloved of counterculture-influenced hackers who often delighted in setting themselves against an AT&T corporate vision of UNIX they regarded as narrow and timid.

The BSD system and this attitude became well-established at UNIX sites with very technical and demanding missions; users in scientific, graphics, CAD/CAM, and other engineering areas gravitated toward it. Commercial shops, on the other hand, tended to go with "safer" AT&T versions descended from System III. The rivalry became more intense after 1982, when 4.2BSD introduced changes that made the semantics of BSD system calls incompatible with the AT&T versions in some important areas. The success of 4.2BSD vendors like Sun Microsystems raised a serious possibility that the UNIX market would be divided and possibly badly hurt by the schism, with two different and even possibly mutually hostile UNIX communities heading off in divergent evolutionary directions.

From 1987's perspective, it is clear that this has not been and probably will not be a significant problem. Starting with the System V release 2 announcement in January 1985, AT&T has successfully moved to co-opt the most attractive features of the BSD releases. Berkeley's vi editor, the csh shell, its mailer, and a near-equivalent of its job control facility have been added to the System V toolset. An enhanced version of BSD's term-cap/curses screen-handling libraries is supported, and equivalents of other important BSD library routines are promised for System V release 3. And the System V C compiler has been enhanced to permit the use of BSD-style flexnames.

Meanwhile, the original Berkeley team has broken up. The Fast File System, a 4.2BSD enhancement intended to speed up system throughput, has turned out to be considerably slower at supporting a typical multiuser job mix than the code it replaced; it is now widely considered a technical failure. Legal problems with the networking code delayed the release of 4.3BSD, which has failed to generate much interest, even for the existing 4.2 user base.

Berkeley UNIX, source of so many of the improvements that make recent AT&T UNIX versions more comfortable for developers and users, may be destined to pass into history, or survive mostly as an alternative mode on SVID-compatible systems. To regain the initiative it held in the early 1980s, the BSD environment would need to host some radical new development in software technology (but see the last section of this paper for one system that may point in that direction).

Some vendors now offer double-headed implementations that can appear as either a System V or 4.2BSD, at the user's choice. This may represent a significant positive trend for BSD UNIX's future.

Related Developments in Languages and Applications Areas

As mentioned earlier, UNIX is one of the classic case studies in the success of open system standards. It is not surprising, then, that users and vendors in the UNIX community have led the industry in the development of such standards in several applications and development-related areas.

C Language Standardization

The original standard for the C language was Kernighan and Ritchie's *The C Programming Language* (often called simply the "White Book"), which described C as it existed at Bell Laboratories around 1978. Though it had become something of a classic in the literature of computer science during the ensuing five years, the text contained a number of ambiguities and was beginning to show its age.

A new description, updated to take account of the evolutionary changes in the C language, was needed. Accordingly, the X3J11 committee of the

American National Standards Institute began work on a formal international standard for the C programming language in late 1983.

The committee's aim was to specify a language that would be upward-compatible with that described in original Kernighan and Ritchie C book, but also include more modern features, such as enumerated types, the void type, and structure passing.

The ANSI draft proposal introduces some entirely new features as well. One introduces a method for declaring expected types of function arguments that can be used to check the correctness of function calls across module boundaries, bringing some of the functionality for the UNIX lint program checker into the compiler for non-UNIX environments. Other additions allow finer control of the extent to which a compiler can optimize code and reorder expressions. Still others enhance the capabilities of the C preprocessor.

The ANSI effort was endorsed by the International Standards Organization (ISO) and assisted by close cooperation from AT&T and major hardware vendors. Given the wide and increasing popularity of C as a development language, the standard can be expected to have a significant impact on application portability across the entire computer industry, particularly (as with MS-DOS) on systems already supporting some UNIX-like features.

The ANSI committee has been very successful at mustering support for its work even before of issuance of a final document. Many C compiler developers (including Microsoft, Lattice, Manx, and other key vendors in the MS-DOS world) have already incorporated support for the new language features in their products and for the standard's C library routines, which are explicitly modeled on those found in the SVID.

The X3J11 Proposed Draft C standard is now in its second cycle of review. Completion is expected sometime in 1988. Close liaison is being maintained between X3J11, AT&T and the POSIX group in an explicit attempt to keep all three standards compatible and cooperating (to the point where the POSIX draft refers to the X3J11 draft and vice versa). Among other things, this should tend to accelerate the traditional synergy between C and UNIX, creating more and more situations where adoption of C as a development language smoothes transitions to an open-system UNIX environment.

The C++ implementations now reaching commercial availability also will conform to the X3J11 standard (Keith Gorlen's paper earlier in this volume conveys some of the exciting possibilities of this new language). It is expected that an ANSI X3J11-conforming C++ compiler will be released as part of the standard development toolset of System V release 3. ANSI C conformance should make the transition from C to C++ almost painless (and correspondingly more rapid) to the net benefit of application developers and users.

Open Systems Standards in Networking

Local and wide area networking continues to make technical progress in the face of a wait-and-see attitude from most major commercial customers. Open system standards are important in these areas because they determine the extent to which equipment from different vendors can be made to communicate with each other without special translation facilities. The IEEE 802.5 "thin Ethernet" cabling scheme has been steadily gaining user and vendor support against numerous alternatives (including IBM's Token Ring network and the AT&T Starlan). Charles Spurgeon's paper in this book addresses technical issues connected with this type of network and touches on some of the reasons for its increasing popularity.

The major ongoing debates in the network standards world center around the International Standards Organization's seven-layer Open System Interconnection (OSI) model for network protocols. This model provides a framework for compatibility and gatewaying between different network protocols. As with UNIX itself, General Motors and the U.S. government are among large customers pushing the transition to an open system model.

Multivendor factory-automation demonstrations of robotic fabrication featuring the GM-sponsored, OSI-conforming Manufacturing Automation Protocol (MAP) have become a fixture at major trade shows since early 1986. GM's MAP factory software runs under UNIX System V.

The Berkeley UNIX versions supported pioneers in the network world with kernel code for TCP/IP, a non-OSI network protocol developed in the late 1970s by the Department of Defense (DOD) for use in its ARPANET project, a nationwide network of DOD contractors and university research sites. Though TCP/IP retains a large and vocal constituency in the networking world, its advocates suffered a major defeat in late 1986, when a U.S. government multiagency task force on network standards issued a policy recommendation specifying OSI as the preferred framework for future federal government networking. The report also dealt something of a blow to IBM's SNA (Systems Network Architecture) proprietary standard by recommending against further SNA procurement.

The Domainizing of USENET

A less visible—but possibly equally important—development has been the absorption of the UNIX world's uucp network into the Internet addressing scheme (for more on USENET, see Harry Henderson's paper). The Internet, originally an outgrowth of the Department of Defense's TCP/IP and ARPANET projects, is a network of networks defined by a tree of cooperating gateways and a set of address-handling conventions.

Before uucp became an Internet zone, uucp email had to be explicitly routed through a chain of machines from source to destination, requiring users to know the topology of the uucp network. Now, an increasing number of UNIX users can use position-independent Internet addressing and expect the routing to be handled by a smart mailer. All the software to do this is in the public domain, freely available throughout the UNIX community.

These Internet conventions are organized around the concept of a *domain*, a collection of machines that some given gateway machine will always know how to reach. For each domain an Internet mailer knows about, it must know either how to route to every machine in that domain or how to get to a another machine that is a gateway for that domain. This lets users send messages to other machines without caring about the route.

This is an important demonstration of principle. It proves that smart nonproprietary software can bridge between physical networks using different transport media and protocol standards. It strengthens the Internet's claim to have set addressing and message-format standards applicable to future public wide area networks (such as the Integrated Services Digital Network (ISDN) being developed as a common digital protocol for the U.S. and international telephone net). It may, in fact, have given Internet the critical breadth of support needed to establish it as the nucleus of a uniform addressing standard for worldwide networking.

PostScript: A Standard for Desktop Publishing

The original UNIX applications area in the early '70s was document preparation, and most UNIX versions include powerful document formatting tools. These tools ran essentially in batch mode and were driven by a macro language of rather intimidating complexity. Though quite effective for the expert user, they did not tend to appeal to novices and clerical users.

More recently, UNIX has been second only to the Macintosh environment as a platform for cutting-edge activity in desktop publishing. The trend toward graphics-driven What You See Is What You Get (WYSIWYG) systems has been expressed most elegantly in a generation of packages (beginning with the ground-breaking Interleaf composition software) that were designed to run on UNIX workstations with bit-mapped displays. That area is expected to be one of the strongest growth areas in commercial UNIX systems during the next five years.

The state of open system standards in desktop publishing, then, can be expected to have powerful effects on the UNIX market. Recent developments look quite promising.

In early 1987, IBM committed to support Adobe Systems, Inc.'s PostScript language for laser printer control on its laser printer product line. PostScript, a procedural image-description language first implemented on the Apple LaserWriter, has more recently found increasing success as an bitmap-image description standard on a number of higher-end nonimpact printers from U.S. and Japanese manufacturers.

The IBM endorsement ratifies PostScript's claim to be the dominant open system standard for control of nonimpact printers. Rival claimants such as Hewlett-Packard's Printer Control Language (PCL, used on the popular LaserJet printer series) will now face more difficult futures.

Printer cost may drop dramatically as generic PostScript control hardware becomes available. Phoenix Technology, the major manufacturer of IBM PC and AT clone BIOS chips, is said to be presently at work developing the first non-Adobe PostScript-on-a-chip hardware.

These developments can be expected to speed the transition of the high-resolution printing peripheral into a commodity technology, accelerating the growth of the desktop publishing market.

The X Environment: A Nonproprietary Windowing System

The first months of 1987 have also seen an explosion of interest in the X windowing system released late last year by the Massachusetts Institute of Technology's Project Athena. Project Athena is an attempt to built for MIT a complete campus network, integrating hardware from many vendors through use of open system standards including UNIX. X is Project Athena's windowing facility; it provides source tools for a powerful, hardware-independent window system interface reminiscent of the Smalltalk or Macintosh environments that can be run on either BSD or AT&T UNIX versions.

One interesting aspect of X's recent history is the way it has affected Sun Microsystem's goal of establishing a proprietary standard in windowing with its recently announced NeWS (Network Window System). NeWS has an edge in power and flexibility over X, but X has the advantage that full source is available for nominal fees, and MIT's policies are aimed at encouraging low-cost or no-cost redistribution. Following weeks of vigorous technical debate on USENET and in other forums, Sun has now publicly committed to support X and develop means to permit X facilities to be used within a NeWS environment.

Trends in UNIX Hardware

One major impediment to the spread of the UNIX OS and related open system standards has been the expense of the computer hardware required to support them. As a multitasking operating system, UNIX requires relatively sophisticated hardware support including a memory management unit (MMU) and real-time clock. For reasonable performance, a large (full 32 bit) address and at least a megabyte or two of main store is important (smaller systems tend to be brought to their knees by the cost of swapping processes in and out of RAM).

Until very recently, hardware this capable was priced out of reach for many small-business and personal users, and the lowest-end UNIX systems were sold into the engineering and scientific markets at a minimum of $10,000 a unit. With the advent of 32 bit very large scale integration (VLSI) chips like the Motorola 68020 and Intel 80286 and 80386, this situation is rapidly changing. These chips have the features needed to support good performance of a UNIX environment.

At the same time, increasingly sophisticated users in the MS-DOS, IBM PC/XT/AT world are finding the single-tasking nature of MS-DOS too restrictive for their application requirements, creating a natural market for cheap UNIX hardware. This section looks at recent developments in that area and what they suggest about UNIX's future.

The Macintosh II: Apple Enters the UNIX World

Apple Computer recently announced the long-awaited Macintosh II for July release. The new machine will be an open-architecture, Nu-Bus based 68020 box with Macintosh Finder Environment and UNIX (SVID) support (via an optional MMU), 8 Nu-Bus expansion slots, color graphics, and an optional slave 80286 board for running MS-DOS software. Nu-Bus, originally developed by Texas Instruments for its microcomputer hardware, has become an IEEE-sponsored open system standard. The Macintosh ROM software, of course, remains proprietary. It is not yet clear to what extent UNIX tasks will have access to the Macintosh ROM facilities, but rumor has it that the Mac toolbox ROM is to be made reentrant.

The Macintosh II breaks new ground in that it is the first offering by a personal computer maker (other than IBM) of a machine clearly positioned to compete in the color workstation market. It will be instructive to see how it fares against offerings from (on the one hand) traditional workstation vendors, and (on the other) the oncoming horde of 80386 clones (discussed later). Its existence has already pressured some major workstation manufacturers to cut prices on their products by as much as 36 percent.

The combination of relatively low-cost access to the huge array of UNIX tools, and the added value of the excellent Macintosh user interface could give this machine huge potential. In particular, Apple may well be able to use it to consolidate its lead in desktop publishing and related areas into a commanding position in that rapidly expanding market.

AT&T: What Comes Next?

In the two years since AT&T's watershed announcement of System V release 2, the company that nurtured UNIX has been less than successful at selling UNIX hardware. Indeed, AT&T's performance in the hardware market has made a sharp and ironic contrast with its success in establishing UNIX as an open operating system standard.

Sales of the AT&T 3Bx minicomputers are sluggish. The otherwise excellent UNIX PC product was weighed down by high pricing and a buggy DOS bridge option; it has fared so poorly since its introduction that AT&T has canceled its contract with the machine's builder, Convergent Technologies. AT&T's desktop computer line now consists entirely of foreign-made PC/XT and AT clones.

Much of this can be attributed to AT&T's lack of experience in competitive markets; most of the rest can be blamed on mental and organizational habits retained from predivestiture days. The pattern of reorganizations and executive departures at computer-related AT&T divisions also suggests that attempts to define a mission for them have been hampered by political infighting.

In sum, though Bell Labs has remained a very influential backer of UNIX, the larger AT&T seems unable so far to integrate this advantage into a consensus about corporate goals.

IBM Drops the Other Shoe: The Personal System/2 Announcements

In April 1987, IBM made its long-awaited announcement of the replacements to the six-year-old PC/XT/AT line, revealing at the same time that it has already ceased production of the PC and XT. As had been widely expected, the new machines depend on IBM-proprietary technology and are aimed primarily at the Fortune 500 market; but they do offer compatibility modes that will support software developed for PC/XT/AT machines.

Unlike the IBM PC, the PS/2 machines were clearly designed to push the state of the art in microcomputer hardware. Extensive use of surface-mount components and custom VLSI enabled them to build graphics support, serial and parallel port, clock/calendar, and other features onto the motherboard itself, obviating the need for many expansion slots (this is also expected to increase reliability). The on-board graphics capability, which is equivalent to the now-discontinued PGA but supports CGA and EGA as well, is truly impressive. Disk throughput and general system performance is also substantially better than equivalent machines in the older line—and the prices of the new machines are lower.

The Model 30 replaces the old PC and XT. The three new high-end models are the ones that can be expected to affect the UNIX market. The Models 50 and 60 are AT equivalent; the Model 80 (release scheduled for mid-1987) is an 80386-based machine. All three use a new proprietary bus structure called the Micro Channel Architecture (MCA) that is expected to be quite difficult to clone.

These machines will run an MS-DOS version, but the intended native environment for them is a new single-user, multitasking operating system called Operating System/2 (already dubbed OS/2) which is not scheduled for release until early 1988. The base version of OS/2, which includes a graphical, window-oriented Presentation Manager similar to but more powerful than the present Microsoft Windows, will be made available to third parties by Microsoft. IBM plans an "Extended Version," including database and SNA facilities.

The PS/2 line's effect on the future of UNIX will largely depend on the extent to which IBM can draw present MS-DOS users into using proprietary features of OS/2. As a single-user system, OS/2 is at a significant disadvantage in many computing environments. If OS/2 nevertheless becomes widely established as a multitasking system, IBM may lock in a large part of the microcomputer market for the next decade and seriously impact UNIX's growth. IBM's strategists appear to be attempting a microcomputer reprise of the System/360 strategy that cemented IBM's mainframe dominance in the mid-1960s.

On the other hand, IBM promised that AIX, the System V-style UNIX supported on the RT PC (which remains in production) will also be supported on the PS/2 Model 80. DOS tasks in an AIX window will be supported.

In fact, initial reaction to the PS/2 line from both technical and financial analysts has been lukewarm. Having been given both plain DOS and UNIX-with-DOS-tasks as alternatives on these machines, it seems unlikely that either users or developers will rush into the embraces of a new proprietary operating system with the speed or unanimity IBM is hoping for. And the proprietary nature of the MCA may actually protect the clone makers, giving them a natural market among micro users that want to continue using the existing AT-bus hardware.

The year-long lag time between OS/2's announcement and expected commercial availability is a serious weakness (it may be that the release of the PS/2 line was moved up to position the PS-80 directly against the Macintosh II). The clone-makers now have nearly a year to reverse-engineer the PS/2 before IBM can sell OS/2's proprietary features. For now,

IBM will have to fight the Macintosh II with DOS 3.3 only. And neither the Macintosh II nor the PS/2 machines will offer true multitasking in their native operating systems until 1988 at the earliest. The only operating system guaranteed to run on both machines (as well as older AT-class hardware) is UNIX.

IBM clearly wants very much to re-establish the dominance of the microcomputer market that it held from the release of the IBM PC in 1981 up to the great clone wars of 1985–86. It is especially sensitive to the erosion of its market share and influence among large commercial customers. The PS/2 line is built and positioned as a tool to lure large users back into the embrace of IBM-proprietary environments.

Accomplishing this won't be easy, even for IBM. To create a market-dominating constituency for OS/2 on IBM hardware:

- Users must be persuaded to throw over their investment in less expensive PC/XT/AT clone hardware and turn their backs on compatible generic 80386 systems.

- OS/2 has to offer enough added value over DOS to justify the building of many non-DOS-compatible applications, which must then displace well-entrenched MS-DOS software in corporate routines.

- Users and developers must be persuaded to ignore the fact that by moving to UNIX they get a common system between the the AT, the 80386 clones, the PS/2 machines, and the Mac II that will still allow use of old MS-DOS software.

- Clonemakers have to fail to reverse-engineer the PS/2 ROM and MCA bus.

Under current market conditions, it seems most unlikely that all these conditions will be satisfied. In particular, the OS/2 Presentation Manager (from which IBM and Microsoft clearly expect to derive much of their edge) may well turn out to be as much of a nonstarter as IBM's previous attempt in that direction via Topview; Microsoft Windows, on which the Presentation Manager is based, is becoming better accepted among developers, but it is not yet used by any MS-DOS product with significant market acceptance.

Within weeks of the PS/2 announcement, a consortium of PC-clone manufacturers announced that they are ready to produce equivalents of the VLSI glue logic on the PS/2 motherboards, and the interface specifications of the PS/2 ROM and MCA have been published by IBM. The manufacturers variously estimate that six to nine months will be required for reverse-engineering and production design of the clones. It is therefore expected that PS/2 look-alikes will appear on the market before OS/2's commercial release, and possibly before the end of 1987. This would have the effect of forcing the PS/2 market open and might leave IBM with the same unpleasant choice between all-out price war and abandonment of the market that it faced against the PC/AT clones.

It is also a strong possibility that Microport or some other low-cost UNIX vendor might take advantage of IBM's publication of the PS/2 ROM interface specification to release a PS/2 System V with DOS task support months before OS/2 or AIX become available.

Generic 80386 Systems: The End of the Processor Wars?

A little-noted event that is a first for the UNIX world is the recent first appearance of generic 80386 systems that are both UNIX-capable and BIOS-compatible with the huge pool of 8088 and 80286-based MS-DOS and PC-DOS machines.

These 80386 clone machines follow on the tremendous early success of the Compaq 386, but they are much cheaper. At the time of this writing, one company in Florida offers a complete 14.2 MHz 386 system (board, power supply, case, monochrome monitor and floppy drives) for around $2800. At current prices, a 40 megabyte hard-drive and UNIX system software could be added for a total cost of less than $3500. And prices are certain to go down, not up, as the "rice-box" clone-makers of the Pacific Rim get into the market.

This hardware can be used with new, inexpensive UNIX ports such as Microport V/AT, which offers configurations costing as little as $149 and no more than $350 that adhere strictly to the System V Interface Definition and offers the latest System V release 2 features.

The 80386-based clone systems will offer desktop-computer buyers exactly what they've been wishing for—low-cost, full 32 bit, multiuser capable systems that:

- are not controlled by any single vendor
- can use all the peripheral hardware designed for the IBM PC/XT/AT market
- that can run all the old MS-DOS software inside a UNIX window

Current 80286 UNIXes from major vendors (Microsoft, SCO, and Microport) and their applications will also run on these machines without modification. These systems offer perhaps the stiffest competition IBM's PS/2 line will face, and may create enormous opportunities—and enormous dislocations—in the wider UNIX marketplace.

Technical Futures

Leading-edge operating system development in the UNIX community is taking three major directions. The first, commercial enhancement of UNIX by AT&T, has already been discussed. This section covers the second and third streams: academic efforts to move UNIX to exotic architectures and two "UNIX-for-the-people" projects that aim to create nonproprietary emulations of substantial pieces of the UNIX environment.

UNIX on Exotic Architectures

In 1986 and 1987, the leading-edge work in UNIX-like operating systems has been more and more concentrated in the area of UNIX implementations adapted for networks, distributed systems and non-von Neumann architectures. This trend well reflects the dominant concerns of the computer science research community in the 1980s so far.

AT&T's own contribution is, of course, the streams abstraction and remote file system facility of System V release 3 (see John Emrich's paper for more details). The powerful new interprocess communication mechanisms in System V also address these areas.

While sufficient to enable major advances in networking, however, AT&T's advances don't tackle the fundamental reorganization of the UNIX kernel needed to support true distributed systems. Various university research teams are doing just that, with encouraging early results that are being watched carefully by commercial vendors. These may well lead to significant commercial uses and software standardization within the next three to five years.

At the time of writing, the most mature of these projects appears to be the Mach system under development at Carnegie-Mellon University. This system, which is source-compatible with 4.3BSD UNIX (and even binary-compatible on the DEC VAX minicomputer), reorganizes the kernel as a group of communicating "lightweight" (that is, low-overhead) tasks suitable for distribution on a loosely or tightly coupled multiprocessor architecture (see Tom Jermoluk's paper for discussion of some technical issues in such systems). Similar aims and approaches can be found in other projects such as the Stanford V Kernel.

The lowest level of the Mach system is a spare but powerful set of communications, memory management and task-spawning primitives that together constitute a sort of subkernel layer on top of which 4.3BSD-compatible kernel calls are implemented. This approach would be just as applicable to an SVID-compatible system.

This arrangement has numerous advantages over conventional kernels beyond its suitability for multiprocessor environments. One is that dynamic configuration of device drivers and other "kernel" services such as process scheduling and file-system management is made much easier; versions can be plugged and unplugged from the kernel process cluster. Another is that the system is inherently event-driven, and so more suitable for real- time programming (but see Geoff Kuenning's paper for discussion of the inherent problems with mixing real-time and time-sharing functions in an operating system), communications and similar applications areas.

The Mach project is now maneuvering to put as much of its code as possible (given the limits of AT&T and BSD source licenses) into the public domain. This is an explicit attempt to stimulate development of UNIX workalikes based on the Mach kernel structure. It may point the way to the next major evolutionary change in the UNIX operating system.

Free UNIX: Some Radical Alternatives

UNIX's peculiar history has given many of its partisans a strong (though generally unstated) belief that, though UNIX's name and sources may legally belong to AT&T, UNIX rightfully belongs to the community of hackers that built it and proselytized for it. AT&T has been aware since UNIX's earliest days that the hacker community is a critical factor in UNIX's success; accordingly, UNIX source is widely available for inspection on publicly accessible university machines, and AT&T has a long-standing tacit policy of winking at technically illegal possession of source by UNIX aficionados as long as such sources are not directly used for commercial gain.

As a result of this process, AT&T may have failed the legal tests necessary to retain trade-secret or copyright control of the UNIX source. But AT&T has enough lawyers and influence to make a test case very costly. The situation is fraught with moral and legal ambiguities that neither AT&T nor the hacker community wants to risk seeing resolved in favor of the other. The result is a delicate balance of power, an understanding by which most hackers accept AT&T's continuing to profit from the system while they continue to exchange system fixes, enhancements, and lore in ways that technically violate the AT&T license terms.

Some UNIX aficionados remain more radical. Richard M. Stallman, inventor of the tremendously popular EMACS editor and one of the leading researchers in the heyday of MIT's famed Artificial Intelligence Labratory (and more recently the subject of a special section in Steven Levy's book *Hackers: Heroes of the Computer Revolution*, Doubleday, 1984) is one of them. He has founded and run a project called GNU (for "GNU's Not UNIX!") that in fact aims to produce a complete, portable emulation of the UNIX kernel and toolset that will be available for the cost of source duplication. Volunteer assistance has come from many members of the UNIX community, including myself and others who do not share Mr. Stallman's motivating belief that proprietary control of software is morally wrong. GNU can at least provide a hedge against possible future attempts by AT&T to take the UNIX software under stricter control.

At the time of writing, the GNU project has produced a nearly complete set of utilities. The GNU C compiler has just been released for beta test, and work on a full kernel is proceeding. There are obvious problems with the concept of a shareware UNIX; in particular, maintenance and debugging of the system will be up to its user community and may be spotty. New hardware standards and a sufficiently large pool of talent may reduce these problems to manageable size, but what effect the system will have on the general market remains to be seen.

Andy Tannenbaum's MINIX project is less ambitious (Tannenbaum works for AT&T!). Like GNU, it is a user-maintained look-alike of the UNIX OS. Unlike GNU, it is intentionally restricted to one hardware family—the IBM PC, XT, and AT—and consequently accepts some significant limitations in features and performance. The main intended use of MINIX is as a teaching tool and vehicle for casual hacking, rather than as a serious alternative to larger UNIX implementations. Nevertheless, MINIX has developed a large and active community of codevelopers during the year of its first release.

The Near Future in UNIX Systems

One important trend, particularly in the microcomputer market, is that all major manufacturers are being backed into supporting an SVID-compatible operating system standard by market pressures. Another is the rapid advance of powerful generic 32 bit microprocessor hardware, particularly in brandname 68020-based systems like the Mac II and (perhaps more importantly) cheap generic 80386 hardware. Any important constraint on near-future developments will be the demand for continued support of old MS-DOS applications.

This combination of forces has very definite implications for near-future design and purchasing decisions. This last discussion offers some observations and predictions of the effects of this new technology.

The development of a true commodity market in no-compromise UNIX-capable micros, paralleling and absorbing the present commodity market in MS-DOS micros and competing with IBM's new PS/2 series and the Mac II, may be well begun by the time this text reaches print. This will have several important consequences:

- The UNIX workstation market established by Sun, Apollo, and a host of small 68000-box vendors (and recently entered by DEC and IBM with the MicroVax and RT PC respectively) is in for a massive attack from the low end. Small companies that get most of their margins from hardware and can't afford the re-engineering to reposition their products outside the 80386's performance range will get plowed under; a few larger companies may get their fingers burnt and back out of the market. Sun and a few others will probably continue to do well, though at much lower margins.

- Barring the discovery of some crippling implementation bug in the 80386 (something more fundamental than the known problem with 32 bit multiply in early releases of the chip) the era of the 68000 family as the microprocessor of choice for UNIX boxes is probably over. The 68020 is comparable in performance with an 80386, and the 68030 will be much better—but now that Intel offers a real 32 bit address space, the 68000 family's superior programming model may count for very little against the prospect of running MS-DOS tasks in a window, the weight of IBM's marketing muscle behind the PS/2 machines, and the sheer volume of the clone avalanche.

- UNIX and open system standards of all kinds (C, PostScript, OSI networking, X, and others not discussed here) will continue to increase in technical and market importance. The commodity PC/XT/AT hardware market has come to depend on the existence of public hardware standards and non proprietary software standards; the nascent 80386-clone market is founded on them. And UNIX is the only common operating system for the AT, the PS/2 machines, the Mac II, and the clones.

Conclusion

Technology, economics, and user awareness are driving the mainstream computer marketplace toward a single global programming environment standard. Industry observers have also seen that UNIX is the operating system best positioned to meet this need. But this much has been clear to those who would see for a long time; it's old news.

UNIX has been an up-and-comer for 10 years now. Many reports on its technical successes have predicted a central position for it in utopian visions of the computing future. What is new in 1987 is that a critical level of standardization and vendor acceptance has been passed, and the remaining political and psychological obstacles left to a UNIX-based, open system computing future are visibly crumbling away. It's an exciting time to be in the industry, because those utopian visions are beginning to come true.

Index

Timing facilities of real-time applications, 362
"Tinker-toy approach" of UNIX, 7, 12
Todino, Grace, 89
Torbett, Michael, 191
Transaction-processing systems, 345–47
Transparent mapping, 274–75
Transport Level Interface (TLI)
　activities, 297–300
　connection establishment on the, 299
　connection release on the, 299–300
　data transfer on the, 299
　defined, 261
　local management on the, 298–99
　overview of the, 295–97
　RFS using the, 281
　role of STREAMS with the, 296
　summary of the, 300
　time diagram example for the, 302–3
Transport Library Interface, 296
trap built-in command in the Bourne shell
　to write scripts that can trap signals,
　135, 431
Traps, 388
Truscott, Tom, 50, 51
TTY architecture, 278–79
Tty driver, 284
typeset built-in command in the Korn shell
　to change shell attributes, 144–46

U

ULTRIX version of UNIX, 321
Unified Electronic Messaging Facility, 114
UNIX
　changes for multiprocessors
　　incorporated in, 472–79
　as a cross-development system, 365
　on the 80286 microprocessor, 387–96
　environment standardization, recent
　　developments in, 489–91
　Ethernet compatibility with, 336,
　　338–39
　exotic architectures to run, 501–2
　file system of, 32–33
　free, 502–3
　future of, 39–40, 486–504
　genealogy, 27
　hardware trends, 495–500
　historical development of, 2–40
　multitasking model, 468–72
　not suited for demanding real-time
　　tasks, 364, 365
　performance on the 80286, 395–96
　portability of, 24–25

　portability of an application running
　　under, 487–88
　portability of C and, 23–24
　processes in, 387–90
　real-time, 342–69
　user interface problems with, 3, 4, 12,
　　18
　workstation market, 503–4
UNIX Communications, 60, 74, 90
UNIX mailers, 93–121. *See also* Electronic
　mail (email)
UNIX Programming Environment, The, 13
UNIX System User's Manual, 182
UNIX User's Manual, 182
UNIX World, 90
UNIX/RT real-time UNIX, 369
"UNIX/370," 480
UNOS system (Charles Rover Data
　Systems), 365
Upstream queue, 291
USENET news network, 42–90. *See also*
　Newsgroups
　asterisks for emphasis in, 78
　background, 50–67
　bug fixes and software revisions
　　discussed using the, 46–47
　CompuServe and The Source compared
　　with the, 52
　convention for emphasizing text in the,
　　44
　cooperative structuring of the, 52–53
　creative punctuation in the, 78
　domainizing of the, 493–94
　filing and saving articles on the, 72–74
　as forum for discussion of political,
　　social, philosophical, and religious
　　issues, 47–49
　joining the, 52–53
　"netiquette" of the, 89
　news reading and writing process for
　　the, 59–66
　newsgroups and their organization in
　　the, 53–64
　no printed manuals for the, 43–44
　orientation for the, 74
　posting original articles in the, 82–85
　product or vendor information obtained
　　from the, 45–46
　"quoting" mechanism of the, 77
　reading articles on the, 67–72
　replying to an article on the, 74–78
　samples of messages in the, 44–50
　sources of information about, 88–90
　spread of the, 51
　UNIX file hierarchy to store and
　　manipulate news articles in the,
　　64–67

Tricks of the MS-DOS® Masters
Angermeyer, Jaeger, Fahringer, and Shafer, The Waite Group

This reference provides the personal user with advanced tips and tricks about the operating system, including advanced tips on using popular software packages such as dBASE III®, Lotus 1-2-3®, and WordStar®.
ISBN: 0-672-22525-5, $24.95

Soul of CP/M®: How to Use the Hidden Power of Your CP/M System
Waite and Lafore, The Waite Group

Recommended for those who have read the CP/M *Primer* or who are otherwise familiar with CP/M's outer layer utilities. It teaches how to use and modify CP/M's internal features, including how to modify BIOS and use CP/M system calls in your own programs.
ISBN: 0-672-22030-X, $19.95

CP/M® Bible: The Authoritative Reference Guide to CP/M
Waite and Angermeyer, The Waite Group

Already a classic, this highly detailed manual puts CP/M's commands and syntax at your fingertips. Instant one-stop access to all CP/M keywords, commands, utilities, and conventions are found in this easy-to-use format.
ISBN: 0-672-22015-6, $19.95

CP/M® Primer, Second Edition
Waite and Murtha, The Waite Group

This companion to the CP/M *Bible* is widely used by novices and advanced programmers. It includes the details of CP/M terminology, operation, capabilities, and internal structure, plus a convenient tear-out reference card with CP/M commands.
ISBN: 0-672-22170-5, $16.95

Desktop Publishing Bible
The Waite Group

A collection of essays by experts in their subject areas, these are the nuts and bolts of desktop publishing. Concentrating primarily on the technical aspects of the hardware and software, this book will be useful to anyone planning to buy a personal publishing system.
ISBN: 0-672-22524-7, $22.95

PC LAN Primer
Kleeman, Anderson, Angermeyer, Fisher, McCoy, The Waite Group

PC LAN Primer explores the Token Ring — IBM's grand strategy to tie together IBM micros, minis, and mainframes with Local Area Networks providing the communication feature.
ISBN: 0-672-22448-8, $22.95

68000, 68010, 68020 Primer
Kelly-Bootle and Fowler, The Waite Group

Beginning with an introduction to the 68000 chips, this book is written to introduce novice or experienced programmers to the instruction set and addressing modes common to the 68000 family.
ISBN: 0-672-22405-4, $21.95

Pascal Primer
Waite and Fox, The Waite Group

This primer will swiftly guide you through Pascal program structure, procedures, variables, decision-making statements, and numeric functions.
ISBN: 0-672-21793-7, $17.95

Printer Connections Bible
Marble and House, The Waite Group

This book contains all the information necessary to make the proper connections to get a printer printing. It focuses on the hardware side of connecting, particularly the main interface — the cable itself.
ISBN: 0-672-22406-2, $16.95

Modem Connections Bible
Curtis and Majhor, The Waite Group

This book describes modems, how they work, and how to hook ten well-known modems to nine name-brand microcomputers. It also features a "Jump Table" and an overview of communications software, the RS-232c interface, and a section on troubleshooting.
ISBN: 0-672-22446-1, $16.95

Inside the Amiga™ With C
John T. Berry, The Waite Group

This book is written for the experienced computer user who wants to put the powerful programming features of the Amiga to work using the C language.
ISBN: 0-672-22468-2, $22.95

Artificial Intelligence Programming on the Macintosh™
Dan Shafer, The Waite Group

Those with a basic understanding of computers and programming will be fascinated by the possibilities of music generation, robotics, and problem-solving available on microcomputers, and this book will show you how.
ISBN: 0-672-22447-X, $24.95

BASIC Programming Primer, Second Edition
Waite and Pardee, The Waite Group

A cornerstone of the Sams/Waite Primer series, this classic text contains a complete explanation of the fundamentals of the language, program control, and organization.
ISBN: 0-672-22014-8, $17.95

The Official Book for the Commodore 128® Personal Computer
Waite, Lafore, and Volpe, The Waite Group

This book examines Commodore's powerful computer with its three different operating modes, details how to create graphics and animation, and how to use the 64 mode to run thousands of existing Commodore 64 programs.
ISBN: 0-672-22456-9, $12.95

These and other Sams books are available from your local bookstore, computer store, or electronics distributor. If there are books you are interested in that are unavailable in your area, order directly from Sams by calling toll-free **800-428-SAMS** (in Alaska, Hawaii, or Indiana, call 317-298-5699).

PLACE
STAMP
HERE

Howard W. Sams & Company
Department DM
P.O. Box 7092
Indianapolis, IN 46206